Collected Writings of William Still

Volume 3:
Genesis and Romans

Collected Writings of William Still

Volume 3:
Genesis and Romans

Edited by
Sinclair B. Ferguson
and David Searle

Christian Focus/Rutherford House

© Rutherford House
ISBN 1 85792 571 8

Published in 2000
by
Rutherford House,
17 Claremont Park,
Edinburgh, EH6 7PJ
and
Christian Focus Publications,
Geanies House, Fearn,
Ross-shire, IV20 1TW,
Great Britain.

Cover design by Owen Daily

CONTENTS

GENESIS

ROMANS

GENESIS

Genesis 1

The Beginning

1:1 There are two preliminary considerations. The first is the relationship of Genesis ch.1 to other creation stories; and the second is its relationship to modern science. As to the first, no one with any spiritual insight or the slightest appreciation of moral grandeur could be confused by a comparison of the 'Enuma Elis' (the Babylonian creation fragments) with the Genesis creation story. It would be as sinful to drag Genesis 1 down to the level of these as to drag Jesus down to the level of the common sinner. The natural origin is not denied, but the supernatural origin lies beyond it.

It therefore ill behoves laymen in these fields to read their own prejudices into the biblical account. The only way to discover new truth is to preserve an open mind. Much truth doubtless still lies hidden in the profound simplicity of the great story, which when discovered may be as different from human speculation as were the discoveries of the Copernican revolution or the theory of relativity. The problem for us is whether Christians can commit themselves to a view of our origins in which humanity rises physically and intellectually, but falls morally and spiritually. We shall return to this question later.

Although the author of 1:1 must have known he was inspired, he may not have been conscious of the full grandeur of the truth he was uttering. Nor may it have occurred to him that future generations would increasingly lay hold as an anchor upon these opening words of Scripture, 'In the beginning God.' Note the simplicity of truth. It does not need a flourish of trumpets: it is a flourish of trumpets, although it may not have been recognised as such at the time. It is interesting to speculate on how simply and naturally the mightiest truths in the Bible, which have engaged and thrilled the profoundest minds, dawned on their human authors and may well have been written down in contexts of domestic simplicity. How happy this should make us! It is in the common ways of life that God reveals himself to us, and it is at the drabbest street corner that we meet the Almighty (if we may say so reverently) in 'working clothes'.

The first four words are one with the beginning of John's Gospel and first Epistle: 'In the beginning God...'. God was, before he worked, and our probing minds must not only go back beyond his work to himself, but forward through his work to himself. He is the beginning and the end and although we can only know God through his work of creation, revelation, and redemption, he is himself our redemption – first, last, and all through (1 Cor. 1:30). It is therefore good to ponder the end at the beginning, and focus our thoughts upon the person of God.

The question may be raised whether 1:1 is an introductory summary of the chapter, complete in itself, or whether it declares creation (out of nothing) of the chaos in verse 2. Both would seem to be true, for the verse is great enough to stand by itself yet also to lead us into verse 2. If we accept this subtlety, remembering that simplicity of mind is necessary to understand, we must nevertheless allow nothing to detract from the emerging, unfolding and evolving nature of the narrative.

The word 'create' may be contrasted with the word 'make' as in 2:3 and throughout the story. It is used three times only, in 1:1 of the heaven and the earth, in 1:21 of animals, and in 1:27 of man. The word is used 'exclusively of divine activity', contains the idea of 'novelty' or 'extraordinariness', and of 'effortless production' (Skinner). It is obvious that 'create' in 1:1 must have a slightly different connotation to that in 1:21,27, these latter uses not referring to creation ex nihilo but rather to the creation of something new (Kevan).

The first verse, having declared the being of God, goes on to show him to be a creative God. Let us not miss the significance of this. His nature is to create and therefore it is impossible to come into contact with him and not encounter his creative activity. This gives scope for the widest exercise of our creative powers of thought, imagination and inspiration, though always strictly within the canons of truth. Therefore, a Christian ought never to be dull nor the Christian life ever drab. Even in a prison cell, the believer sees stars, whereas others may see only mud. We may endure much pain, but pain means life and hope. (Let us never forget that God has an enemy who seeks to usurp and displace him by imitation. The devil has no creative power – he has cut himself off from its source – and is therefore driven to the low cunning of deceitful imitation and counterfeit. That he succeeds in this so well is the measure of how fallen we are).

1:2 The second verse is charged with atmosphere, which only those who read the Hebrew can fully appreciate (cf. Jer. 4:23). The principle notions of this word-picture of chaos (out of which the cosmos – order – was made) are Confusion, Darkness, and Water. Not even the most creatively-minded scientist can go back beyond this vaporous waste. 'It is believed that the stars, our own sun included, were formed by condensation from the collection of gases...' The same writer, Rendle Short, following a consideration of the views of Jeans and Hoyle, goes on to suggest, 'The planets, our Earth included, must have passed through a definite cycle of changes. When the Earth began to solidify and to cool down, quantities of gases would be evolved, mostly carbon dioxide and water vapour. The surface would be covered with thick cloud, and beneath this would be a primeval and universal ocean. As further contraction took place, the surface would be contorted, and the primitive continents and mountains ridged up. The rocks, at first, would be crystalline, as having solidified from a molten magma. Eventually the clouds would clear sufficiently, under the influence of the sun's rays, for the sun and stars to become visible from the earth's surface.' While we reserve our judgement on such speculation, these words at least show that scientists are no more embarrassed by Genesis 1:2 than is our Bible. However, we would venture to suggest that it is perhaps just here at this primeval stage that there is most scope for backward penetration and inspired discovery.

The text goes on to say that the Spirit of God – 'not, as has sometimes been supposed, a wind sent from God to dry up the waters' – was brooding, like a bird over her nest, on the undeveloped chaos. The translation of the Spirit of God 'brooding' or 'hovering' (NIV) is to be preferred to that of 'moved/moving' (AV, RSV) not only because it suggests the purpose of God in terms of millions of years but also because it is evocative of the ongoing work of the Spirit among the people of God. One of the lessons we learn in Christian life and work is that God is not in a hurry. If we think of him brooding over the primeval chaos for millions of years, we will no longer be disquieted or embarrassed by the discoveries of the scientists, but will rather thank them for bringing forth dimensions of truth from the Word of God hitherto undreamed of.

No doubt many still read the first chapter of Genesis as if it described a course of mechanics which God suddenly, albeit not unexpectedly, undertook and carried through at top speed, and then sat down panting for breath. Looking at the creation this way involves telescoping aeons of time and 'evolvement' and has no warrant in the sacred Record. Let us ponder God brooding, rather than moving with quick, crisp, almost mechanical steps. Not only is our conception of creation and its majestic progress enhanced but also our thoughts of redemption and our whole attitude to the Christian life in time and in eternity. 'When the time was fully come, God sent his Son' (Gal. 4:4).

1:3-5 Verse 3 tends to impress believers with its obvious spiritual truth and the connection with John 1:1-5 is quickly made. 'In the beginning was the Word Through him all things were made; without him nothing was made that has been made. In him was life and that life was the light of men. The light shines in the darkness but the darkness has not understood it.' The fact that the Babylonian tablets characterise the appearance of light as a victory of the god of light over the god of darkness casts our mind back to verse 2 and the chaos, making us wonder about the time of the origin and intrusion of evil (see Ezek. 28:1-19 and Isa. 14:9-17). But these are speculative thoughts and unresolved questions which we venture to raise without prejudice in such a controversial field.

The grandeur of verse 3 should not blind us to the problem it raises with verse 14 as to how there was light before lights. Two principal explanations of this have been given. The first explanation of light before lights is given by a former astronomer at Greenwich, E. W. Maunder: 'The order is entirely appropriate from an astronomical point of view, for we know that our sun is not the only source of light, since it is but one out of millions of stars, many of which greatly exceed it in splendour. Further, astronomers consider that our solar system existed as a luminous nebulae long aged before the sun was formed as a central condensation.' Other writers who make the same point could be cited.

However, in opposition to Maunder, the view is as emphatically expressed by others that the first light was our sun which along with other light-bearing heavenly bodies was obscured by vapours until the fourth day. The geologist Beasley in *Creation's Amazing Architect* says, 'It is essential for us to understand here that the sun was never absent from its place in the heavens. It was, however, unable to penetrate the thick darkness of vapours which "swaddled" the earth. It is, therefore, not surprising that some of the ancients and not a few moderns used the idea of "chaos" when writing of this period, as no doubt the earth seemed chaotic and God-forsaken. Possibly its intense and gloomy darkness made it appear as an habitation and battleground of fiends.' (The present writer here begs leave to interpolate that this is what he suggested above – not however a battleground between fiends but a pre-historic battle between God and evil. This may be scorned by some and may prove to be quite untenable, but we do not know when the angelic beings were created or when they fell. Their creation may be provided for in the 'heaven' of verse 1, and their fall in verse 2. This may displease Christian evolutionists, but they must reckon with both the angelic and the human falls somewhere and sometime!)

To resume Dr. Beasley's account: 'The scientists would now have us understand that with the continued cooling of the crust eventually the rising clouds of gas and vapours ceased, and there came a time when the sun was able to shine through to the earth.' Beasley quotes Prof. J. W. Gregory, 'The cloud belt which surrounded the early earth was removed by chilling and condensation.'

The average reader may now feel more rather than less confused. If however we have helped such readers to see that the answers to these questions are not necessary to faith we will have done them a service. We do not abandon the rock of the Word of God because we speculate with the aid of modern knowledge as to how things came to be. Indeed, we stand more firmly on the rock and speculate the more because we are sure that what light may yet fall will bring out the hidden truth of God's Word, rather than contradict it.

It should be stated however that the latter theory of the disclosure rather than the creation of the lights in verse 14 better suits the division of light from darkness into day and night in verses 4 and 5. This does raise the question of whether the 'days' of creation were of twenty-four hours duration. In view of the millions of years mentioned earlier this seems unlikely. A recent suggestion makes them 'days' of revelation of the creation to the author. Perhaps the most acceptable view is that they are 'days' of geologic ages. The revealed Word of God proves however so complex and capable of parallel interpretations that this may not exclude the revelation of our ordinary day and night. The one could fit it with the other, but only if our sun is present from the first day. Otherwise, our natural day and night would have begun with the fourth geological day.

1:6-8 Skinner dismisses this day's work as a description of primitive cosmogony, the world being a sort of structure supported by pillars with 'windows' or 'doors' in the roof, 'opened or shut by God' for the descent of rain. This is found in Egyptian pictures and in the Babylonian creation-myth. The believing scientist, however, finds that the 'literal Hebrew ('firmament' AV, 'expanse' NIV) expresses a profound fact about the atmosphere' (Beasley). It declared the Earth to be unique among the terrestrial spheres because of its atmosphere which supports animal and plant life. The separation of the waters, under from over, provides the vital atmosphere – 'that mysterious blending of oxygen, nitrogen, and other elementary gases which constitute the earth's envelope of air' – in which alone we can survive. The marvel is that the clouds are supported upon a 'substance so light that on certain days we are scarcely conscious of its presence, yet so powerful as to be able to bear upon its bosom billions of tons of water evaporated from the ocean.'

In view of modern explorations in space-travel, it may be worth quoting the following statement: 'It is interesting to realise that our atmosphere is spread out like a blanket, or tent, around the solid earth.... Our atmosphere is said to have a mass of about 5,500 million tons and this extends upward to between 200 and 300 miles. If all the atmosphere were of uniform density, as it is at sea level, it would only be about 5 miles thick, but the pressures are not uniform, and so living things cannot exist beyond about 4 miles without artificial means. When human beings go to the fringe of the "tent" or "expanse" of atmosphere they must take a supplementary supply of oxygen with them, or die' (Beasley).

Many today who read Genesis 1:6-8 in the light of scholars saturated with ancient pagan lore may equate the passage with Babylonian myth, and interpret its primitive conception of the universe as a box structure with roof shutters through which rain is poured. We prefer to read the verses in the light of the content modern science offers. This fits the passage far more naturally than the other without a trace of embarrassment either to the Bible or to science. Who should have an awe of the Creator more than the scientist?

1:9-13 The third day follows naturally without raising any particular problem either to faith or general understanding. The geologists come into their own here, laying their findings alongside the sacred record most harmoniously and enlighteningly. With regard to the appearing of the earth out of the waters we are told: 'Earth movements of great intensity occurred. A "creep" in the rocks, brought about by pressure, forced the sediments into folds. These positive movements lifted the sea floor into dry land and mountain ranges, and the sea retreated.' Again, 'Towards the end of the Cambrian times the seas began to retreat and areas of the sea floor became dry land.' And again (of Silurian times), 'in some regions there was a periodic alternation of level of land and sea; new land areas were slowly emerging and new mountain ranges were beginning to form.' Dr. Beasley comments, 'Have not these research workers given us in these phrases fundamentally the same ideas as the sacred writer who has recorded the command given by God: "Let the waters be collected into one place and let the dry land appear (out of the water)"? Could any correlation between scientific and sacred writers living many centuries apart be expressed more perfectly'?

In verse 11, 'grass' (AV) may better be translated 'vegetation' (NIV). Probably another genre of vegetation is indicated by 'seed-bearing plants according to their various kinds' and yet another in the 'trees bearing fruit with seed in it.' 'Fruit' here need not mean edible fruit but would include trees which have covered seed such as conifers. We would resist any involvement in controversy concerning the question of evolution from sea weeds to land plants. Such a discussion is fraught with problems beyond us. It is best simply to note the measure of agreement between the Biblical record and certain recent scientific findings. But with or without such findings we are nevertheless moved to exclaim with God that everything he made was good!

1:14-19 We have nothing to add to our comments on verses 3-5 regarding the relationship of the First Day to the Fourth Day. However, in spite of the view expressed above that there could have been light before the sun, it does seem unlikely that there was an earth at all without our sun. It further seems to us that 'day' must have a double reference applying both to geologic ages and to natural days. This is certainly not straining the language of Scripture – see Amos 5:18 and 2 Peter 3:8. If this is so then the cycle of natural days would have begun their motion before the sun became visible, within the infinitely slower motion of the creation days of the geologic ages. The lights therefore which were already dividing the natural day from night would at this stage be made manifest for signs and seasons, as well as for the days and years marked by the earth's double revolution of itself and round the sun.

What a beautiful symphony of evolving creation this presents! Acknowledging our severely limited understanding of a subject so vast and complex that it still defies the most brilliant of scientific minds, we suggest that this account of the Fourth Day should be read with deepest reverence (our merely inquisitive faculty in firm control), in a profoundly spiritual frame of mind. These verses should inspire in the reader adoration and worship of the Creator!

In this context what is meant by 'signs' – 'let them serve as *signs* to mark seasons and days and years' (14) The answer may lie in the gracious authority of the word 'rule' (AV), 'govern' (NIV) in relation to our constant experience of sun and moon (16,18). Consider also how the outer universe is 'thrown in' almost as an afterthought in that sentence of superb musicality, 'He also made the stars.'

'O Lord, our Lord, how majestic is your name in all the earth! You have set your glory above the heavens. When I consider your heavens, the work of your fingers, the moon and the stars, which you have set in place, what is man that you are mindful of him, the son of man that you care for him?'

1:20-23 There are certain writers who appear determined to equate the account of these early chapters of Genesis as near as possible with ancient eastern mythology. One consequence of this is that they exclude the findings of modern science almost entirely. They therefore refuse to concede to verse 21 any relation whatsoever to the pre-historic monsters of geological discovery. To them the 'great creatures of the sea' (NIV), 'great whales' (AV) are merely mythological creatures. Surely such an understanding is far too restricting and binds the Word of God.

The AV translation of verse 20, 'Let the waters bring forth abundantly the moving creature that hath life' is better rendered by the NIV, 'Let the water teem with living creatures.' The geologist Beasley reflects this same sense of the original in his own translation of verse 21: 'And God created great monsters and every swiftly gliding living creature with which the waters swarmed.' Thus the gigantic reptiles of the geological eras are fully provided for in the sacred record. Less is said of the flying creatures which apparently are 'not birds but flying reptiles, some of which measured up to 25 feet across the wings. However, the first created birds also belong to this era. The complete skeleton of one known as Archaeopteryx, or "Ancient Wing", has been discovered' (Beasley).

However, the most interesting word in these verses is 'created'. This is the second occurrence of the distinctive Hebrew word *bara* (only here and in vv.1, 27). It is generally held that 'to create' holds the sense of 'out of nothing' – *ex nihilo*. These three acts of creation, of inanimate, animate, and the man and woman, boldly challenge the hypotheses of speculative modern science, and provide those who set the sacred writings above (but not over against) science with the fascinating occupation of watching for the ultimate synthesis of the two. This may well yet involve science in not a few jolts. For our part, it may not be assumed that it will not also involve believers in a few jolts! We are only learning what the Word of God says. True science has its part to play in this. Only those who are humble will learn.

1:24-27 The great sea reptiles (20,21) were produced from the waters, but the cattle or 'livestock' (24), from the earth: 'Let the land produce living creatures.' Note also 'according to their kinds.' Again, there is agreement between the records in the Book of the Rocks (geology) and the Book of Genesis. Many scientists place the new era of mammals *after* the reptilian monsters and *before* the arrival of humankind. If the order in Genesis is right, the groupings of that order are remarkable. Reptiles on the fifth 'day', and mammals followed by humans on the sixth.

It has to be admitted that the pleader for special creation of man would have been better pleased if the reptiles and mammals had been grouped together on the one day and humans by themselves on a separate day. Nor could it be argued, surely, that the time factor was greater between reptiles and mammals than between mammals and humans. The Biblical case for the special creation of humankind stands upon something far more important which leads us beyond all speculation: 'So God created man in His own image male and female he created them.' Note in passing that the plurals in verse 26 do not refer to a council of angels but must be taken as an implicit reference to the Trinity: 'Let *us* make man in *our* image, in *our* likeness.'

(Remember the incipient Trinity of God in 1:1-3 where God creates, the Spirit broods and the Word speaks.)

'This only have I found,' says the Preacher. 'God made man upright; but men have gone in search of many schemes.' (Cf. Isa. 53:6.) This is not a fall upwards, but downwards. And if it be asserted that men and women have made and are making real progress, it has only to be stated that their refinement in evil keeps pace, at the least, with their good. The higher we go, the wickeder we grow. Whether this is an argument for the contrary motion suggested earlier (see above under 1:1), we are not sure.

The scriptural statements concerning the creating and making of man are clear and emphatic. We are made in the image of God, after his likeness, to have dominion over the earth and all that is in it. This betokens a heavenly origin and while the creation of humankind is the summit of the divine work this is not only a process of divine evolution, but an act of divine devolution! We are told the mountain peaks were primevally forced upwards from the bowels of the earth whereas the snow-caps descend from the heavens. Likewise, humanity was formed from the dust of the earth, but then 'God breathed into his nostrils the breath of life; and the man became a living being' (2:7). Our physical constitution may be earthly, but our distinctive affinity is with heaven. Our antecedents may be the mammals, but our 'prototype' is the Christ. (Cf. 1 Cor. 15:45-50.)

1:28-31 The close of the chapter pictures the ideal situation of the completed creation. There is harmony and peace because there is beneficent governance for the mutual good. Food is produced for the man and woman by fruitage (not by the destruction of living things), by seed-bearing herbage (particularly cereals), and by fruit with its seed within itself (29). A somewhat querulous scholarly note remarks that there is no mention of milk or honey, but whether or not these and similar foods are implied for a balanced diet, destruction of life is not involved. The food of the beasts is green herbage (30). This suggests there were no carnivorous (flesh-eating) animals – no beasts or birds of prey. This idyllic scene of peace and plenty gave God pleasure and he saw that it was very good (31).

In Isaiah 11:6-9, we are reminded of the prophesied return to this happy state of affairs when the kingdom of Christ comes. Then there will be mutual respect between all the orders of created life from the lowest to the highest. Then also our original dominion will be restored so completely that a little child will be able graciously to lead a whole menagerie of animals in perfect docility. The intention of this picture is doubtless to show how completely the sting of evil will be drawn from creation (Rom. 8:19ff.). It reminds us of the manifold work of redemption by which sins are not only put away but sin is destroyed and the dominion of evil (when God has used it to the full) broken.

We are further reminded of the graphic picture in Zechariah 3:1ff. of the Lord rebuking Satan and removing the high priest Joshua's filthy garments without Satan having power to interfere. That which universally and absolutely will be accomplished when Christ takes power and reigns, may in measure be our experience now as we seek to defeat him on the ground of Christ's victory. We overcome by the blood of the Lamb both in our confession of faith and by following Him into that suffering and death in resistance to sin which Satan is not able to combat (Rev. 12:11).

Chapter 2

2:1-3 This is the point at which any serious study of the question of a Sabbath of Sunday observance must begin. Not only was the Sabbath given to man as a blessing (Ex. 16:23-26) before it was enjoined as a law (Ex. 20:8-12), but it was 'discovered' by God Himself and used for the divine satisfaction and enjoyment—grace, as ever, being prior to the law. (Note that while in Exodus 20:8ff., the Sabbath is traced back to creation, in Deuteronomy 5:12ff., the Sabbath is directly linked to the redemption from slavery.) It is true to say therefore that the pleasure of the divine Sabbath derived *primarily* from the accomplishment of and satisfaction with creation and from the rest which its completion provided and justified for happy contemplation of a week's work well done.

Though the lesson is obvious it may fail to come home to those living in the modern (and postmodern) times who on the whole do not, as those of earlier generations did, work hard enough to be glad to rest on the Sabbath. This is seen in the high energy requirement of so many of the current weekend and leisure activities. But God found the Sabbath to be a blessing to himself, and if he 'needed' it and delighted in it, how much more we frail and fallible mortals. This blessing he graciously offers us, and having blessed it, to this end sanctified it (set it apart).

Now there is no threat in this. Therefore it is a mark of how far we have gone astray from God that Sabbath observance has come to be viewed as a foreboding of doom which frumpish and reactionary Christians are accused of suspending over the heads of innocent, pleasure-loving people. That is the distorted picture which completely fails to comprehend the grace and blessing of the Sabbath as enjoyed and provided by God. It is a distorted and false picture, because those who must be driven to it by the rod of the law are also those who will not accept the happiness graciously provided by God. They fail to grasp that because joy is the end of the divine being, it is necessarily also the end of his creatures.

It is also a false picture because those who reject the sabbath rest are not innocent pleasure-seekers but wantonly astray from God. If the divine delight in his Sabbath was satisfaction and rest, his pleasure and purpose in ours lies in the particular opportunity it provides us to offer our worship to him. So that the divine argument for our observance of the Sabbath is not only, far less primarily, 'This is good for you,' but rather, 'This is good for me; my greatest pleasure is derived, not from natural creation, but from the glad, free offering of my people's worship.'

Little need be said of the objection to the Christian Sunday from the Seventh Day (Saturday) advocates. Those who so passionately advocate it are so far astray on other matters of Christian faith that their arguments carry little weight. Because the permanence of the Sabbath provision is established on sound, foundational scriptural grounds, it is surely a particularly happy and divinely inspired idea that the injunction legally laid upon us should further be 'engraced' by joining it to the celebration of the Lord's resurrection. How happy we should be that what was first offered in grace and then because of human sin was enjoined by the law is now again provided for in grace by the Christian Sunday. Those who do not see this and rejoice have unhappily imprisoned themselves in that grimmer part of the Word of God which, for all its necessity, is bounded both before and behind by primal and Christian grace.

Adam and Eve

2:4-7 Standing between chapters 1 and 2, verse 4a looks both ways. It sums up what has gone before and prepares the way for new truth. It is of little importance to the reverent reader whether or not chapter 2 is another account of creation from another source. Any of the sacred writers except the earliest might use sources, therefore even the likelihood or possibility of a multiplicity of sources (although we are sure such theories can go too far) does not embarrass the believer in the divine inspiration of the Scriptures. The God who dares to use the devil for his holy ends (although a very different thing from this) is not to be restricted in his use of people and material for his purposes – even in the production of the sacred record. 'Through him all things were made; without him nothing was made that has been made.' This does not commit us to any view, but allows us simply to accept what God has revealed.

The further account begins in verse 4b, 'In the day that the Lord made the earth and the heavens...' (RSV). This translation brings out the difficulty of the passage in relation to the unfolding account in chapter 1. The forming of man before the plants (5) at first seems to contradict the account of the third and sixth days (1:11ff., 26ff.). Many commentators hurry on to verse 7 without dealing with the awkward verses 5 and 6. Perhaps the difficulty is to be solved in accepting the *new subject* of the second account. Chapter 1 dealt with creation in general from nature to man, whereas chapter 2 deals with man in Eden including his creation. The absence of bushes or shrubs may be simply horticultural rather than absolute. Better to translate verse 6, 'But streams came up from the earth' (NIV) rather than, 'But there went up a mist from the earth' (AV). Perhaps the meaning of verses 4b-7 is simply that God made man before he made the garden in which he was to live and work. However, even this suggestion is not without its difficulties, but we await and welcome further light from any quarter.

2:7 Nothing could be plainer than the Scripture's insistence that the human body is of the same substance as that of the rest of the material creation. No less than the beasts we are formed of the dust of the ground, to which at last in mortality we return (3:19). But to say that humans are simply continuous with the animals is not only to go against the accumulated evidence and experience of human history but also to ignore the third distinctive creative act of God in 1:27 (cf. 1:1, 21). If, as is somctimes asserted, verse 7 simply declares natural vitality given to man in common with the beasts, this does not exclude the superior and superlative terms of the third distinctive act of creation in 1.27. Further, if we assume that here in the context of man in Eden (there is no reference to the animal creation) verse 7 is a simple description of the animation of man as an earthy creature, we are bound in our minds to supply the content which in the other place (1:27) asserts man's creation in the image and likeness of God. Demolish 1:27 and man in verse 7 may be a mere animated creature. But if we cannot demolish 1:27, we must either admit the simple inadequacy of verse 7 and/or supplement its statement from the earlier verse.

It would, however, seem to us odd that a statement which associates man with the first creative act (the material universe, 1:1), should assert the second (the animal kingdom, 1:21), and ignore the third which makes man man (1:26f.). Even in terms of the Edenic account where, until the serpent appears, the only mention of animal life is the naming by the man of the beasts and the birds (19f.), it is hard to think of creatures belonging to the second creative act being given the care of the garden (15)! But this drives us back to the word 'man' itself in verse 7 – it has already been given a distinctive and transcendent content as created in the image of God. Even if chapter 2 is from another source, the compiler of the record would certainly read the meaning of 1:26f. into 'man' in verse 7 and could hardly fail to do so also with the latter part of that verse: 'and man became a living being.'

2:8 * Now we are in Eden! That might not be a very happy place if we let our minds stray to all that is to be. Best just now however to stay in Eden, not because we are afraid to face facts, but because we prefer to look through them to that happier Eden beyond, where serpents cannot come. In Ezekiel there are some lovely references to Eden, the delightful garden of God. Admittedly there is a sinister reference in them all to lurking or strutting evil. However, we are not concerned with that but with the conception of the garden of God (see 28:13; 31:3-9, 16b, 18a). In Revelation 22:1-5 the Scriptures have another picture of the garden

---

*The commentary on 2:8 was originally a Christmas Day daily Bible reading note, hence the clear references to the Incarnation.

of God and amongst its beautiful pictures are these words: 'No longer will there be any curse. The throne of God and of the Lamb will be in the city, and his servants will serve him. And they will see his face.' This is the Eden God intended for us, and intends!

It is therefore good to dwell on its beauties and its glories, and upon him whose presence makes it a perfect delight. For those who have lived all their lives in the crisp (usually) cold air of northern Scotland, the thought of living in an eastern and somewhat tropical garden strikes a cord with those who read in the Scriptures of the heavenly Garden. 'The throne of God and of the Lamb' – the Lamb, let us not forget, was once a helpless Child cradled in a manger. 'He came down to earth from heaven, who is God and Lord of all.' The stable may seem a far cry from Eden, but there are strong connections – earthy and animal connections. There is however no serpent there, either animal, human, or diabolic, just those who love the Child, like the shepherds, the wise men, and the dear, holy family themselves. Heaven on earth, in a garden, or a stable, or anywhere else on earth, because He is there.

2:9-17 There is much speculation concerning the location of the garden of Eden. The details given offer some clues. It was 'in the east' (8) and the four headstreams (10) flowing from the garden's river included the Tigris (AV, 'Hiddekel') and the Euphrates (14). This is a specialist's field and we cannot comment further on location.

Note that pleasure in beauty comes before necessity of food. If it was a question of either/or, necessity would come first, but in an ideal world of superabundant provision, perhaps pleasure is more important. Does not the worship and adoration of God offered by the twenty-four elders in Revelation 4:11 suggest this? What can the tree of life (9) symbolise but eternal life? And what can the tree of the knowledge of good and evil represent but that all-important choice which God lays upon dependent creatures to test them?

It is not necessary to review the theories and ideas concerning the tree of knowledge of good and evil since the prohibition in verse 17 and the result of disobedience in chapter 3 define the meaning for us. Despite the attempts to give it a merely 'intellectual' or 'general' sense and even the suggestions that the 'non-ethical sense is fundamental', we stand by the principle that Scripture interprets Scripture, and asserts its plain moral import. That brings us to verses 15-17: 'The Lord God took the man and put him in the Garden of Eden to work it and take care of it...'.

First notice that this establishes the true and right relationship. Man is a creature in the hand of God. God took him in all free grace and put him in the midst of a beautiful place with all provisions for his pleasure and necessity and gave him work to do to impart purpose to his life – the immediate purpose of maintaining the beauty of the place and ensuring the provision of his needs. Within that framework of ample and gracious provision and supervisory responsibility only one prohibition was laid down. It therefore stands to reason that accepting the creatorship and dominion of God and the dependence of man, he could not have found more freedom and independence. The essential moral difference in heaven will be that man will gladly accept his own place, unmolested and unmolestable by any evil power.

Second we should also notice that work is by implication a necessary occupation before the fall. God himself had been at work and we must not fall into the error of those who wrongly assume that 3:17ff. introduces work into human living as the result of the Fall. Rather work was intended to fulfil and (as we have just commented above) to impart purpose to life.

The further question arises as to what 'die' means (17). Is it mortality, or spiritual death? Surely both. It is inconceivable that the consequences of defying God's warning would not affect the totality of man's being, however delayed some of its effects. The suggestion of some who aver that man fell 'up' physically but down morally and spiritually, is that mortality in common with plants and animals is natural. This is a serious question, which is not answered by the retort that surely the plants and animals are fallen, too. Do the processes of growth, decay and new life springing out of death belong to nature? Or are they procured by a fall angelic or human? Indeed is there ground for the question 'whether animal and plant mortality are necessarily the result of the fall also' or that 'immortality may have been offered to man conditionally by God and that he may have rejected the offer by not eating of the tree of life'? In that case the active sin of disobedience may well have sprung from the passive sin of neglect.

What is not in doubt is that man is mortal and by nature lies in spiritual death, and the awful heinousness of his sin is in its revolt amidst such lavish grace.

2:18-20 Skinner and Driver read verse 19 as naively implying the formation of the animals from the ground after man, claiming that grammar excludes the meaning held by Calvin, Delitzsch, and Strack that they had been already created. (Cf. NIV translation, 'Now the Lord God had formed out of the ground...') This practically exposes the record to ridicule as nothing more than a piece of mythology. Note however that the forming (not creating – 'forming' can be used in Hebrew of the work of a craftsman fashioning and perfecting something over a period of time) of them 'out of the ground' seems to be quite incidental to the present account. Moreover it would appear to be inconceivable that the Spirit of God would have allowed, let alone intended, such a manifest contradiction of the order in chapter 1.

To accept the human fragmentation of the records of the Word of God does not and must not commit us to the view that they are mere disordered fragments without homogeneity, any more than scholars would have us think that their cullings from various sources were series of unconnected quotations without rhyme or reason. No one having read chapter 1 would dream of giving any other content to 2:19 than in accordance with it. Even if we assume a compiler of these records, we do not believe he read it otherwise, else he would not have written it down.

We repeat therefore that the subject in chapter 2 is man, not natural creation. Although the record has its artless naivety, it would be even more naive to fail to see the broad fundamental principles of human life which are being laid down. The record is not trying to say in embarrassing innocence and ignorance that the animals were an afterthought, in a vain attempt to provide a companion for man. Rather is it declaring their limitations as a lower order of creation on the one hand and on the other hand the necessity, on every level of creation, of equal mating for a full and proper life. (This is true even within the human order, for we believe that in his wisdom God ordains a man and a woman of approximate intellect to be together. This is certainly the case in the godliest and heavenliest of marriages, and is one of the safe guides in the problem of choice.)

It was doubtless in seeking to know the various levels of understanding of the beasts that man was able to give them truly descriptive names. The same instinct for the companionship of animals exists today in those who for one reason or another are lonely or alone.

The dangers are that either we transgress the boundaries, elevating in our minds the brutes beyond their level or else dishonour our humanity by coming down to theirs. Both of these are inclined to increase in an apostate day when the fundamental principles of the Word of God are despised or unknown. We have to be on guard against this both with regard to domestic animals, and in the undue sentimentalism of television nature study programmes. Some people long to escape from the world of humans to that of animals, but it is not a right longing. All God's creatures abide within their divine order. This is cosmos, the opposite of chaos.

2:20b-25 Verses 21 and 22 describe a sort of supernatural anaesthesia ('hypnotic trance') with a view to surgical operation. Is it strange that it took so long for the woman to be formed, coming as she apparently does after the naming of the birds and beasts? Note that man believed what the divine Surgeon had done, and accepted that woman was not only brought to him, but had been taken out of him. 'This is a profound mystery' (Eph. 5:28-33), and we must not pry into it, but ponder, wonder and worship. It speaks of the solidarity of the human race as an order of creation (Acts 17:26) and therefore of the rightness and suitability of union and fellowship of man and woman in marriage.

Here we also have the statement upon which marriage as a divine institution is founded (24), and from which all arguments thereanent arise. It is a fundamental instinct of a man to seek for union with the complement of his own nature and to depart from the shelter of the parental home in order to do so. The strength of the instinct in maturing manhood is immense. They shall be one flesh. Though the seventh commandment prohibiting adultery is yet to come (Ex. 20:14), the principle laid down here excludes promiscuity as a means of satisfying a noble instinct divinely ordained. Here then is another ordinance of God which is first given as a blessing and then enjoined on fallen man as a law.

It is not insignificant that these two creation ordinances, the Sabbath and marriage, are representative of the two parts of the law of God, the first four pertaining to our relationship with God and the remaining six to our relationship with man. Grace precedes the law. Verse 25 indicates the pure sweet innocency of marriage before the fall, and this proves the honourableness of true marriage (Heb. 13:4). False shame and

perverse modesty about the physical relationship in marriage is neither
of God nor of man before the fall, but of sin and for the Christian must
be shed with the whole life of sin.

In view of the fundamentality of the marriage instinct in man, a
word may be said concerning those to whom marriage is denied. Jesus
said. 'For some are eunuchs because they were born that way; others
were made that way by men; others have renounced marriage because
of the kingdom of heaven. The one who can accept this should accept
it.' We recall that a convention preacher of godly reputation castigated
his fellow in public for not being married, concluding with these words,
'A man is only half a man until he is married.' The castigated one was
covered with confusion and deeply wounded in spirit, until a thought
occurred to him. It was this: Poor Jesus!

Chapter 3

The Fall of Man

3:1-6 The fact of evil is a subject of particular interest to all students of
scripture and a burden on the hearts of Bible teachers to declare.
Nevertheless, we despair of dealing adequately with it here, restricted
as we are by the space available in a work of this nature. In seeking to
understand these verses, one must take care not become bogged down
with questions of symbolism. We will assume therefore that this is
history, and that in simple categories it describes the first intrusion of
evil. However we yield to none in our forwardness in spiritualising the
account, but we do not thereby reduce it to mere myth, either ancient
or modern (see 2 Cor. 11:3). The origin of evil is nowhere factually
stated in the Bible, but verse 1 should be read along with Ezekiel 28:12-
19 and Isaiah 14:12-15, which also employ natural categories to teach
supernatural truth. Evil emerges in the person of its prime mover, Satan,
appearing in the garden as a serpent (cf. Rev. 12:9).

It is impossible for the thoughtful here not to speculate on the origin
of the devil, if only to question how long evil lurked in the shadows
while God was creating all things good. If we believe that God not
only permits and uses evil but even righteously and holily ordains it
for His glory, we cannot refuse the implication of untriedness and
innocence in man before the Fall. Therefore, to speak of man's 'original

righteousness' before the Fall is to use words which cannot have the same content of meaning as righteousness tried and proved in Jesus. In this connection it is important to note that in Christ we are not merely restored to our Adamic nature before the Fall (did Adam fail to eat of the tree of life in the garden?) but to eternal life and to a new order of personhood. (See 1 Cor. 15:45.)

The serpent does not approach the man but the derivative creature, woman, and questions the Word of God. This is always his trick. God's word was the beginning of all things including the devil. To question what brought us into being and sustains us is surely to bring ourselves into question. To ask, 'Why have you made me like this?' is to presume that the Creator can create someone greater and better than himself, which is nonsense. The claim of the creature's superiority to the Creator is obviously the sign of inflated and frustrated ego which the woman must have recognised, but swept aside under the impulse of a new self-exalting idea. 'Ho!' said she, 'This opens up new worlds of thought and action. Is there more to life than God is revealing? Is He hiding something from us that is in our interests to know?'

It is not enough to say that she was disloyal and utterly ungrateful to God to whom she owed all – that is a common failing – but she entertained presumptuous thoughts inspired by a mere fellow creature. Dr. Campbell Morgan preferred to read 'shining one' instead of 'serpent' in verse 1, assuming that he appeared to the woman as a resplendent angel. There would have been more excuse for her if he had! But it was a beast she listened to, speaking as if he were and knew more than beast or man.

The fact that the serpent took to itself such authority ought to have suggested to Eve something out of the natural order. This makes her fall the more responsible and reprehensible. She should not have been deceived, allowing the facts of God's goodness to be wiped from her mind, and receiving in their place alien thoughts that manifestly contradicted God's word. She should have questioned the serpent's right to speak as a superior being. It was out of order for a snake to do and say such things. Thus the whole story, although it plainly and rightly lays the initial blame upon the devil, brings out the full heinousness of her deliberate and presumptuous sin. This cannot be over-stressed. It was a wicked, graceless thing to do by any standard, and this we must see if we are to understand the perversion that is our fallen nature.

3:2-6 We are astonished to read one scholar saying, 'The woman's first experience of falsehood leads to an eager repudiation of the serpent's intentional calumny, in which she emphasises the generosity of the divine rule' (Skinner *in loc.*). That is not how we read verses 2 and 3, or their context. Certainly the woman adds weight to the prohibition, 'You must not eat...' by her '...you must not touch it' (3). But surely this could have been 'loaded' either way. In view of what she did we draw our own conclusions.

Are we to say it was her protestations which emboldened the serpent, or her co-operation? Should she not have reported disloyalty, especially in the lower order, to Adam and to God? Alas, she engaged in discussion with this unnatural serpent, which led to her undoing. Let this lesson not be lost on us. Those who temporise are lost, for the diabolic power of persuasion far outmatches our resistance when it has been compromised by such temporising.

Next comes the bold, flat contradiction with a 'reason' given: 'You will not surely die ... For God knows...' By this time the serpent has not only reared himself from the dust, but has taken a place far above God (read 'God' in verse 5 as in NIV rather than 'gods' as in AV). From this (false) high ground he affects to expose the divine deception! 'God is suspicious and envious, Eve, of your potential powers and is keeping you in the dark lest you challenge his seat. If you take my advice you will surprise him in his own domain!' That was the suggestion to which the woman, having already lent her ear, succumbed. It is a common trick of the devil's to impute to his Enemy his own evil designs. It was he who was jealous of God – that was the trouble in the first place as Isaiah 14:13-14 and Ezekiel 28:17 clearly show.

3:5 There is perplexity in the idea of one tree possessing the properties of knowledge of good and evil, which two concepts are self-evidently complete opposites. But is it not knowledge of their interaction which is meant? If so, there is a determinative world of difference between God's knowledge of good and evil and disobedient man's. Assured that the good will triumph unsullied, God sees that interaction from above and bravely commands his good to go into battle against the evil which free will has made possible. In sharp contrast, man can only see this either by sharing in God's life and perspective (did Adam fail to eat of the tree of eternal life?), or by plunging himself disobediently into the battle at the call of the beguiling voice. Within the bounds of his own order, the man in the garden knew what was good, although he did may not have realised it. It was the evil he learned by his fall and then, in sad comparison, the glory of the God and his good that he had despised and lost.

3:6, 7* The shadow of the Fall cast over all humanity is a truth which becomes more apparent with the passage of the years. Yet for the believer there is a happier truth which enlightens every day – the coming of the Saviour! Thus it is that Grace is prior to sin and, foreseeing and permitting it, is able to save us from it although each of us is deeply entangled in it by ages of engrained habit and corruption. This is our only hope of future happiness for we Christians do not depend on chance but on divine grace. Indeed there is no chance for although the world seems a hopeless tangle of good and evil, in the mind of God they are not confused, and in the end the good will go to its place and the evil to its place. Thus perfect justice will be done. The difference between one sinner in hell and the other in heaven will be the difference of repentance toward God and faith in our Lord Jesus Christ.

See how deceived the woman is here. The forbidden tree was good for food, pleasant to the eyes, and desirable to make one wise – three excellent objectives of which none would approve more than the blessed God. Alas, the appearances were deceptive, for she now saw them with the eyes that the serpent had discoloured and distorted. So it was she ran into hell, certain that it was heaven, taking her husband with her.

The first realisation came in a dreadful sense of negative incompleteness and positive shame which it is impossible not to associate with that wonderful gift by which the race is perpetuated. We cannot but note that their realisation of nakedness has total implications for humanity. They at once tried to justify themselves by attempting to hide their shame. This shows almost at once that the spirit of the serpent had not only entered into but had begun to work in the human mind. They began to deceive first by trying to cover themselves and then by hiding in the garden.

God's word is our only guide – not our eyes, or our taste, or any of

---

* The comment on 3:6-7 was originally written as a daily reading note for New Year's Day, January 1st, 1961.

our senses. These all constantly deceive us and lead us into wrong reckoning. Whereas to live by God's word preserves us from these and from the misuse of our senses. Mere feelings by themselves will invariably lead us astray. Only God's word can lead us safely.

3:8-13 We may think of the coverings (AV, 'aprons') and the hiding as two different aspects of their attempts to hide from God. Alternatively we may think of the coverings as shame in respect of one another. Skinner comments this is 'not true to experience' and so understands both the coverings and hiding as shame in respect of God. C. S. Lewis has somewhere pointed out the tremendous strength of the sex instinct compared with that of hunger. However we must not try to equate the holiness of Christian marriage with the state of the first pair in their fallen condition. Although marriage is natural, even to fallen man, the holiness of Christian marriage does not come naturally, but only by Christian grace.

The 'cool of the day' (8) suggests a world of disillusionment. The guilty pair are not the only ones who are distressed. God has felt the shock of the fall. Although he foresaw all from the beginning – we must not impute to him our narrow experience of disappointment – we may nevertheless justly meditate upon his grief. Well did God know where Adam was in both place and condition, but the fall of this glorious creature, the crown of creation, must have been a great 'blow' to the Almighty.

Some may think we are humanising God too much? Surely not! If someone spoils something you have made and prize highly, does the thought that it can be repaired again dispel your disappointment at seeing it in ruins? Caring costs, and we would most heinously sin in perusing this record if we did not pause to lament with God his grievous disappointment. To lament with him thus leads to repentance.

Adam revealed where he was (10). He was consumed with shame and hiding in consequent fear. All this God knew, but brought the truth home by questioning. The man is not condemned until he has had opportunity to speak for himself, but it is in the act of attempted defence that he exposes his guilt. The form of the question in verse 11 is interesting. Does it imply that the pair were naked before the Fall but were not aware of it, at least in a shameful sense? If so, does this imply the failure to eat of the tree of (eternal) life and does it therefore

limit the meaning of the term 'original righteousness' in the
Westminster Confession of Faith (VI.2)?

The guilty secret having been exposed by God's searching question,
the man ungallantly blames the woman (12). How guilt unmans man!
And she, when she is cornered, also has someone to blame. Thereby
we hope to drown our own complicity in the sins of others. But no,
each pays for his own sin (God is not a fool), and the punishment fits
the crime. Principal Kevan has an excellent word here. He says,
'Punishment is primarily retributive: it is only in a secondary sense
that it is correct to speak of it as reformative or deterrent. Punishment
is vindictive rectitude not vindictive passion, and it is the reaction of
the holiness of God against all violations of it. Sin and punishment are
not arbitrarily connected but are conjoined by the spiritual laws
according to which man has been divinely constituted. Punishment,
however, is not simply the natural process that is set in motion by
sinful action; that is to say it is more than a natural penalty ... Suffering
for sin is a judicial penalty, a penalty inflicted by divine judgement,
and belongs to the moral realm.' Well and needfully said!

3:14, 15 Accepting the historicity of the story of the Fall there is a
curse both upon the serpent (14) and upon the devil (15). What effect
this supreme curse had upon the form and mode of movement of the
serpent we may not know – perhaps it had none. It seems inconceivable
that snakes were ever naturally upright though some evolutionists have
apparently postulated the theory that originally they may have had legs
(cf. the centipede). It is more likely however that the curse casts it
back to its own environment but now with shame, and invests the whole
circumstances of its life with new base, sinister and retributive
significance.

Those who dwell in snake-infested terrain testify to the enmity
between man and the serpents. Nor is the greatest danger from meeting
a snake the rearing of its head, but of its swift and silent striking of the
heel with its fangs. When a potential victim discovers this dangerous
enemy in time, it is not its tail or body which must be attacked but its
deadly head. Thus *homo sapiens* has the advantage, even in danger,
because the bruised heel is less deadly than the bruised head.

It is a fact that the devil who prefers to rear himself like a superior
being and talk with grandiloquent deception is nevertheless a noiseless

slithering snake who eats the dust. Further, all his conquests, however exaltedly gained, drag their victims down to the gutter (see Rom. 1:23). The truth about the devil, that consummate gentleman(!), is that he is a guttersnipe and the fact that he hates the gutter and tries so assiduously to dissociate himself from it only proves the point.

In spiritualising the physical characteristics of the serpent and applying them to the devil, how may we understand the word 'seed' (NIV margin) in verse 15? Is there any evidence that the devil reproduces his own kind? In spiritual application this is perhaps to be thought of as imitative rather than derivative (a tentative suggestion). Certainly the ultimate meaning of the enmity, and the victory of the seed of the woman over the seed of the serpent is Christ's victory over evil on the Cross. This is invariably the starting point of the traditional Nine Lessons and Carols so beloved at Christmas. Compare the word 'seed' in Galatians 3:16.

It is important to note that the first Biblical prophecy of a Redeemer promises not victory over sin or sins, but over Satan. This is right, going to the very fountain-head of the bitter fruits of the Fall. Nor is the problem of sin and evil adequately considered, however otherwise it may be exhaustively investigated, until the ultimate clash between Jesus and Satan is acknowledged and given its due place in the doctrine of the death of Christ. See Luke 10:18, Romans 16:20, Colossians 2:15, Hebrews 2:14, Revelation 12:7-11 and many other references.

3:16 Note that the order of the judgements is the reverse of the interrogations, and follows the order of implication – the serpent first, then the woman and then the man. If the curse on the serpent (we mean the reptile here) be thought of as a relegation to its own sphere with shame and disgrace, the curse on the woman surely means more than this. The pain associated with child-bearing (which naturally should be an experience of supreme bliss as the spiritual symbolism of marriage implies), cannot be thought of as natural in the Edenic sense. Nor is the rule of the husband over the wife natural headship, but that burdensome subjection which is too often the lot of wives through the Fall.

That this is not unfallen nature is made plain by Paul in 1 Timothy 2:13-15. In verse 13 Paul argues that as first-born, there is a sense in which the man has a priority over the woman – most probably a priority in terms of responsibility, hence leadership. This is a fact, and no shame attaches to the woman in respect of it. In verse 14 he states that woman is subject to man on account of her prior sin, and this (according to Gen. 3:16) involves travail which having been incurred by the sin of the Fall may, at least, be eased by womanly grace and godliness. The apostle's commentary in 1 Timothy on the Genesis verse must be taken fully into account for a true doctrine of woman in respect of creation, the fall and redemption.

3:17-19 It becomes clearer that these judgements affect rather than change the environment of those punished. In the case of the woman and the man (for there is no redemption for the devil) spheres are provided in which the fruits of redemption may be seen and recognised as witnesses. Work is not a judgement but is ordained as a privilege and source of total health and blessing for the highest dependent creature set in authority over the natural creation (cf. 1:26, 2:15).

In view of the charge of disobedience laid upon Adam (17a) and not Eve, it may appear that in our comments on earlier verses in the chapter we have imputed too much responsibility to Eve. If so, what would have been the situation had Adam resisted Eve and failed to succumb to her enticement? We ask this question not of mere speculation on a hypothetical situation, but only in order to understand the nature of the man's responsibility. Doubtless there is no satisfactory answer but to think of it may help us see more clearly the nature of the truth which is given us. It is not without significance that the devil tempted first the woman rather than the man!

Before the Fall the ground naturally produced food but afterwards, of itself, thorns and thistles. The implication is that the invariable tendency to return to the wild, which every gardener knows and which the sight of a long-neglected garden proves, is not originally natural but a curse. Therefore there is that vivid contrast between him happily tidying and cultivating on the one hand, and laboriously struggling against rank, unfruitful growth on the other. In the latter rigorous and demanding conditions his kinship with the dust is uppermost, until at length he slaves himself to death and lies down in it.

The question of whether death is natural is again raised by the fact that the ugly word is not mentioned in verse 19. We have already discussed this question, which, we think may not be unconnected with that of the possible failure to eat of the tree of (eternal?) life (see above on 3:8-13).

It is a woeful life for the serpent – that is why he has to work so hard, and often appears to be far busier than God; he has to be! It is a woeful life for the woman – in her travail and her trauchle! And it is a woeful life for the man – in the struggle for existence and to wrest a living from the unwilling soil. The only lasting hope is the Christian hope which brings into human life wonderful palliation of these severe necessities. Yet it is a hope that is set beyond this world. We cannot therefore be other than pessimistic as far as this fallen order is concerned (2 Pet. 3:10). This is Christian realism. Its hope of unmitigated bliss is all yonder.

3:20-21 Some commentators object to the placing of verse 20 between the sentence on the man and woman and the execution of that sentence, especially before Eve's actual motherhood. But surely this inter-weaving of judgement, mercy, grace and faith is true to life as seen in the light of the Gospel. Was this an act of faith on Adam's part? Or was it an outworking of his new found knowledge from eating of the forbidden tree?

It is surely impossible for anyone searching for authentic Gospel insights in the Word of God, to miss the significance of verse 21. Perhaps the first thing we should see is the fact that it was God who first shed the blood of his creatures, and that he did so out of pity for man to provide covering for him. This is the first sign of death in scripture, not following naturally and directly from our first parents' sin, but wrought by God at cost to provide a remedy for sin. The animals were sacrificed to provide adequate covering for the naked man and woman.

We need not speculate as to how this was done; it is stated to be an act of God. However it is important to remember that the meaning of the word 'atonement' in the Old Testament is 'covering'.* The idea of

---

*A comment about the occurrence of the word 'atonement' in the New Testament may be helpful. In the AV 'atonement' only occurs once as a mistranslation in Romans 5:11 where it should read 'reconciliation'. It never occurs in the RSV, but is found several times in the NIV where it is used to translate the Greek *hilasterion*, 'atonement cover' (Rom. 3:25; Heb. 9:5), *hilaskomai*, 'make atonement for' (Heb. 2:17), *hilasmos*, 'atoning sacrifice' (1 Jn. 4:2, 4:10). *Ed.*

covering to hide sin and shame gives place in the Gospel to the higher and more glorious one of removal of sin with a view to re-covering with the glorious garment of Christ's righteousness. (Cf. Zech. 3:1-7, Is. 61:10, Jer. 23:6, 2 Cor. 5:21, Phil. 3:9.) To be over-fastidious about reading this into Genesis 3:21 is surely to partake of that hyper-critical spirit which suspects all Old Testament hints or shadows of truth (we need not go to the other extreme) and regards the dwindling body of truth with dismay. Often precious little is left – little enough, indeed, to make men cynical of all. How terrible!

3:22-24 Verse 22 is notoriously difficult. The words 'like one of us' can only refer to certain attributes of god-like beings – in this case possessing the knowledge of good and evil. We are certainly not to understand the man and woman had attained the plane of God or of the holy angels (as we have shown), but rather that they had come to the sordid realisation of evil as opposed to good.

What God means by the possibility of the fallen pair snatching unlawfully at eternal life is hard to understand. We can only speculate within categories which are proper to Scripture, and assume that it would have invested the two sinners with immortality as spiritual beings. What relation such hypothetical creatures would have had to fallen angels or demon spirits we do not know, but it is inconceivable that the man and woman could have snatched at eternal life in Christ against the will of God and added that to their sinful nature. Perhaps the Lord is simply dramatising the fact and statement of human exclusion from eternal life, and showing that presumption never wins with God, but always drives itself further away, whether by man or devil.

The subject of the cherubim (24) cannot be profitably pursued beyond a comparison of the Scriptural references to them. Whatever sort of beings they are (some say they are not angels, but surely the word 'angel' = 'messenger' is general enough to cover all supernatural beings?), their work is plain, both here and as golden symbols on the ark (Ex. 25:18ff.). Their office is to guard the precious things of God from presumptuous violation, and their weapon of attack at the gate of the garden is 'a flaming sword flashing back and forth' – a revolving sword-flame. All this vividly portrays the fact that the man and woman are now excluded from the privileges which were theirs by divine grace.

The irony of their plight in exclusion is that only now do they realise what they have lost, and the motive to regain it becomes perversely strong.

This is frustration, one of the most painful parts of our evil inheritance by the Fall. Further, the world is no longer a happy productive place any more, but a hard unproductive wilderness mutely threatening human life; it has to be delved and weeded into producing the bare necessities for survival. 'Woe is me!' must have been Adam's bitter cry as he departed from the garden, 'I am undone and that by my own disloyal and complacent folly.' Thus God stands in the shadows of his mysterious Being and calls creatures to their account.

Chapter 4

Cain and Abel

4:1-7 What are we to imply from Eve's acknowledgement of the Lord in the birth of Cain? Perhaps we are to understand there had been both repentance and faith, and a recognition of continuing grace in the midst of judgement? Surely the two sons are taught to sacrifice to the Lord. So they each offer of their produce to Jehovah.

The story is complicated by the difference in their occupations, Cain's being the primitive one, but neither being apparently superior to the other. Indeed, we may ask what the purpose of Abel's flock was but to provide first clothing and milk, and then food by their slaughter. The onus would seem to be upon Abel to justify his occupation. Yet it is his sacrifice, not without blood, which is accepted. Why?

We can only answer that behind the difference of their occupation lies an insight of faith which Abel possessed and Cain lacked. But Cain is responsible for his lack, as we see (7). We need not assume that Cain gave less than the best of his vegetables. Was it the failure to symbolise costly sacrifice in blood which was his sin? We can only infer that Cain offered to God gifts in the arrogant complacency of sin, whereas Abel 'spoiled' his sacrifice in token of his penitence, and was accepted. When Cain expostulates, God exposes the speciousness of his anger and dismay. Cain's heart well knew why his offering had not been accepted. He was not in it – it was a kind of concession, whereas

Abel was in his sacrifice as a humble, believing sinner. There is all the difference in the world!

The textual problems of verse 7 are great. There are at least three possible ways of understanding it. First, it has been suggested that 'sin' should read 'sin-offering', as if grace was providing an animal for sacrifice and laying it at his door (cf. Abraham's ram caught in the thicket, 22:13). Second, a less speculative view is that God is warning Cain of the danger of his jealous anger leading to murder. In this case it would be the sin of fraticide (i.e., the devilish suggestion of it) that was lying at his door so that the remainder of the verse would not apply to Abel, but to whether the sinful suggestion would master Cain, or he it. A third alternative is that the last sentence could connect with the first, promising that if Cain did well in offering sacrifice to God and restraining his anger from his brother, Abel's subjection as the younger brother would be assured. All these views have something to commend them Christianly speaking, and perhaps the obscurity or corruption of the text permits us to engage sanctified imagination upon it, though of course always strictly within the canons of scriptural truth.

4:8-15 In the Hebrew, the sentence telling of Cain's conversation with Abel is broken off. The conversation would have been specious (cf. Absalom, 2 Sam. 13:23-29). See again how the Lord graciously permits a defence (cf. 3:9, 11, 13) by his question, but sin has grown bolder in Cain and he lies flagrantly. Yet incautiously he adds an unbrotherly justification of his professed ignorance. Even if God had not known the lie – which He did (10) – suspicions were aroused by his heartless attitude to his brother, especially when linked with his angry envy of him. Even then the question is asked, 'What have you done?' albeit it is answered immediately to show God's knowledge and care for righteous Abel (cf. Matt. 23:35, Heb. 11:4) and his just concern over the sin which ended his mortal life. God knows and cares what men do to his righteous children, and he will deal with them.

We need not strain the idea of Abel's blood crying from the ground, or of the ground reacting in a curse against Cain. God's nature reacts in sympathy with His judgements. Therefore Cain is prohibited from pursuing his primitive occupation by the natural retribution of the ground, already cursed to Adam, becoming doubly cursed to him. Whereas the ground hardly yields its fruits to Adam in the sweat of wearisome toil, it yields nothing at all to Cain and he is driven out a wanderer and a fugitive.

His punishment is greater than he can bear. This is not repentance but remorse. Yet God is merciful and imposes a restraint upon any who would wantonly take the vagabond's life. What mark or sign was appointed we do not know, but it must have been some apparent indication that God still cared for Cain and would deal vengefully with anyone who slew him. (The question of what other people were upon the earth need not disturb us. It is foolish to make difficulties for ourselves when several possibilities are open from the descendants of Adam and Eve.) We do not know whether Cain had cause to fear his murder, but it is suggested that his fear arose from the guilt of this very sin of murder which his wounded conscience would impute to others. It is guilt which allows entrance to the horrid imaginations of craven fear, which fear (we know whence it is) can only be dispelled by seeking refuge in the mercy of God. Ponder that mercy which hears cursed Cain when he cries in an agony of mere remorse. What have we to fear who are sheltered by holy blood spilt to protect us from our enemy?

4:16-24 See how sin develops, and multiplies manifold. Cain is now twice removed from God (16). Many defensive questions are raised by scholars against a condemnatory attitude to these verses. We do not wish to condemn city life or the institution of the arts and crafts of 'civilisation', but to our mind it is significant that they arise in this evil context (cf. vv.19, 23, 24). E. F. Kevan comments, 'It is not justifiable, however, to argue that these arts are of evil origin because they arose in this quarter.' It would be difficult to disagree with him, and yet – considering the rise of these communities and Cain having gone out from the presence of the Lord – we think it would be very misleading if not dangerous for our view of Christian civilisation to dissociate the 'civilisation' from the sin.

In this passage we have the first mention of polygamy (19), such an idea being unthinkable in the plain terms of 2:24. We also have Lamech rejoicing in murder and boasting to his wives of the multiplicity of his vengeance (23f.). Cain, too, has gone a long way astray between vv.13 and 24. The 'civilised' portion of the narrative (20-22) may stand by itself, but it is within the larger context, and it was out of the first polygamous home that art and craft came. This is not, of course, to impugn creative and inventive powers (we have already rejoiced in these), but to note the environment in which they emerge and mark its significance, though we may not be able to define what it is.

However, is it so difficult to define the significance of creative and inventive powers? There is a right and a wrong questing spirit, and the devil is too often behind the inventor. After all, wasn't it he who made our first parents dissatisfied with the life of the garden? No doubt the Spirit of God is not excluded from, or inactive in, exploration and invention—he is the only Author of it. Nevertheless we are sure that it is divine discontent which he inspires in men and women, causing them to yearn to come back to the original, not move away from it.

Perhaps we can look at the record more discerningly. Presumably Adah was Lamech's lawful wife, and his sons by her became the fathers of the nomads (or bedouin) and of musicians (note 'harp and organ', AV, are better translated 'string and pipe', which with percussion largely comprise non-vocal musical sounds). It is the son of the second woman Zillah (22) who becomes the artificer in metal. Does this make the smith a worker of the devil? No, but it may have affected his use of his craft. There has been an 'almost universal' assumption, although some have questioned it, that Tubal-cain used his craft to make weapons which Lamech his father then used in murder.

Apply this to the misuse of atomic power! In the renaissance (the rebirth of the arts following the dark ages) religion was the principal theme. However in our modern world (to say nothing of post-modernity) it is not God who is the centre of life, but man. The greatest danger to Christian civilisation is, as ever, not in the gutter but in the salons where those with guttersnipe minds purvey their filth and lawlessness under the guise of art. It is not for nothing that so many of the world's entertainment idols when they are sated with the false glare of city life run and buy farms and cottages in the heart of the country. And some of them, like the prodigal son, feed swine, for a change.

4:25, 26 There is not only an aesthetic but a moral and spiritual fitness about the close of chapter 4. It has been a sore chapter in which evil has developed enormously, and fastened upon the birth of invention to pervert it to perpetual human disgrace. But it doesn't end that way – there is hope! Poor Abel dies for doing good as his Saviour did; but the good is not lost for we have its insight today. Thus Abel is not poor, but where he now is he is rich and righteous (Matt. 23:35) and a seed has been given to replace that which was 'lost'.

What a mighty principle of truth is enshrined in the words, 'The blood of the martyrs is the seed of the Church'! 'At that time men began to call on the name of the Lord' (Jehovah, or *Yahweh* properly called). This is stated by the commentators to indicate the beginning of the worship of God by that name. Doubtless, but if our notice of the turning point of this unhappy chapter is valid, these words mean more than this. Does it not mean that after an age of lawlessness men became sick of sin and turned back to God? Or rather that Seth, the first of the godly seed of hope, saw the mess man had gotten himself into by his sin, abhorred it and turned with his family, and eventually his tribe, to God? At least that view does justice to the purpose of the Bible and does not reduce the religion of its first pages to a sort of mere improved or superior paganism. For surely Seth is a type of that other seed, Christ himself. Read right through the paraphrase of Is. 9:2-7, which appears in most Church Hymnaries and begins,

The race that long in darkness pined have seen a glorious light;
The people dwell in day, who dwelt in death's surrounding night.

Chapter 5

From Adam to Noah

5:1-32 In comparing the genealogies of 4:18 with those in chapter 5, similar names and even identical sequence of names (cf. 4:18 with 5:25) should not confuse us. After all, an important task of Bible scholarship is the distinguishing of those of the same name in different generations and even in the same generation. The literary or poetic patterns of the Genesis' genealogies should be noted. For instance, subsidiary genealogies are disposed of first. For example, Cain's comes before Seth's, 4:18 (and see 5:6-8); Ishmael's before Isaac's, 25:12-19; Esau's before Jacob's, 36:1-40. Also, the genealogies are sometimes grouped in uniform numbers (note the 'tens' in chapter 5, e.g., verses 3, 4, 5, 9, 19 etc. and chapter 11:10ff., e.g., verses 10, 11, 14, 17 etc. and three 'fourteens' in Matt. 1:17 which latter excludes several kings). This clearly means that the genealogies are not calculations of generations or years. The arithmetician who would turn the Bible into his kind of scientific text book must be restrained. Not thus do we lead others to faith!

We now come to the significant line (3ff.). It is distressing to find scholars stripping the documents of any but the most primitive import, or of any connection with each other. Are we not to assume and 'read in' any of the later Biblical light to these earliest records? What then of the spiritual purpose and unity of the sacred volume?

The two significant things in this genealogy are the extreme longevity of the patriarchs, and the monotonous repetition – with one exception (24) – of the death formula, 'and then he died'. Many reasons are suggested for the great age of these men. For example, it has been argued they were tribes, not individuals; or the years then were shorter than ours (aren't unbelievers ingenious?); or the numbers given are mystical (the figures are certainly too unruly to be called poetic); or the years are unhistorical exaggerations, as found in literary works 'incorporating the primitive traditions of a people' (Ryle, quoted by Driver, quoted by Skinner). It is further asserted that 'the study of science precludes the possibility of such figures being literally correct'.

We understand that the longevity of our early ancestors indicated the slow progress of human corruption following the fall, which slowness gave plausibility to Satan's lie, 'You will not surely die' (3:4). We are unable to verify modern science's views on this at the time of writing. Do Isaiah 65:20 and 2 Peter 3:8 help? Meantime, the certainty of death is most funereally driven home. To gain the full savour of this, read the chapter aloud. It needs but little or no increase in emphasis on the words 'and then he died' well and truly to nail down the coffin of our mortality. It is, as so often, a historical comment upon the devil's lie.

5:21-27 The case of Enoch who did not die is a most remarkable and surprising inclusion in this genealogy – but not to faith. This is in keeping with the design of God as we see it, to provide the most revealing light on his ultimate purposes in the most primitive records. Enoch (Heb. 11:5), a historical character, is along with Elijah a type of those who by faith 'shall never die'. Note that Enoch had not only that initial faith (which grasps the 'simple gospel'), but faith to progress into a profound knowledge of and fellowship with God. That is to say, his faith led him on to that end for which the divine gift was given, namely the pleasure of God. It is for this God has saved us, that we might walk with him. Enoch did so, and, as we have otherwise suggested, was wonderfully helped over the stile of mortality, closer into the arms of his Beloved.

Methuselah, Enoch's son, is the oldest living man on record. (How long godly Enoch would have lived had he not been taken we do not know.) Is his longevity not related to the godliness of his parentage and upbringing? What, then, does the fifth commandment mean when it promises days 'long upon the land which the Lord thy God giveth thee' (Ex. 20:12) as a reward for honouring parents? (Cf. Deut. 4:40, Prov. 10:27, Eph. 6:3, etc.)

Chapter 6

The Flood

6:1-8 There seems little hope that Bible students will cease to take sides on the question of whether the 'sons of God' were men of the godly line of Seth or were angels. Professor E. J. Young is uncompromisingly categorical: 'The "sons of God" are not angels, but the chosen race'; but if there is even a remote relationship with similar tales in ancient mythology, the evidence would seem to be the other way (see Jude vv.6-7; 2 Pet. 2:4; 1 Pet. 3:19). 'The "sons of God" are everywhere in the Old Testament members of the divine order, or "angels"' (Skinner). The very grotesqueness of the giant off-spring suggests phenomenal creatures, although what connection those destroyed with the flood would have with those in Numbers 13:32-33 and with Goliath, we do not know. The idea of marriage between sinning angels and women seems fantastic to the sober-minded; but the Jude reference is very apposite and convincing, as is 6:4.

Chapter 6:3 is as interesting as it is difficult. But even if we omit the insoluble 'contend with' (AV 'strive with'), the verse still makes good general sense. Suggested alternatives to 'contend with' are 'rule over' or 'abide in', in which case 'My spirit' is the divine principle of life in man.

The remaining question is whether a hundred and twenty years refers to a new human life span (cf. the ages in chapter 5) or the years of respite before the judgement of the flood. Scholarship on the whole seems to favour the former view, although the latter is peculiarly appropriate to the age before the deluge (notwithstanding the excess of twenty years, cf. 5:32 with 7:6). It is not possible to give further guidance on this matter. This fact affords opportunity for practice of that excellent exercise of weighing judgement and yet suspending decision on questions which do not enter into the substance of the faith. What is important and in no doubt is God's wrath with that wicked, albeit renowned, 'civilization'. Verse 5 might well be paraphrased, 'And God saw that man's wickedness was so great that he was wholly bent upon evil.'

The question of how the Lord can repent (cf. 1 Sam. 15:11), i.e., change his mind, is perhaps best answered by observing that his repentance in such cases is not absolute and exclusive, inasmuch as he foresaw the wickedness and provided the ark for the salvation of righteous Noah. We must not read verses 5-8 as if the Almighty deliberated with himself and was subsequently dissuaded from destroying the human race by his observance of grace in Noah's life. Besides, the grace is not in Noah but in God. It is only possible to expose the tension between justice and mercy in the heart of the Eternal by an anthropomorphic show of human deliberation. The fact of God's long purpose of redemption is not affected by this 'interplay' of 'Shall I?' or 'Shall I not?'; but the reality of the divine grief and wrath and his determination to destroy the abandoned generation are thus solemnly brought home.

The 'But' of verse 8 is not of human initiative, but divine. It was not God who had found grace in Noah, but Noah who had found it in God. Noah found grace but he did not create it, and he found it where it was, ever had been and ever shall be – in the eyes of the Lord. That certainly is a great discovery which only faith can make; but it is humbling to think that it is always there before it is seen.

6:9-13 The heavy emphasis on Noah's discovering grace in the eyes of God (see above) may be considered by some too Calvinistic, as witness verse 9. But it makes nonsense of grace to think that God chose to save Noah because he was a man of righteousness and integrity and walked with God. Of course he was, and God was pleased to make him the father of a new generation of humanity because of his godly qualities; but these were the effect of God's prior or prevenient grace, not the cause of it.

God both grants his grace sovereignly to whom he will (Seth, for instance), and rewards him for responding in faith to it. Thus the believing godliness of some never puts God in debt to them – although God may graciously reward them for it – because it had its beginning in the mind of God not in human minds. For we have *two* causes of submission and dependence which preclude us for exalting ourselves in God's sight: we are *creatures* and *sinners*. Wherever authentic good is known, inevitably God has been there, working. Both prevenient grace and gracious reward are therefore seen in this account of God's selection of Noah to establish a new generation.

The corrupt and violent state of humanity on the earth is further brought out by verses 11-13. This could be well understood if it were the result of marriages between the godly seed of Seth and the ungodly seed of Cain. For the ungodly are seldom as depraved and reckless as when they are corrupting the godly. Nothing gives the devil and his agents more pleasure than to contaminate holy seed; for one thing, it destroys the witness to their condemnation. But if we maintain the view (not least in the interest of 1 Pet. 3:19-20) that the marriages were between fallen angels and women (2), are we to equate or associate fallen spirits with demon spirits and assume a tremendous invasion of humankind by demon forces? Is this the hideous state of affairs which God was obliged to punish with the overwhelming flood?

6:14-22 If the cubit is the ordinary Hebrew cubit of 6 handbreadths (about 18 ins or 45 cms), the ark was a craft of 450 feet long by 75 feet wide by 45 feet high (140m x 23m x 13.5m). It would be wrong to assume the style of a modern ship. Perhaps we should envisage something in the form of a gigantic raft or house-boat. The pitch or bitumen is natural to the east (cf. Ex. 2:3). The window would be above, probably the open sides of a raised roof, 18 inches high (.5m) going round the ark, and the door would possibly be in the long side.

There is endless scope for sanctified imagination to picture the witness of Noah preaching and building the ark for a hundred years in face of a wicked generation (cf. the mediaeval miracle and morality plays!). Note that the 'floodwaters' (17) is prophesied to destroy all living creatures on the earth, that is, to cover the inhabited earth.

Verse 18 sees the first mention of 'covenant'. Not the first covenant – that was the covenant of works in 1:26, 28; 2:8, 15-17, by which the man and woman in the innocency of Eden were committed to the gracious work of obediently tending the garden while walking in fellowship with God. We have also the covenant of promise of a Saviour in 3:15 as well as the further personal covenant of God with Cain in 4:15. Now, following the act of grace in providing another seed instead of Abel, the covenant is confirmed with Noah and his family. This is a major type of salvation (cf. Heb. 11:7; 1 Pet. 3:20; 2 Pet. 2:5). The flood is the type of God's total and implacable judgement against sin, salvation from which is altogether in his hands as an act of sheer, free grace.

Though God by his eternal purpose has committed himself to bring a chosen race to glory, he could have annihilated humanity and begun again. Rather, he chose by the gift of faith to lead a remnant freely to commit themselves to him for salvation. While it would be unwise to dogmatise on the tiny proportion saved from the flood – only eight of all humanity (cf. 'few' in 1 Pet. 3:20, also see Matt. 7:14), the elect family is surely an authentic type of the idea of the preservation and deliverance of a remnant. For example, compare the captivity and return from Babylon, the apostolic deliverance from Judaism and also the Reformation. Yet this does not justify sectarianism as Jesus, Paul, Luther, and Wesley made plain in their attitudes and as the decay of exclusive sects confirms. Nevertheless in the Gospels (the idea of) the Kingdom (even after Christ revealed his power by excursions into miracles of nature) remains a mystery – the (hidden) massing of the saints in heaven, who with the King are at last to take the earth by sudden, glorious storm (cf. Matt. chs 13 and 24).

Chapter 7

7:1-24 Here we encounter many difficulties which will not be solved by unbelief. In face of much hitherto in the holy record which has eminently appealed to faith, that would be the coward's way out! The fact of an ancient deluge of great magnitude has been proved by archeology. It undoubtedly covered a great area of land in, at least, the Babylonian region of the Middle East. (We may not be impressed by repeated assertions that a wooden structure apparently embedded among the snows of Mount Ararat may be the ancient ark. We do not need to see the ark to believe in it, any more than we need to see the tree upon which our Lord was crucified to believe in his cross (cf. Heb. 11:1, 3).

Note the unleashing of subterranean waters as well as rains from heaven (11): 'Outbursts of subterranean water are a frequent accompaniment of seismic disturbances in the alluvial districts of great rivers ... The Flood is thus a partial undoing of the work of creation...' Note also the perfect number seven in the pause before the flood and in the number of clean beasts (2, 10). This tempts us to theorise but we do not need to over stress to the believing mind the perfection of God's works of mercy and of judgement.

The question of the clean and unclean beasts is difficult. 'Perhaps the distinction was between edible and inedible, or tame or wild, or sacrificial or non-sacrificial. It probably does not refer to the laws in Leviticus 11. By sevens ... might mean seven pairs, but more probably three pairs, and an additional one for an offering.' (Cf. 8:20.)

It is neither necessary nor possible to assume that a totality of the species of animal life entered the ark, any more than to assume the complete inundation of the whole earth. 'When Luke says "all the world was to be taxed", he obviously did not mean South America. Nor, when we are told that "all the kings of the earth sought the presence of Solomon" is it meant to include Japan and Australia. Genesis says that all the high hills "under the whole heaven" were covered. Amongst St Peter's audience on the day of Pentecost were men "from every nation under heaven"; in each case it obviously means all the then known world' (Rendle Short).

The Lord shut these eight persons in, and the waters began to rise. Note that no children were born to Noah's sons until after the flood. Thus the waters of judgement and destruction to all other men became the waters of salvation to those in the ark. The death of Christ seals the doom of the evil angels and all who side with them, but is the salvation of all who believe. See Isaiah 43 and Hebrews 11:7.

Chapter 8

8:1-14 E. F. Kevan concludes that the 'flood occupied exactly one
solar year'. This is arrived at by elaborate calculation.

We should notice the literary beauty of the narrative here. There
may be typical significance in the raven which did not return at all and
the dove which did. There is certainly plausibility in the thought of the
two birds contrasting the 'old nature' – satisfied with the world under
judgement, and the 'new nature' – finding satisfaction only in the things
of the new creation (albeit we would put the former negatively and
note the raven's lack of homing instinct towards the ark). The
symbolism of the dove's three excursions is beautiful. Its return empty
reminds us of the hymn:

> Happy birds that sing and fly round Thy altars, O Most High!
> Happier souls that find a rest in a heavenly Father's breast!
> No repose on earth around, they can to their ark repair,
> And enjoy it ever there.

Its return with the olive branch reminds us of the familiar symbol
representing peace used even by people who do not know its origin.

We understand that the olive does not grow at high altitudes and is
said to flourish even under water. This links the refuge of the ark with
the world renewed after judgement, and leads to the dove's non-return.
The most delicately suggestive symbolism is thus presented to the
imaginative Christian mind as also in the completion of God's vast
and overwhelming judgement on the wicked earth. Following the
climax of the flood, the rain ceases, the subterranean waters return and
the earth is dried up.

8:15-22 This thought occurs to us: was it not impossibly hard for God,
who knew beforehand what man's sorry history would be, to be
enthusiastic about this new beginning? The answer is: No! He was not
looking at the evil but at the good. Yes, he sees all the evil but he does
not set his gaze upon it. This is the difference between human short-
sighted optimism which would peremptorily exclude all evil forthwith,

and God's long-term assurance which lets avalanches of evil come, and from the havoc they wreak works out his purposes of everlasting good. More, see how the righteousness of faith shines in the dark. What pleasure God must have had of Noah and his family riding high on the rising deluge! His emergence into the new world must have rejoiced the divine heart even to the eclipse of the 'loss' of his other creatures.

God's command is now to multiply and be fruitful. There is no command to build an altar and to sacrifice the clean beasts from the ark. That was Noah's idea. Not that it was not God's. It was. But it flowed from the living, creative faith by which this man freely responded to the overwhelming grace of God. When God reveals the glory of his salvation in a solicitude prepared to manipulate the creation to succour his chosen, it inevitably evokes a response which fittingly seems to read his mind and sees the right thing. The right thing here was the altar, the sacrifice and the sweet smelling savour in the nostrils of the Almighty. It was worth a hundred floods and the loss of generations of people dear to the heart of God to evoke this one response. It was this in Abel which delighted the Lord and maddened Cain. Here it is again in Noah. The Almighty is overjoyed. A fallen man – not unfallen Adam and Eve but – someone wrought upon by the serpent and already far on the road to corruption (albeit another seed and a chosen godly line) has made response to God, not only in saving faith but in token surrender.

God's pleasure is seen in the promises he makes. There will not again be a universal judgement until the earth is burned up and renewed (2 Pet. 3:10-13). Until then, the cycle of seasons and the rhythms of nature proceeding from the beneficent inter-orbiting planets of the cosmos will not fail. The 'mysterious universe' itself is directed towards the glory of God in the preservation and redemption of men. Although man does not live by bread alone, he cannot live without it. Therefore in that economy there is nothing more important than seed-time and harvest. 'Give us this day our daily bread,' is a request we must make and do all in our power to implement, for it flows from the gracious promise of a faithful providence. Nevertheless it is a promise in the context of fallenness and the curse of the ground. If famine comes – and its threat today increases in the face of the growing world population – it will not be God's fault, but ours by our sin, not least our pursuit of non-productive occupations. If the world starves it may not be on account of the lack of bread-winners, but of bread-makers.

In our land we have become so sophisticated that we need immigrants to do our chores. This affords us time for the refinements of life. But how many patrician civilisations have been swept away when the common people survived! Is it because patricians tend to become parasites?

Chapter 9

God's Covenant With Noah

9:1-7 Noah emerges to a new world order in which former strictures are relaxed and the human dominion over the creatures, apparently forfeited by sin, is partially restored (2). Noah and his family are permitted to eat flesh to supplement their vegetarian diet (3). Was this the divine sanction of a liberty taken by man? Or is it rather that flesh-eating commenced with Noah's post-deluge sacrifice? In view of the typical nature of the later Old Testament sacrifices, the symbolism of the Christian sacrament (Matt. 26:26; 1 Cor. 11:24) and the mystery of the believer's union with Christ (Jn. 6:47-58), it is hard to think of flesh-eating as a concession to wilfulness, like the sanction of the monarchy (1 Sam. 8:7).

Yet it remains true that human beings were ideally intended to be vegetarians. Whether fallen humanity should try in God's name to recover that ideal is very much an open question. Certainly Jesus ate boiled fish. Perhaps the question concerning the inappropriateness of eating meat is answered in the prohibition of eating blood (4). Compare the divine scruple concerning the eating of the blood out of respect for the creature's life with the hygienic practice of blood-letting in slaughterhouses. It must be significant that the blood which is the life of the body accelerates decomposition when it is dead! Thus the divine prohibition of eating the blood of both man and beast is approved and practised in the interests of hygiene. The Bible is true and its religious practices have implications which are not only moral but also hygienic.

9:8-17 The question arises as to whether the rainbow is recorded as only appearing after the covenant. Those who closely equate the record with pagan mythologies have no difficulty in supposing that it does so. But even stone-age man need not know the scientific cause of the rainbow to see it! It is impossible that at this advanced state of the earth's evolution the rainbow had not already been seen. What is to hinder the Almighty appointing something already familiar as a sign and token of a gracious unconditional covenant? Note that verse 13 in NIV reads, 'I have set my rainbow in the clouds', not, 'I do set...' as in the AV.

We have used the word 'unconditional'. Some think the covenant is bound up with the conditions prescribed in verses 1-6. An attempt is made by some to distinguish a promise from a covenant: the former a 'bare' promise, the latter an agreement with a token or sign. This is groundless. It seems that the attempt to make the Bible more systematic than it is leads to arbitrary distinctions, not only between promise and covenant, but between man's co-operative involvement or non-involvement. The terms of the whole passage convey the undoubted impression that this is an unconditional and absolute covenant. The original covenant of works (Gen. 1:26, 28; 2:8, 15-17) required co-operation but the promise of Cain's protection (4:15) or the creatures' dread of man (9:2) or of the rainbow as a sign that water would no more devastate the earth (15b) required no human co-operation.

Also some covenants are with signs and others not. When they are with visible signs we may explore the meaning and purpose of the sacramental principle and the relation of the word of God to the sign and the reality it represents. The outward and visible sign is a legitimate concession to man's corporeal nature which is intended to lead faith from the seen to the unseen. To unbelievers the sign may become a stumbling-block which ends in idolatry of the symbol. Nonetheless, signs are legitimate and intended as tokens to believers and as encouragers of faith already there. The sign does not create faith. Faith is not generated by outward or visible signs!

The Sons of Noah

9:18-29 Modern scholarship flatly contradicts the statement in verse 19. This is one of the places where we must take a stand against the voluminous speculations of the learned and abide by the word of God. We are told: 'As a scientific account of the origin of the races of mankind, it is disqualified by its assumption that nations are formed through the expansion and genealogical division of families; and still more by the erroneous idea that the historic peoples of the old world were fixed within three or at the most four generations from the common ancestor of the race ... Whether a single family has ever, under any circumstances, increased until it became a tribe and then a nation, is an abstract question which it is idle to discuss: it is enough that the nations here enumerated did not arise in that way, but through a process analogous to that by which the English nation was welded together out of the heterogeneous elements of which it is known to be composed.'

We make no comment upon this but standing upon verse 19, although without prejudice as to how it should be interpreted from subsequent hints in the record, we proceed to the unhappy incident of Noah's sin. The RSV renders verse 20 as if Noah was the first farmer (*Noah was the first tiller of the soil. He planted a vineyard...*) but surely 2:15; 3:19; 4:2; 5:29 disprove this. The NIV translation is to be preferred: 'Noah, a man of the soil, proceeded to plant a vineyard.' It appears rather that he was the first to cultivate the vine (see NIV footnote). That was no sin. Nor was it a sin to drink of its fruit. But to drink too much until he shamefully unmanned himself was a grievous sin which was the occasion for the lewd ridicule of his offspring (cf. Hab. 2:15). The sin of Ham's attitude and action (22) is heightened by Shem's and Japheth's chaste, respectful behaviour (23) and is shown to be both the cause and effect of a baser moral outlook. (There may be the suggestion in verse 22 that Canaan, Ham's son, had something to do with the unseemly incident and consequently incurred the curse along with his father.)

The curse in verse 25 is very serious. There seems to be no ethnic reason for not accepting the spreading of the Semite races eastwards (from whom Abraham came) or of the Indo-European races north and westwards, or the Hamite races southwards, particularly to Africa (see Pss 105:23, 27; 106:21, 22). Therefore, we believe it is not too much to say that the whole vexed question of colour bar arose from this sin. Not that this excludes the effects of the sun, it is simply that exposure to its intense rays in tropical Africa was part of the judgement. This will horrify some, but we have read too much already in the brief compass of nine chapters to doubt the far-reaching effects of sin!

Chapter 10

The Table of Nations

10:1-32 In this chapter we have the overspreading of the (known) earth. The chosen seed comes last according to the pattern of the Genesis' genealogies. Japheth is first with the Indo-European nations, here 'chiefly concentrated in Asia Minor and Armenia, but extending on either side to the Caspian and the shores of the Atlantic'. Some find it an interesting study comparing the names of Japheth's sons and their tribes with modern place names and ethnic groups (cf. also Ezek. 38:2, 3). Ham is second and, since the truth is often more complex than systematisers like, we find that his sons do not only overspread Africa ('Mizraim' is Hebrew for Egypt) but also Arabia and beyond – the region from which Abraham the Semite emerged.

It appears that Nimrod was not only a man of renown but, as often goes with it, a great show-off. Jehovah would not be taken in although his people often are by sheer human prowess. Nor ought ordinary human beings to be cynical about human achievements – we have one in the next chapter in the tower of Babel – but they do not propitiate or gratify God. Shem is the elder brother of Japheth (21). 'Eber' was Shem's great grandson (11:10-14). Note also in connection with Asshur the son of Shem (22) that verse 11 should read, 'From that land (Shinar = Babylonia) he (Nimrod) went to Assyria where he built Nineveh...' (NIV). The genealogy of Shem is not pursued beyond Peleg on his side, although the genealogy of his brother Joktan's sons is given at length. This is because the line is extended to Abraham in chapter 11.

What does 'the earth was divided' mean in verse 25? Are the two brothers another Cain and Abel? (Cf. Jacob and Esau and the prodigal and his elder brother.) The earth is divided indeed and the division is by sin. The puristic refusal to accept the recurring fact of the prodigal brother (or nation) is part of a romantic idealism which is foreign to the realism of the Bible. Sin is something wrought into human nature, although initially foreign to it, and it will take the whole of time to work it out. This does not call in question the efficacy of Christ's redemption but indicates the divine patience in its outworking.

Chapter 11

The Tower of Babel

11:1-9 Chapter 10 has given an account of the descendants of Noah's three sons and their distribution over the known earth. Some object to the contrast between the gradualness of the dispersion in chapter 10 and the suddenness of the judgement in chapter 11. But surely history is an interweaving of crisis and process. Nor need we exaggerate the suddenness of the judgement. We have learned in the creation account that we must 'extend the telescope'. Even in the account of the fall we are not necessarily to attribute catastrophic events to swift, clockwork action. Nevertheless, as man can turn the whole course of history by the decision of a moment (cf. the decisions relative to the Crucifixion), much more can the Almighty do this in judgment and so instantly confuse the whole human situation.

We do not believe the story of the Tower of Babel (cf. Nabel = folly) to be a mere myth, even 'myth' in the technical sense. However it is a parable of God's advancing judgments upon sin as the cursed presumptuous spirit of fallen men develops. The account is embedded in history as the findings of archeology confirm. Photographs of the ziggurat uncovered at Ur show lines of modern pilgrims ascending its various stairways, just as men of Abraham's day may have done in their ascent to worship the moon-god. Skinner says, 'The most conspicuous feature of a Babylonian sanctuary was its ziggurat – a huge pyramidal tower rising, often seven terraces, from the centre of the temple area, and crowned with a shrine at the top ... the ascent of the tower was a meritorious approach to the gods; and the summit was regarded as the entrance to heaven ... the resemblance between the language of the inscriptions and that of Genesis is too striking to be dismissed as accidental.'

Note in verse 4 that the gradual dispersion implied in chapter 10 is seen as a bad thing to be resisted. There is no need to assume that dispersion of itself is a judgment of God. Surely before man fell it was envisaged as an expansion of the garden of Eden. It is the resistance of it for ambitious and presumptuous reasons which is sin. The judgment therefore was not the dispersion which would seem to be inevitable in a growing population, but the confusion which separated man, not only by distance, but by language and customs and which rendered it harder for him to mass himself together and assume arrogant, godlike powers.

Note that the succession of world empires which arose between David and Christ were God's answer in judgment to the backsliding of Israel and Judah. The modern tendency towards world empire doubtless arises from the same cause in Christendom, the New Testament Israel. Think of the confusion which followed the decline and fall of the Roman empire (the last of the great five), a confusion which lasted until the Renaissance, the Reformation and beyond until in our day world-empire has again become a realisable dream and ambition.

God could confound the nations again, not by water or speech, but by fire and begin once again with a remnant (the prophesied final judgment is by fire, 2 Pet. 3). We see therefore the movements towards world unification (perhaps even in a world church whose aims could be more political and sentimental than Biblical) as a stratagem to take the rule out of the hands of the Almighty. If we look at our Guide Book we shall see that, due to sin, God has ordained that his kingdom shall come in hiddenness and mystery (Matt. 13). But Christendom will not have it so and non-Christendom has its own ideas. The end of all these things may be envisaged therefore as it is described in one verse of the Revelation (20:9), 'And they went up on the breadth of the earth, and compassed the camp of the saints about, and the beloved city: and fire came down from God out of heaven, and devoured them'.

From Shem to Abram

11:10-32 We come now to that genealogy which may be said to follow on from that in chapter 5. Its form is similar, and, like it, steers a straight (although not necessarily an exhaustive) course from one point to the other. The first genealogy is from Seth to Noah; this second genealogy is from Shem, Noah's son, to Abraham. Note the decreasing ages and the younger parenthood.

There are two Nahors (24f, 26f.). There is debate as to the order of the sons of Terah. In a note on the older Bible chronologers in his commentary on Acts, F. F. Bruce holds them to have assumed that Haran was the eldest. The order in verse 26 would therefore be that of the brother's importance. Haran, by his death in Ur before the family moved, no longer appears in the record. Nahor married his cousin, as

Abram married his half sister (20:12).

What did Terah know in departing from Ur? We are told in Hebrews 11:8 that Abraham 'obeyed and went, even though he did not know where he was going'. The purpose 'to go to Canaan' (31b) may have been Terah's own. If so he changed his mind half way at Haran (no connection with Terah's deceased son), probably due to advancing years, and remained there. But the Lord had said to Abram (12:1) to leave his country *and* his kindred; the latter he apparently failed to do, wishing to remain with his father as long as he lived. This at least is how Stephen reads the history (Acts 7:4), influenced as he may have been by a variant reading in the Samaritan Pentateuch. The difficulty in Genesis is then solved by assuming that Abram was born sixty years after Haran (cf. 11:26; 12:4; Acts 7:4).

Of one thing we are sure: the call came originally to Abram in Ur, 'before he lived in Haran' (Acts 7:2). Did Abram insist on taking his whole family against the Word of God? Or did Terah insist that they should all come? Possibly the former, so that when Terah settled down in Haran, Abram allowed his earthly ties to silence the Word of God.

We are so serenely sure that we can make God's will unite with what is against God's will, and we delight in our ingenuity in serving God and ourselves; but it always turns out that it is God who is forgotten. God knows this, and wants to save us the shipwreck we make of trying to reconcile the irreconcilable. The plausibility of saying, 'There is no harm in this', or, 'Surely this can dwell together with God', is plain when we realise that what we want along with the Lord is really another god who will not be content with second place, or even equal place, but intends to oust the Almighty altogether. We see therefore that Abram's undue attachment to his family was inspired by God's enemy to frustrate the divine purpose concerning Abram and the promised land.

Chapter 12

The Call of Abram

12:1-3 Acts 7:2-4 reveals the moral and spiritual tension underlying Abram's removal from his country and his departure from his kindred. This is only hinted at in Genesis 12:1, where the pluperfect 'had', although not grammatically in the text, is true to the course of events. It is clear from the Acts, Genesis 15:7 and Nehemiah 9:7, that the call came to Abram in Ur, whereas it is also clear in Genesis 12:4, 5 that the call also came to Abram in Haran. For some reason which we cannot determine (it is suggested that a general migration took place), Abram's kindred left Ur with him, and all 'settled down' (*katoikew*, Acts 7:2, 4) in Haran, and prospered, whence God had to 'remove' Abram after his father had died, or, perhaps, by the death of his father!

We stress this wrench and struggle of Abram to break away from his kindred because it shows how powerfully Satan acts in and through God's children when major strategy is involved. For this is one of the major turning points in sacred, indeed in world, history. God had before chosen a seed and a family through which to fulfil his purpose, but those not chosen were swept away as in the judgement of the flood. This singular choice of Abraham is different, in that a saving purpose through him to all nations is expressed. Even the first promise of a Saviour (the *protoevangelium* of Gen. 3:15) concerns judgement. This provides the first clear expression of a mediatorial redemptive purpose, and it contains very great promises. The land was to be shown, in which Abram's seed would become a great nation. But 'great' does not mean merely numerous, or worldly famous, but *known to be made great by the blessing of Jehovah.* See 14:17ff., (cf. 2 Chron. 9:6).

Nor was their greatness to be merely a boast anent other nations, toward the evangelistic purpose of leading them to seek and find the Hebrew's God (e.g., the queen of Sheba). This nation which was to be Jehovah's evangelist to the whole world would be the touchstone of weal or woe for every nation. Those who acknowledged the Hebrews as blessed of God would be blessed, for God would be pleased with them and those who cursed them would be cursed by God. Nor was this a mere threat to try to advance the Hebrews' prosperity, but objectively expressed what would happen to each nation as the

Almighty pursued his sovereign and invincible purpose of blessing the whole world through them. Resistance to his purpose would be crushed. See Matthew 25:31-46, especially 32, 33, and cf. Revelation 7:9.

12:4-7 On the construction of this great story which we have tried to build up from the scriptural evidence it appears that Abram may have been the son of Terah's old age, and, although already married when they left Ur, was either completely devoted to his father or entirely possessed by him, possibly both. When God cannot separate us from our dear delights, he must take them away from us in the interests of his kingdom, and in our interests. It was said of a deceased business man he had not left his money, but that he had been taken away from it!

Abram, bereft of his father – he still had Sarai, and Lot, and 'all the possessions they had accumulated' and 'the people they had acquired in Haran'—at last strikes out on the God-directed path and reaches Canaan. Passing through the land he came to Shechem, a place whose history it would be fascinating to trace with the aid of a concordance (see e.g., 35:4; Joshua 24). Shechem means 'shoulder', and refers to the ridge which connects the two mounts of Ebal and Gerizim (the latter the place of the Samaritan temple in our Lord's day), which stand about two miles apart overlooking a fertile valley.

In verse 6, 'the plain of Moreh' (AV) should read with NIV 'the great tree of Moreh', or 'the oak of Moreh' (RSV). 'Moreh' means 'teacher' and some have suggested the name came from soothsaying in the shade of the great oak. However, it may be that Abram sought in the place used by soothsayers to teach the Canaanites of his God. The place name is not again in Scripture connected with teaching, but references to Shechem may be referred to for further enquiry into this.

It is not likely, however, that Abram, even if he had friendly contact with the Canaanites, confided what the Lord said to him there about his seed and the land. That was something to keep to himself and cherish, not only for future reference, but to guide his immediate footsteps. For how far it did so, see on 12:8-10 (below), but Abram, the father of those who have faith, is also (as we shall see) Abram the wilful. Meantime he built an altar to the Lord who had appeared to him in the land.

'To obey is better than sacrifice', but we often want our religious experience before we obey. Not so: our religious experience is often a reward. The great deeds of faith are not done in a flush of religious emotion, but in the cool conviction of a bare word spoken by a still small voice. Nothing else, within or without, may encourage, and all others may call us fools, but the 'death' of *pure obedience* is the only way to authentic religious experience.

12:8-10 It was natural to go on moving south exploring the land. Few things are so exciting as exploring new land, especially if it is little known even by hearsay. Abram travelled twenty miles south to Bethel (these first emplacements became focal points in the Hebrews' history), and built another altar to the Lord and called upon his name. The first altar was built *in response* to the Lord's appearing to him, which could only take place 'in the land' when obedience had been fulfilled. The second is built with a view to *Abram calling* upon the Lord.

We do not wish to press distinctions where there may be none, but in view of verse 9 and what follows we do not think it unwise to try to discern where Abram began to go wrong. It was not in seeking reassurance that the Lord was still with him twenty miles away from the place of his appearing, but in the exploratory spirit which seemed to inspire it, and which led him on 'towards the Negev (south)' until it took him out of the land altogether and into Egypt.

This is one of the major typical lessons in the Old Testament. Its relevance can hardly be overstressed. Read from Abram's, Joseph's and Jacob's experiences, to Jeremiah's (Jer. 43, 44) – not to mention the dispersion of the Jewish intellectuals to Alexandria, the centre of Greek and Jewish culture in the centuries before Christ, especially the Seventy (LXX) who translated the Old Testament into Greek – and you will find that going on 'towards the south' is always against the will of Jehovah. Even the captivities are towards the North, as the final onslaught of evil is from that direction. By contrast Egypt, for her sins against Israel, is precluded from again becoming a great power (Ezek. 29:14-15). Do we not see the continuing force of this prophecy in the current decline in Nasser's power? The questing spirit of Abram has, by the will of the flesh, passed over that scarcely perceptible line between faith and presumption, between the bold, humble, and purposive act of faith, and the impertinent, aimless curiosity of the tourist.

However, if Abram wants to explore the far South and has no reason beyond his inclination for doing so, the devil will soon oblige. There was a famine in the land of Canaan, and of course Abram could not remain with his people in a land of hunger. Apparently he had always been accustomed to plenty, and could not face starvation, not even to please the Lord. Besides, why had Jehovah brought him to such a land and given him promises concerning it? Why, indeed? That is what Abram had to find out. We never find out why God brings us into unhappy circumstances by getting ourselves prematurely out of them. We must wait in our plight until we see what they are for. This is faith. Anything else, by whatsoever name designated, is disobedience.

Abram in Egypt

12:11-13 We may be tempted to wonder whether the famine was as sore in the North as in the arid Negev (south) into which Abram had come, albeit the 'remains of buildings and irrigation works prove that it was once much more extensively cultivated than at present' (Skinner). The outcome of remaining in the land was seemingly hunger, whereas the necessary outcome of going into Egypt was ungallant, not to say cowardly, conduct on the part of Abram along with the unworthy resort to half truth (cf. 20:12). It would appear that the judgement on Ham has apparently already taken effect and the Semite woman is fairer than the Egyptian women (Gen. 9:24f.).

Our so-called self-preservation often excludes the miracle of divine intervention; besides it is not necessary that we should continue to live in the flesh, but it is necessary that we should abstain from sin or from the appearance of sin. Abram felt it so necessary to flee the land of famine into which Jehovah had led him that he was prepared to sacrifice his wife's honour if need be. What option had she?

This is the ultimate in human selfishness, and a man may not see it until he has taken his first Christian steps and is faced with the challenge of faith in God versus love of self. How can he face the fact of self until has seen the possibility of another sort of life which begins and grows by the death it dies? He sees it in nature (Jn. 12:24), but not in himself, until he is confronted with the divine. Some people then expect the Christian to grow up at once with never a stumble, which is as unreasonable as expecting him never to grow up. The man of faith makes many blunders before he fully learns that the power of mere faith in God is far stronger than the power of self, even when it is reinforced by the devil's aid. The strength of faith is hid in the necessity of dying to exert it. 'These all died in faith.' There is no other way to prove it.

12:14-20 Abram was right about the Egyptians. They did as he predicted. Sarai was taken into the house of Pharaoh and Abram was given lavish presents. The half-lie had worked and all was well: Sarai might even become Queen of Egypt, and Abram was a wealthy man in a great country. But the Lord – he is the hidden factor who puts his head out of his heaven when all our ungodly arrangements are made and to our confusion and dismay says, 'Not quite!'

To many it hardly seems fair that Pharaoh and his household should suffer for Abram's sin (17), but that is too superficial a view. Pharaoh is bound by the fundamental laws of human life which, when not utterly darkened by sin, impinge upon the human conscience. If the son of Ham has strayed far from the monogamy of his father Noah, that is the son Ham's fault, not God's. He must suffer for taking the wife of the Lord's chosen, even if Abram concurs, and it is thus that Abram is appraised of Jehovah's disturbing part in the proceedings.

How often a man's judgement for his sins is wrought out through others with whom he has to do, and who face him with the fact he is unwilling to face himself! However deadened Pharaoh's conscience as to the immoral foundation of his harem, Jehovah makes him see that the plagues are for his liberty with Sarai, and he expostulates with Abram (18). What a disgrace for God's chosen man to be dismissed from Pharaoh with the whole sordid tale of his duplicity, greed of gain, cowardly self-regard and dishonouring of his God exposed to public view! 'Be sure your sin will find you out.' Such exposure is inevitable, although God resorts to the use of the most unexpected means – even the reproach of the ungodly, or the speech of an ass. Be warned!

Chapter 13

Abram and Lot Separate

13:1-4 Abram returns to the land though we are not told whether or not the famine had ended. Accompanied by his wife and Lot, and taking back with him not only all that he had had originally, but also now considerably richer than before, Abram came back to Canaan with something else he had gained in Egypt of far greater importance. He had learned a new and precious lesson about the Lord's hidden working to bring him from his trespassing into forbidden territory back on to the right track again.

Was it gain all round? No. God turns our ill into good for his glory, but the lesson of trusting God in the famine has still to be learnt. It is all very well to be taught by our sins that God's laws are inexorable, but to abide and endure in God's appointed wilderness is a far better lesson to learn. Believers may become aware of the many ways in which the Almighty can check them, but it is far better to prove him in those crises which are divinely ordained to test mettle and upgrade faith. Abram missed that refining of his faith and, with his little spiritual gain where it could have been much, goes back to the altar he made at Bethel to call upon Jehovah and make a new start.

A new start. We are forever making new starts, but the Christian life does not consist in making new starts. The writer of Hebrews says we must 'leave the elementary teachings about Christ and go on to maturity' (6:1). We shall not do this by constantly missing our cue and running helter-skelter to this and that new exploit when the opportunity to make a major stand on faith is before us. The obstacle, we complain, is too big. It is too big for chronic infants, but not too big for growing sons and daughters who want to try their strength in God. Our obstacles are our opportunities. They may determine our advance in faith. But if we avoid them, those same obstacles may be lost opportunities resulting in our remaining infantile – for ever.

13: 5-13 Scenically, Bethel is 'one of the great viewpoints of Palestine'. We can see the two men viewing the 'whole land' (9) and Lot arriving at a decision as he also viewed the 'well watered' 'whole plain of the Jordan' (10). But our study of the foregoing passages has also helped us to understand the spiritual topography of the scene so that we may guess at the cause of the strife between the herdsmen. The record may not explicitly tell us that the trouble arose because of Abram's sin in going down to Egypt and behaving unworthily there. However if we are not to empty it of all moral and didactic content, it as good as tells us so.

God's judgements are never 'out of the blue', but are woven into the web of time. One thing we know when we face it, there is no sin without cost, even if the price is paid, as in this case, after Abram is back in the promised land. This lesson is itself worth its weight in gold to those servants of God who would walk in the paths of righteousness and eschew ill consequences to themselves and their calling. It is not insignificant that the strife arose through wealth which had been greatly increased in Egypt through Abram's subtlety.

We should also note that the problem, having arisen, could only be solved by a humbling on Abram's part and separation from his beloved nephew. It is plain that Lot was in no mood to yield, and was determined to extract the greatest possible advantage from the situation. But Abram, after the Egyptian escapade, had sought to right himself in Jehovah's eyes, and now rose to his full moral and spiritual stature, giving the choice of pasturage to the younger man. This should have shamed Lot, but did not: self was in the ascendant, and whether he had been encouraged in the acquisitive spirit by Abram's unworthy greed in Egypt or not, he is now consumed by a desire to 'get on' and increase his already considerable flocks and herds. The determining factor in his choice was material, not spiritual. It was not even social. He did not love Sodom's evil ways, but had his cattle-breeder's eye upon the fertile plain. He apparently thought the material advantage outweighed the spiritual.

We only need name the places, with their vile associations, to see how wrong he was. For this is a long story, and we can but assess the importance of each event in the light of the sweep of the patriarchal history. The lessons here are chiefly that magnanimity pays in the end, and materialism runs up a huge account. Before any of us can say of our human situation, 'The boundary lines have fallen for me in pleasant places' (Ps. 16:6), we must take spiritual, as well as material, stock. The end of the same Psalm says, 'You will fill me with joy in your presence, with eternal pleasures at your right hand'. This means only 'in your presence' and 'at your right hand'.

13:14-18 Dear Abram! The greatness of the men of God in the Old Testament is not their invariable rectitude (e.g., Jacob and David), but their aptness to repent when they saw their mistake in the light of God's word. The consequences of his sin have taken their course, and Abram has lost the fellowship of a virtual son or younger brother – though it will not be long before Lot desperately needs his uncle. Yet God has always something larger and better for those who take the lowly, sacrificial place in crisis and patiently defer to the arrogance of youth.

Lift up your eyes now, Abram. Lot thinks this most favourable plain is now his. (We shall see!) Not only what remains, but the whole land, north, south, east, and west, is yours and your offspring's. As to family, you think you have lost the only 'son' you are likely to have. That is a greater mistake. Your descendants will yet be as numerous as the particles of the dust of the earth, and if they can be numbered, so shall your descendants be numbered. The direct fulfilment of this, still a prophecy although progressively being fulfilled with the conversion and death of every saint, is found in Revelation 7:9, 'After this I looked and there before me was a great multitude that no one could count, from every nation, tribe, people and language, standing before the throne...'

The nearer promise concerned the land. Abram was to traverse it to see its extent (17), but whether he did so is not stated. He had learned a lesson concerning inquisitiveness and acquisitiveness, and, believing God in the more exciting exploration of the divine will relative to His astounding promise, he humbly sought a place in which to settle down. He found it in Hebron, round the other side of the Dead Sea from Lot, near the great trees of Mamre. There he worshipped the Lord.

The simple narrative reads like a homecoming. How could a man who had been given such amazing promises contemplate a simple domestic life? Well, if he were to become the father of an innumerable host, it would have to begin with a family. Besides, those who are content to dwell simply with God, and willingly renounce the bizarre and demonstrative, may soon find themselves in the midst of momentous events, playing leading, directive roles. Those who take the long view and humbly accept a present, lowly station may find themselves catapulted into most dramatic and significant events. We die to live.

Chapter 14

Abram Rescues Lot

14:1-12 As we study this fascinating chapter, let us keep constantly in mind the moral and spiritual government of the world lest we miss the instructive interactions of cause and effect. When we read that Lot chose Sodom and Gomorrah we immediately think of their destruction by fire, but that was the final outcome of God's judgement for sin. Lot and his family had sorrows enough before that. His chief concern was for the prosperous area, not the people, or their moral or political condition. The difference between Abram and Lot as they stood on the vantage point at Bethel is that Abram had the long view that faith affords, whereas Lot's view was blocked by selfishness.

Concerning the five petty kings of the southern Jordan valley, sin and wickedness had led to carelessness and to the wanton casting off of the yoke of their overlord. Indeed, their position is a miniature of Israel's in the captivities: foreign occupation, resisted, leads to devastation. The judgements of God operate against the heathen as well as God's own people. Twelve years the cities of the plain submitted to Kedorlaomer of Elam (beyond the Persian Gulf), then rebelled, and in the fourteenth year Kedorlaomer came with his vassal kings (5). They came from the east in a magnificent sweep northwards along that belt of fertile land which, turning down from the Euphrates through Syria and Palestine in a huge elbow, skirts the Aramaean desert. They carried all before them in a major campaign of conquest which proceeded southward through Bashan and the Amorite territories as far as the hill country of Seir and the Paran wilderness (6). Then they turned up the eastern side of the Salt Sea to Hazezon Tamar (Engedi is on the western side), beyond which this all-conquering army was bravely met by the kings of the Jordan plain.

It was not merely a daring, but a foolhardy thing to do, and it ended in disaster, for they were overwhelmed and shattered, their cities plundered, and Lot, his family, and his wealth carried off as well (12). This is as plain a judgement upon sin as may be seen. It falls upon the wicked of Sodom and Gomorrah whether or not they see it. Note that God is often more concerned with the act and fact of judgement than with its explanation – many people never know that their trials are divine judgement. However believers should perceive it for what it is.

The divine judgement falls also upon Lot who had gone there to prosper. How quickly God can take away all that we devote our lives to amass, and how quickly he can take us away from its enjoyment whether by sickness or sorrow, or with it by manifold disaster and death! Follow on a map the sweep of Kedorlaomer's triumphant campaign and see how inexorable are God's judgements, even from afar and by circuitous routes.

14:13-16 It is an interesting reflection that the great army of Kedorlaomer had passed close to Abram in its northward march but had not touched him or his wealth. Our God is an accurate marksman. Who was the 'one who had escaped'? Was he a servant of Lot? If so, could he possibly have been one of those who quarrelled, perhaps the first instigator of the strife between Abram and Lot (13:7)? If so, it was exact justice that sent him to appeal to Abram, and if he was sent by Lot himself it was a further irony that made the independent nephew utterly dependent upon his uncle for his very life.

How often those who spurn God's chosen are made to turn back to them again in misfortune as their only help. Whatever Lot had felt on leaving Abram for the fertile plain, there was no bitterness in Abram's heart, only sorrow. As soon as he heard of the younger man's plight, his whole estate was geared to pursue Kedorlaomer and recover him. This is part of the cost of being a man of God. He has to bear the slights of those who think it rather weak and simple – not to say disadvantageous – to abide by the narrow way when there are pleasing prospects beyond. More, when the short-lived pleasures which are out of the will of God have harvested their own sorrow and loss, he must be the first to retrieve the lost, not out of duty or out of the gloating revenge of 'charity', but out of that compassion which genuinely cares for a brother in need.

It was a long road from Hebron to Damascus, and a force of 318 trained men seems pitifully small by which to relieve the Elamites of their prey. Note however that Abram's force appears to have been increased by his allies (24, cf.13b), though Abram appears to have been the leader and commander. We need not speculate as to how it was done, though it is clear that Abram was not without ideas of military strategy. The God who preserved Lot, his people and his goods, was well able to enable Abram to do this (20). We may reflect on the courage and assiduousness of Abram in pursuit of the conqueror of nations with an apparently significantly smaller force. The very idea seems preposterous, but that is the faith that 'laughs at impossibilities, and cries, "It shall be done!"' It is also a faith which worked by love and by a forgiving spirit.

14:17-20 The kings of Sodom and Gomorrah fled and fell into tar pits (10). 'Fell' here evidently does not mean 'slain', therefore it must surely have been a shamefaced king who met Abram on his return from the defeat of the all-conquering overlord (17). We see how a life lived in too salubrious circumstances, slumping into over-indulgence impairs the mental powers, saps the will and renders men unfit for the battle of life. When Kedorlaomer came, the kings of Sodom and Gomorrah appear to have run for their lives, whatever they may have been worth!

The King's Valley (17c), if it is the same as in 2 Samuel 18:18, according to Josephus was 'two stadia from Jerusalem'. So Abram, who in his exploratory travels southward probably did not touch the Judean hills, came for the first time within distance of the destined holy place of Jerusalem. But grace was there before him. Melchizedek, whose name means King of righteousness, presumably lived on the high ground of the crag of Zion (perhaps the same as – or certainly nearby – Mount Moriah, cf. 2 Chron. 3:1). The name of the place was then Salem which means peace. There is a parable in this, not unconnected with the hidden strength in the word 'comfort' (comfort derives from the Latin *cum*, 'with' and *fortis*, 'strength', and hence originally meant 'strengthen') and in the word 'Comforter' (Paraclete = a supporter).

Jebus, as it was later called, was the last Canaanite stronghold to be taken in David's day (2 Sam. 5:6-9). Its peace therefore derived from its strength. Melchizedek was a king-priest, a common combination in ancient times, who worshipped the most high God, Creator (rather than 'possessor', AV) of heaven and earth. He brought out bread and wine (18), primarily for sustenance, but in honour of the doer of an illustrious deed, and doubtless with religious significance. Melchizedek blessed Abram, as having been blessed in his pursuit by the most high God. Happy are those who bless whom God blesses, because they recognise God's blessing when they see it. By contrast, unhappy are those who do not (cf. 12:3).

Now review the significant points in verses 18-20, and see how perfectly both the place of Salem and the name and character of its king speak of the great King-Priest, Christ. No wonder David in Psalm 110, the most quoted in the New Testament, discerns Melchizedek's significance. Hebrews 5-7 bring out this fully in a wealth of typical lessons. For his part, Abram, his action done in the hiddenness of faith (cf. 'what we do not see', Heb. 11:1), discerned a fellow believer in God singularly manifesting divine grace, and gave him a tenth of the spoil. Thus when God's man meets a type of God's Son, he behaves becomingly. This is always the response of God's people when, however surprisingly, they meet authentic grace.

14:21-24 We must not depreciate the generosity of the King of Sodom, even if his offer was the usual custom of war. The man is at least shamed into magnanimity, but it is when the pagan is thus moved that we see how short he falls of the nobility of an Abram. It is the difference between those who possess an ethically effectual religion, and those without it. It is on a religious oath sworn to El Elyon (the Most High God) that Abram disdains the spoil. And the reason? Lest he be put at a disadvantage by the heathen.

This attitude must be distinguished from that of our Lord in seeking the favour of a drink of water from the woman of Samaria. Both attitudes are a witness, but why so diverse? Christ's was his first personal contact with an ostracised woman, and generosity was something she did not know. Her only knowledge of men was as creatures of prey. A man who respected her was something new to her. It impressed and drew her. With the King of Sodom it was different. His knowledge of men who worshipped the Most High God was confined to Lot, and his witness had been neutralised by the common failing of a love of wealth – there was nothing morally distinctive in Lot to impress. Now Sodom would see a man who evangelised by keeping his garment clean of the common taint.

This is the only witness that can shock the worldly wise, whereas with their victims (e.g., the woman of Samaria) it is the opposite action which tells. Yet both witnesses have a common element, namely that both Jesus and Abram stood clear of the common sin, lust in the one case, materialism in the other. We may assume that the king of Sodom had never seen such a combination of altruism as in Abram's pursuit of Lot and his refusal of the spoil. Who could not but be curious concerning a God who inspired men to act thus? It is the nobility of Christian deeds which witness to the power of our Christian God. Men may hate Christians for them, but they cannot but acknowledge the power by which they act in uncommon generosity and high minded altruism. This God is no idol to kneel before and make ineffectual obeisance to, but a God with both eyes open, watching his children both critically and kindly. This mixture of grace intrigues the beholders, both repelling and attracting them. The question is whether repulsion or attraction will prevail.

Chapter 15

God's Covenant With Abram

15:1-5 'After this...' – what did Abram fear? Was it reprisals from Kedorlaomer and company? Or do the Lord's words of comfort in here (1) imply that he had unwise second thoughts about his loss of fellowship with Lot and of the spoil? This is a common depressive reaction following an experience of utter exhaustion. The whole world suddenly seems 'blue', the prudence of one's ardent and noble endeavours is called in question, and God himself appears to become little more than an unproved hypothesis. It is sleep and rest that the exhausted believer needs, and, possibly, that direct appeal to the innermost self which by-passes the turgidity of grosser emotions by means of a dream or trance (see verse 12).

Abram's fears were quelled, not by the promise of a specific gift, but by the assurance that God was God and would be God to him. This is the first thing those who are dispirited need, for with it they can brave anything; without it there is no alternative to despair. Then follows the negative promise that God will protect him: he has nothing to fear. Yet even when fears are quelled, mere safety is a bare prospect. It takes more than this for a full life, especially when driven by faith to do noble deeds. To what end the sacrificial endeavour and costly self-denial? God is the reward.

Is this 'pie in the sky when you die'? Even if it is food for the soul while the bodily state is poor, is that a timely reward? It is not a matter of either/or, but of priorities. How can we know that God is the prime essential if we do not go back experimentally to his existence (Heb. 11:6)? And if he was enough for himself before the worlds began to be, is he not enough for us?

Nevertheless we cannot stifle the aggrieved question, 'Is that all?' The answer is that it is more than enough, but it is not all. 'But seek first his Kingdom and his righteousness, and all these things will be given to you as well' (Matt. 6:33), for those who are in union with God are always fruitful (John 15:1-5). Beyond the mere protection there is God to enjoy, and the sure hope of perpetuity and abundant spiritual offspring. The three essentials of a worthwhile life are God, protection and a future – in Abram's case a son. No sinful life which has these three has any right to complain. The scope is infinite and the prospect glorious.

15:6 It was enough for Abram that beyond safety and fellowship with God, a son was assured– what is the purpose of life if not to perpetuate it by transmission? But assured by what? By God's Word. But that has to be believed. Abram believed God's Word. What is the essential content of a faith which God honours, counting it for righteousness? It can be expressed in terms already used: it is founded upon the assurance that God is himself all-sufficient and all-efficient. He could in fact as easily place a son on Abram's lap without his co-operation as he caused Mary to conceive without human aid. 'Not by works of righteousness which we have done, but according to his mercy he saved us, by ... the Holy Ghost.'

But the merest faith is never alone. The classical insight of the Reformation is that we are saved by faith alone, but not without the exertion of its moral power. Faith without works is dead, because it is not faith at all. The value of *sola fide* is not inertia in the sight of God, but that it firmly believes its co-operation is as much of God as if it left it all to himself. There is therefore no taint of supposed merit in its works of faith. Abram is 'saved' as absolutely by faith only when he gets Isaac, as when he merely believed God's word. Our purpose in making this alignment of faith and works of faith is to combat the antinomian and unethical believism. Such believism equates salvation with two objective experiences, one when we believe and are 'saved', the other when we are 'carried to the skies on flowery beds of ease'.

The tragedy of this view which sees salvation in these two easy stages is that what happens between them is thought to be irrelevant. One jump and you are 'saved', two and you are in glory. The *quality* of the believing life between times does not matter.

This is one of the most pernicious heresies of modern evangelicalism. The truth is that the moral life is all-important, proving or disproving the reality of the first stage of mere faith unto salvation. If faith without moral works is dead, it cannot be the instrument of salvation at any stage. For faith, however rarefied by submission to God, has the seeds of all moral endeavour within it. This is what Paul is protesting to the Romans when he turns from the subject of justification by faith to sanctification by faith. To the question following all he has outlined in chapters 3-5, 'Shall we go on in sin?' he answers, 'You have failed to understand what I have been saying' (Rom. 6:1). The fact that you think easy believism permits you to go on sinning indicates that your believism is not faith at all.

I repeat: faith is moral, and involves moral transformation, however long it takes to accomplish it. God credited Abram's faith as (unto) righteousness because he knew that it contained the germ of moral action. Those who most believe that only God can save, co-operate the most with God in his salvation. Nor do they take credit to themselves. None knows better than they that it is all of God. It is when we work hardest at our salvation (Phil. 2:12f) that we know it is not our work, but his.

15:7-17 We read several times that Abram built an altar to the Lord and called upon him (12:7, 8; 13:4, 18), but this is the first recorded time that Abram addresses God in direct speech. He calls him Adonai Elohim, even after God has identified himself as Lord (7). What this shows we are not sure. Radical critics would say it shows the 'discontinuity' of the text! Our view of inspiration leads us to ascribe more intelligence and breadth of purpose to the Holy Spirit than to jumble the names together in a patchwork text. The first use of the name 'Lord' in direct speech is by Sarai – not in a worthy cause! (16:2). In 17:1 God reveals Himself to Abram by another name, 'the Almighty' (*El-Shaddai*). From this we infer that God is gradually leading Abram to a knowledge of different attributes of his divine character. (See also 16:13).

The name 'LORD' (7) (Hebrew *Yahweh*) appears to be explicitly associated with the land. This was to be the name by which other nations came to know the Hebrew's God – a tribal god like their own as they thought, but with a force reaching beyond national boundaries as they found out because he is God of gods, not only possessor, but maker of heaven and earth.

Apparently the promise concerning the son was more credible than that concerning the land (8). We fail to see the grounds upon which Abram in his request for a sign is absolved from doubt and uncertainty. The different reactions to the two promises (cf. v.8 with v.6), surely establishes the fact that they were received differently. Observe how God accommodates himself to the prevailing contractual practices. Normally the two parties to a contract would walk between the divided pieces of the sacrifice as a sign of mutual obligation. The birds were not divided (cf. Lev. 1:17: is this a symbol of the impassability (not subject to suffering) of the Spirit?) Some have suggested the 'unclean birds of prey' (11) may typify the demonic attempt to interfere with a divinely significant event. Nothing supernatural happened until Abram was drawn into deep sleep in the twilight of the day. Whether the experience of 'a thick and dreadful darkness' (12) was connected with the doubting demand for a sign we cannot say, but the revelation to Abram is of dire events (13f.).

The alternation of moral cause and effect in the Scriptures and in experience forbid our ignoring the possibility of a connection. The dark experience of Egyptian bondage is prophesied in comprehensible terms, which help us not only to concentrate that sweep of Hebrew history into a concise and significant statement, but also with it to prefigure the later Israelite and Judaic captivities as a telling repetition of history. The variations in the comparison between the Egyptian and Babylonian enslavements do not affect the similarities of their significant features.

Here there is enshrined a philosophy of the history of God's people (13-16), and it is for want of an application of this to the contemporary scene that the Church seems so irrelevant and lacking a word for the hour. What Abram sees, he knows will only be fulfilled long after he has died in faith (cf. Heb. 11:13, 39). After the dark experience, the Lord himself symbolically in a representation of fire (cf. Exod. 3:2), passed between the pieces of the sacrifice alone. The meaning is that this is not a contract (between equals), but a divine covenant in which God himself takes the initiative.

15:16, 18-21 The 'Amorites' is a general name for the inhabitants of Palestine. Their iniquity provides the moral justification for the Israelite conquest of the land and the liquidation of the Canaanite nations. The books of Joshua and Judges, not to say all Israel's warlike projects, should be read and understood in the light of this all-important statement (16). It is part of that truth which issues from the fall, that humanity in its best state is not only altogether vanity, but deserves nothing but judgement and hell. Indeed, human sin which always deserves hell is still part of a potion of judgement which may take a long time to fill up before it is drunk. The time God's enemies take to fill up their cup is generally the time of his people's bitterest affliction. During it, God waits to be merciful to the few who may repent, for they have a conscience and cannot be absolved from responsibility even if they make it as dark as night! Further, he also employs the time to humble, purify, and mellow his people – it was a wonderfully united and submissive nation that escaped from Egypt.

We do not forget that Abram's request for confirmation related to the land. The covenant statement concerning the extent of the promise is now made. The land promised is from the river Euphrates to the Nile. (Cf. Num. 34; Josh. 1:4; Ezek. 47:13-21.) This was to be possessed by conquest, the classical statement of which is found in Joshua 1:3: 'I will give you every place where you set your foot.' Here, in a few simple words, the sovereign grace of God's provision is perfectly married to the challenge of man's action, obedient faith. God offers, his people accept. His people fight, God helps them and gives them victory.

Actually Israel never possessed the whole land offered her, which fact is a parable. It was when she nearly did so that she was most effectually God's evangelist to the Gentiles (see 1 Kings 10). The correlation between sanctification and evangelism (not to say their due order) is thereby typically established. Evangelism in the main is not the work of babies, but of spiritual adults. It is not a diverting pastime from the claims of maturity with its constant painful deaths, but a task for the full-grown.

Chapter 16

Hagar and Ishmael

16:1 Take the promise of 'a son coming from your own body' as Abram's heir (15:4) with the statement here that Sarai 'had borne him no children', and see this couple's dilemma. The assumption of Genesis is that domestic life is monogamous (2:24). This is supported even by the account of Lamech's bigamy (4:19-24), and the baneful associations of the only statement he made to them sufficiently noteworthy to be recorded! Undoubtedly the implication in 15:4 is that the promised seed would be not only by Abram, but by his wife Sarai. Barrenness was no barrier to Jehovah. 'Sing, O barren woman, you who never bore a child … because more are the children of the desolate woman than of her who has a husband' (Is. 54:1; cf. Gal. 4:19-31).

The woman takes the initiative (cf. 3:1ff.). How often in history initiative is born of impatience and of failure to understand the rough road by which God reaches his goals. The royal road is the hard road whose glory is hid under 'blood, sweat, toil, and tears'. God never subverts his own laws to accomplish his will. He has no need. All power is his, and although his economical use of it is marvellous, it is always instantly at hand. He loves a tight corner.

We are not so adventurous. We lack not only the daring, but also the abandon with which he flings himself into a 'fix' with a gleam in his eye, which says, 'Now watch me get out of this impossible situation!' Those who are for ever running to 'help' him spoil the fun of seeing him undo the snags and run panting and laughing home. Oh, Sarai meddlesome creature! This is not God's way. Little do you know the trouble you are posting to yourself and to your race by the birth of Ishmael, the father of the Arabs!

16:1-4 Sarai had asked for it, although in adopting the customs of the day she had probably given little thought to consequences. If when tempted to fall away from God's laws, we took time to think through the obvious consequences of our deeds we would see how unpropitious they are. Sarai's intention was to use Hagar as a chattel. But this is *the* sin against God and our fellow-creatures. Whoever commits it discovers the dire consequence that the creature, being a person in her (or his) own right, asserts herself to the confusion of the user. Even an Egyptian maid was no mere surrogate mother for Sarai, but had a life of her own which when debased, naturally – albeit sinfully – reacted against the contempt of the barren woman.

This compensating adjustment of God was mercy to Hagar, although she used it spitefully to despise her mistress. She had the inner satisfaction that she had an ability which her mistress had not. This was God's gift in kindness to her. She should have rested humbly in this knowledge. But sin intruded and the conflict that resulted was part of Sarai's judgement for her forwardness. Thus sin begets sin until it produces an innumerable progeny – none of which dies – until our world becomes so full of frustration that God's purposes have little apparent hope of survival.

This is the kind of situation in which God chooses to work. No one can read the Bible with open eyes without seeing the growing odds which God allows against himself. Sinners may do their worst, but God masters all. He might have revealed himself to Sarai or Abram and said, 'This is not the way. If you take Hagar and beget a son by her he will become your nation's greatest enemy and cause your people untold suffering.' He didn't, because he chooses to teach his people not only by words but also by experience. Such a learning process is the only satisfactory school. Indeed, the only way for the wilful self-assured children of God to learn to hate sin is to stew in its juice. This is what Sarai and Abram and their progeny will do. But they *will* learn at last. God is sovereign and easily overrules what he allows. Even though we reach it by a hard road, the final end is glory.

16:5-16 Everything goes wrong, as it must when those who are enlightened by God revert to the ways of the world. Sarai blames Abram which, on the face of it, is unjust. But she had a grievance, not only in the pleasure her maid now had in her husband as well as in her conception, but in Abram's failure to refuse the suggestion in the first place. In the fall, although the primary human blame attaches to Eve, the man as head of the woman bore his own responsibility. It is the same here: Abram stands accused before Sarai of not resisting the offer she now so deeply regrets.

There is a word here for the Christian married. However much the dominance and initiative may lie with the woman – and men love to be mothered – the man is not absolved from his responsibilities of headship. In this case the prospect doubtless pleased Abram. But it was wrong, being both adulterous and presumptuous. Abram should have said, 'No'. If we rightly catch the undertone of Sarai's charge (5), it is that she wishes he had!

Abram's rejoinder makes matters far worse (6). The awkwardness in finding that even a slave-girl has feelings is got over by putting her more firmly in her place and reducing her again to the status of a maid. Not likely! Why? Because both nature and God is against the violation of anyone's personhood. It is not that God condoned Hagar's flight although it was his judgement against her master and mistress. Rather that he makes it the occasion of wise advice and a gracious promise to Hagar (11f.).

This is the first mention in scripture of an 'angel of the Lord'. However we may speculate as to the nature of the theophany (appearance of God), we must be in no doubt as to its divine authority. 'Ishmael' means, 'God hears'. He had heard the distracted woman and in sending her back to submit to Sarai made known to her what a significant, illustrious, and aggressive character her son would be.

We may ask the question, 'In what proportions did Ishmael's maternal ancestry or his upbringing under a sense of his mother's grievance (cf. 21:9-21) breed in him such aggression and defiance?' The name Hagar gives to God and her explanation of it (13), both indicate a God who not only sees (that is always true), but who allows himself to be seen. The name she gives to the well (14) carries the meaning further, for he is the seeing God who in letting himself be seen does not consume the see-er, but permits her to. (Cf. Gen. 32:30; Ex. 3:6; Judg. 13:21-23.)

We have in this incident the whole gospel of grace. There is the sin, both her own and that of those who had brought her to her present plight, her desperate need and destitution, the divine pursuit of the 'hound of heaven', the visitation with its fearsome sense of awe, the grace of the divine care and the wonderful promise, but also the requirement that she return and submit. How often after a divine visitation the Lord requires in the first place that we return to our arduous and irksome lot to see him work out his purpose there, and from there. Is this a word to you?

Chapter 17

The Covenant of Circumcision

17:1-14 Attempts have been made to improve on 'Almighty God' as a translation of El Shaddai, largely without success. Perhaps the context helps as much as the meaning of the words, for the covenant is of gracious promise involving moral and religious obligations (symbolised by physical rite. For the spiritual significance of circumcision see Lev. 26:41, Deut. 10:16, 30:6, Jer. 4:4, etc.). God's might is controlled by his love and his strictures are all in the interests of becoming fit for his loving fellowship.

Note here the difference between a mutual pact and a divine covenant. Abram is not invited to agree, or to say anything at all. His co-operation is assumed and required, yet it is by complete consent and persuasion of his feelings, mind and will that it is to be engaged. The change of name from 'high father' to 'father of many (tumultuous) nations' implies fruitfulness and an issue which will include rulers of nations and a land, all of which are bound up in a covenant of everlasting validity.

The significance of the *everlasting* covenant could be discussed under various historical references, Old Testament, New Testament, and subsequent history, but we grasp its precise meaning only as we relate it to the spiritual import of the rite enjoined (11). The everlasting covenant is not in the end with any ethnic group as such (cf. Rom. 2:25-29), or with any ecclesiastical division, but only with those whose *hearts* are circumcised. This is the Old Testament counterpart of baptism in the New Testament, which baptism both in Colossians 2:11-13 (where circumcision and baptism are identified) and Romans 6:2-11, symbolises our death with Christ to sin. It is far more important to see this than to comb the text for points of contact with pagan mythologies, for inherent in the rite is the message of the Cross, salvation by death and resurrection. The everlasting covenant is not with nations or denominations, but with those who die with Christ to the world, the flesh, and the devil. (Note the 'demand' of the Church of England baptismal service that godfathers and godmothers 'renounce the devil and all his works'.)

It is necessary to consider the significance of the physical act of circumcision. It was not uncommon in Abraham's day, but this does not disturb us: the distinctiveness of biblical symbols is not that they are new (a fact which leads many students of comparative religions astray, as they see nothing more in biblical religion than an improvement on paganism), but that they are given new meaning through historical focus and divine intent. It was imposed upon unsuspecting infants of Abraham's line to bring them within the covenant (cf. Ex. 4:24-26 where Moses is all but slain by Jehovah for neglecting the ordinance in deference to Zipporah's delicate sensibilities).

What was its meaning? First, it was a bloody act, speaking of sacrifice. Second, the completeness of the act as implied in the 'circum' of 'circumcision' symbolises the radicalness of Christ's death unto sin, and our participation in it by faith. (Note carefully the follow through of the argument in Rom. 6:5-11 where Christ's death unto sin on our behalf is described as 'once for all'.) Third, it was performed on the organ of procreation, bespeaking new life. Fourth, it resulted in better physical hygiene, thus its spiritual meaning was also a cleansed life. (See Col. 3:1-11.)

The New Testament application should be obvious. The old covenant was for those of natural descent along with all incorporated into the community by whatsoever means (12, 13). The new covenant is for those of spiritual descent, both within the Christian family and incorporated into Christ by whatsoever evangelistic means. As all within the old covenant were not ultimately accounted to be of the Israel of God (Rom. 2:25-29), no more are all within the new covenant! (Ponder the implications of circumcision for our ecclesiology.) Grace is ultimately a mystery, therefore mystery to some extent enshrouds the critical spiritual issues of the faith which underlie the performance of the rite. This mystery does not absolve us from the responsibility of faithfully performing the Christian rite. Nor dare we assume a lack of faith where the rite seems ineffectual. This also is mystery.

17:15-19 Sarai's name is also altered to suit the mother-to-be of nations. Abraham laughed. God was being far too heroic. He had a son already, by the only means possible. It was awkward, indeed, foolish of Jehovah to pursue the matter of Sarai! But it was Abraham and Sarai who had been awkward and foolish. They believed God as far as they could understand him, yet could not trust him beyond that, but supplemented

– even corrected – that by their reason and by the adoption of prevailing customs. Poor God! pinned down by man's reason and never allowed to do something extraordinary. Most extraordinary!

This same restriction of God is rife in the Kirk, where convention is made to rule all. In the sphere where creative action is most possible and seemly it is excluded by the 'decencies' of the 'done thing'. What a pious fraud is this restrictive 'rationality'! God wasn't doing an unnatural thing, but simply extending certain normal functions beyond the usual age. Yet, Abraham excluded it. He argued: 'We have had a long marriage and there has been no fruit at all. God is not going to wait until the unlikely becomes the impossible and then do a spectacular thing. He is economical of the miraculous.' 'Yes, Abraham, but it can never be ruled out! Less and less so when major works are afoot and a whole series of races are being fathered. It is you who have done the unusual thing by adulterously disrupting your domestic life. God's miracles may break out of the conventional patterns: they never violate His moral and spiritual principles. You are the innovator, Abraham, not God. You foist this ill-begotten Ishmael upon him as a fait accompli. But he will have none of it. That is your affair. The son of hope God promised through you is also by your wife, not her maid. You must readjust your mind to this immediately.' The child's name was to be Isaac which means, 'he laughed'.

Why do we perversely run ahead of God, assuming we know what he will do? He will do what he says, but our rational interpretation or extension of it is as likely as not to be disastrously wrong. Keep by his word. Take it seriously, but do not go one iota beyond it.

17:20 The strictures of the legal mind are far too rigid and hopelessly inadequate to cope with the complexities of good and evil in the divine struggle. 'God should not give sin licence to manufacture so much embarrassing evil,' we say; 'and where he does, should he not more strictly define its limits? Should not Ishmael be kept down?' No. This is the way of the coward who does not believe in the righteousness of his cause, and has to underwrite and prop it up by various defensive means. Not so God. His cause is forged in the crucible of opposition and impossibility. He casts it to the dogs, exposes it to the winds of adversity, and lets all the fiends of hell fasten on it to its destruction. Thus he shows its inherent and invincible superiority.

Nor is this done quixotically. God does not add to Ishmael rumbustious power: nature and sin attend to that. Ishmael is a son of his 'high father' Abram, and of his run-away Egyptian mother, and these qualities combine to make him a mighty character. (Compare Absalom.) Ishmael is destined to become the father of 12 nations. Thus God allows nature and sin to multiply the opposition in his invincible purpose. This is the involved nature of God's battle for the victory of his will.

Let us absorb this lesson into our systems until we see its long-term confidence in every page of the Scriptures until all our impulsive, defensive, and defeatist reactions are curbed, and we leave the outworking of hell's destruction and the divine victory to God. Meanwhile let us get on with the simple task of daily living by the power of the Spirit fulfilling holy laws.

17:21-27 God repeats in plain terms the promise of the birth of Isaac, and departs to let Abraham fulfil the ritual part of the covenant. This he does 'on that very day'. This is the sort of obedience God likes. We have already said the practice of circumcision was probably widespread in Abraham's day. Josephus gives the age of thirteen as the point of circumcision amongst the ancient Arabs, and Ambrose as fourteen amongst the Egyptians. It is suggested that the notice concerning circumcision in this passage is based on knowledge of ancient custom. 'Anthropological evidence shows that it was originally performed at puberty, as a preliminary to marriage, or more generally, as a ceremony of initiation into full religious and civil status of manhood' (Skinner).

We should not, however, assume that the Hebrew's practice of the rite had no influence subsequently on surrounding peoples. On the other hand we should reflect on God's adoption of primitive religious rites as symbols of the highest biblical concepts. Some students on finding Hebrew and Christian rites and sacrifices amongst pagan peoples either drag them down to the heathen level or frantically try to dissociate them for them. No need. Why should we not allow the glimmerings after religious truth of even the vilest heathen nations? That they have a little light does not detract from the full light! (See Rom. 2:11-16.)

Return to Abraham's instant obedience. Although the practice was doubtless not unknown, surely it was remarkable that he organised the operation for all his considerable personal estate 'on that very day' (23). His uninhibited alacrity is telling. We read many stories of the opposite sort in the Scriptures, and in subsequent religious history, in which the called servants of God are initially obtuse. All the more evident is it that lack of inhibition in obeying the commands of God is a sign of a superior quality of faith. It is true those who have it may still occasionally lapse and fall away, but when confronted with the challenge of the Word of God they have no hesitation, but plunge their personality into co-ordinate and purposive action. This is the mark of a promising servant of God. However, when that hesitation and inhibition tends to have the upper hand in our lives, the hopes and prospects of fruitful service are undoubtedly diminished.

Chapter 18

The Three Visitors

18:1-8 This is one of the loveliest and most instructive stories in the Bible, which we must take by itself. The comment in Hebrews 13:2 about hospitably entertaining strangers because some have thereby entertained angels 'without knowing it' is important, especially the 'without knowing it'. We are reminded of the practice in certain business circles of sending representatives incognito to test the quality of service in their own establishments. Then there are those who surreptitiously classify hotels. Here in Genesis 18 God comes down to see how Abraham treats wayfaring strangers. To profit from this lesson is far more important than to argue about who the three were.

As to the visitors' identity, the text permits us to take high ground, since they are a trinity initially addressed in the singular as 'My Lord' (3). Surely the simple mind accepts the record as it stands. One of the three is repeatedly called 'the Lord' as the story proceeds (vv.10, 13, 17, 20, 22 etc.). Further, two of the three go on to Sodom (vv.16, 22; 19:1) while Abraham remains standing before the Lord who stays on longer with him (22). However, the important thing is that the authority, discernment, and power of God is vested in the visitors (cf. also ch. 19). The lesson is that Abraham, aware of no more than that three passers-by were in need of 'entertainment', gave of his time, energy, and substance to his utmost. The details may be compared with ancient

and modern bedouin custom. He could scarcely have done more –
'Abraham hurried ... ran ... selected ... gave ... brought ... set'.

Ultimately he discovered he had been personally serving God. We
are reminded of the words of Jesus, 'Whatever you did for one of the
least of these my brothers, you did for me' (see Matt. 25:31-46). The
difference between the two passages is that in the Old Testament God
is being served, whereas in the New Testament it is his needy ones.
However from Jesus' point of view there is no difference at all – it was
done for him. Therefore to treat a person with scant attention or respect,
say, at the door or on the telephone, and then find that they are of some
importance and change one's tone, is simply to show the limits and
inadequacy of our charity. We are all guilty here, and the standard is
high.

Furthermore our time, energy, and substance is limited (although
not always as much as we claim!). Our only hope of attaining God's
standard of practical charity is to be so at leisure from ourselves that
we are ready to serve to our utmost whenever that may be called for.
We must learn to trust God will give us the needed discernment, lest
we cast our pearls before the brutish and waste our substance on the
devourer. Yet, think of the 'waste' of God's love. Our lovely story has
turned into a tremendous challenge. God help us!

18:9-15 Here begins Abraham's realisation that the strangers are no
ordinary visitors. It was perhaps not surprising that the name of the
wife of such a prominent man as Abraham was known to travellers
through the land, but perhaps the rather obvious addition of 'your wife'
made Abraham start a little. The words spoken by the Lord (note the 'I
will surely return' in verse 10) are meant for Sarah's ears, for the tent
where she thought she was concealed was immediately behind him.
Perhaps she was listening in any case, especially when she heard her
name.

The astonishing thing about the story is the combination of sheer
homeliness and divine momentousness. Sarah is behaving like a coy
maiden eavesdropping behind the door while God is making a solemn
pronouncement concerning his eternal purpose. Life has always that
complex of mundane and momentous for the believer, only we do not
see it. Not that God is always making strategic pronouncements, but
he is always *there*, and never standing idly by.

It has been suggested that Sarah regarded the visitors as three ordinary wayfarers. So did Abraham, we believe, until they began to talk, but as that idea was soon dispelled from his mind by the words in verses 9f., so surely from Sarah's mind also. The laughter, we aver, is not dissociated from that sinful preoccupation with the most intimate relationship of life which so often mars its holiness. Whatever Abraham or Sarah knew by this time, it is clear that the Lord expected them to understand who was talking to them. This fact points a most relevant lesson to us. In guidance, how are we to know that the Lord is speaking? Faith, which rises with purity of heart, will know. God may come in the homeliest guise and in the most ordinary surroundings, but the 'pure in heart shall see God'. The question, 'Is anything too hard for the Lord?' (14) indicates in what dimension the man and his wife should have been thinking. The emphatic words that follow the question certainly brought Sarah to her senses, and she began to fear and tried to cover up (15). That was the most imperceptive reaction of all.

What is the nature of that laugh which echoes in our hearts when God says something big to us? Is it cynical, as if we are saying, 'I have been straining after that all my life and now you come when it is beyond possibility, and say to me that I shall have it?' Ah, but we forget that only when we renounce our too dear desire can God give it with his blessing. God could easily let us have what we want without his blessing, and often we are eager enough to snatch at it on those terms. But God does not permit us to have our own way. He has made us for himself and also for his blessing. Without that dimension of deepest and sweetest fellowship with him, all the dearest delights on earth are missing his loving purpose.

Abraham Pleads for Sodom

18:16-19 It was while Abraham was performing the final courtesy to his guests, conveying them on their way, that they came to a point whence they could see the Dead Sea and Sodom beyond. Jerome calls the place Caphar-Barucha, a deep ravine over 3 miles east of Hebron. There the Lord begins to speak. (How wonderful it is to visit the place and confirm geographically the authenticity of the narrative!) The Lord says he will not hide from Abraham, destined to be the father of many nations, what he will do in respect of Lot's home town. But the divine confidence is not shared as a reward for Abraham's faithfulness (19), but with a view to that faithfulness continuing. God is not previewing Abraham's life and rewarding him beforehand; rather is he ensuring its quality by his knowledge of him. Thus the beginning of verse 19 should read, 'For I know (NIV, have chosen) him *in order that* he will direct his children...'

This is the knowledge of God which is not, like ours, a mere factual affair – God is no spectator – but creative, purposive knowledge (cf. Amos 3:2, AV). Therefore God is no mere judge (like an umpire or referee) who waits to see how men will do, or even predicts what they will do, in order to reward them; but *pre-determines* what they will do to accomplish His will. It may be helpful to understand the verb 'know' (translated in verse 19 by NIV as 'have chosen') in its common Hebraistic sense of 'enter into intimate relations with', as in Genesis 3:1 (AV), 'Adam *knew* his wife ... and she conceived...' God was not asking Abraham to be a good man or even bribing him to be so, but was entering into a deeply personal relationship with him so that he would be.

This is the kind of constructive psychology which on the human side galvanises men and women into obedient action. Thus Abraham, even if he had been unwilling, is engaged and involved, covenant-wise, up to the hilt, and has no option but to listen with a full sense of responsibility. But his will is not over-ridden. It may seem to be at first. But consider what is set before him to encourage his hearty consent – his high destiny, and the knowledge that every nation on the earth will be blessed through him. No man who saw this could do otherwise than leap to it with all his powers.

It is thus God commands us, not without showing us the eventual advantage of obedience. That his command engages our will does not detract from its freeness. Rather does it set us free from our own narrow, blind, injurious wills, to devote ourselves wholly to 'his good, pleasing and perfect will' (Rom. 12:2).

18:20-23 The difference between the 'outcry' of Sodom's wickedness and the angelic testing of it is not a difference in factual, but in deliberative knowledge. This is the force of the verb, 'I will know' in verse 21. God will give them one more chance, so to speak. Not that he has hope – He knows them too well. Why one more chance? First that justice may be seen to be done. Second, in circumstances most conducive to decency, if there is a spark of decency left, it may be they themselves might discover their depravity. Certainly it is clear from the context that Abraham understands God's, 'If not, I will know' (21) to mean punishment unto destruction (23).

We are here (22) obliged to think of the three visitants as Jehovah himself accompanied by two angels (see above on vv.1-8). As the men turn away to go to Sodom, in his distress of heart for Lot, Abraham detains Jehovah to plead for the place on his nephew's account. The terms on which this is done elict a principle upon which in subsequent history God deals with wicked nations, his own or others: he is willing to withhold judgment upon any nation, however wicked, if there be a sizeable remnant of righteous folk within its bounds. This principle would have operated savingly in Sodom's favour if Lot had gained even a few converts to righteousness. It is later applied to Israel itself in both the northern and southern kingdoms, whereby the divided nation is saved several times by reason of the righteous in the midst (cf. Elisha and Hezekiah in 2 Kings 6:8–7:20; 9:1-37; 19:14ff.). We have ample reason to believe that the British nation has been so saved twice in living memory.

This story of Abraham's pressure of intercession teaches us two lessons about the Lord. First, his wonderful patience with the righteous intercessor: 'The prayer of a righteous man is powerful and effective' (Jas. 5:16b). Second, there is a limit to the divine patience, even with a righteous man, if he pleads for a nation beyond that minimum of righteous people within it. The minimum in this case was ten (32). Whether Abraham was satisfied that he had reduced the odds to realistic and safe proportions, or whether he knew this was God's limit, is an open question. If the former, he was sadly wrong, for only four essayed to escape and one turned back. If the latter, Abraham contented himself, knowing that he had done all he could for Lot. But if Abraham thought that Lot's safety was dependent on saving Sodom, he did not know the individual selectiveness of the Lord's righteousness. (See below on 19:1ff.) Sufficient to conclude that we learn God will save a nation for his remnant's sake even if it be an ineffectual remnant and has to be prayed for by another righteous man; but it must be a sizeable remnant.

Chapter 19

Sodom and Gomorrah Destroyed

19:1-11 The two angels proceeded to Sodom. What was Lot doing at the gate of the city, the public place for meeting and transacting business, in the evening? In David's day it was first thing in the morning that judgement was done at the city gate, and it was when David's zeal languished in this respect that Absalom was able to steal the hearts of the people. Compare also the Jeremaic phrase for Jehovah's earnest appeals to ungodly Israel: 'rising up early and speaking (or sending)'. Was there a more sinister reason for Lot's presence there in the evening? It is hardly likely he was aimlessly or complacently enjoying the evening sunshine. Was he in fact anxiously watching the beginnings of the night life of the city? The New Testament refers to him as 'a righteous man, who was distressed by the filthy lives of lawless men' and 'was tormented in his righteous soul by the lawless deeds he saw and heard' (2 Pet. 2:7f.).

The importance of Sodom's critical test is that the angels doubtless appeared there, as they had to Abraham, as men of the highest quality to be held in honour. If there was any restraint of the perverse lust of the Sodomites, it would be exercised in favour of such honourable visitors, men whom it would be the greatest shame to corrupt, or to whom to suggest such corruption. But there is no restraint (5). Indeed, their lust doubtless burned fiercer for these worthy men, because it is the particular pleasure of diabolical wickedness to defile the purest. This gives the devil his greatest satisfaction.

So far, then, from this wickedness being a matter of degrees of badness which had shreds of decency that would stop at certain enormities, it was of the nature which delighted most to do the worst. There is no hope for this absolute badness which would defile the Holiest himself. God can only destroy it. The angel-men were resolved to remain in the street all night (2b). This would be common for travellers who found no hospitable roof in a city and could not afford to pay for lodging. The text indicates the divine intention is not to think the worst of the city, but to give it a fair trial, assuming that it was possible for wayfarers to remain in the city square unmolested through the night (cf. Moffatt's translation of 1 Cor. 13:7, 'always eager to believe the best').

Lot himself admits how impossible it is, and urges them to accept his hospitality (3a). He therefore takes the greatest pains not only to deal with them honourably, but to pay due regard for their safety. It is in these circumstances in which the most favourable opportunity is provided for any moral restraint on the part of the Sodomites, that they reveal the enormity of their lust. It is typical of such consuming passion to suppose that all men are as obsessed with it as they themselves. Doubtless they assumed that no one would lodge for the night in Sodom for any other reason. The two men's rebuff would not only incense them, but fill them with a sense of injustice that any should come to the city to incite them and then frustrate them. (This is common amongst shameless people. One of the most despicable features of the lewd exhibitionism of actresses is that they can be the most cold and passionless creatures who calculatedly inflame men's lust.)

The imperiousness of their lust is seen in that after being smitten with (probably temporary) blindness (cf. 2 Kings 6:18-20), they still wearied themselves to find the door (so AV). This is the awfulness of sinful craving of whatsoever sort, that it grows beyond all control, and at last finds itself in hell where it is cut off from any fuel for its devouring. Hell is therefore the place or state of unfulfillable desire. Note in verse 3, 'bread without yeast' or 'unleavened bread' is suggestive of Lot's personal righteousness; and also in verse 4, 'from every part of the city – both old and young – surrounded the house' is by contrast suggestive of the totality of the depravity of the place.

19:12-15 The divine urgency is impressive. The scoffers in Peter's Second Letter say, 'Where is this "coming" he promised? Ever since our fathers died, everything goes on as it has since the beginning of creation' (3:4). Just so, but when God at last rises up to punish, although there be no outward sign of it in the earth, it is well to heed the slightest hint of divine warning, for God's judgments are swift and sudden – the more so when they are long delayed. Patience held in, bursts at the last, with fearful consequences.

Nor have these wicked ones any excuse for complacency. As Peter goes on to say in his Second Letter, they are willingly ignorant of the fact that God had already devastated the earth by the flood. Although that form of judgement was thereafter excluded by the Word of God (Gen. 8:21), other forms, including fire, were not (2 Pet. 3:3-7). One pattern of divine action which will not change in any age is that moral wickedness, when it has adamantly refused to repent, will be visited with full consequences. This has nothing to do with different ages, dispensations, or eras, but with the eternal inviolability of the law of God. As neither God nor the abiding precepts of his law change, no more does his dealing with those who refuse his grace.

Lot pleaded with 'his sons-in-law who were pledged to marry his daughters' (14). Why did such young men desire a righteous man's (presumably) righteous daughters? For the reason given earlier, that the devil loves to defile the pure far more than further corrupt that which is already corrupt. Does this not explain, beyond all natural attractiveness, why wicked people love to corrupt the young and innocent? There is in the heart of the depraved a particularly diabolical satisfaction in introducing the innocent into vile practices. This should be understood, for it explains a great deal, although it excuses nothing. We are not suggesting that the men's desire to marry Lot's daughters was of itself depraved. Rather we are wondering what sort of a life the women would have had with these wicked men, not unlikely to have been storming Lot's door the night before along with their associates?

The mockery – they treated Lot as if he was joking – is something which we should understand and expect. The ingenious perversity of the whole community had become so 'natural' to them that it was inconceivable that any judgement should fall on them for it. Why should they be so spiritually blind? To be fully initiated into the devil's ways and to know no other, is to become implacably and, apparently, 'rationally' opposed to God's. For Lot to plead with such men was truly to cast pearls before swine. It was a waste of time, and an offence to God.

It is like this to some extent with the wicked today, not least in our own land. It is almost a sin to waste the holy Gospel on them. They are too far gone to do anything but trample it under their feet. They should not be given the chance. To speak to them of the love of God in Jesus Christ is only to cheapen holy things, and God's children may have to answer for doing so. All we can do is warn them of coming judgement and then flee, and leave them to stew in their unholy juice. That is what the Lord commanded Lot to do.

19:16-23 It is not easy to determine accurately Lot's attitude to the divine summons. He had been living in a cesspool of unrelieved iniquity; yet as we have already seen, 'that righteous man living among them day after day was tormented in his righteous soul by the lawless deeds he saw and heard'. Was the love of worldly gain which first enticed him there still holding such an powerful fascination for him that he continued to live in Sodom in spite of its hideous evil and had to be half dragged out of it before it was enveloped in flames? What other explanation can be offered than that he was in a daze of the devil? The very mood of the narrative in verses 15 and 16 suggests the angels are aware that they are speaking to a half-crazed man whose mind is hard to penetrate with the stark truth. It is perhaps not too much to say that we have a fleeting glimpse of the 'panic' in heavenly beings at the thought of the destruction of a bemused believer.

How doggedly persistent is the Almighty in saving us despite our chronic provocations. 'The Lord was merciful to them' (16b). Even after Lot has left the evil place, he is not convinced that such drastic steps were necessary. The angels bid him escape for his life, neither lingering nor looking back (17). Yet complacent Lot remonstrates with them, as if to say, 'Tut, tut, Sirs, you are very urgent! There is really no need to be so alarmed. Surely if I go a little way from the place that will please you. You don't expect me to make for the bare mountains infested with brigands!' At this point we expect the angels almost to sweep him and his women-folk off their feet and carry them to the safety of the mountains. But no, the Almighty in face of bland obtuseness is almost exasperatingly patient – at least *we* think so when he is dealing with others! Like an indulgent grandfather, he says, 'Well, I will let you remain near at hand, and will save the place you choose (Zoar) for your sake.'

Then came the fire, and at last Lot knew the awesome truth. He feared, then, so much so that he could not remain at peace in Zoar, but made for the mountains with his daughters. Alas, had not his wife, turning back, remained both in body and mind too near the area of destruction? Henceforth for Lot it was not to be as near to destruction as was safe, but as far from it as possible, even if it meant the bare mountain side and the fruitless end of his line.

19:24-38 To those who need natural explanations of Old Testament miracles there is no lack in the case of the fire, brimstone and salt. The plain where Jordan runs into the Salt Sea is volcanic and sulphurous. Any one who have seen clips of film recording volcanoes in eruption from close quarters will realise how terrible the destruction of the cities of the plain must have been. The miracle lies in God's timely harnessing of nature for a moral purpose.

It would be easy to exaggerate the sin of Lot's wife, but she is surely in Scripture a type of those who look too lingeringly back to the sinful world and are ultimately engulfed in its destruction. How far was Lot spiritually conditioned by his wife? We do not even know when she first came on the scene. What was her nation? Did she influence Lot to choose the prosperous but wicked plain, or had she even a hand in the strife between the herdsmen? We do not know, but it is obvious that she was more at home in Sodom than her husband.

Lot and His Daughters

It appears that Lot had no son. That could easily have been a judgment. He who would gain the best of this world generally finds he loses the best of both. And Lot did. For all the intercession of Abraham (who, although he did not gain his request yet gained his object – God often answers our prayers differently to our asking (29) for he knows all the facts!), and for all his personal righteousness, Lot ended his days as a cave dweller in the company of two depraved daughters.

Whatever privations these three endured, they were able to make wine. People will satisfy their lusts at any cost and in the most adverse circumstances, even 'turning' furniture and other basic necessities into strong drink. For a time these three may have thought the whole world had been destroyed, as in the flood. They may even have assumed that the whole world had lived like Sodom and had therefore deserved destruction, although surely Lot knew better. So often it is part of the curious blindness of evil people that they assume that their vile world is the only possible world. How wrong they are!

It only remains to remark the kind of nations Lot begat. Old Testament history shows Moab and Ammon to be the vilest of Israel's neighbours, whose respective gods, Chemosh and Molech, involved apostate Israel and Judah in the most revolting sins. Moreover they were among her bitterest foes. It is fearful to think that from the line of Abraham arose practically all the surrounding enemies who distressed Israel and Judah in the days of her later backsliding. How strange that the family of God's man should beget in sin almost as many as his spiritual children, to the latter's great confusion (cf. Gal. 4:29).

Chapter 20

Abraham and Abimelech

20:1-6 Critical scholars hold that this narrative is a variant of that in chapter 12:10ff., the difference being 'petty'. One of the most plausible arguments is that Sarah is 'conceived as a young woman capable of inspiring passion in the King'. On the other hand, the allotted span is not yet reduced to 70 years, and the beauty and attractiveness of Sarah, extolled in secular literature, may still have been very evident at the age of 90.

The man who left the urban civilisation of Ur has long since become a wandering master-shepherd, and must necessarily seek pastures new for his flocks and herds. Strange that after God's promise of a son in old age Abraham should still think it necessary to resort to the former agreed subterfuge of calling his wife his sister (cf. v.13)! Surely the Lord would preserve him! It may be significant that we hear of this artifice only when Abraham journeys south. Was there a sinister pull to take precautions for his own safety? If Abraham knew he was being drawn southwards against his better judgment and against the Lord's will who had made such a wonderful promise to him, he knew he could not call upon him to protect him from other sheiks who would seek to slay him for the sake of his beautiful wife. Sarah was therefore to be exposed to defilement after Isaac was promised.

There must have been a very evil pull to drag Abraham and Sarah into such a dangerous and compromising position. As we meditate on the Scriptures, how soon we see the shadow of evil appearing. Then takes shape the design to frustrate or corrupt God's purpose. Nevertheless, the Almighty can allow the wayward wills of his children to go far from the prescribed path, yet prevent calamity overtaking them. How would he do it?

Well, what did Abraham think about Abimelech taking Sarah at such a time? Did he not fear her corruption? Did he not pray to God? We do not know, but God who does not force the wills of his children has other ways of thwarting the results of their folly. He spoke directly to the man (3), although beyond words he safeguarded Sarah by visiting Abimelech and his people with a deadly sickness. There were thus two safeguards, probably three, against Sarah's defilement: first the disease with which Abimelech was smitten, then associated with that his disinclination for intercourse, and thirdly the warning to the man.

God knows His own business best, and will not let his cause suffer. He can come far nearer to the ruin of his purpose than we dare to imagine, yet by his mighty hand retrieve it. Thus he frustrates his children's foolish tricks without violating their wills. The result is that he educates their wills, rather than coercing them. An all-significant distinction!

20:7-18 Gerar is not as far away as Egypt, and Abraham's waywardness is not as great as when he went there. Furthermore, God had a purpose in allowing him to get into this tangle, namely to show him that, singular as was God's call of him, he had no monopoly of the knowledge and fear of God (cf. John 10:16). Abraham had not only discountenanced the possibility that Abimelech knew the Lord, but also the possibility that he knew the one true God under any name or form. He was wrong. Abimelech, if he had not known God before, which is unlikely, now responds to him with the greatest ease and naturalness as if he had viewed his integrity and innocency of heart as in God's sight all the time (4).

It is an unwarranted assumption that the singularity of our divine call excludes his knowledge in others. It is not a false assumption, of course, that the world is very pagan, yet in the most pagan places God is sovereign. Even if our motives for being in wrong places are mixed (or wickedly unmixed), we must not assume that God in his providence may not confront us with some pagan with a real knowledge of God and far more righteous in his moral life than we. This could be exaggerated, and must not be; but we must never exclude the possibility that in the most unexpected places God's righteous man will be there. God is so often found in the unexpected. We should look for him there. This is the spirit of the true evangelist.

The fear of Abimelech and his people is impressive (8). More so his generosity to Abraham. He is not only righteous, his conscience being open to the word of God who in mercy visits him with corrective judgment (always a sign of mercy and of a purpose of grace), but he is instantly repentant when he realises what he has done, and makes all the amends he can in restitution for his wrong to Abraham and Sarah. Verse 16b should read as in the NIV, 'This (the gift) is to cover the offence against you before all who are with you; you are completely vindicated.' There is a wonderful interchange of spiritual benefit in this intriguing story. While Abraham learns from Abimelech, Abimelech also learns this man's standing with God. Abraham prayed to God, and God healed Abimelech and his people (17f.). It was a pity that Abimelech found out the man of God not only with a lie, but with ungodly cowardice. What righteous pagan today would have reacted so graciously? The whole thing is woven with judgment and mercy. Is it not wonderful to find so much of the New Testament in the Old, and the message of Genesis so contemporary?

Chapter 21

The Birth of Isaac

21:1 We almost feel that we have dealt with verses 1-8, so factually have we believed the promise. But our 'faith' is after the event. In a real sense Abraham and Sarah did not 'know' they would have a son until she had conceived, and until the child was safely delivered (though see Heb. 11:1). Think of the number of fears which could have intruded between the one event and the other – that she might miscarry, that the child might be still-born, that it might be a girl (who would in those days continue her husband's line, not her father's).

The test of whether our acceptance of the promise was as believing as theirs (and we have seen that they both had their difficulties in believing) is whether we believe an equivalent promise of God to us, not yet fulfilled. The primary spiritual lesson here, and it is one of the greatest importance, is that the word of God is to be trusted. (We are not here going into questions of how in our day we may know God's word to us. When asked the stock question, 'What constitutes a call to God's service?' I usually answer, 'A call!' To say that God speaks in any day so that we may miss his word or not hear or understand it is surely to put the power of God – not to say his intelligence – at a low level. But some are too anxious to know the word of God but for entirely the wrong reasons: they fear lest it interfere with their plans!)

One of the most serious examples of a servant of God not believing God's word of promise and command simply and exclusively is Gideon. See the number of quibbles he introduces in Judges 6:13, 15, 17, 22,

23, 36, 37, 39; 7:10. All this is not unrelated to Gideon's subsequent backsliding after the victory over the Midianites and his renunciation of the leadership of the nations (see 8:27). The stature of a man of God has much if not everything to do with the simplicity of his faith. The lives of some are dogged by problems of faith, whereas the only real problem is accepting and obeying the revealed will of God. All other problems are mere intellectual sport for our leisure moments – a bit of fun to sharpen our wits.

Given that simplicity, although life still contains sorrows and trials and is far from easy, it is essentially simple. The issues are heaven and hell, God or the devil, faith or unbelief, obedience or disobedience, black or white. There is no grey! Happy are those who can separate the black from the white amidst the infinite greys of life. They will die a thousand deaths. But they will rise from them all, to steer a straight course Home!

21:1-8 Abraham and Sarah now laugh on the other side of their faces. This phrase is usually used the other way round, the 'too happy laugh' first and the 'laugh' of dismay afterwards. But 'he laughs longest who laughs last'. It is only due to the patient love of God that the cynical laugh is ever turned into the happy one. When it is, there is nothing so heart-humbling and softening. Just to picture this old woman with her son is to encompass a whole world of pleasure. To the Heavenly Father, if not to the earthly father, the most significant thing about the child was something that had been enjoined of God and was duly performed by Abraham, his circumcision (4). He was a child with the mark of death upon him, a good and godly death (see again Col. 2:11f.).

There was therefore manifold satisfaction at the birth of Isaac. God was satisfied, and Abraham, and Sarah. And the child grew. Of course, because heaven and earth were conspiring toward his health and prosperity. When heaven and earth agree, what can hell do? We heard recently of a Christian professional man who had inscribed in large letters on his waiting room wall the words from Romans 8, 'If God be for us, who can be against us?' Rather disconcerting for his rivals! It is worth ensuring that God is for us, however long we have to wait for him. That is everything. But if in impatience we attempt a short cut to his will, see our mistake and take the long way round after all, we have still the Ishmael or our mistake to reckon with. And Hagar. What regrets

Abraham and Sarah must have had amidst their pleasure that they had not waited! So may have some reading these study notes. They are written that others reading them may not thus live to adulterate their pleasure in the day of God's fulfilment. Wait on the Lord.

Hagar and Ishmael Sent Away

21:9-14 How sin comes home to roost! Sarah should not have offered her maid to Abram. Hagar when she had conceived should not have despised her mistress. Sarah should not have dealt hardly with her and caused her to flee. Hagar should not have incited Ishmael to mock at Isaac. Sin reacts against sin and evokes more sin to increase sorrow and distress. 'A man reaps what he sows' (Gal. 6:7). Sarah is now in the vastly superior position, not only because she has a son and can now laugh at Hagar, but because her's is the son of promise. Hagar will now suffer for her sinful influence upon her son Ishmael, but if challenged concerning her folly, she would doubtless have said, as many do today, 'I could not help it. The feeling was too strong for me.' But then look what our strong feelings lead to. What a trouble-saver is a forgiving spirit!

Notice that God makes no distinction between the sins of Sarah and the sins of Hagar: both suffer according to the measure of their sin. Yet they are not treated equally, for Sarah the wife of Abraham is a chosen vessel of God. She has therefore the right to demand the expulsion of Hagar and her son from Abraham's household. And Abraham, for all his grief, must comply (11). Here we see how unexclusive is the love of a true parent for his children. Sarah could now do without Ishmael, but not Abraham. His joy in the birth of Isaac did not quench his love for his growing son Ishmael. This God understood, though Sarah did not. Yet God's declared purpose must take precedence over every other consideration, human or otherwise.

God does not say to Abraham, 'There should not have been an Ishmael!' But the unhappy events say it loudly. We must pay to the end for our presumptuous follies. And so the lad and his mother have to go (14). It is a poignant story, one calculated to draw compassion from the hardest heart. Yet, for all Hagar's plight, we can sympathise with Abraham. These two were going out into the wilderness and would know soon enough what would befall them of good and evil. But

Abraham wouldn't know. There would be nothing for him but the haunting fear of their slow starvation, their capture by robber bands, or even their violent death. Not quite! God had spoken, and it must be done.

But surely with Abraham's obedience, seldom so noble as here, came the assurance of God's word. While God proclaimed the clear priority of Isaac, he also found a place for Ishmael in his prophetic word (13). Where was Sarah when Abraham was providing for the woman and the lad? Apparently she wasn't interested. They could die for all she cared – better to die. 'Ah, Sarah, you should not be so cruel. God's command to Abraham to do as you have said contains a hidden judgement for you. One day, when your child is a youth, Abraham himself will take him from you in response to God's command (ch. 22). There will be servants with the father and the child, and wood for a burnt offering. But no lamb for sacrifice. What will your thoughts be then? Perhaps you will then know something of Hagar's feelings, and Abraham's now.' Our sins come home to roost.

21:15-21 Calculating from 17:24-25, 21:5,8, and assuming that the Genesis record is chronological, Ishmael was between sixteen and seventeen when he was cast out with his mother. It must be remembered that longevity was greater then than now, and children would therefore take longer to come to maturity. Note that the age of weaning an infant (8) was about two and half years and that Isaac was forty before he married. This must be borne in mind in reading the record lest we wrongly assume Ishmael as a helpless infant. Further, although Hagar would doubtless quench her son's thirst before her own, the woman would have more stamina than the lad.

It must be emphasised that the lesson in this story has nothing to do with the lad's age. Its first point is the marvel that God allowed the mother and child to come so near death before he relieved them. Was he unable to help until in their extremity they cried to him? That may be so. Certainly God cannot assist our wilful self-reliance. This would lead to our walking home to heaven hand-in-hand with God, saying, 'He has helped me to save myself!' The gates of pearl are absolutely barred to that. 'Nothing in my hand I bring, simply to thy Cross I cling.' But we are sure God was bending down watching what would happen, with the tenderest interest.

It was the boy's voice God heard (17). Was this because his promised purpose concerned him rather than his mother? Was it also because her sin had brought upon her this plight? Note that it is Jehovah (Lord) who deals with Hagar in chapter 16, but Elohim (God) here. Certainly God's care is for the lad and his future. Was there water there and she did not see it (19)? Apparently, for hatred and bitterness are blinding, and hide from us our greatest good. The woman was saved for the son's sake.

It was natural, especially in the circumstances, that she should seek a wife for him in her own land (21), but it was a pity. From Ishmael and his twelve sons (25:13-15) sprang many of the Arab nations who eventually as Muslims became the bitterest opponents of the Jews. Note that according to the historic pattern of the book, the story of the lesser son is again dealt and disposed with before that of the greater son proceeds.

The Treaty at Beersheba

21:22-34 Abimelech is obviously a considerable figure in the land, with a commander-in-chief for his army. The grace of both these men is astonishing. It is to be remembered that when Abimelech remonstrated with Abraham for deceiving him, he took no offence when Abraham said he assumed there would be no fear of God in the land, although Abimelech was clearly a God-fearing and upright man. Abimelech must have accepted Abraham's explanation as truth and completely overlooked the slight. Now the two men testify that they see God is with Abraham in all he does. This does not exclude evidence of Abraham's moral rectitude, but it is different from it.

Had Abimelech been perverse, he could have held up Abraham's lapse as a sign that God was *not* with him, ignoring the manifest evidence of his prosperity. He did not, but with his chief captain confidently approached him, acknowledging the evidence of the divine favour. It is not easy to discuss this without seeming to elicit from the Scriptures an antinomian flavour, as if God had overlooked Abraham's deception of Abimelech. There is nothing of the kind in the Scriptures, nor would we commend such a thing. Indeed, such an intent could hardly be charged on those who are constantly drawing attention to the judgments of God which are abroad on the earth! Nevertheless, God, in His purpose of making men righteous, must begin with unrighteous men who have been forgiven over and over again.

In certain circumstances, therefore, and at certain stages, the evidence of the favour of God may be more important than evidences of strict righteousness. To recognise this fact does not glorify unrighteousness, but sees the persistent grace by which unrighteousness is eventually overwhelmed. Note that Abraham appears less gracious than Abimelech. Was he on the defensive? He certainly deals faithfully with Abimelech about the servants' strife over the well. But Abimelech is able to profess ignorance, and the two men proceed to a covenant.

What sort of covenant is it? Note that the initiative in the interview is Abimelech's. He asks Abraham to swear kindness to him and his prosperity. Abraham does, but reproves Abimelech concerning the seized well (25), and when Abimelech professes ignorance, Abraham takes the initiative in establishing a covenant by a gift of sheep and oxen. This could be viewed as a return gesture for Abimelech's earlier gifts to Abraham (20:14), although that may not have been in mind.

Was this, then, a one-sided covenant in which Abraham did all the giving? It seems so, for in addition to a general gift, he sets aside seven ewe lambs (28). Abimelech does not understand what these are for, but Abraham tells him they are a witness that he dug the well in question. The place is therefore called the Well of Seven, Beersheba. Notice, however, that the name Beer-sheba is found earlier in the chapter (14). This does not necessarily mean that the place had the name before the incident. History is written after the event, and however chronological it purports to be, it is easy to anticipate in the matter of names. We shall look at this more closely when we come to 'Amalek'.

The significance of the perfect number seven is obvious, but not the tamarisk tree which is planted or its apparent link with the 'new' name for God, El Olam. It is hardly new when we think of the emphasis on 'everlasting' in Genesis 17:7, 8, 13. The word Olam is used in the Old Testament of hidden or secret things, and of indefinite time. The Greek synonym which is very common in the New Testament is 'aion', meaning an age.

Chapter 22

Abraham Tested

22:1-3 The word 'tempted' (AV) should read 'tested' as in the NIV. God tests. It is Satan who tempts, although God may use Satan to this end. James points out the blessing of perseverance in testing and then contrasts testing or trials with temptation, by implication tracing sin back through temptation to Satan (Jas. 1:12-15; 3:6). It should be realised that in spite of God's words, 'Now I know...' (12), this is not an attempt to add to God's knowledge of Abraham, but to reveal Abraham's heart to himself. (Cf. Exod. 16:4; 20:20; Deut. 8:2, 16; 13:3; 33:8; 2 Chron. 32:31; Prov. 15:11.)

No reference is made to Isaac's miraculous birth, although this is clearly in the patriarch's mind (Heb. 11:17-19), only to Abraham's love of him as his singular son (2). Abraham's obedience is therefore seen to be not of that stolid, stoic sort that steels itself to any sort of sacrifice, but of that higher sort which by its faith can penetrate the wall of death and see the purpose beyond. The question for Abraham was whether the Lord had taken leave of his senses after all his wonderful leading and guiding. The answer was an emphatic, 'No!' If God's word seemed mad, then there was method in his 'madness', and it was altogether to be followed, whatever the cost. He therefore did as he was bid, without question.

Some people can only obey God when it goes with the 'grain' of their inclination: God can only be right when *they feel* that he is right. This is simply to set ourselves above God when his way is not our way. If we argue this out fearlessly enough, we shall come to a discovery as deep as our destiny; we shall know whether we have at all the faith which saves, or not. This is the only way to look at this event. All appeal to tender emotion and fine feeling is beside the point. Not that these heart-breaking sensitivities do not matter, but that something matters more – the will of God. If the will of God is paramount in our lives, although God may wrack us with pain (and very likely he will at some points), we shall bear it and obey.

22:4-9 There is no need to make too much of it, but the verb 'come back' in verse 5 is plural: '...we will come back to you'. One of the

most trying parts of Abraham's experience must have been Isaac's
questions. There are wonderful depths in Abraham's answer, 'God
himself will provide the lamb for the burnt offering, my son' (8). What
did the dear man know? A careful study of Hebrews 11:17-19 suggests
he expected not Isaac's escape from death, but his resurrection out of
it – 'Abraham reasoned that God could raise the dead'. Two things he
knew. First, God would make a mighty nation of Isaac. Second, God
now demanded his death by sacrifice.

It is because logistic men will not bring the seemingly opposing
members of such a contradiction together, that they are never permitted
to clash and thus to conceive a new idea. The ruling idea is the promise
of a mighty nation. The demand for death is an inter-position, not to
frustrate the ultimate purpose, but, by deflecting it, to drive it on to a
higher plane of fulfilment. This must have been something like
Abraham's thoughts as he trudged his way to Moriah. Mighty thoughts
from our ancient father! Thoughts worthy of the place.

Liberal scholarship tries to tell us that there is no ground for
identifying Moriah with Jerusalem. Nor is the much later reference to
Moriah in 2 Chronicles 3:1 (cf. 1 Chron. 21:18-24) thought to be reliable
(though it is interesting to note modern Jewish scholars have no doubts
as to the location of Moriah as the Temple Mount). Liberal scholars
even suggest that Moriah was introduced into the Abraham story on
the strength of the chronicler's note just referred to. How clever! Thus
those who refuse the inspiration of the Bible stand on their heads to
refute it. Josephus has certainly no doubt (cf. Ant. 1, 13, 1), although
the sacred text, not to our knowledge questioned, is enough for us.

How appropriate that the awesome prefiguration of Christ's eternal
sacrifice should take place on the same mount! However, it is not that
the same place was the location of these events which gives the events
their relationship, but the quality of their sacrificial demand and cost.
So every elect child of God must go to his Moriah or his Calvary. It
matters not whether in time it is before the great Sacrifice or not. Our
'sacrifice' follows his, for his is the pattern which gives meaning to
every sacrifice demanded of God, whether BC or AD. Our sacrifice –
even Abraham's (Jn. 8:56) – must follow Christ's, for his is the
prototype. Yet there is that fundamental element in his sacrifice from
which all of our sacrifices are necessarily excluded: 'There was no
other good enough to pay the price of sin'. We can therefore only

follow him into sacrifice because he has laid the foundation of its acceptance with God. It is ours, then, with the great Apostle to 'fill up in my flesh what is still lacking in regard to Christ's afflictions for the sake of his body, which is the church' (Col. 1:24).

22:10-14 We have seen from Hebrews 11:17-19 that there is no reason to suppose that God expected anything less of Abraham than Isaac's sacrifice, or that Abraham expected to escape the actual deed. Verse 10 can only be read therefore as Abraham's full and active intent. Indeed, the indication that the angel's voice 'called out to him from heaven' (11), perhaps hints at how emphatically Abraham had to be deterred from the deed. He may well have expected a voice from another quarter trying to dissuade him from doing God's will!

We learn that in moments of high destiny the true servant of God must know the voice of God from that of other voices. We may say reverently that it is God's business to make his voice distinct from other voices. We have no reason to doubt, either from faith or from experience, that he does not do so, especially at critical times. It may seem strange to draw from the angel's words (12) the meaning that now Abraham knew he feared God. But what else can they mean? There is never anything experimental or tentative about God's knowledge. The purpose of history is not to prove anything to God. If it were, how could he be assured of the outcome and therefore how could he be as assured as He is?

Rather is history's purpose to show to men and angels the glory of God's grace. It is as if the Almighty is saying to Abraham: 'I am sure you are astonished that you have been able to go thus far. You may well be, for you could not have done it apart from my grace. Now you know, not so much what you can do – of yourself you can do nothing – but what I can make you do. Nevertheless, my grace is such that I will reward and bless you, as if it had been all your own effort, and not of my power. Now take the ram, and offer him for a sacrifice.'

To a natural man, the relief would have excluded all else and the sacrifice would have been performed, perhaps, heartlessly and hurriedly. Not so with Abraham. It must have been one of the deepest moments of his worshipping life. He offered his sacrifice as if it had been the bleeding and smoking flesh of his son. Yet more: it was actually a sacrifice which God himself had provided. Thus by this primitive incident we enter into some of the meaning of the idea of substitution in sacrifice. Refusing to waste time with considerations which quibble over it, we affirm that the substitute is greater than any mortal can give because it is given by God. We may therefore offer it in the confidence it will be accepted by God and he therefore will pour his blessing upon the offerer.

This substitute does not exclude our sacrifice; it not only involves it, but also demands it before the saving purpose is revealed. Hence the conviction of sin in times of revival could be so great that men and women almost died under its weight, and needed a ministry of great grace and persuasion to lead them to peace with God. From now on Isaac was to Abraham not merely a miracle son of promise, but a son given back from the dead. He would regard him as Jairus, or the widow of Nain, or Martha and Mary, regarded their revived loved ones – as lives precious enough to God to be brought back from the dead, and therefore too holy for anything but God's highest will.

Is not this how those of us who have been led to absolute self-denial (not the giving up of things, but of ourselves), regard our lives in and after Christ's sacrifice? Life is then too sacred for anything but his will. Now, for all Satan's attempts to drag us down – how he loves to do this above all! – it becomes inconceivable that we should live for anything other or less than God's revealed purposes. To have been through this death (and far too many Christians have never come near it), is to be done with all specious forms of piety. All artifice is swept away by reality. Men and women who have died this death may not appear religious at all; certainly they abhor sanctimoniousness. You need to be with them and hear them in prayer 'on the mount' to know how real and deep their religion is.

22:15-24 The result of this transcendent experience is that the Lord, having formerly repeated his promise to Abraham in most solemn circumstances (17:3ff.), now swears by himself (cf. Heb. 6:13-20) that he will bless Abraham and his descendants and by it all nations. The sworn promise is now, as at the first (12:1-3), of unqualified blessing. But it would not always be so (cf. 15:12-16), and we know that that blessing fulfilled in Christ (cf. 'seed' in Gal. 3:16) came by way of many disasters to Israel on account of her sin. It is because of failure to see in what unruly and uncertain context the promise is fulfilled that men have despaired of the sanguine hope. But there is no despair in Abraham, nor in any of the believing line who followed him, before or since Christ. These all died in faith believing (Heb. 11:13, 39), and did not doubt the promise of the coming of the kingdom, not least because they felt its hidden power in their souls. This hidden power is the reality of their spiritual experience of death and resurrection with Christ, and they died in faith having trumpeted forth its message, because to them the kingdom was as real as if it had already come. For 'faith is being sure of that we hope for and certain of what we do not see' (Heb. 11:1).

The chapter closes happily and appropriately with the family record of Isaac's bride-to-be, Rebekah (24:67), daughter of Bethuel, son of Nahor, Abraham's brother.

Chapter 23

The Death of Sarah

23:1-20 Sarah is disposed of in two short verses. It would appear the older a person lives, the less notable, generally speaking, is their demise. It is sad to see how insignificantly some old people are 'put away'. Doubtless that is understandable when their contemporaries are all gone. But when the departed have served their day and generation well, it is hard that the busy world should not take time to pay their respects. There is a lesson in this. The final assessment is not in this ungrateful world of unremembered service, but on that farther shore where godly souls receive their meed of praise, and are welcomed into a community of abiding respect and love. Not that Abraham is casual in his grief: it is too deep for public exhibition. He 'went in' (AV) to mourn and weep for Sarah. Then, like the man he was, 'rose from beside his dead wife' (3) to dispose of his beloved with despatch and dignity.

There are different views of the underlying ethos of this transaction. One view is that the sale of the burial place was implied from the beginning of the negotiations. Another view is that the Hittites were reluctant to give Abraham a legal title to land by purchase (Skinner, *Comm. in loc.*). We are impressed by this, although we should not minimise the honour and affection in which Abraham was held: while he says, 'I am an alien and stranger among you' (4), the Hittites reply, 'You are a mighty prince among us' (6). Likewise Sarah had been a famous beauty in her day. The free offer of a sepulchre may be regarded either as an act of spontaneous generosity, or as an expedient to prevent Abraham becoming a landowner, or a mixture of both.

Abraham accepts their generous offer, made in the hearing of the community, and comes at once to the point – he knows what he wants! With the courteous manners of the east, Abraham requests they intercede with Ephron on his behalf (8), while the same Ephron was sitting among those engaged in the negotiations (10). While Abraham asks only the part of the field with the cave, Ephron offers the entire plot (11). Note the suave deprecation of the offer. However when Abraham makes known his desire to own the land and insists on a business transaction (13), Ephron in the same deprecating manner names a high price as if to say, 'But what is that between friends?' As a matter of fact it was nothing to Abraham, and he clinches the deal at once (16). If Ephron wanted to make money, he did, but if he and his Hittite compatriots were trying to prevent Abraham becoming a land owner by polite means, Abraham was too astute for them. Besides he had Someone working for him.

There comes a time in negotiations with smooth and oily men when the only thing to do is to drive one's bargain hard, like a coach and horses through the facade of their selfish objections. There are modern examples of the high business acumen of Christians, and although that can and sometimes does deteriorate into worldly and un-Christian practice, it ought not to; when however high ethical standards of true godliness are maintained, it is a testimony to the business training that the practice of Christianity affords.

Perhaps the important thing about Machpelah is that Abraham has now a stake in the promised land, although it is only a burial ground for his family. Sarah, Abraham himself, Isaac and Rebekah, and most significantly of all Jacob – when Joseph was given permission by Pharaoh to lead a funeral procession from Goshen (50:5ff.) – were all buried there and Leah also (49:31). However the embalmed body of Joseph appears not to have been buried in exactly the same cave, as some suppose (cf. Josh. 24:31 with Acts 7:16). Verses 17ff. read like a legal document, including the contract or deed of purchase. A final thought to ponder is whether this stake Abraham now had in Canaan contained in it the hope of a resurrection!

Chapter 24

Isaac and Rebekah

24:1-4 In this chapter there is undoubtedly a beautiful illustration (rather than typology) of the romance of Christ and his bride, the church. We will refer to it here and there, but it should not be indulged in at the expense of the historical truth of the text. That would be to make the same mistake as the mythologisers which would be a strange association indeed for pietists! Commenting on the chapter, Skinner says, 'But if such a historical kernel existed, it is quite lost sight of in the graphic delineation of human character, and of ancient Eastern life, *which is to us the main interest in the passage. We must also note* the profoundly religious conception.' (*Comm. in loc.* Italics mine). It is an interesting confession for Skinner to make that the chapter is not primarily valued for its religious content. We can hardly be blamed if we take this view at its own valuation, accepting valuable insights here and there which illuminate parts of the text, but not looking for much spiritual help from Skinner's commentary. This is what we do.

The summation of Abraham's life that 'the Lord had blessed him in every way', is impressive. We have seen something of how this works. It is by God's sovereign, electing grace, into which Abraham's discerning faith and acts of obedience – elicited by grace – dovetail in perfectly. There is a wonderful balance between grace and faith: they are both authentic. In our walk with God, we discover the one is mysteriously a response to the other, a real response, so much so that perhaps our strongest impression in the midst of an act of faith is the full persuasion of our whole personality; thought, feelings and will.

Abraham is now an aged man, possibly bed-bound. He calls his oldest, most trusted servant (whom we take to have been Eliezer), his heir according to contemporary custom if he had no son (15:2). Abraham commands him 'to swear by the Lord, the God of heaven and the God of earth' (3) a most sacred and intimate oath, involving the issues of life and posterity, that he will not take a Canaanite wife for Isaac. There is nothing inadequate about Abraham's basic conceptions of God (cf. 14:22, 22:14). The Lord is Maker and Sustainer of heaven and earth, and it was undoubtedly this noble conception of God as the One Who made and controls all things which gave him his superior moral purpose. Naturally, he would not want his significant son to be joined with a woman of Canaan, however advantageous to Isaac's congenial establishment in the land that might appear to be. Such a woman would have no higher conception of God than a tribal spook.

Some today might well argue that Isaac ought to have been able convert a Canaanite wife. But the record of Israel, especially of Solomon, shows that God does not bless with conversion marriage unions which have been founded on carnal, or even adulterous, desire. First things first. From the consanguinity (nearness of blood) viewpoint some would say that Abraham suggests a worse thing than marriage to a heathen. That is not so. The spiritual is more important than the physical, and where that has first place, the dangers of the physical are well covered by God. Abraham is quite explicit as to what Eliezer must do. Faith knows what it is about. Until it does, it waits. This is because in fruitful action, thought and deed go together.

24:5-9 Eliezer's doubting fears (5) are not those of a meddler, but of one called to find and bring the bride home. It is interesting to find such consideration for the woman's inclination. This in the ancient East surely shows the influence of Abraham's godly household. The aged patriarch had no doubt that the woman would come, for was not the idea from God? But he deferred to his servant's delicate sensibilities and explained his assurances. Before doing so, he was quick to dispel the notion that if the woman would not come, Isaac should return to the land of his fathers. To suggest such a thing would be to fail to understand God's purpose. Isaac must not marry a Canaanite, but one of his own line and of a higher civilisation than that in Canaan (Abimelech presumably being an exception to the general standard of morality in the land). Isaac's bride-to-be must come to Canaan!

She must be willing to be a missionary! If she is not willing, Eliezer would be clear of his oath. However, Abraham is quite sure this will not happen. And he should know. We believe his words in verse 7 were spoken with feeling and conviction, for did not God take Abram's father away to constrain him to continue his journey whither he should (11:31f.)? The God who got him out of the land of his fathers, would incline the woman destined to be Isaac's bride to come also: '– he will send his angel before you'. But should Abraham's faith be misguided (8) – and we see here the doubt which tends to mingle with the purest faith – Isaac was not in any circumstances to leave the land of Canaan for Haran. So the servant made the oath.

Reflect how difficult it can be for those who lack faith, even those who like Eliezer are most faithful and obedient, to be convinced that true faith cannot fail. The outcome is so obvious to those whose reason is God's reason. To others such (seemingly blind) faith leads to the most hazardous actions. Strange!

24:10-14 Taking with him 'all kinds of good things from his master' (10), Eliezer set out with a caravan of ten camels for Aram Naharaim, which is North-west Mesopotamia. The name Mesopotamia means 'the land between the two rivers', the Tigris and Euphrates (consult a map to ascertain the location); the word is a transliteration from Greek, not Hebrew. Nahor had apparently migrated from Ur to Haran later than the rest of the family. We have already been told that Abraham had had news of his family which doubtless included their approximate whereabouts (22:20ff.).

We now see a little of how the divine 'coincidences' are arranged. Eliezer who clearly knew what he was doing, made for the city of Haran, and sat himself down at the local well (apparently the only well in the area, discovered last century by archaeologists) in the evening with his camels. He then prayed to his master's God, in his prayer suggesting a test of how he should know Isaac's chosen bride. Note carefully that it was a moral test which had nothing to do with physical beauty or signs of wealth, but rather with kindness and the desire to go the second mile. It was indeed a long second mile to offer to provide sufficient water to satisfy the thirst of a caravan of ten camels!

There is a real kinship between this incident and the Lord's approach to the woman of Samaria (John 4:7). The initiative is with the divine purpose, but it takes a natural and sociable form. This is extremely important for Christians to learn. The true witness for Christ does not approach with his evangelistic banners flying! These are a poor substitute for the grace of moral character. They make the wrong appeal and often attach the wrong sort of folk to the Christian cause. One of the major tragedies of modern evangelicalism is that it distrusts the witness of Christian moral character because such an appeal does not create an instantaneous sensation. But God prefers to work through the natural, unforced, unselfconscious witness of those whose life is suffused with the grace and truth of Jesus Christ.

24:15-27 Eliezer's prayer is not long in being answered. 'Before they call, I will answer; while they are still speaking, I will hear' (Is. 65:24). The damsel appears: she is beautiful, and pure (the latter seems notable), but her spirit of cheerful and willing service is the appointed test. Eliezer is astonished. This amazement at the speedy answer to our prayers is a strange phenomenon of the human heart. Try as we will to assure ourselves that we should not be surprised by God's timely goodness, we are. As far as the astonishment arises from unbelief and incredulity, we must be ashamed of it, but when it arises from feelings of joy and gratitude, we must be glad. 'When the Lord brought back the captives to Zion, we were like men who dreamed. Our mouths were filled with laughter, and our tongues with songs of joy' (Ps. 126:1f.).

But Eliezer was not rash: too much hangs upon the question. Most men would have been too elated to contain their story any longer, and would have sought at once to know her family. Not this man. He waited and wondered (21), but said nothing until she had completed her self-appointed task. All the time he was searching critically for a clear sign of the Lord's will. When the task was done, he offered her gifts, not an ear-ring, but a nose ring (!), and bracelets. These may have been rewards for service. Then came the all-important question (23). Notice that Eliezer presses the point. If this is the right woman, not only will she be of Abraham's family, but her father's house will be a hospitable place, with ample provision for a worthy traveller.

Was this Eliezer's conversion (26f.)? It could have been. Eliezer loved his master, and if his master's God was good to Abraham, he would be the servant's God, too. Certainly his prayer in verses 12-14 was not directed to a God he himself appeared to know but was to the 'Lord, God of my master Abraham'. His petition was that God would show kindness to his master (14b). Eliezer had doubtless seen the goodness of God to Abraham many times; but the seeker after truth may find other explanations of godly prosperity. There comes a moment, however, when the explanation of 'chance' does not cover the wealth of facts. It is not necessarily that there is a predisposition to disbelieve; rather a dislike of coming to rash conclusions which may have to be changed. But when the goodness of God not only dispels doubts but satisfies reason, then the seeker is faced with the plain alternative: 'If the Lord is God, follow him' (1 Kings 18:21).

Eliezer 'followed': 'Then the man bowed down and worshipped...' (26). Some have tended to think of the word 'worship' as referring only to singing and thus have emptied it of its biblical meaning (see Ex. 20:5; Matt. 4:9-10; Rom. 12:1); but we should recognise that this statement denotes an act of deep commitment. Yet he is filled with joy at God's goodness to his dear master and by the fact that, as he kept strictly to a godly course of action, he had been led to the very place and person of Jehovah's choice. 'As for me, the Lord has led me...' (27b), is a great text, and contains endless variations of practical application. But it does in general proclaim that the wonders of God's goodness are only fully proved by those who keep to the narrow way (it isn't really narrow at all, but seems so because there is only one good way over against many bad ones) of God's spacious purpose.

24:28-50 Rebekah had a brother. It is alleged that his greedy character appears at once. At all events, when he saw the gifts Eliezer had for his sister, Laban gave him a most expansive welcome (30f.). Note that he uses the name 'the Lord', and it sounds natural and spontaneous. Compare this with Joshua 24:2. Nothing was left undone for Eliezer's hospitality but, grateful as he is, he is not forgetful of his mission. He cannot relax until its burden is unfolded and its issue settled. Wise are those who do not allow themselves to become unduly indebted to a wily host too soon. Business before pleasure, especially when it is divine business. 'The King's business requireth haste.'

Eliezer rehearses the whole story beautifully. Now, what do they think? There is no need to 'think' when the Almighty completes a project with perfect precision. All man can do is marvel. Perhaps the greatest lesson the Christian can learn in a world of mistakes, mishaps and mis-timings is to watch and wait for the Almighty's perfect deed. To see how perfectly the Lord works is surely to begin to learn that it is better to let him do all and co-operate simply and trustfully with him. We shall never do better. We shall never do as well. This humble obedience is the one lesson we are here to learn. To learn it fits us for heaven, for it lets God be God, and that is all he asks.

24:51-60 It has been supposed that there are some contradictions between verses 51 and 58. Perhaps the intervening verses help to reconcile them, especially the suggestion that Rebekah remain for some little time before leaving (55). It appears that by next morning Laban and his mother had agreed to delaying tactics. Even carnal folk can at first be persuaded to the Lord's will when the audacious sweep of its power and glory is revealed (cf. Matt. 13:5f.). It is only on reflection that its personal cost weights heavily against their approval of it. Eliezer will not delay.

This was bold and unsociable behaviour (contrast Jacob at Haran, ch. 29-31), and only a strict sense of his mission could have constrained him to act so. But he doubtless discerned the intent of the hindering tactics, and his very sympathy for the mother must have lent wings to his desire to be off before his resolution was overborne. By then the house-hold's resistance had stiffened, and they forced their eastern minds to the most unusual expedient of asking the will of the prospective bride! Note, Rebekah is not asked if she will delay departure ten days, but if she will go with this man. Her answer is clear and unequivocal: 'I will go.'

At this point it may be profitable to consider what in the past has been seen as the 'typical' nature of the chapter, but which we prefer to see as an eloquent illustration of the gospel messenger. When Christ's servants are sent to invite sinners to be his bride, the chosen have no doubt: the response is, 'I will go.' This does not exclude the struggle to decide, for the devil fights for their souls. But when eyes are truly opened, there is no doubt, only serene assurance. Here is an illuminating parable on deliberate evangelism. (Serious and mischievous misuse is made on the writer's views because we are alleged to disown evangelism. Rather our ministry aims at that unconscious evangelism which is the native air of the mature and living Christian. See Matthew 5:16.) Deliberate evangelism is initiated by the Master, and gains its end, however many refuse by the way.

Milcah and Laban, having asked Rebekah's will could hardly ignore it, and they send her away with good grace, finding some consolation in the prospect of her destiny – the mother of thousands upon thousands. To what extent this was an informed prophetic utterance? 'May your offspring possess the gates of their enemies' (60b) is very like Genesis 12:3, but not untypical of common usage. Or were their parting words merely an ambitious hope? We can't be sure. Bible characters often speak greater than they know, for God's purposes for his line are often 'immeasurably more then all we ask or imagine, according to his power that is at work within us' (Eph. 3:20). Thus God gets his way, and enables his appointed servants to get their way for him, against all odds. Let the fearful who are truly called to deliberate evangelism take heart, and let all others look to the witnessing quality of their lives and concentrate on that.

24:61-67 This passage begins with a beautiful simplicity. The departure is described as if it were a matter of daily routine. Thus by almost effortless acts of choice God's chosen move into the stream of his will. They know that there is destiny in every act. While their sentimental selves may tell them that they should be churned up with emotion, they are not. Grace overwhelms all.

Isaac has removed further into the Negev (south). The absence of any reference to Abraham has led the 're-arrangers' of the record to assume his death in the interim, but there is no need of this. (We should be careful of those who 're-arrange' the Word of God, e.g., Moffatt's translation. Not only is the biblical material sacrosanct, but its arrangement is surely by the Holy Spirit. This is especially so in the Gospels where, following an understanding of individual incidents, the very sequence of the material may yield instructive and significant patterns of teaching. Indeed an awkward joint, or an unexpected change of subject may have something deep to teach us if we are prepared to meditate upon it in the Spirit. This may apply less to the Epistles for the obvious reason that they are mainly spontaneous effusions in which the Holy Spirit's design may be less calculated.)

Isaac had settled at the place of Hagar's well (cf. 16:14). The simple description of Isaac meditating in the fields at the close of the day is beautiful (63), tempting us to allegorise, or at least to allow the text to direct our thoughts onwards in the biblical story of salvation. Does the 'evening' suggest the marriage supper of the Lamb and his Bride at the end of the age? Certainly the circumstances of the meeting of the bridegroom with his bride are suffused with holy light. The whole is done in the light of the Lord.

Christian marriages are made in heaven, and should be left to heaven. God will not give his best to over-eagerness which does not wait his will and time. Even allowing for the longer patriarchal lifespan, forty years was a long time for an eastern young man to wait for a bride. To hear young Romeos talk, one would think the Almighty had no sense of romance and would deliberately choose an unsuitable mate for them. How perverse and absurd! No mistake was made with Isaac's romance: 'he loved her' (67b). So it is, always, with those who humbly and sweetly defer to the Almighty in the serious and delectable matter of marriage. We could give instances, but perhaps the imaginative reader may catch the echo of fervent 'amens' which the reading of these sentences will evoke in many happy Christian homes. There are several other intriguing touches to note in the narrative, such as the modesty of the veil, and Isaac's comfort in taking his bride to his mother's tent. Very, very beautiful. And true to Christian life – even in a dark world of sin.

Chapter 25

The Death of Abraham

25:1-10 The question arises whether Abraham had Keturah as a wife before or after the death of Sarah. The natural conclusion is after, in spite of his great age and Keturah being called his concubine in 1 Chronicles 1:32 and here in verse 6. The matter is not of great importance, perhaps indicating the need of the old man for help and support in his closing years. His life's mission is now largely accomplished.

The issue of the marriage with Keturah is clearly not as vital as that of Sarah, or for that matter, of Hagar. A descendent of Shuah may be found in Bildad the Shuhite (Job 2:11), and there are significant links with the Midianites when Joseph was sold by his brothers (37:28 and note the reference there also to Ishmaelites), and also in the account of Moses finding in the land of Midian a godly priest whose daughter he married and who later was of great help to him in his administration of the people (Ex. 2:15ff.; 18:1ff., 24ff. We wonder whether Jethro's godly influence descended from Abraham?) Another reference to the Midianites tells how sadly they drove the Israelites into 'mountain clefts, caves and strongholds' (Judg. 6:2).

Notice that 'everything' (5) is comparative. Abraham was not unkind or ungenerous to his other children, but his chief care was for the son of promise. When Isaac's welfare is fully provided for, the old man can die happily 'in faith'. The meeting of Isaac and Ishmael at their father's funeral (9) was probably their last. At such times the distance between kith and kin is seen for what it really is, and after coming together briefly the family members leave knowing their several ways are growing ever further apart. This is not necessarily a bitter realisation, but a sad and wistful facing of a fact. When we are thus brought back to the memory of earlier years, emotions can run high and we may become exceedingly sentimental. But reason need not be affected and we return to our own sphere and vocation, not desolate or bereft, but with the high conclusion that while blood is thicker than water, Spirit is thicker than both!

25:11-18 We are here reminded that the responsibility of godly parents for a child of the covenant is of a certain order and is limited (1). When that responsibility is fulfilled, the parent may die peacefully, assured that neither God's mercy nor his purpose will fail.

Ishmael's Sons

The genealogy of Ishmael now follows, intervening in the account of the continuing history of Israel, according to the method of the book which disposes of lesser figures before proceeding with the chief characters in the divine purposes. There is even a spiritual lesson in this for it shows the manifold grace of God who seeks the salvation of the Gentile as well as of the Hebrew. A most illuminating reference to the Ishmaelite genealogy is to be found in Ellicott's commentary, so helpful that it may be useful to quote it in full.

'Of the Arabian tribes sprung from Ishmael we read of Nebajoth and Kedar (Is. 60:7) as pastoral tribes, rich in flocks. Dumah is deemed worthy of a special prophecy (Is. 21:11f.), while the people of Tema are described as generous and hospitable (Is. 21:14), and in Job 6:19 they appear as active traders. (See also Jeremiah 25:23, 35f.) Jetur, Naphish and other Hagarite tribes were conquered by Reuben and his allies (1 Chron. 5:19), and Jetur became the Iturea of Luke 3:1. For the occasional references made to these and other sons of Ishmael in classical writers, the reader may consult Smith's Dictionary of the Bible or other similar works. The abode of the twelve tribes sprung from Ishmael was the northern part of Arabia, whence gradually they extended their influence, and apparently soon absorbed the Joktanites (Gen. 10:26-30), themselves a kindred Semitic race. These genealogies would be inexplicable if we did not remember that successive waves of people occupied these lands, and that while the old names remained, the dominant race was new. So the rapid growth of individuals into tribes (as of Midian, 25:2), was the result of higher civilisation and greater energy subduing feeble and less highly developed tribes. Hence in verse 16 the sons of Ishmael are called 'princes' ['rulers', NIV]. We gather from this that Ishmael had gathered round him a body of men of the Semitic race, of whom large numbers were constantly on the move towards Egypt (cf. 12:10ff.), and by their aid had established his rule in Paran, and handed it on to his sons.'

This necessarily shadowy outline of Ishmael's descendants is interesting not merely as a foil and background to the high story of Messiah's line, but as tracing the rise of those nations who provided the divine goads and chastening strokes of judgement on Israel when she went astray. Where the AV has, 'he died' (18), we should read with NIV, 'his descendants settled'.

Jacob and Esau

25:19-26 The barrenness of Rebekah (21) is of a whole series of similar difficulties which the Lord allowed his chosen ones to encounter in the fulfilling of his historical purpose. (Cf. 16:1; 29:31; Judg. 13:2; 1 Sam. 1:2; Lk. 1:7.) This shows the divine policy of permitting evil its full resistance to his holy will in order that God's victories may be seen to his glory, and also that the faith of his chosen ones might be tested and strengthened. Man's co-operation against the hindrances of evil is therefore engaged so that by the prayer of faith he also gains victory over the evil. It is suggested that the verb 'prayed' (21) may derive from a word for 'incense', in which case the prayer of faith is not only a victory over evil but, much more important, a source of pleasure to God.

There were twenty years between the marriage of Isaac and Rebekah and the birth of Esau and Jacob. We do not know when Isaac began to pray or whether he prayed all those years, but if he did then the answer was a long time in coming. Why does God often delay the answer to our prayers? Does he wait until we are fit for his answer?

Rebekah was also driven to prayer by her distressing experience (22). It was an astonishing answer God gave her, explaining both what she was suffering and the far-reaching destiny of her offspring. In the divine preference of the younger to the elder we have again one of a series of similar events which strike at the immemorial honour of the first-born (primogeniture). There are Abel, Isaac himself, Judah, Levi, Joseph, David, Solomon. However, note that while none of these seem to have an innate tendency to advance themselves at the expense of their elders, Jacob's tendency to outstrip his brother seems to have begun before birth.

Does Jacob's cunning arise from a sense of inferiority to his brother? Or is it that he had superior intelligence? Cunning and intelligence are not the same thing, but rather opposites, the one being a diabolical substitute for the other. If God's preference of Jacob was irrespective of his physique or intelligence (Rom. 9:10-13), how sad that he was so innately inclined to snatch at his place by artifice. The chosen of God has no need to struggle with a sense of inferiority, only to wait in patience. Indeed we know that the mark of the true children of God is not any tendency to snatch at their rights, but like Christ (Phil. 2:6ff.) to yield them in the interests of others, and thus receive them with greater glory. We can only say that Jacob became Israel (32:28) in spite of himself, and not without mortification which overtook him all the more painfully because he fled from it.

25:27-34 The word 'cunning' is sometimes used to describe Jacob's character. It is strange to find the av using it to describe Esau's hunting (27, cf. niv 'skilful'). The question arises whether was the same strait in each son, in Esau directed to the pursuit of game, but in Jacob directed towards ensnaring his brother. Humanly speaking, Esau is the more admirable type with his healthy, athletic interest in the outdoor life. By contrast, Jacob was a 'quiet (douce?) man' who loved the home life in which he apparently over-exercised his furtive mind at the expense of his body. Note, however, that he was to be subjected to a very physical life which stretched his endurance to its utmost in the years ahead (31:40-42).

Was there something inverted about Rebekah to prefer the son who sat around the home with her to the one who did a man's job – even if

Esau did pander to her husband's inordinate love of savoury meat? Jacob does not seem to have been able to produce the food – that was a man's responsibility in those days. But he was able to cook a stew (29), though the narrative suggests his mother normally prepared the meals (27:9). Is the text hinting that he knew how to trap his brother and was ready when the opportunity came?

The implication may be that Esau would not have despised his birthright (the headship of the family) had he not been in physical distress. This by no means exonerates him but shows how easily his resolution was distempered by his physical condition. He had that simple sort of mind which deferred to his body. This of course is the wrong order. We expect it in animals, but not in those created in the divine image and who are given minds to control their bodies.

Jacob made him swear an oath (33). He knew how to clinch a deal so that there was no retracting. He need hardly have bothered. Esau rose from the meal and went off as if nothing of importance had been lost. What a thoughtless 'animal' – governed only by his immediate bodily desires! Which of the two men do you prefer? Neither? We agree. But God who knows the end from the beginning chose one and rejected the other. This not only challenges our spiritual discernment, but shows its limitation. God is able to take the most unlikely material and fashion from it a new thing. If we could always see what he was doing, we would be near the level of his divine thoughts. But there is little chance of that, so limited are we by our myopic view of his ways and purposes!

Chapter 26

Isaac and Abimelech

26:1-5 The similarity of these incidents to those recorded of Abraham incline some scholars to assume that they are duplicates with variations (cf.12:10ff., 20:1ff.) However, this ignores the plain statement in verse 1, 'besides the earlier famine of Abraham's time'. We are clearly intended to understand this was a mistake repeated from earlier times.

The principal locations of Canaan in patriarchal times may be found in most maps of Canaan in Old Testament times. Hebron, Beersheba

(Lahai-roi or Beer-Lahai-roi) and Gerar form a triangle adjacent to the Salt Sea and south of Jerusalem which is easy to trace. Note that while Isaac was obliged to move from his well-loved oasis at Beersheba due to famine through drought (those who have visited Israel will have witnessed the awful aridity of the Judaean wilderness), he refrained from going southwards towards Egypt, but moved north-west to Gerar in Philistine territory bordering the Mediterranean Sea.

The Lord then confirmed to him that he was not to go down to Egypt (v.2). Why this seemingly unnecessary advice? It is not likely that fear of Abimelech would have driven him south since Abraham earlier had had the same difficulty in Egypt (Gen. 12:10-20). Was it the difficulty of the wells (v.14f.)? We can only conjecture but since this is the first recorded time the Lord speaks directly to Isaac, we assume he rehearses to him the terms of the covenant made with his father Abraham (cf. v.24). Divine blessing to the patriarchs and their successors is related to location: only in the land of promise can Jehovah bless them with His presence and His prosperity. Recall that Abraham partly learnt this lesson following his escapade into Egypt, for next time he journeyed towards the south (Gen. 20) he did stop well short of Egypt! Isaac now keeps within the bounds of the land, but there is the same wayward tendency of his father. It is this which Jehovah bestrides with his prohibition and astonishing promises of blessing.

These things are a parable. The place of blessing for us is within the shelter of Christ's death for sin and his rising to life eternal. Both the pictorial history of the Hebrews and the dramatic history of Christ's deeds have their counterparts in our lives. On account of the devil's enticements, there is always the tendency to escape from the feared famine conditions of the narrow way but both blessing and security are to be found only within the confines of the death-life of Christ. While involving real self-denials we find this leads us into streams of experience so broad and deep that they not only transcend space but time also, and we become one with the warrior-saints of all the ages, even with the holy angels in their mysterious missions.

26:6-11 The repetition of this expedient in two successive generations is remarkable to say nothing of the astonishing lack of gallantry. We would have thought that, despite the eastern attitude to women, Isaac would have cherished his beloved Rebekah who had been given to him in such divine and romantic circumstances. 'Abimelech' is a title, like Pharaoh or Caesar and means 'father-king'. The 'window' (v.8) implies a permanent building of some pretensions, whereas Isaac's entire household presumably still lived in tents in spite of the text indicating a fairly permanent stay in the area (v.12). The translation 'caressing' (NIV) is better than 'sporting' (AV) in verse 8.

Isaac had far less justification for calling Rebekah his sister than Abraham. Sarah as well as being Abraham's wife was also his half-sister (11:29), whereas Isaac was second cousin to Rebekah. As with his father, Isaac is put to shame by a pagan king with a high moral code. Had Isaac not known of Abraham's experience and his unwarranted fears? Not only is murder unthinkable to Abimelech but adultery also (vs.10-11). Abimelech's injunction to his people is that none should touch this man or his wife on penalty of death. There is nothing higher in any moral code than this – and long before the Mosaic law! It is as if the Lord, unable to dispel Isaac's apprehensions, convinces him through the noble ethics of the very persons he is afraid to trust. This is both a rebuke to the fears of the elect, and a challenge to their prejudices against the 'pagan'.

26:12-14 Cultivation on a small scale is still occasionally practised by the Bedouin in Israel today. It would seem that we are to think of Isaac's lifestyle as being similar in many respects to that of the Bedouins (see 30:14; 37:7). Certainly it was remarkable that when Isaac sowed 'the same year' of famine the Lord blessed him with a wonderful harvest. Whatever the shortcomings he had advertised to the highly moral Philistines he was nevertheless chosen by God for blessing and prosperity. This is not to say that God's blessing makes the moral law irrelevant, but that the greater encompasses the lesser and aims to reach it by a higher road.

Now comes the test of Abimelech's morality. If morality is related to Jehovah at all it will not only acknowledge divine blessing when it sees it but also desire it. But as Isaac's prosperity increased the Philistines became more envious of him. Whether Abimelech thought it unjust that God should bless someone less moral than himself is not clear, but it is possible that a sense of injustice was an element in the Philistine jealousy. The importance of this is that the blessing of Isaac during a famine, perhaps because he refrained from going down to

Egypt, was the Lord's means of evangelising the heathen. But the moral heathen is always the hardest to evangelise! We are justified in asking if Abimelech in asking Isaac to leave on account of his prosperity was refusing to learn the lesson of that prosperity's source.

Surely this is part of the great refusal of the 'easy yoke' which the Lord graciously imposes upon His chosen. Jesus commands us to let our light shine before others that they may see our good works and glorify our Father in heaven because they see God is behind those good works. The question is whether we Christians realise just how widely this sort of spontaneous, unconscious evangelism operates. In fact it is in action wherever Christians are showing forth God's blessing on their lives. If someone asks why it does not have greater effect on the world the answer is because of the great refusal. Many are unchristian not because they do not know (although that is true of a growing number), but because like Abimelech although they know, they do not want.

When will this fact strike the false optimism of those who want to 'evangelise to a finish' (whatever that means) 'in this generation'? To see this truth should not discourage biblical evangelism which is to let one's light shine. Rather should it encourage it. If there is a light and we allow it to shine, it will shine! Our first concern should be that there is a light in our life, and the second to see that we neither quench nor hide it.

26:15-25 It is a possible inference from a comparison of verses 1, 15, and 18 that Isaac moving westwards from the famine stricken area came upon Abraham's wells stopped with earth and was driven nearer Abimelech than he wished. Afterwards, when his deception was discovered and then he became too prosperous, he was bowed out and retired to his father's wells to dig them out again.

We are to learn that behind the careful morality of Abimelech lay a spirit of envy and hostility toward Abraham and Isaac. After Abraham's death this showed itself in stopping the wells in a deliberate attempt to edge Isaac out of the land. Fair enough if the wells belonged to the Philistines, but rather serious if they belonged to God and it was his people who were being excluded. We hear much about people's rights today and at times when Christians who are being blessed materially and spiritually come embarrassingly near, there are some who claim the right to keep them at arm's length as if to say with Abimelech, 'We would have a greater distance between you and us!' Alas, such people fail to reckon with the Lord. The sad thing about Abimelech and those like him is that, seeing plainly God's blessing on his people even in difficult times, they react with envy instead of eager interest. Worse, they go on to set themselves against those who would gladly live peaceably alongside them and so they forfeit the favour which God would have shown them for his people's sake.

Isaac shook off their dust from his feet and began to re-open his father's wells. It becomes clear the dispute was whether the land around Abraham's wells belonged to Isaac or the Philistines. The Philistines apparently did not interfere with the wells while Abraham was alive but after his death they seemed to think Isaac an easy prey. Isaac called the first well Esek (v.20), which means 'dispute'. The second well he called Sitnah (v.21), which means 'opposition'. The third he called Rehoboth (v.22), which means 'room'. Was this God's way of driving Isaac back to the place of blessing? God uses his enemies not only for the severe chastening of his children but also for more gentle correction. If only we could see this, we would be humbly delivered from all bitterness against our opponents, and be graciously led back to the place of blessing.

Some have suggested that Isaac should have stayed where he was at Beersheba and endured the famine. There may be truth in this, but if so it is doubtless a counsel of perfection. Nevertheless we should stay in the Lord's will however severe the test may be. If we do not he himself has his own way of leading us back.

26:26-33 The unselfconscious evangelistic witness has told after all! What has Abimelech seen? First he saw Isaac's deception – the witness started off on the wrong foot! Then he saw his prosperity. Most of all, however, he saw Isaac's meekness when being nudged out of the land. Abimelech's behaviour is typical of many convicted by the gracious evidences of a believing life: 'Why have you come to me, since you were hostile to me and sent me away?' (v.27).

It is the effect of that strange inner repulsion-plus-compulsion complex which wears down the smitten conscience and against all human pride and reasoning forces the scorner to capitulate, if only to avoid mental and moral disintegration. We have already quoted in this connection our Lord's words about others seeing the Christian's good works and glorifying our Father in heaven (Matt. 5:16, see above on Gen. 26:12-14), and now Abimelech's testimony bears it out abundantly. This glorious confession towards the close of this distressing chapter makes the heart sing because of the fulness and wisdom of its application to the modern scene.

This is evangelism which does not set out to attract but to live its own distinctive life amongst and over against the unbeliever leaving that to have its effect. Jesus urges us to have faith in God and assures us that all things are possible to those who believe. But if we set out to witness to Christ by flag-waving it must be because we underestimate or even discount the distinctiveness of the Christian life and think it needs to be dressed up to show. We only succeed in caricaturing it! The one thing we should fear is indifference. Certainly we see here that opposition is a most promising sign. How many of us are happy to count amongst our Christian brothers and sisters erstwhile enemies? This is the most intriguing aspect of all our work for Christ.

We are now ready to withdraw our earlier suggestions that Isaac's was a colourless life. Although not without fault in the situation of famine, Isaac avoided going into Egypt at a testing time, and he was used, albeit in humiliating circumstances, to glorify his God in the eyes of Abimelech.

The rest of the story is obvious sequel. 'We've found water' (v.32). Of course, things tend to go well for those who are on the high road of God's purposes. The new well was probably the old one, or at least one in the same seam of water (cf. 21:22-33). Is this not another parable for us? God would have us go back to the place where he first blessed us and where our love for him was unalloyed. Is this a word to you?

26:34-35 In 35 read, 'They were both a bitter disappointment to Isaac and Rebekah.' NIV has, 'They were a source of grief to Isaac and Rebekah.' We imagine that a man of Esau's nature would unthinkingly rebel against the restraints that Jehovah's covenant and commands imposed upon him. Perhaps these women had a wilder beauty which attracted him (cf. David and his wives, esp. Maacah, Absalom's mother: 2 Sam. 27:2-5; 1 Chron. 3:1ff.), but it can hardly be doubted that his natural lawlessness was aggravated by his mother's favouritism of Jacob, whom Esau heartily despised. This must have created a major tension in Isaac's mind, for beyond his natural admiration for his lusty son, he may well have been seeking to compensate Esau's lack of mother love, although this could have been more covert than overt.

As Esau made choices more and more contrary to the pattern commanded by God, Isaac would have to admit, far more reluctantly than Rebekah, that Esau's way of life was a bitter disappointment. To the extent that Rebekah was to blame, the motions of Isaac's affections for his family would increase in complexity. Thus it is that even the happiest marriage in the Lord can at last produce a home situation which defies unravelling. Why? Of course sin is the cause but who shall say whether it is sin in our own generation or earlier? We hardly know what our children will become. We can but commit them to the Lord in faith and by prayer, example, and precept, in that order, work towards their growth in godliness. Compare the two basic factors of human responsibility and divine predestination as set forth respectively in Exodus 20:3-6 and Romans 9:11-23ff.

Chapter 27

Jacob Gets Isaac's Blessing

27:1-10 We are left to speculate as to the connection between the meal and the proposed blessing, but it seems to have been close. It appears that Isaac in his decline let his human affection over-ride his knowledge of the divine will (25:23). This was a serious lapse. It is sad when the Lord's servants live long enough to undo the work of their glorious years (cf. Hezekiah, 2 Kings 20). But the Lord has means of intercepting their folly, although we are sure he is never driven to subvert his own law. As we understand it, Isaac had forgotten himself as God's man but Rebekah's favouritism of Jacob came to the rescue.

The question arises whether God approved the deception of a deceived and misguided man in the interests of his declared purpose. Perhaps it is best to say that the devil outwits himself in the sphere of his own disintegrating bedlam. If this is so, then when God allowed the devil in Rebekah to thwart the devil in Isaac he himself was deliberately involved only in the prophetic blessing falling upon Jacob's head.

If you think this sounds like casuistry, look at the Cross. God would have his Son die for the sins of his people – but how? The righteous God cannot slay his holy Son! No, but sin does it for him. God has no part in the sin. Yet he uses it. Does this still sound like casuistry? I know of no other way of resolving the problem. This is the nearest I can come to an explanation of the intricate perfections of God's holy will in action. Instead of presumptuously cutting the Gordian knot of the problem by pronouncing the story a moral tale, we must patiently try to understand how God's perfect will is done in a fallen world where men and their actions are riddled with evil. God will take care of his integrity in his use of evil. For our part we must beware lest we underestimate his daring. We cannot argue with him. 'Shall not the judge of all the earth do right?'

Therefore as far as we may it is ours to unravel the holy and the unholy in those circumstances and events in which the will of God inexorably is done. What other purpose could God have for allowing evil than daringly using it to serve His holy will? That is the fun of it all. To grasp a biblical worldview we must see God laughing (Ps. 2:4) at the devil working overtime with excessive zeal, rashly overstepping himself in his uncoordinated efforts and consequently undoing his own work. Instead of entitling this story 'The Stolen Blessing', we would rather call it 'The Blessing finds its Proper Head'.

27:11-29 Rebekah had thought of everything. Beyond the daring of mother-love is a curious kind of faith which was willing to bear the curse (vv.12-13) that her favourite son should have the blessing. The 'best clothes' (v.15) denote the religious nature of the occasion. Once ready, Jacob made his entry. Had he forgotten about his voice or did he attempt to change it (v.22)? At all events the old man is uncertain, the more so because his faculties are unreliable. He questions him and as his suspicions are increased by Jacob's explanation he seeks closer proof. What is it he most suspects? The speed with which the wild game has been found or the mention of 'the Lord your God'? Some have suggested that Esau would not use religious language. But might he not use it for an admiring father's sake? If he did, it would sound awkward and unnatural rather than merely glib, whereas religious Jacob would lie smoothly as in the manner born.

Isaac's sense of touch was now satisfied, but that voice...! Trusting his sense of touch rather than his hearing he called for the food and drink and ate, still questioning (v.24f.). The smell of the clothes suggests not only that Esau wore them frequently but that they had acquired the odours of an outdoor man. Taken together with Isaac's words in verse 27b, this suggests an instructive identity of religion with vocation.

Isaac began his blessing with material things (was he still uncertain?), but then proceeded to the spiritual as if the firstborn still retained his birthright (v.29). Consider how much Isaac was overriding. First, the promise to Rebekah and the strange token of it in her own body (25:23). Second, Esau's own disregard of his birthright (25:32ff.). Third, Esau's ungodly and unpromising marriages (26:34f.). Is this not part of the disconcerting perversity which overtakes the aged when their powers begin to fail?

We should be on our guard against the temptation to misjudge Christian people who in their dotage contradict the whole former tenor of their lives. It is painful for loved ones to see a dear one acting so distressingly but it is a reminder that the devil does not easily let go and may be especially malevolent when the worn-out body is too feeble to resist. Nevertheless, the blessing descends on Jacob's head and the devil with all his accomplices, witting and unwitting, is foiled. It is a very human and intriguing story. Truth is not only stranger than fiction but far more wonderful. Is it not pathetic to see some of the supposedly clever attempts to concoct stories for public entertainment which have nothing of the solid substance of a biblical drama? What food for thought is contained in our Book! Not much wonder it grows fresher to us and we grow fresher in it.

27:30-33 Did Rebekah help Esau to prepare the savoury meat, or did his wives? Does Isaac's question, 'Who are you?' suggest his disillusionment on hearing the authentic voice of Esau? The violent trembling shows how fully Isaac realised what had happened. Wily Jacob had not only overreached his brother and deceived his father, although only just, but had received his brother's blessing – 'and indeed he will be blessed'. The irrevocable nature of the words of blessing can only mean that Isaac knew the prophetic spirit by which he spoke came from God. We can only faintly imagine the rage which convulsed him as, frustrated and rebuked, he realised the Almighty had used his trickster son to thwart his dottled disobedience.

What reckonings follow our wayward attempts to manipulate the Lord's will! He is always Master in his own House. This should make us very humbly reticent about any project of human enthusiasm which does not have the stamp of divine authority. It should also assure us that however insecure and uncertain the cause of God may appear amidst the welter of our mixed motives, God has many agents of veto to prevent his purposes going awry. At this point we must stand apart from Jacob and Rebekah silently gloating in the background over their successful stratagem. However we cannot resist an inward chuckle at the spectacle of disillusioned Isaac and chagrined Esau bewailing their misadventure. It is a poor heart that never rejoices and he is a sour, humourless Christian who has not a hearty laugh at the expense of these two. However disconcertingly bigoted and bombastic the course of it may be, this is the ultimate outcome of every attempt to make God serve our wills. Thank God his salvific purposes rise above the shambles of human wilful folly.

27:34-40 One commentator has written: 'Those tears of Esau, the sensuous, wild, impulsive man – almost like the cry of some "trapped creature" are among the most pathetic in the Bible.' But for all that he is fully responsible for his plight. Hebrews 12:16f. tells us that it was his contempt for his birthright which brought about his undoing. Of course he sought the blessing 'carefully with tears' (AV), 'diligently with tears' (NKJV), but he found no place to change his mind about the birthright which was the cause of his being 'rejected'. The reason he could not have the blessing was that he wanted it without the responsibility which went with it.

How like the unregenerate world this is! They want God's blessings in this life and in that which is to come but at the cheapest price. They forget that although salvation is free, having been purchased at infinite cost, the acceptance of that blessed gift is the most costly decision of life. Indeed the price is to follow our Saviour to the furthest limits of His exemplary death (we cannot follow him into His substitutionary death for that is a finished work), and that calls for total response to His call (cf. 2 Cor. 4:8-12; Col. 1:24). 'If any one would come after me, he must deny himself and take up his cross and follow me' (Mk. 8:34). Unwilling for such cost, there grew in Esau that root of bitterness which poisoned both Esau's own life and also the whole history of

Edom until the Hasmonean dynasty gave way to the Herods of our Lord's time.

It is exceedingly pathetic to listen in to Isaac and Esau commiserating with one another on Jacob's subtlety. They may well wrap themselves round with self-pity as far as that wily rascal is concerned (Jacob's name is variously translated 'Over-reacher' and 'Supplanter'). But the father and his cheated son miss the point. This is not a mere human mischance, but a divine retribution for irresponsible carnality. Esau is obliged to plead for any blessing Isaac has remaining, and receives one (39-40). Surely that also was declared under the influence of the same prophetic spirit, as history confirms! Read it in a recent translation to discover the majesty of the words and their fullest expression. The ungodly history of Edom may be traced with the aid of a concordance (but especially see Num. 20; Judg. 11:17-18; 1 Kgs 11:14-16; 2 Kgs 3:8-26; Ps. 137:7; Jer. 49:7-22; Ezek. 25:12-14; Obad.).

Jacob Flees to Laban

27:41-46 The text apparently intends us to understand that Esau had secret intentions: 'He said in his heart' (AV), 'He said to himself' (NIV). The question then arises as to how Rebekah knew. Some have suggested verse 42 implies that what Esau said in his heart was also spoken of confidentially to those close to him. This is the simplest explanation. Of course it is not impossible that the Lord himself communicated to her his murderous intention. Indeed, it is quite possible that she discerned what was in her son's mind, although the text suggests such maternal discernment was then confirmed by verbal reports of his intentions.

Was Rebekah surprised at Esau's reaction? Possibly. Those caught up into intrigue can become blind to reality. She was instantly apprehensive for her favourite, and her inventive mind soon devised a plan. A 'few days' (AV), 'for a while' (NIV), is doubtless a euphemism (v.44) to ease the parting, although Rebekah may have expected her fickle son's anger to be short-lived. She might be deprived of them both (v.45b) either by Esau's banishment from the household or because of his death by blood revenge should he kill Jacob (cf. 2 Sam. 14:7) – though in the latter case one wonders who would have been left to do the slaying!

Rebekah was ingenious in covering up her reason for Jacob's departure. But her ingenuity would have been seen to be flawed had Isaac recalled his father Abraham's emphatic instruction to Eliezer when he sent him to find a bride in Haran, 'Only do not take my son back there' (24:8). However it could be argued the situation was different now in that Jacob was related through his mother to the other branch of the family and knew exactly where he was going. There was not the same danger that he would be spiritually lost by the way. If Isaac had forgotten his father's fear of him leaving the land (assuming he knew of it), Rebekah's earnest hopes that Jacob would not marry a Hittite as Esau had done were sufficient to persuade him.

The old man co-operated beautifully. The Lord was behind it of course, not only in the interests of Jacob in whom the divine purposes lay, but to work out that retribution which must fall upon Rebekah and her favourite son for their sin. Mother and son would never meet again! This is how the Almighty breaks up associations so exclusively close that they injure others. A very different example is that of Herod and Pilate who became friends over Christ's trial – but not for long. While intimate relationships can be one of God's sweetest gifts to his people, there are other relationships which stray into forbidden areas and are therefore displeasing to God. Beware!

Chapter 28

28:1-9 Notice two things in Isaac's charge to Jacob. First, he appears to have no qualms about sending him out of the land. Second, there is no recorded word of rebuke for his disgraceful deception. It may be that through the painful incident the old man had a new experience of God. He may have repented that he had ignored God's revealed will for Jacob and thereby discerned (notwithstanding the necessary judgment on Jacob for his unworthy trick), the glorious future that lay ahead of his younger son. Therefore, when Jacob appeared before his father to receive his final charge, that unusual spirit of grace Isaac had known in the blessing again took possession of him and made him prophesy expansively the blessing and fruitfulness of Jacob and his posterity in the land.

Was Esau constrained by a complex of motives to seek another wife? There is no hint of murderous hate in verses 6-9. The passage reads as if Esau suddenly realised that he had displeased his parents in his marriages, and accepting the ostensible reason for Isaac's sending Jacob to Paddan Aram, tries to please them by seeking a wife of nearer kin. Perhaps the simple truth is that Esau's temper cooled as quickly as it flared up, and so he took steps to prove that he was a dutiful son. Poor Esau. It was hardly the way to correct what was wrong, and besides it was scarcely to be expected that a daughter of Ishmael would be a particularly godly woman, even though she was a granddaughter of Abraham (v.9). Abraham had some sorry descendants!

These considerations, however, would not appeal to a man of the mental age of Esau. His actions would seem to him altogether laudable. Had he been reminded he already had too many wives and that this new one was not of promising stock, he would have lifted up his hands in despair as if to say, 'You spiritual people are never pleased! Here am I letting bygones be bygones with my wily brother, and am seeking to contract a more suitable marriage, but it seems all I do is insufficient to win even your mildest approbation.'

'Quite true, Esau, but you are doing it all from the wrong motive. You have no principle in the matter. It is at the point when you see your course of action leading you into unpleasantness or inconvenience that you employ a little religiosity to give yourself the semblance of a spiritual man. But it is only to wriggle out of an unhappy situation. At the moment it is necessary to placate your parents, and you do it the best you can, with never a thought that its moral inadequacy is obvious. But like all carnal folk turned religious for convenience, your motives are showing.'

Esau's attitude is still all too common today. His successors make a token appearance at Church before a special occasion which they intend will serve their purpose in some way. They are saying in effect, 'I'll attend next Sunday so that they cannot say I never come!' But their disguise is totally ineffective. One reason why such folk ultimately become antagonistic is because they suspect they are seen through. They certainly are!

Jacob's Dream at Bethel

28:10-13a Jacob in his flight from Beersheba was overtaken by the darkness at a particular place, and lay down to sleep with a stone for his pillow. He may have done so in spite of his fear of brigands or wild beasts. If so, the dream God gave him was all the more wonderful. The moral and spiritual symbolism of a ladder from earth to heaven appears to suggest reaching God by some sort of effort and not therefore a particularly evangelical concept. But see John 1:51: '... you shall see heaven open and the angels ascending and descending on the Son of Man', and John 3:13: 'No one has ever gone into heaven except the one who came from heaven – the Son of Man.' We learn that the ladder is not in fact from earth to heaven but rather from heaven to earth!

However, the ladder with its two-way traffic of angels here would seem to symbolise not so much salvation as an auxiliary ministry. At the top was the Lord surveying and seeing all, and the ascending and descending angels were in constant communication with the wayward child of God in the moment of his deepest agony. If ever there was a picture of grace overreaching sin, it is here. Of course we do not exclude the repentant thoughts of Jacob as he hurried northwards, banished by his folly from all he knew and loved, albeit incited by an unworthy mother. He may even have wept himself to sleep. Whether he did or not, it was at this point the Lord, standing at the top of his stairway, might have lectured him roundly on his wickedness. Instead he gave him this gracious vision.

Ah, the righteous soul who seeks always and only to deal with the erring one in terms of exact retribution knows nothing of God's real mind towards sinners. Where he pursues his purposes of grace, no barriers can stand in the way. He pours his grace into the heart of the prodigal with seemingly indecent extravagance. Not that repentance is foregone but rather that it is evoked by grace. Could grace not have done the same for Esau? The only answer is that it didn't (cf. Mal. 1:2-5 and Rom. 9:10ff.). True under-shepherds will keep close to their Master in the care of the flock that they may do His inscrutable will, not theirs. Left to ourselves, many of us would have opted for Esau, not Jacob. We do not know, and need to depend upon One who does.

28:13b-15 It is more than interesting, it is instructive to ponder the interplay of judgment and grace in the life of a wayward elect soul. Is there anything in the comparison of God's act of judgment (Jacob's flight) with his words of promise recorded here? We might wonder what Rebekah would have thought of her favourite, pampered son lying all night under the stars at the mercy of the elements and wild creatures.

Yet it is in these miserable circumstances that God fills his mind with the most astonishing promises of his coming greatness and of the significance of his posterity.

God's favour can be very sore for it calls to high destiny but bids us wait for it, making us pay to the full for the sin of every short cut to its attainment. It happens, therefore, that for our over-eagerness we may find ourselves in a howling wilderness in the dead of night with a stone for a pillow. It is there that the heavens open and the glory of our service is revealed with its expanding significance. This miserable context in which the hidden glory is revealed is not always of the soul's own making. It was not by sin that our Lord found himself in the agony of the garden that night, but because he refused to sin. Thus we learn that the agony which the evil one thrusts upon the righteous may be far more costly than that which we bring upon ourselves by our sins.

However, there is one area which cannot be touched – that of conscience. Jesus suffered infinitely more than Jacob in his cold night experience and yet paradoxically less, because He suffered with a clear conscience. If Satan cannot get us to sin by trying to run ahead of God he will make us pay for it but he will not be able to make us sully our souls, and when the agony is over the peace which flows from the knowledge that we possessed our souls in integrity will be inexpressibly heavenly. More, the prospect ahead will be bright!

Finally, notice that Jacob was going out of the land of promise to be prepared to inherit that land. The chosen one would have to spend an exiled lifetime learning to die that death to self which he refused in his youth. God's will will not be frustrated. It may take longer that way, but God is not in a hurry. All will be fulfilled when the death has been died (think of Peniel, 32:22ff.), although the callow youth may be then an old man. The high road is better than the low, for the long way round is the shorter cut home.

28:16-19 Do Jacob's words (vv.16, 17) indicate that as he had fled in despair he had left God behind? He could hardly believe that the Lord's promise to Rebekah concerning him was cancelled by his sin, but apparently he assumed that while he was banished from the land he was also separated from the divine presence. What a wonderful discovery for a desolate penitent to make, that the Lord was with him in the place of his cold despair! This lesson to Jacob is one which we need constantly to re-learn. God is not put off by our sin. He can deal with it, as he deals with us in it.

More, the Lord's presence is not to be judged by our senses. Perhaps Jacob's fear when he woke was that he had behaved as if God was not there when he was. This need not mean that Jacob had done anything sinful (we guess he would have been too repentant for that), but that he had in effect ignored God, assuming his absence! We've all had the experience of being upset when we discover we have ignored someone dear to us because they were in an unfamiliar place. We fear we may have offended them and so we go to great lengths to prove that we did not know they were there. This was Jacob's fear, but infinitely greater because it was fear of God. Jacob would never forget the place where in a state of cold despair God revealed Himself wonderfully to him – thus the name Bethel, 'House of God' and gate of heaven.

Bunyan tells us there is a slippery path which runs to hell from the gate of heaven. But there is also a gate to heaven situated at the threshold of despair. The discovery of this grace when least expected is a most solemnising experience, inspiring moral and religious responses which thereafter govern our lives dutifully and benignly (see below on 28:20-22). Thus see how Jacob marked the place and occasion by setting up and anointing the stone. This is later forbidden (Lev. 26:1, Deut. 16:22), but that there was no superstitious or idolatrous significance in Jacob's act is seen in his moral response to God's grace. Where there is such moral response, there is no fear of mere idolatry for the Spirit sanctifies all.

28:20-22 The fruit of God's astonishing and persistent grace (assuming Jacob's prior genuine repentance) is that Jacob in godly fear and unbounded gratitude vows a vow. It is not a bargain made on the fundamental question of accepting Jehovah as God, (as made to read in the AV, NIV and the 2nd paraphrase) but rather a pledge both to set up a house of God at Bethel if and when he returns, and to give a tenth of all his prosperity to God. I prefer to read: 'If God will be with me ... so that I return safely to my father's house in peace and the Lord be my God, then this stone which I have set up as a pillar shall be God's house, and of all that you give me I will surely give you a tenth.' I am sure this is the intended emphasis.

With regard to the tenth, note first that Jacob regarded all he should acquire as from the Lord and therefore stewardship was required. To give God a tenth did not absolve from wise stewardship of the rest: 'But remember the Lord your God: for it is he who gives you the ability to produce wealth' (Deut. 8:18), and, 'Every good and perfect gift is from above...' (Jas. 1:17). It is all his. Note also that Jacob asks only simple things: that God would keep him in his journeyings, provide food and clothing, bring him home again in peace and be his God.

Was it because Jacob did not ask wealth that he got it? Compare Solomon and God's words to him: 'Since ... you have not asked for wealth, riches or honour ... I will also give you wealth, riches and honour ...' (2 Chron. 1:11f.). God daren't give us something we want too much if it is not himself we want, for he is a jealous God and there is no love without jealousy. Further, we are not to think of the tithe as Jacob's own idea. It is clear from Genesis 14:20 that it has divine sanction, and inspires the godly in a moment of unusual blessings to offer it to God as a sacrifice of thanksgiving. Indeed, at the close of the Book of Leviticus the tithe is enjoined as a command (27:30-34).

The blessings which result from tithing when it is undertaken out of gratitude to God and not as an irksome discipline are seen in Malachi 3:12. There the failure to tithe is characterised as robbing God, and the restoration of tithes which have been withheld brings blessings beyond the capacity of the Lord's people to receive them. Many could testify to this. It should also be noted by those contemplating the practice that not the least of its blessings is that it frees the Lord's work and his servants from preoccupation with material things. No true servants of God enter God's work for money. They should not therefore be obliged to be preoccupied with making ends meet which has the effect of making them more money-minded than they desire to be. Where the Lord's people tithe, there is no shortage of money and there is ample to provide for His servants which is the first purpose of the tithe. The tragedy of the service of many who are said to 'live by faith' is that money is obviously a principal preoccupation of their lives. This is plainly wrong and, alas, can often arise because of the earlier wrong of niggardly giving by those who are in gainful employment.

Chapter 29

Jacob arrives in Paddan Aram

29:1-14 We have already noted (see above on 24:10ff.), that last century the only well in the district of Haran was re-discovered. When we were last at this place a man was looking for a wife for his employer's son. Now that son's son is here, looking amongst other things for a wife for himself. There is no word of a great stone (v.2f.) at the well's mouth in Rebekah's day. Jacob addresses the men, 'My brothers.' Did he assume they were his relatives? He is told that Laban his uncle is well, and that his daughter Rachel the herd maid was approaching with her flock (cf. Ex. 2:16-17). Did Jacob violate the local custom in watering Rachel's flocks before all had gathered? We can almost excuse him his gallant eagerness. We can certainly understand his emotion on meeting his cousin. Think of his flight and the night at Bethel, the fear of his uncertain future as it vied in his mind with his faith in God's promises, the loneliness of his journey into a strange land – then meeting his cousin in the pastoral normality of her daily duties and finding her such a delectable person. It was all too much for him, and his feelings welled up and overflowed in what for us with our western outlook might appear to be astonishing behaviour – he wept and kissed her.

We are not aware of any such thing as 'platonic affection' in pagan lands of these times but would acknowledge a far more open and explicit expression of family affection. In the eastern culture of his day Jacob's tears would not have demeaned him in the eyes of Rachel and the herdsmen. But whatever the onlookers thought, the meeting was far more than an occasion for the emotional expression of family affections. Clearly it was the first sign in his own life that God was as true as his word that he would bless him. The first experience of that in any believer's life marks a red-letter day.

The account of Jacob's meeting with his uncle is depicted in scenes of deep emotion. Again, such behaviour was typical of the culture of those times, but even so we suspect this whole family sensed a divine destiny among them. How could they have been unaware of it? Are we not aware of the Lord's calling when a member of our family is selected for divine service? The question arises whether those who fail to recognise such intimations from God are not in some jealous or perverse sense against God's purposes for a life he has chosen. Personal happiness and well-being may depend on acknowledging the divine will and gladly embracing it. God will not be deflected from his plans by the blind wilfulness of a stubborn soul.

Jacob Marries Leah and Rachel

29:15-24 Laban is manifestly a smooth and consummate schemer but as he bows and scrapes, ingratiating himself into the young man's favour, we also see him rubbing his itching palms behind his back. We suspect his leading thought is, 'I can use this young man,' and he means 'use'. For his part, Jacob is in love with Rachel. Without any material resources for a dowry, Jacob is going to have to pay by service. So Laban agrees and makes his consent appear as a gracious gesture to his guest. However, Jacob's deep attraction for Rachel has by no means escaped her father's notice. He would not tell him that local custom forbade him giving his younger daughter in marriage before the elder. Rather he would lead him on to procure him by deceit for another term of seven years service for the younger.

It was a brilliant scheme, the kind that looks easy in theory but fails in practice. Therefore it ought not to have worked. But the duplicity was by divine permission to requite Jacob for his own base trick on his brother. No one is safe in a family or community where deceit is rife. Ultimately, social life breaks down because no trust can be placed in any one, and without trust people cannot live together at all.

Jacob had an eye for beauty and Leah had sore eyes. Nor is it always the younger God chooses to favour, although that may have been what Jacob presumptuously assumed. He wanted Rachel because he loved her as he could love no other (cf. the spiritual meaning of verse 20 with 2 Cor. 4:16-18). Alas, sin had already put its spoke in the wheel of Jacob's life, and his plans would go sadly astray – notwithstanding God's promises, which would be fulfilled. The story unfolds. Laban used the custom of bringing a bride veiled to her bridegroom in order to thwart his nephew's expectations. Jacob unwittingly married Leah, and she became the progenitor, not only of Reuben and Simeon, but of Levi and Judah.

God's ways are past finding out – we cannot fathom them. The surest way to be in line with the unknown divine will is to ensure we are in line with the divine plans in their plain moral precepts. God may seem at times to be very ingenious, but it is the ingenuity of sinful man which makes him appear so. He is really simple in his ways as his beloved Son must have known in heaven, but he cannot allow his alienated creatures to outwit him. Nor shall they. His seeming tortuous will simply straightens out our tortuosity. (Cf. Isa. 40:3-5, and Matt. 11:28-30.)

29:23-35 The deceiver is deceived. It is rather different to be at the receiving end, and perhaps Jacob now spared a sympathetic thought for Esau in his dismay. Esau for all his bitter tears could not have had the decree of Jacob's blessing reversed. Neither could Jacob's marriage to Leah be annulled although he did not then realise how divinely significant this union was to be. Laban's first concern is lest Jacob ruin the seven days marriage festival (v.27) to which he had invited his neighbours. Rachel he will have when the week's festivities are completed – but as wages for another seven years service. What could Jacob do but submit? Thus in a sort of ancient hire-purchase agreement, one week later he was given Rachel also!

It requires little imagination to visualise Leah's plight. She was the lawful wife of Jacob (Gen. 2:24), but was excluded by his idyllic love for Rachel. So-called 'romantic' love often excludes rightful claims making them appear disreputable and insignificant. Nevertheless the God of righteousness is not only watching, but working. The contrast between Jacob's association with Leah and Rachel could hardly be greater in terms of revulsion and pleasure, but the revulsion was fruitful while the pleasure was barren.

Is God, then, perverse? No, it is sinners who are perverse and God, as we have already remarked, must appear more perverse than they in order to frustrate their perversity. Leah conceives, but not Rachel. Whatever Jacob and Rachel thought of this (would they not try to minimise it?), Leah knew what it meant: it was a triumphant token that the Lord pitied her in her humiliation. The birth of her child did not draw Jacob any nearer to Leah, and the Lord caused her to conceive again. There was still no effect, and she conceived again.

Jacob's Children

After her third child (v.34) she expressed her longing that so fruitful a union will draw her husband's love, especially when his concubine remained barren. The name of the third son (Levi means 'joined' or 'attached') together with Leah's words express the hope that Jacob will be more of a husband to her. Certainly the birth of the fourth son, Judah (meaning 'praise'), climaxes the significance of the family's destiny. Perhaps we may delicately infer that the words, 'Then she stopped having children,' (v.35) indicate the accomplishment of a divine purpose, as usual against tremendous odds, after which Leah might well rest on her laurels. It reminds us of the accomplishment of the Saviour's birth in the midst of the Roman census. The Almighty gets his way!

Chapter 30

30:1-2 On the human level the domestic scene in which the envious Rachel provokes her husband to intense anger may be seen as an understandable reaction to Leah's growing family. But on a deeper level we must also see it in relation to the divine purpose in the birth of Leah's fourth and special child, Judah. While we may do full justice to the human crisis and the tensions arising from the 'eternal triangle', we must not fail to see through the human veil to the spiritual conflict. In stage craft, use is sometimes made of a gossamer curtain which in the absence of light appears thick and impenetrable on its far side, but when light is supplied reveals as if from nowhere a scene scarcely less clear than if there was no veil at all. This is what God does at the beginning of the story of Job. He reveals the heavenly lying beyond the earthly scene.

According to the measure of our insight of faith, it is given to us also to penetrate the veil and see the spiritual conflict beyond the human situation. This is precisely what the Apostle is speaking of to the Ephesians when he says, 'Our struggle is not against flesh and blood, but against the rulers, against the authorities, against the powers of this dark world...' Paul does not mean that we do wrestle on the human level – obviously we do! Rather is he saying there is a conflict behind the conflict, and no one can understand the one who does not see the other.

The conflict in the unseen world gives meaning to our human wrestling.

Those Christian religionists who are puzzled about the course of history and the Church's place in history do not see the hidden conflict and therefore can scarcely see God's sovereign purpose engaging the passionate reaction of the enemy. To see in measure what God is doing and how, is to understand the virulence of human opposition to it. It must surprise the enemies of grace that they become so much more passionate on some religious issues than on others. This is because the devil has a vested interest in their fierce opposition in that field.

Does it seem we have wandered some distance from Rachel's and Jacob's domestic scene? The discussion of the two dimensions of conflict started there, and is certainly not immaterial to it. After all, Judah is Judah – the progenitor of our Saviour – and the evil one must have hated his birth.

30:2-8 Consider the frustration of a lover unable to procure the Lord's blessing on his concubine. It is at such times men realise there are powers beyond their direction and control. Sometimes thoughtful children question the statements in the Bible and the Hymnary about God's provision of our daily bread. 'It comes from the baker,' they say or, 'It comes from the miller and the farmer.' Then we then lead them gently on through the workings of nature to God and the Mind that controls the elements – controlling them at times in relation to human righteousness and unrighteousness.

Jacob is ready to acknowledge that sovereign hand now, but not with good grace. As far as he is concerned God has blessed the wrong woman and all his soul is against it. When his frustrated paramour herself reproaches him and demands, 'Give me children, or I'll die,' his frustration reaches mortifying pitch. But wilful man does not know when he is beaten, nor wilful woman, either. So Rachel tries a legal trick to ensure that a child born on her knees will be hers. Note, however, that the object appears primarily not to have a child upon which to lavish mother-love – a laudable desire and surely more worthy if the little one is otherwise unwanted. Rather was her intention to vie with her sister and show the triumph of her love for Jacob.

It was a poor victory, even if Rachel tried to justify it by giving the child the name Dan which meant 'he has judged' or 'he has vindicated', as if God had vindicated her desire (6). Even so, she appears to fail to understand the Deity working in favour of Leah, for Rachel calls him

Elohim which probably in this context covers gods in general. In contrast, Leah addresses the Lord (29:32, 33, 35), the God of Abraham, Isaac, and Jacob. Rachel did come to understand better as we shall see (30:24). Meantime she is intent upon a competition with her sister Leah. Another son is born who seems to have cost Rachel greater wrestlings than Bilhah who bore him – Naphtali means 'my struggle' (8).

Poor Rachel, how hard it is to get even with God! Our best efforts fall short, but our madness hides this from us and we fail to see how ludicrous and sacrilegious are our attempts to fly in the face of providence. If we saw ourselves as others see us – far better, as God sees us – how differently we would behave! Evil tries to ensure that we don't, but if we walked in the light we would never allow ourselves to be committed to a God-defying course, and thus we would never make an exhibition of ourselves before God, mortals and angels.

30:9-13 There is, no doubt, a divine providence in the twelve sons of Jacob but it seems a pity that that number should be made up by Leah's unworthy resort. There was no need for her to get even with Rachel. Surely she could have allowed her distracted sister that vicarious victory! The book of Proverbs concludes, 'Charm is deceptive and beauty is fleeting; but a woman who fears the Lord is to be praised. Give her the reward she has earned, and let her works bring her praise at the city gate' (31:31-32).

It would appear that Leah's fault here was in fearing she had lost advantage. She had not! If Rachel had borne a son herself – even two or three – she might have begun to fear she was losing, but to descend to Rachel's strategy was an unworthy move for a woman in her position. Doubtless the disadvantages of unprepossessing looks and the disfavour of her husband roused her jealousy, creating the desire to deny her sister even the slightest advantage; but how unnecessary!

If the respective advantages of the worldly and the godly were weighed in a fundamental scale of even human values, it would instantly be seen what a poor figure the former cuts in comparison with the latter. And the worldling knows and senses it. Why then do the godly allow themselves to be led into carnal competitions of unworthy resort? Leah even calls Zilpah's son a name meaning 'good luck' (11)! We foolishly assume disadvantage where there is none and so descend to the level of an unholy scramble, when the reality is that our God-given advantage cannot be gainsaid. The man and woman of God can sit by humbly when the worldling struts and cocks his head towards the admiring public. For although he would be livid with rage to admit it, he is really trying to get even with the godly for the undemonstrative witness of their fruitful life. All sincere Christians tempted to give way to defensive aggressiveness before the world or carnal religiosity take note! Let this lesson penetrate your deepest thought and feeling. 'The meek shall inherit the earth!'

30:14-21 The mandrake or love apple is 'the round, greenish-yellow, plum-like fruit of *mandragora vernalis*, which in Syria ripens in May – the days of the wheat harvest – and is still (superstitiously) sought in the East to promote conception' (Skinner). Poor Leah is still intent on the child-bearing competition and superstitiously sends her grown-up son Reuben to the field to gather love apples. But love apples, even if there were anything in the superstition, will not take the place of an unwilling husband. Therefore when Rachel, who has her Jacob but nevertheless is still barren, sees the love apples she is willing to trade her sister a night with Jacob for the fruit (15), hoping thus to procure conception.

Yet that begrudged night with his lawful wife was right in the sight of God, and he blessed it. This should have been sufficient evidence to Jacob that God was with him in the one association and not the other. The birth of the subsequent children to Leah suggests that he learned this lesson. We can hardly agree with Leah in her interpretation of the name given to her fifth son, Issachar, which means 'hire' or 'reward'. There is no way God blessed her with another son as a reward for her self-sacrifice in giving her maid Zilpah to Jacob (18). Rather the name Issachar fits the grosser interpretation of his having been begotten by hire from Rachel. Whatever Rachel might have mistakenly thought, we cannot allow that the Lord could or would ever bless such a practice.

In our study of these accounts in Genesis, while we admit and make allowances for the primitive standards of patriarchal morality, we must judge them by the fully ethical moral law revealed to us in the Scriptures. It is not that since these days God has improved his standards – they remain for ever the same. Nor is it that he works out the destinies of men and women without regard to their observance of his Law as known in their consciences. Leah is Jacob's wife. Even if their cohabitation is procured by unworthy and superstitious means, it is still lawful cohabitation, deserving of the blessing of God.

The blessing is repeated in another son (19) whose name Zebulon probably means 'honour', because Leah hopes that at last Jacob will treat her with honour as his lawful wife. Thus Leah bore six sons to Jacob. Finally, she bore a daughter, Dinah.

30:22-24 It would appear that in the tremendous strain of Rachel's attempts to justify her love for Jacob, she had explored the whole gamut of human emotions from frantic resentment to sullen despair, until at last (why is it so often 'at last'?) she had been driven to appeal to God. We noted above that there was no prospect of a further child for fruitful Leah if her husband would not come to her. But if God does not will it, neither was there any prospect for childless Rachel even by her pleas to Jacob and his co-operation. The issues of life are still in his hand.

Now we find that when Rachel implores God, he hears and answers. This does not mean that God blesses concubinage, but that he blesses Rachel in asking something from him which she has formerly sought by her own effort. The divine answer to her request must have been a new experience, and is seen in her invoking the name of Jehovah for another son after Joseph's birth: 'May the Lord add to me another son.' If we are not reading too much into the text, it appears that Leah is much more at home with the name 'Lord' or 'Jehovah' (Yahweh) than Rachel, who used the general word for God, 'Elohim' – often in the Old Testament referring to pagan gods. But she appeals to God and He answers her cry, and she is disposed to take the Lord's name upon her lips. While this may have marked her conversion from superstitious to living faith, more probably it marked her consecration to the Lord.

A school teacher in our city recently objected to a child speaking of 'the Lord Jesus', and sharply rebuked her by saying, 'It is not the "Lord Jesus" but "Christ"'! May not Rachel's use of the divine name reflect the same sort of thing? It is significant how mere names become associated with different degrees of intimacy with God, so that people select for their use those names which unwittingly reveal in what relation they stand to him. We give ourselves away by the language we use, so that the most innocent listener can form a fairly accurate estimate of how 'far ben' or otherwise we are.

One or two qualifications must be noted, however. There can be a glib and sentimental familiarity with the more homely, sacred names which is not so much a sign of intimacy as of immaturity. Likewise there is a sweet and precious intimacy found in the most mature that is not at all for the hearing of the cold cynic or distant sceptic. 'Do not give dogs what is sacred; do not throw your pearls to pigs. If you do, they may trample them under their feet, and then turn and tear you to pieces' (Matt. 7:6). (In Greek, *kunos,* 'a dog', was a nickname for a cynic and the word 'cynic' originally came from *kunos*). Therefore the language we use within the fellowship of God's people is not necessarily the language to use in the world.

Jesus spoke in parables to conceal the truth from those who would not hear, but amongst those who would hear the same parables aroused a curiosity which they went out of their way to satisfy. This 'concealment' needs a special sensitivity to the guidance of the Holy Spirit and those who speak of their faith must preserve a delicate balance. There is a message for us in our Lord's method, both in respect of our discernment of people who use remote names for God – such as the Deity, the Supreme Being, the Powers that Be, Providence, the Almighty – and in respect of the degree of freedom we use to speak of our God in the world. Learn from Jesus that discernment to know when it is best to speak of him with wise restraint.

Jacob's Flocks Increase

30:25-31 It would be an interesting psychological study to compare the characters of Jacob and his uncle Laban. They have the same flawed traits. How then is Jacob prosperous and Laban not? Were there other disparate traits in their characters which outweighed their similarities? We hardly think so. The Biblical record clearly intends us to understand that one was blessed of God, the other was not. Was that Laban's fault? Possibly not entirely. Yet when in extremity Jacob was faced with the death to self from which he had run – his flight precipitated by his own folly – he faithfully died the death of repentance and was thereafter open to certain dimensions of the blessing of God.

As a farm manager for Laban God blessed Jacob, until Laban became wealthy. Whether Laban was lazy or stupid, it appeared he had not learned Jacob's techniques, but assumed that by intrigue of one kind or another he could retain his services permanently. It is a fatal fallacy on which wicked men pin their hopes that evil tricks will always work, whereas the Almighty sees to it that they do not. Perhaps even police forces work patiently on this principle and often, in the end, successfully.

Jacob had never settled down (25), although Laban may have thought he had. How could he? He had promises from God (28:13-14) which required his co-operation for their fulfilment; he must start for home some time. He essays to do so now, but Laban is distraught and is forced to concede lest he lose his wealth-maker. However, Jacob will not name even the highest wage – he has a more devastating plan! (See below on 30:31-43).

Meanwhile we see pathetic Laban who has learned by experience that the Lord had blessed him for Jacob's sake (27). Accepting that blessing passively as a permanency, he had done nothing about it. It appears he was an indolent man, who trusted in his wits rather than in his works. There must be a proverb about that! Relying on one's wits instead of applying oneself to honest work does not work indefinitely. Consider how there are those associated with the Christian cause who shelter under its wings and never become imbued with its spirit. Some of them may even be in full-time service. This may go on for half a lifetime or more, but it has an end and the cold winds of reality begin to blow. Ultimately the fact that some have lived off the fruits of other's faith becomes painfully evident. Let all of us beware!

30:31-43 Jacob said, 'Don't give me anything.' Laban had dealt so cunningly that Jacob would not trust his gifts (28), but had his own ideas as to the contract he wanted to make with his father-in-law. The story is curious, and has led to endless speculation. There is a physical element in it involving scientific cattle-breeding, and there is a psychological element involving the effect of visual images during the generative process. Many accept the first but reject the second as fantasy, forgetting that the one claim Jacob would have on the offspring of Laban's flocks was that they were speckled. In the East sheep are generally white, and goats black or brown. Laban would therefore easily concede him a few speckled sheep and goats.

Jacob's handful was set at a safe distance from Laban's and were given into the hands of Jacob's sons (35), while their father continued to tend Laban's flocks and herds. Two suggestions have been made as to the use of the speckled sticks. The first is that the animals gazed upon them in curiosity as animals do when they came to drink, and conceived under the influence of these visual images, consequently producing speckled young. Ellicott who holds to this first suggestion comments, '...with the result, physically certain to follow, that many of them would bear speckled young'.

The second suggestion is that the ewes saw the reflection of the rams in the water, blended with the image of the parti-coloured rods, and were deceived into thinking they were coupled with parti-coloured males. 'The physiological law involved is said to be well established, and was acted on by ancient cattle breeders (see the list of authorities in Bochart, Hieroz. ii. c. 49; and Jer. Quaest. ad loc.)' (Skinner). (There is of course a third and obvious alternative to the above two suggestions. It is that the true source of the outcome of Jacob's deal with Laban was simply God's hand of blessing on this man. See 31:42.)

May we make delicate comment here? Is there not food for thought in this incident? We are thinking of moral and spiritual rather than psychological (though we would not exclude them) conditions of conception. Our suggestion is that 'born in sin' has two connotations: one, the basic fact of human fallenness which cannot be altered; and two, the misconceiving of children through sin prevailing at the time of conception. If the second is as valid as the first, then pure conception in a spirit of holy fear and love, would seem to be a necessary safeguard (cf. 1 Tim. 2:15). Why should this be thought of as over-pious intrusion into a human experience so blissful and holy that it symbolises the union between Christ and His Church? May it not be that the promise of infant baptism is most fulfilled where parents' prayers have been from the beginning?

We return to Jacob. The part of the story which will appeal to the modern cattle breeder is the selection of the beasts for breeding, but this has no meaning in the story apart from the production of speckled young! The record says that Jacob produced large numbers of healthy speckled animals from Laban's non-speckled flocks and herds. Whatever theories may be advanced about the 'science' of Jacob's methods, we must conclude that he succeeded because God was with him. Nor must we forget that Laban too needed dealing with! God's servants who at times are shamefully treated by the world (and even by some within the church), often live to outwit them, for faith in God, seeing this, is willing to wait its time. One of the Almighty's commonest strategies is to allow his enemies to think they have got away with their knavish tricks. They haven't.

> Workmen of God! O lose not heart, but learn what God is like,
> And, in the darkest battlefield, thou shalt know where to strike.
> He hides Himself so wondrously, as if there were no God!
> He is least seen when all the powers of ill are most abroad.
> Ah! God is other than we think; His ways are far above,
> Far beyond reasons's height, and reached only by childlike love.
> Then learn to scorn the praise of men, and learn to lose with God;
> For Jesus won the world through shame and beckons thee His road.
> For right is right, since God is God, and right the day must win;
> To doubt would be disloyalty, to falter would be sin.
>
> F. W. Faber

Chapter 31

Jacob Flees From Laban

31:1-24 Sentimentalists in religion (of whom there are many today – scratch them and see!) will think Jacob's stratagem wholly immoral. Verses 10-13 prove that it was not so. The stratagem was from the Lord. Laban was immoral in using his son-in-law, and in only seeking to recompense him when in danger of losing him. The employer who proves unworthy of a profitable workman deserves to lose not only him, but the wealth he has gained by him. This happened here, and Laban did not like it.

Laban's sons said that Jacob had gained 'all this wealth' from them (1); the AV translates, 'all this glory'. The Hebrew for 'glory' is 'weight'. (Cf. 2 Cor. 4:17 where Paul speaks of 'an eternal glory that outweighs' our momentary troubles.) The Hebrews had the idea of the 'solidity' of the world of the spirit – in a phrase of C. S. Lewis, 'spirit is heavier than matter'. However, Laban's sons misunderstood the situation. It was really the other way round – they and their father had gotten their wealth from Jacob's skill and industry. It was Jacob's comparative abundance to which they objected.

It is futile to argue with the crafty who have been lawfully outwitted. The only sensible course was to gather the God-given profit and depart. This is what Jacob did, having explained to his wives. Note that Leah is consulted (4,14). The reaction of the two sisters is important, not only from Jacob's point of view but from their own, for the women had seen the Lord was with Jacob. Now they not only took his side against their grasping father, but shared the divine indignation with Laban for exploiting his own flesh and blood (14ff.). Was it Rachel who spoke and used the name 'God' (Elohim)? Certainly she did wrong in stealing her father's household gods (cf. Judg. 18:17ff. and 1 Sam. 19:13), not only because it was dishonest but also because she had no need of such superstitious trinkets, journeying as she was to Jehovah's land with Jehovah's chosen servant.

It took three days for Jacob's departure to be known for while he himself had served with Laban's flocks, his own livestock (and probably his household) was largely with his own sons. Having crossed the river Euphrates, Jacob and his substance made for mount Gilead over three hundred miles from Haran. This could not have been traversed by a slow-moving company in seven days. E. F. Kevan suggests that Jacob's sons had been leading their flocks further and further away, while Jacob and his wives made a swift last-minute getaway on camels.

Laban Pursues Jacob

Laban in hot pursuit is intercepted by God and warned (24). While it is a curious but true-to-life story of family intrigue, God is nevertheless in it and there is no doubt on whose side He is. If we can discern both the implications and applications, the unfolding plot throws floods of light on the rights and wrongs of our human relationships.

31:24-55 The inveterate unscrupulousness of Laban is seen in his deliberate ignoring of God's word, his one-sided charges against Jacob and his plausible regret that there had been no farewell party. Even these are self-contradictory, but he plunges deeper into irrational argument: Jacob has done foolishly, and it is in Laban's power to do him hurt. By the standards of God's word these assertions are false. No one is ever a fool to do what God says though all the world may think so. Nor is it ever in anyone's power to hurt God's guided and protected servants whatever others may think to the contrary. But those who live only by their wits need iron control over their emotions and their tongues.

Laban now admits God's word to him of the night before (29f), and concedes that Jacob must needs respond to the call of homesickness, but need not have stolen his gods. It is a weak and confused ending to a blustering beginning. Perhaps in his mind he was heeding the Lord's word and had no hope or intention of persuading Jacob to return but was nevertheless determined to have his angry 'say' before admitting it.

Jacob's answer is strictly honest. By 'afraid' (31) he means the fear of unpredictability. Fear of God is a healthy fear, because we know God acts according to principles of inviolable justice and mercy. Fear of the devil and his agents is not, because their only certain principle is that of unprincipled self-interest ready to do anything to their own advantage. This was Jacob's fear of Laban and his wisest action, therefore, was to depart. Not that the Labans of this world let their prey go easily ('I tell you the truth, you will not get out until you have paid the last penny', Matt. 5:26). Jacob is obliged to have it out with Laban in the end but as it turns out, Rachel's double deceit of the theft and the denial of it tends to put Laban in the wrong. Thus Jacob is given opportunity to wax hot in defence.

He does not mince words but reviews Laban's disgraceful record, ending with a bold challenge concerning God's word the previous night. Laban suavely changes the subject, and makes his claims on Jacob's substance (43). Then he suggests a covenant, whereupon a witness in stones is set up which is to act as a boundary between them. Laban's name (47) is Aramaic, and Jacob's is Hebrew, both meaning 'witness heap'. 'Mizpah' (49) means 'watchtower'. Why does Laban take the initiative in all this (43-53)? Because it is really he who is on the defensive. He is about to lose the chief blessings of his life, which fact he tries to hide under a great show of protecting his interests from this 'plunderer' Jacob. For his part, Jacob humbly co-operates, and shares a covenant meal with him, but well he knows it is a covenant of separation on whose terms Laban goes back to obscurity, and he on to illustrious historicity and eternal destiny.

Do not leave this chapter without noting Jacob's total integrity (38-41). (In 30:33, NIV translation 'honesty' is literally 'righteousness'.) Notice also that his habitual practice (39) was to go the 'second mile' and keep himself beyond any reproach or suggestion of dishonesty. That his testimony is true is confirmed by Laban's silence on the matter for he knows that nothing his son-in-law has said can be denied. God's servants should always be thus beyond reproach.

Chapter 32

Jacob Prepares to Meet Esau

32:1 What a text is verse 1 – not merely for a sermon, which may be only an incident, but for a life! Jacob, after a seeming lifetime of expenditure of energy and pain, notwithstanding his blessings, is going back to the life from which he perforce ran away. But he returns with all the wisdom gathered in the wilderness. Of course, even a life-time's experience in the wilderness will not profit if one has not the knowledge of the land of blessing by which to judge it. Nor is it necessary to be cast into the wilderness to learn the futility of that life. Jacob had apparently thought he could combine the life of self with that of the divine call – indeed he even thought he could thus help God fulfil his will.

This is a great mistake. One of the greatest lessons we learn in the brutally frank record of the ancient patriarchs is that their sins of impatience never help, but rather hinder God's purposes. Some, living by God's word *simpliciter,* learn wisdom in the land of blessing, while some learn wisdom by cruel necessity in the barren wilderness. What sort are you? Do not let us glorify Jacob's obtuseness because of the undoubted glories and emotional thrills of repentance: the years it takes to learn that a great gulf yawns between moral good and evil are far better spent in constructive service, if only we will learn early. Many quickly give evidence that they are going to learn this lesson with difficulty. Far happier are those who early die a radical death to inbred sin: their path is not only easier, albeit costlier (compare what it cost our Lord to resist sin utterly), but more fruitful.

32:2 The word Mahanaim, although its original meaning may have been lost, is generally taken as meaning 'two hosts' or 'two camps', the one the visible host of Jacob, the other the invisible host of the angels. This is highly suggestive, and could tempt us to weave many fancies within the canons of Scripture. One of the more prosaic inferences is that the angels whom Jacob met at Bethel on his departure from the land (28:12) had invisibly guarded him throughout his years in Haran, and only manifested themselves again to his consciousness on his return. This would not mean that the invisible in the wilderness became visible in the land of blessing, but that we become aware of the angelic host in the place of God's choice for us.

We do not know how this is related to the ancient story of Job who apparently was not aware of the unseen hosts during his 'trial' as the later writer of the narrative was (Job ch. 1 & 2). Nevertheless, it is clear from Paul's mighty words of exposure in Ephesians 6:12 we are meant to understand that although the battle for souls is fought on earth, the issues are heavenly. Therefore we must ever reckon on all the armies of heaven, blessed and malign, ranged against each other. Nor is it so much that they sway us for they are not our superiors. Although they may be presently superior to us in many things, in reality they are our inferiors as Hebrews 1:14 asserts. Further study of this subject will need to take in the first two chapters of Hebrews which will reward careful reflection and meditation.

32:3-12 We sympathise with the difficulty some have found in the principle that there is still a price to be paid for sin after it has been forgiven. The narrative of Jacob's life has now reached the stage where this problem clearly emerges. The once-for-all forgiveness which is bound up with regeneration, justification and conversion absolves utterly from the eternal penalty for sin. However, the natural consequences cannot be abrogated so easily. The physically maimed sinner remains maimed after conversion (albeit God can heal that also). Further, the sins of God's elect children sinning against the light are much more heinous than those of the darkened unbelievers, and therefore the moral consequences affecting them and others are allowed fully to work themselves out.

This is judgment. It applies more rigorously to children of God than to others, because the judgment is disciplinary to mould and refine the character. Whereas the natural and moral judgments that fall on finally wilful unbelievers on earth are but a harbinger of the eternal torments of the damned. Although God is nothing less than perfection even in his judgements, we may be assured that he is far more concerned on earth to correct and refine his own who are to dwell with him for ever than to deal with those whose worst and most awful inheritance is hereafter. This being so, Jacob is still paying for his sin against Esau.

We learn that Esau has gone to the remote land which is historic Edom (3), that wild and desolate country round the south end of the Dead Sea (cf. 14:6; 27:39; 36:4-8). Jacob, having delivered himself and his substance from the wily Laban, now faces the brother he griev- ously wronged so many years ago. In fear he sends messengers ahead to plead with 'my master Esau' (4), 'my lord' (5), for acceptance and reconciliation. Could this not have been done years ago? Thus it is we shelve the responsibilities we should face until forced (by God) to do so.

It is a humble speech he sent with his servants, which must have cost him greatly to have them deliver – not least because it shows that this great man had lived with an uneasy conscience all these years. But more, Jacob is going to pay unto the uttermost farthing for his ancient sin. The news from Esau is that he is marching northwards with four hundred men. (It has been suggested that Esau had been engaged on a marauding expedition when he heard from Jacob's servants of his brother's approach). This drives Jacob into panic (7), and we must not miss the significance of this in the sphere of heavenly warfare. Satan uses the news to excruciate Jacob's conscience, but God uses it to drive him to prayer (9ff.) for the complete purging of that conscience.

His prayer follows the expedient of dividing his company. Now we see the man of God utterly stripped before his Maker, with no hope or help but in the 'bare' word of God together with the encouragement of God's many mercies to him in the intervening years. This is the beginning of the death of Jacob from which the new man Israel (Prince with God) sprang. Jacob had died that death potentially at Bethel in his converting separation long ago, but only now is that death being died in actual experience. Jacob plunged into it – he had no alternative, for no one can bank upon God through half a lifetime and then turn back at the crucial issue – and found that there was no hope or help in a critical situation anywhere but in His God.

Where are you in this? You may have died your death potentially by conversion but are you living that death, unto God? If so, when the actuality of it overtakes you, down you will bravely go and find, albeit in agony, that there is firm ground under the feet of your naked faith in God.

32:13-24a We continue to follow the steps in Jacob's repentance. Encouraged by the manifestation of the angelic host, Jacob had boldly sent messengers to Esau with a conciliatory message (3ff.). Whether it was sound psychology to impute to his offended brother an acquisitive spirit which would be appeased by gifts is a moot point. Nevertheless, on hearing the dread news that he was marching towards him with an army (6), Jacob began in great fear to make plans for the encounter. He divided his company in two (7), and fortified himself before the Lord with a humble recital of the gracious facts of his calling (9ff.). He then selected his presents and bid his drovers lead on with their various companies (13ff.). The animals would naturally make better speed in droves of their own kind, but doubtless Jacob had also in view the psychological effect upon Esau of seeing successive flocks and herds appearing (16). Perhaps Jacob hoped that the evidences of his own wealth would impress Esau, and incline him to be reconciled to a brother of such substance. The drovers would be selected with care to present Jacob's compliments worthily and make suitable ingratiating speeches (17f.). When the whole of Jacob's caravan passed through the ravine (the valley is about four miles wide with high ground on the southern side), he himself turned back.

We might surmise that Jacob had done everything possible to prepare for the meeting and now would try to get some sleep, or encourage himself in the company of his most understanding and discerning loved ones. No; his efforts and the prayer he had made were not enough. It was one thing to encourage himself in God, but another to possess the serene assurance that all would be well. Jacob was terrified of his brother, but he intended to conceal it under an exterior of such wealth and generosity as would impress, conciliate and perhaps even humble him. These mixed motives are not the stuff of which deep peace and serene assurance are made. Jacob had to seek deeper, and in his uncertainty was driven to be alone with himself and God to sort things out.

This may seem fearfully ruthless treatment of a panic-stricken man, and we may be tempted to wonder if God is not too exacting with the ancient faults of his children. He is not. This man is called to an exalted destiny which cannot be fulfilled until he is utterly emptied of self and sifted through and through until the last vestige of self-trust and self-regard is rid from his soul. Death to the sinful self is as categorical as Christ's death, but may it not be that there are deaths at different levels, and this man who is to father a nation must be brought down to absolute bedrock?

We cannot have it both ways. If we would have ease we cannot have illustriousness in the kingdom of God. Surely our greatest comfort in the deeper, costlier deaths is the quality of purpose they serve. 'Let us fix our eyes on Jesus ... who for the joy set before him endured the cross...' (Heb. 12:2).

Jacob Wrestles with God

32:24b-28 Jacob's wrestling at Jabbok is an experience of profound significance. It is very sad to read one critical appraisal of it: 'We have to do with a legend, originating at a low level of religion...' We are not questioning the primitiveness of the raw material of religious experience in patriarchal times, but to dismiss experiences recorded in scripture as 'originating at a low level of religion' is like leaving our Lord amongst the riff-raff of his earthly day. There is no doubt that Jacob was engaged in a struggle which proved to be the spiritual birth-pangs of the nation of Israel. This is the only interpretation which does justice to the divine potential in the event. Its profound significance is proved by the unfailing intellectual and theological exercise each fresh consideration of it affords. The very cryptic nature of the account speaks of the mystery, not only of the divine being, but of the divine-human encounter. Read Hosea 12:2-5 for scripture's own commentary on scripture.

What is the meaning of this trial of strength? It is entirely unworthy to believe that Jacob thought he was wrestling with a mere man, even at the beginning. Perhaps it is better to think of the Almighty accommodating himself to Jacob's strength to test how far he would go in sacrificial effort to procure the divine blessing. However, the paradox remains that while Jacob is praised for prevailing over the angel, it was that very prevailing which made the divine one incapacitate him, and caused him to cling and plead for blessing.

It is doubtful if the human mind will ever truly reconcile these two. Perhaps the heart of the lesson is in this, that great as is the power in prayer of those who empty themselves of self to seek God only, nonetheless the supreme thing which must follow is the brokenness of spirit which can do nothing but cling and plead. It therefore appears that the ascendancy of the reformed doctrine of our utter dependence upon God for His mercy and blessing is proclaimed here, not only as the Alpha of our Salvation but as the Omega too.

This is a lesson only for those who have fully repented of the self life, and entered into superhuman wrestlings with God for blessing. Prevail we must, and 'overcome', but it costs terribly, and prince of intercessors though Jacob became he was still only a cripple clinger. Jesus, although categorically different, suffered this injury – and also Paul. So will all who holily aspire to count in the Kingdom.

32:29-30 Verse 29 is curious. Jacob asks the name of the Wrestler, but the Wrestler parries his question. Nevertheless he blessed him there. It was doubtless natural for Jacob to ask the divine Person's name – the unfolding of the revelation in the Scriptures has much to do with the divine names. Was this then a gentle reproof as if to say, 'Name? What have you to do with names? I reveal who I am in my encounters and in my Words.' It is a sad day when we seek to take the involvements of the divine encounter with all their saving power and reduce them to some tabulated formula, as if to say like some messenger on the telephone, 'Who shall I say was calling?' It is like those inveterate note-takers who reduce to writing the very effusions of the Spirit in a season of supreme blessing.

The name then is not necessarily one that we receive as on a divine visiting card, but one we supply from the depths of our transfigured souls. Although Jacob gives the name 'Peniel' to the place, it really applies to the One who met him there. Does this testimony, that Jacob met God face to face, contradict the assertion that 'no one has ever seen God' (Jn. 1:18)? No. The God that no one has ever seen is God in the full outshining of His essential glory – 'our God is a consuming fire' (Heb. 12:29). This is not that, but the manifestation of God accommodating himself to frail Jacob, so that he might bless him, not destroy him. Jacob got the message, so vividly in fact that he knew he had looked on the face of God, yet had not been consumed (30b). The marvel is that we may embrace the God whose full glory would consume our mortality, and yet not die, but live as we have never lived before because we experience lifegiving fellowship in all its transforming sweetness and power.

32:31-32 The Greek word for 'staff' in Hebrews 11:21 is quoted from the LXX (OT in Greek) translating a Hebrew word which may mean either 'bed' or 'staff' (Gen. 47:31). If 'staff' is not the appropriate word, the suggestion that Jacob was a cripple from Peniel to his death need not rest on that comment in both Genesis and Hebrews that he worshipped 'leaning on the top of his staff'. Verses 31-32 do not suggest a temporary injury. Read them carefully.

We have here a picture and parable full of poignant instruction. It is the sort of human experience that could possibly best be expressed by a devout artist – a painting of a cripple man walking bravely away into the sun. Is that a pretty picture? Perhaps not 'pretty', but nonetheless beautiful. Is it necessary that he should limp? Is this not a disadvantage to a man of substance, influence and destiny? No, because it keeps him clinging to the *source* of his substance, blessing and power. The limping is a symbol of Jacob's frailty, not least that sin which the Wrestler may have seen latent in Jacob's power to prevail, namely the pride of spiritual achievement. God wanted him to be fruitful to the end, and the only way to ensure he would not take flight into some self-exalting fancy, ruining the very possibility of spiritual usefulness, was to cripple him.

God did that to another. When three times Paul asked his thorn in the flesh to be taken away, God said, 'No. The privileges accompanying your service for me are too great for a sinner to enjoy without danger of carnal flight. I will pin you down.' God did, with the result that Paul at the close of his life could say: 'I have fought the good fight, I have finished my course, I have kept the faith: henceforth there is laid up for me the crown of righteousness, which the Lord, the righteous Judge, shall award me at that day; and not to me only, but unto all them also that love His appearing.'

No fruit without cost. We cannot have it both ways. If we are determined to be fruitful within the measure of the divine will, we must be prepared to pay – not our price, but his. To be willing to pay is to ask for it. Jacob did when he went back to Jabbok that night on his own. And he got it. If he had not, the whole course of the world's history might have been different. We never know what our rising to full stature may mean. We do not need to know but we dare not be less than our best, lest we sit prizeless throughout eternity.

Chapter 33

Jacob Meets Esau

33:1-4 Chapter 32 began with the two-storey picture of the two hosts, the earthly and the heavenly. Perhaps after our admonition not to forget the heavenly warfare (see above on 32:2; cf. Eph. 6:12), we have ourselves failed to reckon with it in Jacob's wrestling at Peniel. We will make no attempt to synthesise our comments now with what we have already said.

It would appear likely that Esau was marching northwards to Jacob with hostile intention (32:6). If that was so, was it Jacob's intercession at Peniel which changed his attitude? This is a tremendous lesson to learn on the power of God-given prayer. Recall again how Jacob having done all he humanly could to placate his brother by gifts and having made all preparation for his family and substance against a militant encounter, could not rest, but returned across the gorge and gave himself to a battle of prayer which shook him to the depths of his body and soul. There he gained the victory and blessing, and in that strength went forward next morning to face the brother he now feared so much.

We pass over the circumstances of that meeting, including Jacob significantly putting Rachel and hers to the rear, to note only the manner of Esau's approach. What changed a man armed to the teeth approaching with a formidable force to one running, weeping, embracing and kissing him in the demonstrative manner of the East? Surely it was prayer. But not any sort of prayer. It was the sort of prayer that flows from souls who not only deeply repent of all sins and sin, but die a painful death like to that of a woman's pain travailing in birth, until a new thought-life is born in the heart and mind of an adversary. God does nothing by halves. When he changes a mind he does it thoroughly. Although that transformation can be so gradual we are scarcely aware of its extent, he can also do it suddenly, yet just as radically.

This, apparently, is what happened here. It was a certain Esau who set out for the North. It was quite another Esau who fell upon his twin brother in an excess of tender emotion. That almighty battle of prayer at Peniel had not only changed Jacob but Esau as well, so that neither of them bore ethical or spiritual relation to the men they had been during the long years of bitter separation. It is not that the work of transformation was sudden. God uses every minute of time to do his long work, but that work is often consummated in a burst of divine activity which looks as if it has been done through one experience. Life with God is an interweaving of process and crisis. Those who most patiently endure the one are most ready for the other.

33:5-11 Esau is well-nigh incredulous at meeting Jacob's wives and children, his interest showing how graciously his attitude had been changed in the course of his journey. Wonderful! He asks in polite fashion what the 'droves' mean (8), and makes to decline them, perhaps with a flash of independence, refusing patronage from his wealthy brother (9). However, to Jacob it is a debt, not only of obligation for his ancient wrong (discreetly not mentioned on either side), but of gratitude to God and to Esau for the graciousness of the meeting (10). He prevails upon him to accept.

This is the way to patch up quarrels. The circumstances are particular of course and do not universally apply, but whether the quarrel be recent or long-standing, the lesson of overcoming evil with good remains. In other cases Jacob's actions might not procure the same results, but that would be the adversary's responsibility. That possibility did not deter Jacob from going the whole of the second mile. Even if Esau had remained hostile and had caused Jacob to suffer grievously, he would have suffered as one right with God into whose hands he then must commit his persistent enemy. However, in the present case, we are sure the blessing Jacob sought in wrestling with the divine One was Esau's grace and favour towards him.

This lesson we all need to learn at some time or other. Why do we persist in thinking we demean ourselves by humility? Rather we put the onus on our adversary to do likewise. Jesus got the better of his foes by submitting to them and he was never at fault, as we are. The pity is that we see this in him and in Jacob, without seeing that we should do the same, Or if we do, we refuse it instantly, not as a death that has to be died to self, but as that death we must die under any circumstances. How wrong! The Christian should never be afraid to be stripped of the rags of his self-esteem, for underneath are the garments of Christ.

33:12-20 Esau assumes that Jacob will settle beside him at Seir (South of the Dead Sea), or at least he will visit his settlement and sojourn there for a while. This Jacob knew could not be. Esau might be personally converted to him, but the whole course of their lives was different. There could be no reunion of interests. Yet Jacob is afraid to say so and takes refuge in lies. His pretext is plausible. What did Esau and his marauding horde know about the gentle pastoral art? He is bid lead on with his soldiery, and they will follow with the families and the flocks at an easier pace. Esau insists on providing an armed escort (15), but Jacob declines the need of it. So Esau marches away as loved ones and friends take leave of one another for a few hours, never to meet again – other than at a funeral (35:29).

Meanwhile, Jacob sets out to build 'a place for himself' (AV, 'a house'). The word 'place' or 'house' (17) has a double meaning – not that the narrator necessarily intended it, though the divine Writer did! The map shows that Jacob made little pretence of following Esau south, but struck west over Jordan. He may have remained at Succoth for a considerable time then moved to Shechem (18f.), where he bought land (see John 4:5). The significant thing is that he did not return to the stone at Bethel as he vowed to do (28:22). True, Bethel was further south and would have taken longer to reach, but he is clearly trying out places, and at last erects an altar to the God of Israel at Shechem. This is not in accordance with his vow and, as we may assume without reading on, things will go wrong.

Before we develop that further, let us pause to reflect that wrong is wrong in itself before ever its consequences come upon us. Yet it is only when they do that we seem to know and feel the heinousness of sin. This should warn us not to judge our state before God by our frame of mind, but by our acts of choice in relation to him. Jacob should have made for that stone at Bethel as fast as his family and flocks would allow him, but other considerations intervened. They usually do, but our well-being and safety depend upon keeping to the high road of God's revealed purpose. Why should we spend our life discovering that God is not mocked? How much better to prove his kindness to his obedient children!

Chapter 34

Dinah and the Shechemites

34:1-31 It all started innocently with the young girl newly arrived from another country going out to see the maidens of the new land (1). But she shouldn't have been there, because Jacob should have been at Bethel. When we are out of God's will, things most innocent in themselves become fraught with evil possibilities because the devil closely watches our slightest straying from the divine protection. Our safety is in obedience. To Shechem, seduction may have been no more than an incident, but his pleasure in Dinah was more than a passing attraction (3). Seeing her distress, he spoke tenderly to her. Why did Jacob wait for his sons (5)? Hamor is more forward but as the fathers talk, Jacob's sons appear and angrily take over (13).

The astonishing feature of the story is Jacob's weakness. Is this the disarming of sin which robs even the strongest man of his resolution? How well the devil knows his business! Jacob has no will to act with calm judgement, but Hamor and Shechem know exactly what they want (11f.) and ask for it in no uncertain terms (cf. Deut. 7:3 and Josh. 23:12f. with verse 9). Shechem offers to the parents any dowry they wish and a gift to Dinah. (Cf. 24:53, but Ex. 22:16, 17 and Deut. 22:28, 29 are more applicable.)

The deceitful sons of a deceitful father see how they can trick Hamor and the men agree to circumcision as the condition of alliance of the tribes (18, 24). Do they not know a good thing when they see it? This Jacob is a wealthy and prosperous cattle breeder, and are not his womenfolk fair (21, 23)? Yes, but they little know the intent of Jacob's sons. The massacre is wrong (25), not only in fact because of Jacob's supineness, but in degree according to just retribution (see Ex. 21:23-25; 22:16, 17, Deut. 22:28, 29). The horror of Simeon's and Levi's outrage is described by dying Jacob (49:5-7) and we later learn of the apparent consequences to the tribes concerned (Num. 18:1, 2, 6, 20-24, Levi; and Josh. 19:1-9, Simeon). Yet the only height Jacob's resentment can now rise to is remonstrance with his sons for the inexpedience of their action at a time when he is trying to establish himself in the land (30). In motive, the sons are more righteous than their father, albeit their revenge is out of all proportion. At least they see the wrong, whereas Jacob is blinded to all questions of honour by the prejudice of his self-seeking heart. Is this the Jacob of Peniel? Yes, and *after* Peniel – a most perilous time!

Chapter 35

Jacob Returns to Bethel

35:1-5 The Lord intervenes. Reminding Jacob of his personal history, he bids him do as he had vowed years ago and go and settle at Bethel. This blunt advice is appropriate for all fevered souls restless to make the most of life who scurry hither and thither seeking to find a sphere large enough for their talents. Our brief time on earth is but the preparatory school and, vital and decisive though it is, real fulness of life lies beyond. Anything we seem to miss here by keeping to what may seem the too-narrow way of the Lord's will, we shall enjoy in much greater fulness and without distraction there. The Lord's servants who would fulfil their calling must be prepared to let a lot go by them in which they long to share. Yet one of their inestimable gains is a true appreciation of pleasure, which is all the more truly felt for being within the divine pleasure, and all the more keenly enjoyed for being a rare experience.

One of the shocks which awaits the sampler of infrequent simple pleasures is the cynicism and boredom of those who indulge without restraint. It is not so much that we can have too much of a good thing. Rather is it that the good things are packed too tightly into what our Scottish forefathers called an 'ill skin', and the pleasure-lovers being right neither with God nor themselves nor their companions are in no state to enjoy them. We should train our tastes down here; we shall have ample use of them yonder.

Before they leave Shechem, Jacob, coming to his spiritual senses, orders the surrender of all superstitious objects. These would include Rachel's stolen teraphim (31:19) and all amulets (earrings) and idols, whether brought from Padan-aram or acquired since. These were buried under the oak (cf. Jos. 24:19-32, esp. vv. 26, 32).

The journey from Shechem to Bethel involved an ascent of 1,000 feet (approximately 330 metres), for Bethel was one of the finest vantage points in the land. As they travelled, the tribes they passed were struck with fear, no doubt partly because they heard of the shocking massacre at Shechem, but also because God put a supernatural terror of them in their hearts. God protects those who turn to him with all their hearts, forsaking every other trust as Jacob's family had now done in putting away all their pagan idols. Indeed, there is something awe-inspiring about a faith that has only invisible means of support, yet prospers visibly. Even in Church circles there is an almost superstitious awe of this, but at least it affords freedom to those who live by invisible support to get on with their prosperous work unmolested.

35:6-15 The name El-Bethel (7) is interesting, in that the name of God is repeated – literally, the God of the house of God. It is this necessity to reinforce the divine name which betrays the eventual shortcomings of all symbolism of places, names and things, because the mere commemoration of an old experience, however blessed, is not good enough for the 'here and now'. This fact provides both a hazard and an opportunity; the hazard of merely harking back to old outworn experiences, and the opportunity of new experience of God. 'The Lord's mercies ... are new every morning.' It is as if each new experience of God has discovered a 'new' God. If a personal experience may be allowed, then the use of the sweet and blessed words 'Come to me, all you that labour...' at the Lord's Table are seldom ordinary, because of fresh grace at each new reading. Nor do we ever become accustomed to the quiet thrill of discovering, 'O there you are, Lord: how wonderful to meet You here again!' Is our surprise the surprise of unbelief? Sometimes it may be, but not always necessarily so. We say that because the newness of God in his successive comings is something to which we cannot and ought not to become accustomed.

E. F. Kevan suggests that Jacob may have added Deborah his old nurse (8) to his household when he went to visit and, alas, bury his father Isaac (27-29). The old nurse was buried under the oak of weeping (Allon Bacuth) at Bethel. Here God confirms Jacob's new name Israel (10) with all its implications. The command to be fruitful (11) may have been answered in the birth of Benjamin, but probably more properly applies to the subsequent growth of the nation (cf. Ex. 1:7).

The promise of the land is included in the confirmation (12). We are reminded that although Christ's soldiers are as pilgrims and strangers in a foreign land passing through their evil generations, the

day is coming when the kingdoms of this world will become the
Kingdoms of our Lord (Rev. 11:15). There is no need to bid tearful
farewells to the blessings we too lingeringly enjoy during our brief
sojourn; we shall meet them again more perfectly in the heavenly
kingdom.

It is suggested that the drink offering (14) was a mere libation to the
dead 'according to a custom attested among many ancient peoples,
and found in Catholic countries at the present day' (Skinner *in loc.*).
However, there is surely no need to equate Jacob's action with the
mere superstitions of his day. Admittedly he was a man of his age, but
not merely so. The great thing about the rites of the Christian religion
is not that they are different from those of the heathen – often they are
not – but that they have a different, purifying Object, even the living
God Himself. To see only *mere* paganism in the patriarchal history is
to be spiritually blind.

The Deaths of Rachel and Isaac

35:16-21 It is asserted that Ephrath (16) is not Bethlehem (19) but lies
on the border of Benjamin, between Ramah and Gibeah, as witness 1
Samuel 10:2 and Jeremiah 31:15. Whereas Christian tradition holds to
the text of 35:19 and 48:7. Perhaps a careful study of the context of 1
Samuel 10:2 by one knowing the land could solve the matter, but see
37:14 and locate Hebron and Shechem on a Bible map.

It would be easy to form a perverse inference from the misfortunes
of Jacob and Rachel's association, namely that God is against what we
like, especially if we like it very much. This is unfair, and, in this case,
short-sighted. Jacob's true but distasteful marriage (cf. 2:24) to Leah
was but the deceitful boomerang of his own deceit of Esau. Where
there is steadfast adherence to the abiding precepts of the moral law
(cf. Ex. 20:17), God may graciously entrust us with a generous measure
of human pleasure. But it is sobering to note how old sores open up
again when we stray from the paths of righteousness.

Jacob is off again not to the west as before but to the south, the
direction whence so many of Abraham's and Isaac's troubles arose.
Things are bound to go wrong. Indeed, so great appears to be his
impatience (he had no peremptory call to obey like Mary and Joseph
(Matt. 2:13), only his own questing carnality), that he cannot wait the
birth of Rachel's second child, and the child is born and the mother

dies on the way. Poor Rachel a-dying called the child Ben-Oni – Son of sorrow (18), as well she might, but Jacob called him Benjamin – Son of my right hand. It is suggested that the child by these names is a dual type of Christ, as it is suggested by some that Benjamin was especially honoured among the Gentiles (45:22), although the evidence cited is a rather slender thread upon which to hang such a sweeping generalisation!

Poor Rachel! the woman's lot is hard enough (cf. 1 Tim. 2:14f.), without a thoughtless husband making it harder. Is it a true instinct and not a mere romantic feeling that attributes to Joseph in his enforced journey an exquisite care for Mary? This is one of the sweetest tests of a husband. What a noble thing is the life of a Christian family at all ages and stages and in all experiences!

35:22-29 The notice of Reuben's great sin is decently brief, but none the less significant. Jacob and Leah's eldest, he seems to have been taken into his mother's confidence regarding her struggle to capture Jacob's affection from Rachel (30:14f.), and later thought the strongest blow he could strike for her would be to dishonour Bilhah, Rachel's maid. 'All's fair in love and war' may justify some actions but this was too daring a thing to do, with the consequence that Reuben lost his primogeniture, not only by that incestuous act, but by reason of the weakness of character which it betrayed (see 49:4).

This lawlessness appears again in the subsequent history of the tribe of Reuben, as we see from their wilfulness and plausibility when Israel had reached Transjordan in her long journey from Egypt (Num. 32). This later led to their schismatic altar on the far side of the Jordan after the conquest of the land (Jos. 22, esp. v.10), and ultimately to their being lost as an effective part of the nation. It is also instructive to note that their determination to remain outwith the land of promise meant that they were a prey to the nations to the south, Ammon, Moab, and Edom, as Gad and Manasseh were to the later Syrian and Assyrian hordes from the North.

It might also be instructive to trace the primogeniture through to favoured Judah. The primacy as firstborn lost by Reuben was bestowed by dying Jacob on the sons of Joseph, Ephraim and Manasseh – even there the primacy is reversed! (See 48:14; 49:22-26 and 1 Chr. 5:1f.) However, note that Psalm 78:67ff. asserts that the ruler was chosen not from the Joseph tribes but from Judah. Although Ephraim is sometimes used as a collective name for Israel, especially the northern kingdom after the division, it is clear from the verses cited above that this is not so in Psalm 78. (See also v.9ff. and esp. vv.35-37.) Certainly it is clear from vv.67-72 that the ultimate favoured choice fell upon Judah and David 'his servant' (1 Chr. 5:2). Thus the rash and contemptuous act of an unstable character disposes of its high destiny for ever. This is frightening, not so much as showing the momentousness of an act as the weakness of a character. If we are terrified by its seeming dread fatalism, let us fly to the mercy of God that He may save us from our fatal selves. He can and will.

Chapter 36

Esau's Descendants

36:1-43 The names of Esau's three wives are in confusion, as may be seen by comparison of 26:34 and 28:9 with 36:2-5. Remember that Esau chose the third to try to appease the wrath of his parents (28:8) at his marriages to Canaanite women. She was a daughter of Ishmael, which was nearer kin but had little else to recommend it. Besides, this was simply to go deeper into the mire of polygamy. Perhaps the only name of future significance in the long list is Amalek (12). He was grandson of Esau by Eliphaz' concubine Timna. The question arises whether he is the founder of the Amalekites of whom we read in Ex. 17:8-16, or whether they are descended from a much older people, first mentioned in Genesis 14:7 and presumably referred to in Numbers 24:20. It is interesting to note that they are called Amalek in Exodus (as if with emphasis on the person) not the Amalekites as in Genesis 14. However, in Numbers 24:20 in the reference to their being the 'first among the nations' they are also called Amalek. Nothing is proved, nor is the puzzle solved. No more does the suggestion that the name 'Amalekites' has been subsequently read into Genesis 14:7 as the ancient people who preceded Amalek in the territory south of the Dead Sea. (It is of course possible that in 14:7 the name Amalek is used by a compiler of the area where that tribe later came to live. *Ed.*)

It appears that although Jacob did not follow his brother south, Esau who had come from Seir to meet Jacob tried to settle in the land and become a cattle-breeder like his wealthy brother. He does not seem to have succeeded and although the reason given for his return to Seir is that Canaan was too narrow for two such prosperous men, the dominant reason may well have been Esau's love of the bandit life. The wild rocky fastnesses of Edom need to be seen to realise what excellent terrain it was for a robber chieftain and his brigands. (Cf. Obad.; Is. 21:11, 12; Jer. 49:7-22; Ez. 25:12-14; Mal. 1:2-5.)

Note that 'mules' (AV) in verse 24 should read 'hot-springs' (NIV), an illuminating hint as travellers can aver. But it is sad to think that Esau is returning to his mountain retreat whence at last he would emerge to bar Israel's way through to the promised land. See Numbers 20:14-21.

Chapter 37

Joseph's Dreams

37:1-8 Verses 1 and 2a belong together. Scholars are divided as to whether the formula of 2a constitutes the introduction or conclusion of a genealogy (cf. 2.4; 5:1; 6:9a; 10:1a). Joseph's criticism of the sons of his father's concubines (2b) is given before the remark concerning his father's love for him, as if to establish the lad's integrity. The coat (3) is not of 'many colours' (AV) but of a certain style, a full robe reaching to the hands and feet and not a sleeveless undergarment or tunic. The style denoted unusual honour, as seen in 2 Samuel 13:18. Jacob's favour of his apparent youngest son may not have seemed invidious to his brothers until the lad began to grow up. Perhaps the brothers shared in indulging him until then as older children sometimes do younger. But if they loved him as a child, they hated him as a younger man because of his father's continuing and increasing favour of him, and could not speak civilly to him.

We can neither excuse the father nor the son, for this is favouritism. But the father was surely more culpable than his son. How astonishing are the blind spots of the great ones of the earth! Did it not occur to him that he was endangering his favourite by such open indulgence, or did he underestimate the passionate animosities that can arise between full-brothers, let alone half-brothers? If the father was blind to the hazards of the situation, the stripling could hardly be expected to see it. A fine upstanding young man with none of the family deceit in his nature, but with a high sense of honour, he would expect his brothers to have the same sense of honour, to accept what he said and even take pleasure with him in his prediction.

Alas for the high-minded optimism of 'upstanding young men.' The Word of God does not share their naive and sanguine hopes. Is this a cynical observation? No. There is no limit to the hopes of humanity redeemed but when young men are brought up under the same roof as redemption and yet spurn it, what hope is there that they will live by its precepts? Yet God can use all this folly at length even to reveal and typify redemption by Exodus, albeit Joseph pays sweetly for his boastfulness and errors of judgment. Ah, the justness of God; and, withal his grace!

37:9-11 Joseph had apparently not told his father his first dream – perhaps he knew what to expect – but with the second dream he had more courage and confidence. Jacob's rejoinder is not without its grim humour: the possibility that Joseph might lord it over his brothers was all right as far as he was concerned, but over himself and Joseph's mother (Rachel was, it appears, still alive at this time), that was different! How truly both of these dreams were fulfilled. In a curious way, Joseph's unwisdom in the way in which he spoke of them had a part in their strange fulfilment! It was not that he told his dreams, but the immature manner in which he apparently acted which clearly angered his father.

How strangely is the tapestry of life woven with dark and shining threads of evil and good! Jacob kept the matter in mind. We are reminded of Mary pondering in her heart the events which followed her Son's birth. They were far too great to share with any but God. Jacob must have had some such premonitions. What a pity he did not rebuke his overeager son for the right reason! Yet God had revealed these things to the lad, and it was not only necessary for our appreciation of the romance of Joseph's life-story, but also as a witness against these churlish brothers. After all, the day did arrive when Joseph could say, 'I told you so!' He certainly had restraint, then, and didn't. That condemnation could not have been implied had he not shared his dream. As the Psalm says, '...the word of the Lord proved him true' (Ps. 105:19).

It is all very difficult. The telling of his dream was necessary and yet the manner of his telling appears to have been presumptuous. There are certainly intimations from God which ought not, dare not, be divulged (cf. Dan. 12:4; 2 Cor. 12:4), as there are doubtless intimations which must. What a revelation the final unravelling of good and evil in the human situation will be! Perhaps our own surprises will exclude preoccupation with those of others. God grant that our surprises may not be too great!

Joseph Sold by His Brothers

37:12-30 Jacob has meantime travelled far south to the vale of Hebron (see a map, comparing such places as Shechem, Jerusalem, Bethlehem, and Hebron.) Had Jacob left flocks in Shechem on his departure (34:27-30), or did his sons gravitate towards the place where they had made such a fearsome name for themselves, hoping to subdue the survivors? Or was the pasture better in the north? Jacob is obviously anxious about them, and sends Joseph to find if all is well. Had Jacob no knowledge of the brothers' murderous hatred of his favourite? The poor lad searched the Shechem area without finding them. On enquiring, he learned they were further north at Dothan where at last he found them.

We wonder if there was a divine dispensation in their being so difficult to find. But Joseph was too faithful to return home without word. His father's anxiety would be his spur. He caught up with them, but little did he know what was in their minds as he approached. This was their perfect opportunity. But it is only when events are viewed at short range that the powers of evil seem to gain the initiative. We know too much about the end of this and other history to be appalled by Joseph's plight. The brothers' words about seeing what would become of his dreams (20) may have eaten into Joseph's heart and made him tremble for their fulfilment and his own safety, but doubtless faith in the authentic revelations of God would fortify him. Whether it did or not and whether Joseph panicked or not, made no difference to the ultimate outcome. Our God is far more concerned with what He is going to do with us, than with what we may think about it in an alarming situation.

Was it a sense of responsibility which made Reuben dismiss their plan (22)? Surely there was compassion in his heart. Perhaps Reuben had sons of his own of Joseph's age (cf. 1 Chron. 5:3), and felt for him.

We hope so. It is curious by what complexity of divine 'plot' Joseph came to arrive at Egypt at all. Reuben's plan was to cast his young brother into the roughly hewn-out cistern (these were common in the land as they were used to collect and conserve the winter rain), and to rescue him from it by stealth when he had opportunity. He is stripped of his coat, of course – that offending garment – and cast into the pit while the brothers' sit down to eat.

Amos 6:1, 6, 7, has an interesting sidelight on this where, though 'Joseph' is a synecdoche for the ten tribes, there is a possible backward glance to the complacency of his older brothers. A similar situation is found, spiritually, in the gambling of the Roman soldiers by the cross of Christ. In the meantime Judah also relented, and meeting the caravan approaching, hit on an idea to salve his conscience and make a little money (26).

The difficulty of the three names, Ishmaelites (25, 27), Midianites (28) and Medanites (36, see NIV marginal reading) were all descendants of Abraham (cf. 25:2,12), is surely over-rated when elaborate theories of composite documents are supported by it. Any intelligent child could suggest several plausible ways of explaining the double reference.*

37:31-36 We hope the brothers were satisfied when they had got rid of their brother, boastful in his youthful immaturity, and had broken their father's heart. They did not know Jacob or his love for his favourite son, if they thought they would quench this envied affection for him. He refused to be comforted. This must have galled the brothers more, and may have caused them to wonder whether their action was at all to their advantage. We wonder if Jacob's refusal to be comforted may have contained an element of instinctive knowledge. During the wars many refused to believe that their missing loved ones were really dead. In most cases this belief turned out to be a futile hope. It may have been otherwise with Jacob. Not that he consciously believed his son was still alive – he had seen what he believed to be his blood on the

---

*Apparently Reuben was not party to this plot, and his dismay can be imagined when he returned to the cistern and found the lad gone (29). We are not told whether Reuben was let into the secret, or whether he thought the blood on the coat was Joseph's or not. One other thing not told here but which may be imagined is Joseph's distress, first at being cast into a disused cistern where he was certain to die, and then being sold as a slave to bargaining merchantmen. This is later revealed from the brothers' lips in 42:21f. But such heartless and monstrous injustice of revenge has its retribution, always. (*Ed.*)

robe – but that the higher reason of the heart refused to be consoled by acceptance of something too dreadful to be true. It was the blood, doubtless, which convinced his conscious mind (in modern days that hoax would have been exposed!), but the heart would not take it in.

We feel sure that this was the case, not only because of the masterly ending of chapter 37, but also because of the sweet acceptance of bereavement which God gives to those who trust in him. 'The Lord gave, and the Lord has taken away; may the name of the Lord be praised' (Job 1:21b). The Spirit of God could not give Jacob acceptance of his son's death when he was not dead. Thus God guides his chosen ones according to his knowledge rather than according to their ignorance. This is surely part of living by faith.

Chapter 38

Judah and Tamar

38:1-10 We do not assume the strict chronology of all the chapters in Genesis. For example, compare the assumption in 37:10 that Rachel is still living with the account of her burial in 35:19. However, the opening words of this chapter, 'At that time', seem to indicate the events about to be narrated as following those in chapter 37. If this is so, the fact is illustrated that one sin gives entrance to the empire of evil, so that the divine protection is withdrawn and the soul exposed to a whole world of potential temptation. The sad tale of Judah's shame, one of the most sordid in the book and the more disgusting on account of Judah's high destiny (the devil loves to drag the highest furthest down), is not merely unfortunate, but betrays an intrinsically flawed character ensuring the certainty of Judah's further lapse.

Judah would have regarded his friendship with the Adullamite as not compromising his faith. After all, we must befriend unbelievers if we are to make known the good news in deed as well as in word. That was all right but being in a state of exposure to evil through his sin against Joseph he was liable to fall into any trap. A friendly visit on the one hand and a marriage on the other are two very different things. (Note that Shua is the name of the woman's father). Thus the whole genealogy of Judah is tainted at the source. How fearful! But there is worse to follow.

We do not know Er's sin, although the text (see also 1 Chron. 2:3) indicates that his sin was in the sight of the Lord (7). Since all sin is in his sight it means presumably that he sinned deliberately in front of the Lord. Doubtless it was some shameless act which, in the Lord's sight, made him not fit to live. Onan was also a wilful character and vilely frustrated his father's intention (cf. Deut. 25:5-10)), and God slew him also. Some may think this part of the story a disgusting intrusion into the intimacies of private life (albeit the judgments of God operate there as inexorably as elsewhere), and so may deplore the countless multitudes through the ages who have doubtless made lewd and giggling reference to it. But the record itself gives no licence to such. How otherwise could the necessary facts of the case have been communicated? We may conclude that they are related as chastely and with as little incitement to ribaldry as possible in the circumstances. 'To the pure all things are pure,' to which we may add that to the pure disgusting things manifestly under summary judgment of God are too solemn for any other than fearful thoughts.

38:11-26 Judah's two sons are now dead by summary divine judgment. There only remains Shelah, still a youth. Tamar could not have him, and Judah using his youth as a pretext, sends Tamar home to her own people. It may be that Judah associated the deaths of his two sons with Tamar, the reason for which is inexplicable since it was Judah who chose Tamar for Er (6). It seems clear he had no intention of giving Shelah to her. This would not have been apparent until the lad was grown up.

In the meantime Judah's wife, not named, died. After the mourning was over, Judah went to the sheepshearing with his old friend the Adullamite. Tamar by this time was aware that Judah did not intend to honour his promise and determined not to be set aside. Her shameful resort may give a hint of the sort of woman she was and why she should have been associated with the brothers' death, but we can only guess. Her depraved idea may have been new born in her frustrated mind.

This sordid association illustrates the temptation of the widowed woman left desolate without family or child to resolve her frustration by any means. Tamar is simply using Judah's lust to achieve her thwarted end. Although she has been admittedly wronged by Judah according to the levirate law (14b), two wrongs do not make things right. The wily woman seeks pledges of her hire, which he gives (18). She conceives, and Judah shamelessly employs his friend the Adullamite to deliver the promised kid and receive the pledges, the insignia of his rank. In verse 23 Judah means, 'Let her keep the pledges since you have not found her to exchange them for the kid and we do not want to be shamed.'

We now come to the worst, the hypocritical part of the story. When Judah hears that Tamar is with child, he commands she should be burnt (24). The only reference in Scripture to execution by burning is in Lev. 21:9. (In Hammurabi's code, death by burning is the penalty for incest). The normal Hebrew execution was by stoning. (Cf. Lev. 20:10; Deut. 22:23f; Ezek. 16:40; John 8:5.) David gives us another example of that all too human tendency to condemn one's own sins in others (2 Sam. 12:5, 6). Is not the reason why the grace of God is loathe to condemn that there is no guilty condemnation in his heart to spur him to defensive denunciation? Thus sinners are hard on sinners, whereas those purified by grace and not by self-effort are most loathe to condemn.

Tamar has what the world calls the trump card, these pledges (cf. the pledges of the royal birth of the shepherd's daughter in Shakespeare's *The Winter Tale*). Judah not only acknowledges the sin of impurity (cf. again David in 2 Sam. 12:13), but that of withholding Shelah from Tamar. His comment 'She is more righteous than I,' (26) gives an important insight into the meaning of this complex bible word. He means that her action was done to honour her relationship with her late husband's family, since the word 'righteous' can often refer to honouring a particular relationship. He himself had neglected to fulfil his obligations towards her as his daughter-in-law.

Let us pause, when we rashly think to sin one sin, to consider what tangle of further wrongs involving many it may lead us into.

38:27-30 This account may be compared with that of the travail of Rebekah and the birth of Isaac and Jacob in 25:21-23. Note that in both cases 'red' is associated with the elder. Zerah is pronounced the elder by the midwife's words and action but both he and Esau are supplanted (or 'overreached', in 27:36 by deception) by the younger. It is Perez who breaks forth (his name's meaning) and maintains the line of Judah leading to Messiah. The line between Judah and David may be traced in 1 Chronicles 2:4-15, but more simply in Ruth 4:18-22; see also vv. 11, 12. Thus Messiah's line, which began with a family of deceivers – several generations of them – continues with a case of incest (there is no hint as to the nation of Tamar), incorporates a redeemed harlot, Rahab (see Josh. chs. 2 & 6 and compare with Matt. 1:5), and Ruth, daughter of the vile Moabites – not to speak of David and Solomon's own sins. We therefore learn that he who came to become sin for us (2 Cor. 5:21), incorporates in the line of his human descent a variety of notorious sinners. Is not God daring in the things he does to justify those sinners whom he loves?

Chapter 39

Joseph and Potiphar's Wife

39:1-6 Joseph in Egypt is favoured from the start, by God and man. Normally a new slave would be given the most menial tasks, usually in the field, but not Joseph. He was with him in the great man's house and prospered him. Potiphar saw that the Lord was with him, and that it was the Lord that made all to prosper in his hand, and so Joseph found grace in his sight and was promoted to chief place in Potiphar's household. This brought a special blessing upon Potiphar's house so that he trusted Joseph absolutely. The reference to 'food' (6) may mean that an Egyptian might not allow a Semite to handle what he ate, or it may mean that what he ate was all Potiphar knew about in his own house.

This is true evangelical witness, according to our Lord's own prescription: 'You are the light of the world. A city on a hill cannot be hidden. Neither do people light a lamp and put it under a bowl. Instead they put it on its stand, and it gives light to everyone in the house. In the same way let your light shine (it does not say 'flash') before men, that they may see your good deeds, and praise your Father in heaven' (Matt. 5:14ff.). Perhaps the most wonderful thing about this is that those who see 'your good deeds' connect them with God, and glorify him. And yet it is not surprising, for surely there must be a quality, not to say fragrance, about good deeds wrought in God (cf. Jn 3:21) that characterise them as being from one source only, the living God himself.

This is our first, inescapable Christian duty to others, and it cannot be done by human devising or striving, however ingenious, but only by the good deeds which issue from character. So it was with Joseph. He was totally trustworthy, and withal possessed grace and charm. This is why he is such a beautiful type of Christ, for grace and truth are beautifully matched in him. It is all very well for us to say that Joseph was a specially chosen person, but every Christian is 'specially' chosen – for something!

39:6b-10 Here comes the reason for telling us that Potiphar had committed his whole household to Joseph. Potiphar's wife thought this gave Joseph freedom to do what he desired, and in a manner it did; but what Joseph desired was not what she thought a promoted slave would desire. She lusted after the attractive young man, and could not understand why he did not seize the opportunity offered him. It was certainly not the likelihood that such an association would be discovered if it continued that deterred Joseph. Rather was it something this pagan woman knew nothing about, namely fear of the living God, which gave him such high respect for his neighbour (not least herself), and especially for his master's trust in him. Joseph's religion and life were integrated because religion was not for him a departmental indulgence, but the governing principle of life. Since he saw all things are subject to the fear of God, he ordered his whole life in accordance with that fear of God, to whom he knew he had to give account.

It is, of course, the total lack of this today that makes modern men and women so wanton in their behaviour. They think they can do what they like and get away with it, although they see – or would see if they opened their eyes – that the world is strewn with the wrecks of those who thought likewise and found they couldn't. How true is Psalm 36:1, quoted in Romans 3:18, 'there is no fear of God before their eyes'! It is this which both restrains the presumption of fallen man and leads him into the paths of righteousness and true peace and prosperity, there to discover that the fear of God is the shepherd's rod by which he would lead us into the knowledge of his love. It is only when his love is completely frustrated that it breaks out in wrath and judgement. To say that God may not in the end judge in wrath is a piece of diabolical impertinence; nor would the sentimentalists like the kind of world that would follow if God did abdicate his sovereignty.

Potiphar's wife listened to his reason for not responding, but thought to herself, 'We shall soon overcome his religion. Religion is all very well in its place, but no one lets religion interfere with his life. We shall wear him down.' This is always what the worldling says and by a process of attrition tries to wear the believer down. It is clear that this must be the devil's attempt to shake the person who has achieved integration of religion and life. If a believer wins through here, it is triumph indeed. All our will and effort must be directed to this end of remaining under the gracious domination of the fear of God. However, only those will outlast Satan's attempts at their downfall who see the grace which lies behind the law, and the love which is behind the fear, and realise that wrath and judgment are the last resort of a God whose sovereignty and glory must be advanced at all costs.

When David was accused by the prophet Nathan of the sin against Bathsheba and Uriah, he realised it was 'against you, you only, have I sinned, and done what is evil in your sight...' (Ps. 51:4). Those who fear only God will do no wrong to God's other creatures – not that that will always please them. Potiphar's wife did not want Joseph to treat her with respect as in the sight of God. But that is what Joseph did, and nothing could have maddened her more.

39:11-20 Had Potiphar's wife arranged that no one should be about the house? She must have been sure she could overcome Joseph's scruples, given the opportunity. Thus the lustful mistakenly assume that others only restrain themselves for want of opportunity. How wrong they are! We heard of an actor who having boasted in writing of his own lechery, then offered advice to young women to beware of men, because 'they are all lecherous beasts'. No! This was but a revelation of himself and his 'set'. Equally it would be wrong to impugn the gentler sex under the category of Potiphar's wife, although the lengths to which sex-obsessed women will go have to be seen to be believed. It is not difficult to believe that such women (and men), frustrated on the very lip of their desire, grow uncontrollably mad and are ready to hatch the most diabolical plots to avenge their refusals.

Study the undertones of verse 14 to see the sort of woman she is. To the serving men whom she summoned with her cry of genuine distress – but of frustration, not fear – she contemptuously called her husband 'he' (AV, NKJV, RSV), and appealed to their underling spirit by calling the chief servant Joseph, 'That Hebrew slave', while the plural, 'to make sport of *us*', seems to imply that no woman was safe in the house while Joseph was there. It is almost unbelievable that outwith storybook fiction one could be so evil as diametrically to reverse the truth, but we have seen this enormity in our day raised to the highest peak of refinement in the struggle of fevered nations for ascendancy. It is so monstrous, flagrant, dastard, that we would not think any would dare, but the devil dares all right and his servants too who are hard put to it to gain their wicked point.

So Joseph is cast into a special prison. Jewish commentators have questioned Potiphar's acceptance of his wife's story on the ground that he would have put Joseph to death if he had. It is a moot point. There is no other evidence that he doubted his wife's word, which means either that she had been faithful until then, or else was a consummate deceiver. It was a cruel turn to Joseph's fortune, and all for honour's sake. That at least he had not lost, and to a man as honourable as he that was everything. Indeed, as we peruse the first nine chapters of the book of Proverbs, we can think of one far more worthy to collate and teach these aphorisms about the wiles of wanton women than Solomon!

Yet again, therefore, this paragon of virtue is plunged into ignominious captivity. This must seem unbelievable misfortune to those who think men are essentially decent, but it is quite to be expected if we believe that nothing is so universally hated as goodness. One of the signs that our own nation is heading for disaster is that few things are as despised as sheer goodness. It is all right if people keep their goodness to themselves – that is their affair. But to be indecent enough to show it – that is the final shame. Parade a broken marriage or a shady deal and that is apparently all right. But let goodness shine out and the cry is, 'Away with it, it is not fit to be shown.' Ours is rapidly becoming a community among sections of which our Lord's words in Matthew 5:16 will be impossible to fulfil. When it is so, then our nation will go down, as innumerable others have done, and serve it right!

39:21-23 A great part of the epic history of the Bible could be written under the heading of the 'buts' of the Lord's triumph over wickedness long suffered. One of the most gracious verses in Genesis is 50:20, where Joseph sees behind his brother's wickedness to God's good use of it to save the chosen race from starvation: 'You intended it to harm me, *but* God intended it for good ... the saving of many lives.' It is the realisation of this gracious over-ruling for good which makes Christians strong to face evil. For human beings are not animals living only for the pleasures of the moment, but they have the human gifts of intelligent memory, imagination and foresight. Indeed, by nature they need to have something to look forward to, even when present circumstances are favourable. So it is that faith is a wonderful spur and challenge to adversity, and brings out the very best in men and women, according to their calibre.

God himself is absolutely behind this heroic endeavour and plans with all the love of his fatherly heart to make 'the wrath of men praise him' in the blessing of his bestrewn children. Take the words, 'But the Lord ... granted him favour in the eyes of the prison warder' (21). This is such a sovereign action that no one could calculate it, from which we learn that the overwhelming power of the Almighty is reserved for those who keep God's holy laws in adverse circumstances. It is as simple as that. As children of God (we are not forgetting that God's mercy waits to bless the contrite sinner, but nevertheless forgiven sinners must not 'continue in sin that grace may abound'), if we keep God's holy laws, although all the world should be against us, he is for us. We know that however long he takes he waits to come down on our side with his mighty grace. This is what he did for Joseph.

How many of God's choicest saints have learned the most and best of their God in prison? What a history! And what an encouragement to those often much maligned. Fear not – he purposes good for you! Your vindication and blessing before men is not your motive for standing for the right, rather is it your love of the right which you have learned from him in close fellowship. Nonetheless he may not only make himself unspeakably precious to you in the dark days, but bring you out into the unsolicited light to favour you before all your detractors. It mattered not where Joseph went, they could put him in the worst place imaginable, but by the Lord he would soon be raised to a place of trust and leadership.

Joseph, you may say again, was a chosen vessel; God does not bless all His children so. Perhaps not, but we are all chosen by him for something, and Joseph's blessing was vitally related to his integrity of character. The Lord does not favour anyone. True, his mercy lights upon the meritless unto salvation, but only those who make progress in it by way of Christian character are favoured in his service. That costs something. The first favour (in salvation) is free, unmerited; but the second (in fruitful service) has to be costly paid for. Joseph paid, and got it.

Chapter 40

The Cupbearer and the Baker

40:1-23 We gather that it was not difficult to offend the king of Egypt or his high officers. There are 'Pharaohs' today whom no power on earth can please! These two particular men were given into Joseph's care as being worthy, even in prison, of special attention (4). Where did Joseph come from 'the next morning' (6)? It was not only that Joseph noticed they were dejected – any observant warder or fellow-prisoner, however heartless, could observe that – it was rather his kindly inquiry, showing the terms of cordiality in which he stood with the men, and his concern for their welfare. This was the quality and the spirit of service which earned for Joseph everywhere positions of trust.

Is it not a remarkable thing that a youngster brought up as a favourite son and given every advantage his father could procure, should have such a spirit of trustworthy service to his fellows? Would that there were more Josephs today! The men were dejected because they assumed their dreams had meanings, but there was no one to interpret them. The naive would assume that Joseph thought himself to be God, but he means that he knows God who will tell him what they mean (8b). Who would have associated three branches with duration of time? And how would he have known whether it was three days, or months, or years?

The cupbearer uses an expression in verse 11 which indicates that he hands the cup, having no stem or handle, from his palm to that of the king's. This was the style of some Egyptian cups. Joseph however in his interpretation speaks of handing the cup (literally) 'into' not 'upon' Pharaoh's hand (13). He is so sure of his interpretation that he puts in a plea with the cupbearer to remember him when he again stands before Pharaoh, for, he says, 'I was forcibly carried off from the land of the Hebrews'. His comment has come under criticism from certain scholars as indicating varied forms of the narrative. Joseph only means he was carried away from his father. If he had said 'sold' that might have brought his father into disrepute without elaborate explanations. Besides, in all honesty he would use a word that would evoke sympathy from the cupbearer for his plight. The 'land of the Hebrews' only means the land where the Hebrew people lived. Was he likely to go into a long account of Jehovah's promise to Abraham, Isaac, and Jacob? Really, these critical scholars expect standards of meticulousness which obtain in no civilisation whatsoever. They seem prepared to force the narrative in a most unnatural way!

When the first dream is interpreted favourably (16), the baker is encouraged to press for the interpretation of his dream. The 'three' motif having been established, it would stand for the same duration in this dream also. How brave of Joseph to interpret the dream as he saw it! The question arises whether there is confusion in the narrative between hanging and beheading (19). It doubtless means both, that after death by hanging he would be decapitated and thrown to the dung heap and the scavenger birds. This was exceedingly ignominious in Egypt where they loved to preserve and mummify bodies (we can see these in the British Museum). Even if Joseph knew that Pharaoh's birthday was in three days when in the midst of the celebrations certain amnesties (and apparently judgements) were given, it was not he who first mentioned 'three', but the cupbearer and baker. No, there is no escaping the whole thing as divinely arranged. He is a poor God, out of touch with the needs of his individual and precious children, if he cannot do that. Why do people, chosen and ordained to interpret the Scriptures, want in his own Book to reduce him to less than a cipher. There is a reason for this, hidden in men's hearts. May it not be that in our generations and century there will be few harder censures in the last judgment than against Bible whittlers.

The dreams and their interpretations came true but the cupbearer forgot Joseph. From the rest of the story it appears this was genuine forgetfulness, because he would have assumed that Joseph only anticipated what was inevitable and that all his service to him was simply to ease his mind for three days. He would not have consciously thought this out, but the facts would have caused him to let the memory of Joseph recede from his mind as not being of any more importance to him. This is how many view acts of service and who show no gratitude. But when we know ourselves to be hell-deserving sinners every tiniest favour is a cause of gratitude, so that we spend our life giving thanks, to men and to God. This is the Christian way. But God was in this forgetfulness, albeit not in the ingratitude of it, not only to release Joseph from prison, but to present him to Pharaoh. God's delays always imply more important things to follow. God waits to bless.

Chapter 41

Pharaoh's Dreams

41:1-14 The account is authentically Egyptian. Two full years the cupbearer had forgotten Joseph's plea. That was a long test to Joseph's faith. Think how perplexing it must have been for him to find such favour and prosperity at the Lord's hand and then to come to this. Must not the cupbearer's remissness have tempted Joseph to think Jehovah had set him aside, and make him ask, 'What have I done to deserve this?' God is often slow but always sure, and over-ardent spirits who would consume themselves and all about them with instant zeal need repeatedly to be reminded of it.

At last Pharaoh dreamed – twice (cf. Joseph's two dreams and those of the cupbearer and baker). He was not only puzzled but disturbed because he knew his dreams imported something concerning his person, and knew not if it boded good or ill. The first cattle were sleek and fat, the next gaunt and thin (we need not go into the sacredness of the Nile or of the cow to Egypt: that can be read elsewhere by those interested) but the fat cattle were eaten by the gaunt (4). In the second dream, the plump ears ate the thin ears which had been blasted by the dreaded Sirocco, the south east wind of spring and summer (7). None of Pharaoh's magicians who mixed education with occult dabbling, could interpret the dreams.

It was then the cupbearer remembered. His experience with Joseph had been as a piece of useless mental junk until then – 'keep a thing seven years' says the superstitious adage, 'and it will come in handy'. The cupbearer had 'kept' it two, but in his disinterestedness did not know he had it! But God knew. It would have been difficult for him in Pharaoh's hour of need not to remember his own and the baker's dreams, and Joseph's help. His frank confession (9) shows how completely he had forgotten Joseph in the joy of his restoration. (Isn't it amazing how we can compartmentalise life, so that we easily adjust to very different worlds? Expatriates tell us that after a furlough or two they switch very naturally and quickly from the tropical to the cooler, more urbane life).

Let us again remind ourselves, against possible adversity, how far the Almighty can allow and contain reverses to his servants and his purposes. So that one day, 'out of the blue', when Joseph may have either been despairing or apathetic and not at all expectant, word came to him in the dungeon that Pharaoh wanted to see him and had a job for him to do (14)! From the dungeon to the palace and the royal throne....

Whether or not we think of Joseph's life in general as a type of Christ we cannot miss the suggestiveness of that transition (Phil. 2.8-9). Joseph like our Lord also knew great extremities of experience, and in one day was brought from the mire of the dungeon, clean shaven (as was seemly in Egypt to appear before Pharaoh) and properly dressed, into the royal presence. We are reminded of the bondage of many of God's choicest saints to irksome frailties of mortal flesh. How wonderful it must be one day which may be of perhaps greater burdensomeness than usual, to be suddenly released like a bird from a cage into the presence of the King. 'For our light and momentary troubles are achieving for us an eternal glory that far outweighs them all' (2 Cor. 4.17). Marvellous!

41:15-44 Notice the proud touch of the king in his description of the dream, 'I had never seen such ugly cows in all the land of Egypt' (19). His pride would be taken down a little before Joseph's God was done with him! When Pharaoh had done, Joseph declared that the two dreams were one, and the repetition of the message under different symbols simply confirmed it, and that it would shortly be fulfilled. Having given his interpretation in a few master strokes of description in terms that the king would understand, Joseph proceeded to suggest that what was needed was a man of discretion and wisdom to cope with the situation. But who? Pharaoh must have instantly thought to himself, 'Who in my kingdom will believe this story sufficiently to lay up grain in store for seven years against a famine that may never come? The only man to do this is the one who believes that the prophecy in the dream will come true.' True; Joseph believed it: he said that this was God's interpretation of the dream. He was the very man.

The question we ask is whether Joseph was really suggesting himself for the job? If he was, it was not as an opportunist – it would be no sinecure – but as one who conscientiously believed he saw what was needed to be done. After all, the person who has experience of purveying on a small scale may be as able to do it on a large scale if he can keep his head. Under God, Joseph would do this. So, having suggested officers under Pharaoh (34f.) to gather the fifth part (note that proportion) of the grain, Joseph gets the job. This meant that Pharaoh believed Joseph – after all, he had the dreams! – as indeed he acknowledged that the Spirit of God was in him. What a testimony!

From then onwards Joseph could do no wrong, and would not. He was honoured, not only because he had ideas on how to cope with a forthcoming crisis, but could be trusted to act in the highest interests of the people under Pharaoh. Surely the expansiveness of Pharaoh's advancement of a young Hebrew fellow just dragged from gaol indicates that he manifestly felt the Spirit of God to be on him. This again we note is the quality of authentic godly witness which proclaims itself to partake of a transcendent otherness and which is freely acknowledged. 'Let your light so shine before men that they may see your good works, and give glory to your Father who is in heaven' (Matt. 5.16). We must be so thoroughly Christian that others must see that it is of God. What a challenge!

41:41-53 The ring was the sign of highest legal authority while the word for 'fine linen' indicates that it was material made of a kind of flax of 'great fineness and whiteness'. The gold chain is typical of the exquisite workmanship excavated in ancient Egypt and seen on their monuments. 'Make way' (NIV), 'Bow the knee' (AV) is difficult to translate; the word used is obscure Egyptian, and may mean something like 'Live Long', 'Rejoice', or, 'Be Happy' (cf. *Vivat Rex* or *Vive le Roi*). Pharaoh's name for Joseph (45) is also obscure and there appear to be no grounds for the suggestion it means, 'Revealer of Secrets'. It may rather refer to his new office, meaning, 'Food of Life', or 'Food for the Living'; Jerome's Latin translation has it as 'Saviour of the World', making it refer to his conservation measures. It has also been suggested that Joseph's vestures may have had priestly significance.

'On' (45) refers to Heliopolis meaning, 'City of the Sun God' which was a centre of sun-worship in Egypt. The high priest of On was apparently an important personage in the religion and politics of the land, and we are told that the priestly college situated there was reputed to be the greatest in the country for learning. No censorious comment is made or even hinted at in the record concerning Joseph's acceptance of an Egyptian bride. The reason which underlies all the Levitical prohibitions of marriage with other nations is not racial but religious. In cases where the foreign bride wholeheartedly embraced the Hebrew religion and abandoned idolatry, the prohibition has no force as in the case of Ruth, daughter-in-law of Naomi. There is no evidence that Asenath influenced Joseph away from his strict Hebrew monotheism (belief in the one true God). Indeed, we assume that she accepted her husband's religion.

If Joseph's new position and vestments denoted priestly status, we can scarcely believe this compromised his Hebrew faith. The whole record, not least the names he gave his sons, suggest the reverse. Some have speculated Joseph's Gentile bride is part of a type of Christ seeking his Gentile Church while rejected by his brethren, Israel. We see no objection to this, since it is in accord with Romans chapters 9-11, and does not imply a dispensational view of Scripture – albeit it is held by those with dispensational views.

The seven years of plenty came as prophesied, and Joseph made good use of them to fill the granaries of Egypt. Such a policy, which could have had many influential critics during the years of good harvests – at least until they saw the first part of the dream fulfilled – might well have been difficult to pursue with the gathering in to storage of 20% of the harvest as he had counselled (34). That Joseph carried it out so thoroughly indicates the authority he had in the realm. It is an amazing story of what God can do when he wills. This teaches us many things, not least the lesson of patience and endurance when God chooses not to do spectacular things. There is a reason. Wisdom waits his time.

41:50-52 The names Joseph gave to his two sons are suggestive, not least in view of the reversal of the primogeniture. The first born Manasseh (possibly meaning 'to forget') is associated with Joseph's unhappy past and Ephraim (possibly meaning 'twice fruitful') with the glorious present. But the primogeniture is reversed, so that Ephraim takes precedence over Manasseh (see 48:14ff.).

This has spiritual implications. It is through much tribulation that we enter into the kingdom of God, but these troubles, Paul tells us, are 'light and momentary' in comparison with the 'eternal glory that far outweighs them all' (2 Cor. 4.17), which follows when the positive is seen to be far more important than the negative. If only we could remember this in the midst of our troubles. We are too frail and too often only rejoice when we have had a happy issue out of them. Joseph's rejoicing at the birth of Ephraim by no means implies he had not endured his trials with godly fortitude. But how few of us exhibit his faith! Remember Jesus' words, 'A woman giving birth to a child has pain because her time has come; but when her baby is born she forgets the anguish because of her joy that a child is born into the world. So with you: Now is your time of grief but I will see you again and you will rejoice, and no one will take away your joy' (Jn. 16:21f.).

Jesus, for all his anguish on the Cross did better than this, for he 'for the joy set before him endured the cross, scorning its shame, and sat down at the right hand of the throne of God' (Heb. 12:2). To see that this is inevitably the order of experience should surely encourage us bravely to submit to the trials we endure for Christ's sake, knowing that there is a happy issue out of all our troubles, the happier for our fortitude in enduring them. If there could be any regret in the Kingdom, may it not be because we would return to bear our Christian trials more bravely in order to enjoy our reward more gloriously? This of course cannot be. Faith must see the point and purpose of the trials before the glorious end appears.

However, there is another thought. Joseph said, 'God has made me fruitful in the land of my sufferings.' Some of God's saints, like Jeremiah, had to wait until after death to see the outcome of their faithfulness. It is not always so. God may allow us to be fruitful in the land of our affliction, and triumph in the place where we suffer the deepest reverses. Hope on!

41:53-57 The history of ancient Egypt and the relative chronologies of the Hebrew patriarchs and the various Egyptian Dynasties are all so obscure and uncertain that it is impossible to date Joseph's stay or indeed to infer much. However, the Genesis account with its authentic Egyptian flavour is in accord at this point with the records of the ancient Egyptian monuments. It has been asserted that the advent of Joseph was a major turning point in the administration and welfare of the Egyptian State, and that he was the initiator of the granaries' scheme of which there are subsequent accounts. This would not surprise us. Joseph came to a great Empire, but his sagacity and decisive action suggests he was superior to the best Egyptian statesmen of his day. What more natural than to infer that the Hebrew genius made its mark on ancient Egypt as it has done on all subsequent civilisations?

The astonishing thing is that the critics and scholars incline to reduce this evident superiority to a fabulous pastiche of shreds and patches in which the lowest of motives are sometimes attributed to the 'writers'. They attribute them with taking traditional and legendary accounts of Hebrew sojourns in Egypt and elevating them to illustrious epics, to the glory of the Jews. We must not forget that the world rulers of demonic darkness (Eph. 6:12) from the very beginning are against the Hebrew rise. We are therefore bound to expect that outwith the Scriptures the history of the Hebrews is often contemptuously regarded or even ignored.

Yet it is hard lines that those who deal with the sacred record should take the contemptuous outsider's part. We will have none of this. Although we desire to be unprejudiced enough to accept and integrate the results of all objective enquiries and research, we hold tenaciously to the unique value of the Scriptural record on many grounds, not least our Lord's own testimony, and beg leave to believe that a more satisfactory view of the composition of the book of Genesis must yet be found. It is surely odious to the reverent mind that in a comparison of records, the sacred is judged by the secular, and not the other way round. The fearful thing about it all is that the chief casualty in these critical views is the Holy Spirit who is politely, nevertheless rigorously, excluded. All rightful glory to Joseph, and to Joseph's God!

Chapter 42

Joseph's Brothers Go to Egypt

42:1-6 An ancient Egyptian inscription indicates that it was the practice of Asiatics to appeal to Egypt for food in time of famine. This famine which was predicted by Pharaoh's dream was widespread, affecting Canaan. 'Jacob learned that there was grain in Egypt...' (1). Why should it have been the old man sitting at home who urged some action and not his sons and their families? Does the text suggest that the sons had heard, but were doing nothing about it, or at least were hesitant? If so, why were they unwilling to go to Egypt? We must not read into their minds thoughts which assume they feared what we know happened to them. They were certainly not expecting to find Joseph grand vizier of Egypt, but had they a deep guilt-complex relating to Egypt? Or was it only that they were a purposeless lot, who leant far too heavily on their resourceful father? If so, it needed the old man's word of command to jolt them into action.

Ten made the journey. Benjamin, now his father's favourite both because of maternity and youth, was not allowed to go. Why was Jacob afraid to let him go? Had the brothers developed a jealousy of him? And did Jacob therefore distrust them with the youngster, suspecting his sons were not guiltless of Joseph's loss? Whatever the brother's thoughts, we know God was at work in the circumstances and that their wickedness was soon to catch up with them.

No situation could be more dramatic than the meeting of the brothers with Joseph (6). They had gone down to Egypt, a journey which had caused Abraham to fall away from the Lord bringing him into deep trouble (12:10ff.), and also a journey which God explicitly told Isaac not to make (26:2). Yet Egypt was the land in which enslaved Joseph had triumphed as a faithful servant of God. Although the brothers may possibly have had strong feelings of guilt about Joseph – especially when their father refused to let Benjamin travel with them – and might not have been surprised to meet him in some menial or servile position, they were hardly expecting him to be prime minister. Their very last thought was that he would be personally supervising the distribution of corn to famine-stricken easterners.

Was this Joseph's normal function during the famine? If so, did he take on this role in hope of finding his brothers? It is by no means impossible that underlying his power and great responsibility there was a secret intent in his heart, perhaps not even shared by his wife, to watch for his hungry brothers coming to Egypt for food. It is in circumstances fraught with these involved motives and emotions that Joseph one day recognised his brothers amongst the suppliants for food. Doubtless, there was nothing in all his exaltation in Egypt which afforded him the peculiar satisfaction of his brothers' deep obeisance.

We do not believe his acceptance of their humble submission was either gross or vindictive. While it would have taken a Jesus himself to have borne such a triumph without carnal indulgence, Joseph's chief satisfaction seems to have centred in the vindication of his dream (see v.9). The man who had feared God enough to reject the advances of Potiphar's wife, was obviously governed by that high consideration (39:9b). Even now, in his moment of supreme triumph, fear of God would still be his chief preoccupation. Learn that those whose characters are formed by godly reverence and awe will constantly be guided and constrained by filial fear of their God.

42:7-24 To those who are imbued by the spirit of forbearance and gentleness unto complete pacifism, Joseph's harshness may seem quite inexcusable. But this narrative must be taken as a whole, and we must see his rough speech and stern action in the light of the effect his attitude had on his brothers (21). It is very probable that these men had never been far away from remorse ever since they sold Joseph to Egypt, so that the dilemma they were now in quickly smote their consciences and brought forth among them a flood of mutual confession. But it still needed a touch of their own medicine – some harsh and seemingly unjust treatment – to bring home to them the enormity of what they had done. Joseph provided this. It is doubtless futile to moralise on Joseph's treatment of them from our later and fully Christian point of view, but we see what he meant to do, and do not doubt that God was with him in it, for all its rigours.

We must confess that the thrice-repeated accusation of spying (9, 12, 14) reminds us of modern interrogation techniques, making us shudder, but there is nothing as sinister as that in Joseph's mind. When pressed, the accusation elicits their family history (13), a moving experience for Joseph, but it does not weaken his intention to make them pay to the full for their sin. He swears by Pharaoh (doubtless for their benefit), that they will not be released unless their youngest brother is brought as a proof of their good faith. Notice that Joseph tactfully ignores the reference to the lost brother. Meantime, they are clapped in prison for three days. This was perhaps a little taste of what he himself had endured for long years. It is amazing how frequently our ancient wrongs against our fellows eventually bring upon us some of our own medicine!

Joseph then releases them (18) and alters his plan, but he prefaces his decision with words which indicate the anchor of his life: 'I fear God.' This would assure the brothers that this man would act towards them with integrity. His new demand had a twofold purpose: it gave him the opportunity he longed for, to see Benjamin his only full brother; it would also allow him to test whether his brothers had changed in their attitude towards their half-brother (44:20ff.).

It is interesting to reflect on the effect of this demand on the different actors in the story. There is the dismay of Jacob (36) – that was the cruelest thing, and yet the arch-deceiver was now himself deceived. There is the anxiety and conviction of the brothers (21ff.). And there is the eager longing of Joseph himself (24). Was there ever a story so full of drama? The fact that they believed the man increased their obligation to do as he had said, but it increased their dilemma also. It was this that drove them to acknowledge their sin and pour it all out in mutual confession, knowing not that the 'Egyptian' who had spoken to them through an interpreter understood all (23). Their mutual confession leads to recrimination, and Reuben justly charges them with the cruelty of their precipitate behaviour in selling Joseph when he intended to deliver the boy from them and send him back to his father.

All this Joseph heard, and it was too much for him. He had to turn to hide the tears of emotion which welled up in his eyes. Who shall say what was preponderant in that emotion? Was it the thought of all he had suffered over the years? Was it all he had missed of happy home life and of his father's love? Was it the love he still bore for his brothers in spite of their treatment of him? Or was it the longing to see his father again? Perhaps at such a moment it is the tension of the varied tautened strands of feeling which forces expression. No one knows the almost intolerable burden of high tensile emotion in the person of high moral character. Perhaps we have never realised the extent of this profound tension in the ministry of our Lord.

42:24b-38 Simeon is chosen and bound before the brothers' eyes. Might he have connected this misfortune with his own brutal sin at Shechem (34:25f.)? The brothers set out on their journey home, to discover on the way that the money of one of them had been restored (28). It appears that on the return journey only one sack was opened for fodder, but when the others opened their sacks on their arrival home, to their dismay they discovered all their money had been returned (35). Notice their reaction of fear: 'Their hearts sank and they turned to each other trembling' (28), and, 'When they and their father saw the money pouches they were frightened' (35). We might have expected delight on discovering this kindness rather than their intense apprehension. We are reminded of the fear of the people when the restored demoniac was seen to be clothed and in his right mind (Mk. 5:15), and also the fear of the disciples when Jesus walked to them on the waves of the lake when they were hard pressed in rowing (Mk. 6:50, cf. also Mk. 4:41).

The minds of fallen sinners must be deeply saturated by a spirit of pessimism, defeatism and fatalism to be so unwilling to accept a deed of kindness without suspicion and fear. 'Too good to be true,' say those blinded to the glories of grace. 'Too good not to be true,' say those who believe that at the heart of the universe beyond all evil lie optimism, hope, kindness and largesse. The brothers were too preoccupied with the relation between their strange experience and their chronic guilt to see it. They therefore inclined to assume that everything thereanent boded ill, however good it might appear.

What a distortion of the truth unexpunged guilt works in the human heart! The guilty soul walks down the street and every eye accuses him. Should a friend suddenly clap his hand upon his shoulder he cries out in anguish as if apprehended for the sin which is torturing him. In those circumstances the most needless exposures of sin are made until the whole world knows, whereas not a soul had such a thought in mind until the guilty gave himself away by reading accusation into the most innocent and friendly gestures. 'Not only do all men know, but God knows,' thinks the guilty soul, 'and He is against me!' But the brothers have more to think about than this.

About twenty years before, they had returned home callously bearing Joseph's torn and bloodstained coat to his father. Now they return to him to say that another son is missing. They are going to feel it this time, because Simeon is not lost by their hand, albeit through their old sin. So accurately does sin reproduce itself and spring out to pounce upon us as we once pounced on another! Aged Jacob is not interested in the corn or the money in the sacks, whatever that may mean. Simeon is lost, and they are demanding Benjamin as the price of his release.

We should note that the father does not discuss the Egyptian overlord or his demands (36, 38). Does he not trust his sons, but believes them to be in some sinister league to deprive him of his favourite children? If so, we are reminded that there is in the moral constitution of the world a bias against all sin including favouritism in families, of which sin Jacob is to be purged by bitter loss. Nor does he accept Reuben's quixotic, but ridiculous, offer. They have lost two sons to him: they shall not lose a third, especially this youngest, the only comfort of his aged life. But Jacob, old man that you are, you are far too significant a figure to be left in peace even in your old age. There are mighty movements of God afoot, and you are involved in them. You are yet to see Egypt itself, and Pharaoh. But first, when your family are hungry again, you will deliver Benjamin to your sons.

Chapter 43

The Second Journey to Egypt

43:1-25 Again Jacob takes the initiative when the spectre of hunger once more haunts the family home, but he is reminded by Judah that they may not return to Egypt without Benjamin. Had he blindly hoped the brothers might forget this condition on returning for food? When reminded of it, Jacob protests at their naivety in telling the Egyptian their family history. 'But we didn't expect the man to ask for our young brother,' they exclaim (7). 'There is nothing for it but to allow him to come with us, and I will answer for his life with my own,' urges Judah (9). This is a different oath from that offered by Reuben, and Jacob reluctantly accepts it and lets Benjamin go. Gifts are prepared, and money for the food, both the money returned in their sacks and more for a second supply of grain ('double' in vv.12, 15 means a 'second' payment) and they depart. For Jacob it is a heavy parting, and he sends them on their way with earnest prayer to the all-sufficient God that 'the man' in Egypt may be pleased to send all his children back (14).

The sight of Benjamin makes Joseph give the orders which had no doubt been forming in his mind, and he doubtless prepares with suppressed joy and excitement for the ripening of his purpose. The brothers on the other hand, subjected to a further gesture of generosity in being conducted to the great man's house, are exceedingly afraid (18). Again we remind ourselves of our involuntary distrust of grace – 'it's too good not to be true!' Thus they begin to make placatory overtures to Joseph's steward. The steward is 'in the know' with his master, and speaks graciously to them, hinting that he knows somewhat of the mystery, and there is nothing to fear. 'Your God must have put the money in your sacks, he says, because I was paid all right' (23). Doubtless, but God generally uses human hands to do his good work – Joseph's in this case.

Few things are as telling as the grace of Joseph's servant. He knows that their God is a God of grace, even if they do not! Where did he learn it? Where do you think? This simply means that young Joseph, who had perforce to carry the grace of his religion into his captivity to ease his burdensome lot, also carried it into his high status and responsible office – a much harder thing to do – to grace his home and teach his servants. This is evangelism indeed, unselfconsciously knitted into the fabric of daily life. It is the sort of evangelism the world most sorely needs, and no true Christian is excluded from its service.

43:26-34 Whether Joseph delayed his return because he was occupied with affairs of state, or because he deliberately put off the dramatic moment, he must certainly have approached his home with peculiar excitement. The preliminaries having been completed with due ceremony including the presentation of Jacob's gift, he proceeded to enquire somewhat anxiously of his father, and receives assurance that the old man is still alive and well (27f.). He then turns to his beloved brother Benjamin, trying hard to hide his feelings; it is almost too much for him, and he swiftly withdraws to give vent to his uncontrollable emotions.

What the eleven brothers thought of this sudden exit, or how it was covered up, we are not told; they may have feared even more this man's unpredictable behaviour. For a long moment they must have stood in awkward embarrassment, shifting from foot to foot while Joseph composed himself. When he returned, he briskly motioned them to the food to distract his mind, while the unsuspecting brothers speculated between themselves on the frequent changes in the Egyptian's moods and manners and what it meant.

How different our interpretations of unusual behaviour may be from the hidden truth! Christian social life requires nothing less than complete detachment from self-preoccupation in order that we may project ourselves into the situation of others with imagination and understanding, and yet with reserve, because of our lack of knowledge. We doubtless bring very much less to that task of mutual care and concern than this needed detachment or understanding. Nevertheless it behoves us to become increasingly engrossed with the lives of others that we may less inadequately understand them, and patiently and charitably reserve judgement where we fail.

There were apparently two reasons for Joseph's sitting apart. The first is explicitly stated: since he was now of the priestly castle of Egypt, it would be 'detestable' for him to eat with Hebrews (32). The second is implied in the comment that 'they served him by himself', presumably because of his high rank. The fact of those Egyptians who ate with Joseph refusing to sit at table with Hebrews indicates their religious pride. Herodotus says they had the same contempt for the Greeks. There is a lesson in this for Christians. We see the same worldly contempt for God's elect in every age, whether in Egypt, Babylon, Palestine, or Rome. 'Let us, then, go to him outside the camp, bearing the disgrace he bore. For here we do not have an enduring city, but we are looking for the city that is to come' (Heb. 13:13f.).

What did the brothers think when they found themselves arranged at table according to age? There was no end to the puzzlement this man created in their minds. This may have been more perplexing to them than Joseph's favour of Benjamin. It was customary in the East to send token portions from the chief table to one whom it was desired to honour. Nor would it have been unusual to honour the youngest of a large family, especially one who had been particularly sent for. However, the shrewd unspoken suggestion undoubtedly is that Joseph was thereby testing his brothers to see if the spirit of jealousy of younger brothers persisted in them. Perhaps also Joseph was expressing by his action in serving Benjamin five times as much as the others what the restrained tears would otherwise have shown, namely his love for his young brother. However, the inhibitions and fears were soon overwhelmed in the fellowship of eating and conviviality. Surely one of the strangest scenes in the Bible!

Chapter 44

A Silver Cup in a Sack

44:1-34 Was this sumptuous feast (43:34b) not the moment for Joseph to reveal his identity? Had not the play gone on long enough? It depends on whether Joseph felt he had accomplished his purpose. What, then, was his purpose? There are doubtless several elements in it, implicit and explicit, but does not the next stage, when Benjamin is incriminated, suggest that Joseph is seeking to teach a proper care for younger brothers? He can hardly have been so sick with sentimental love for his young brother as to try to detain him in Egypt. It appears he is intent upon exercising his brothers in those qualities of conscience and fraternal care which Joseph to his cost had found utterly lacking in them.

This intended lesson for the older ten men must have hurt the youngest brother most of all. It was such an unlikely charge. None the less the cup was in his sack. In ancient civilisations the priest's drinking cup was often an instrument of divination. Perhaps they assumed that it was by this means that Joseph knew the brothers' ages. It was therefore a doubly serious crime to steal the great man's goblet and divining cup. Joseph, always the master organiser, had arranged things perfectly. The eleven brothers, homeward-bound, with a sense of relief and an astonishing story to tell, had just left the city when they were overtaken, the charge levelled, and the discovery made. This was the bitterest blow yet. They could only return (13). Certainly it was unthinkable to continue homewards without Benjamin. Better not to go home at all!

Joseph was waiting for them at his house, and they fell before him in despair. Judah takes the initiative, according to his promise to his father (16ff.). Is there a touch of gullibility about the brothers, at this further discovery in their sacks? Would it not have been legitimate to have said, with something less than prostration, 'What's going on, here? Who is manipulating this crazy game?' Such a suggestion may be facile to the scholars, as being violently anachronistic – that is, out of keeping with the times. This may be true, but it shows how far our democratic spirit has travelled from the servile fear of autocracy. Perhaps this process has gone too far. There is no fear of authority before men's eyes today. This is necessarily a bad thing, for where respect is lacking, anarchy is bred.

See how eagerly Judah tries to incriminate all the brothers: 'servants' and 'we' (16; see also vv.19, 20, 21, 23, 24, 26, 30, 31). But Joseph will not have the issue confused. 'Only the man who was found to have the cup will become my slave. The rest of you, go back to your father in peace' (17). Joseph, you are taking a great risk! What if they accept your word and go? Would you really deprive your old father of his boy? Opinions differ as to whether Joseph knew what he was doing, or was simply improvising as the drama unfolded. Some hold that he was deliberately creating this situation to see if the sons of Leah had changed in their attitude towards the son of Rachel. However, if he had intentions of continuing his deception, he little knew the assault about to be made upon his *savoir faire*.

What is Judah's appeal? It is the appeal of truth spoken by sincerity driven in humiliating circumstances to unfold a moving human story. When Judah speaks of Joseph's mother, his father's surmise concerning Joseph's disappearance, his fear of losing Rachel's other son (20), Joseph knows the play must end and the truth emerge. Judah's appeal as to what he would say to his father on returning without Benjamin, what would then happen to the old man, and his offer of himself as a slave in place of the boy (30ff.), overwhelms the great man completely. He prepares to divulge all.

This is a lesson on the superior power of truth passionately felt in the realms of controversy. The brothers were in the wrong from the beginning and Joseph had got his own back as he tested their motives and sincerity. But there came a point beyond which the righteous aggressor could not go without surrendering the righteous initiative to his adversary. When sin is deeply repented of, the penitent one is placed in a strong position! This should not be forgotten by very righteous folk who ruthlessly drive sinners to their knees. What do you do when you get them there, and they turn out to be more repentant than you bargained for, and appeal to your mercy? Are you as merciful as you are righteous? If not, your righteousness is self-righteousness – a vile thing, as far removed from the 'grace and truth' (Jn. 1:14) of Christ's righteousness as heaven is from hell.

Chapter 45

Joseph Makes Himself Known

45:1-6 It has been obvious in Joseph's contacts with his brothers, especially on the second visit, that all the bottled up emotions of twenty years were in danger of exploding. He knew that they would, and the poignancy of Judah's speech showed that he could hold out no longer. He had only time to order everyone out of the room before he broke out into an uncontrollable fit of weeping and wailing in the eastern manner, until either the sound was heard, or the account of it was told, throughout the palace of Pharaoh. The brothers must have been both astonished and terrified at this emotional display by the man in command of Egypt, none of them apparently the least suspecting who he was, until he said, 'I am Joseph' (3a).

It must have been to them a stunning blow which, as soon as they grasped it, would have explained his strange and paradoxical behaviour. Perhaps, however, their dominant thought was of chagrin and dread to find the brother they had sold like an old pair of shoes, now master of Egypt. No words can convey the force and complexity of the shock they must have received – 'they were terrified at his presence' (3b). But they had nothing to fear. Joseph had tested them well, almost too well, and found them in their attitude to young Benjamin entirely different fellows from those earlier years. This was good enough for him. They were completely forgiven.

What had changed them? Was it the inner tribulation of a nagging conscience for over twenty years, especially as they saw how Jacob continued to grieve for Joseph? It was a heavy price to pay for the luxury of a spiteful action, as many have proved. The number of criminals who give themselves up, and even confess to additional crimes, shows that. Of course the impingement of the individual conscience may depend upon the keenness of the communal conscience prevailing. Doubtless for the brothers to live with the results of their cruelty in their father's fretting spirit was like salt in a wound that would at last have to be cleansed by confession.

Note that the context in which complete forgiveness is pronounced, repentance having been established, is the purpose of God which foreordains to his use and glory the very evil he abhors. (Cf. vv.5 and 7 with 50:20.) There is a whole doctrine here of the relation between good and evil which, being worked out and applied, fully satisfies the godly mind as to the problems of evil. Note also Joseph's firm monotheistic faith (belief in one God), and in his acceptance of the prospect of famine for five more years, according to Pharaoh's dream, and his planning for the same.

45:5-8 If we knew the effect of the seven years famine on the people of Canaan, we might better understand Joseph's references here to the preservation of his family's life. As there is in the wrestling at Peniel a paradoxical element which calls for repeated reassessment, so is there in the going down to Egypt. Taking the view we have of Abraham's and also Isaac's tendency to seek the south country, and the unhappy results thereof, we cannot but view the sojourn in Egypt as a dangerous excursion into the forbidden land. The eventual slavery proves that. Nevertheless it must be seen in the context of the family's sin and God's over-ruling and use of it for the manifesting of his greater glory. God did send Joseph to Egypt to preserve Israel and his family in the famine, but it was the brothers' sin which engineered it – to say nothing of the ultimate consequences of their Jacob's own sins.

This, then, may be called expedient grace, although we must not forget the typical teaching of redemption from Egypt which runs through the later Old Testament Scriptures. That is the grace which saves God's people in dire distress; it draws them into a situation which changes in the course of the years from honour, freedom and plenty to shame, slavery and destitution. Just as we must never incriminate the Almighty in that sin which he uses to evoke his glory, so must we never excuse those guilty of the sin by which that glory is evoked. (Read Rom. 3:5-8 and 5:20–6:2). The glories of God's grace would never have been seen in redemptive terms but for the sin of man. That does not glorify human sin, but God's grace. To preserve this fine balance of truth is one of the marks of growing spiritual maturity.

45:9-16 Having tried to deal with the complex reasons in the divine will for Israel moving to Egypt, let us now turn to the joy and eagerness of Joseph's invitation. From Joseph's revelation of himself onwards there is a quite exhilarating pace and grace in the narrative. Both from a literary and religious point of view this is bound to flow from the mounting tension of crisis upon crisis as Joseph reached the climax of his moral and dramatic purpose. However, let us not be taken in too easily by the story's rapid flow. This is no mere artistic effusion, but a pouring out of that grace of God which attends wrongs that have been righted and almost impatiently waits to unleash in divinely acceptable terms its floods of joy on souls reconciled to each other.

It is ours increasingly to prove this astonishing and embarrassing grace as we keep to the right in all we think, say and do and as we seek to right the wrongs that too frequently mar the even tenor of our lives. Consequently, there comes a time when our almost involuntary communications with our Heavenly Father protest the growing lavishness of his grace, in trepidation lest it be a dream from which we wake, not to see a leering devil jeering at us, but the Christ bidding us share his cross more painfully. Indeed, we must not forget the fellowship of his cross that runs through all this extravagant grace. It is the cross that brings the grace out, and it is only because we have learned bravely to bear the disciples' ills, as Joseph did, that we count them as nothing before the oncoming tide of the divine pleasure.

Nevertheless, that cross and the sorrows we may have to bear are not nothing. The cost of Joseph's integrity is not lost on the Almighty, and we can well imagine he spent the rest of his days in virtual, unalloyed pleasure. He had had enough pain. Having seen the humbling and repentance of his wicked brothers and the painful past wiped out, there were worlds of human pleasure to be savoured, and a family life to be established and enjoyed which Jacob and his wives and children had never known. It was Joseph in Egypt who, revealing the highest rectitude of all the clan from Abraham onwards, now points the way to a new happy family life based on mutual trust and affection.

How hardly are such earthly delights come by! It takes a world of woe and crucifixion to call them into being, but it is abundantly worth the cost for its fruits are heavenly sweet. All this and more is singing in Joseph's head as the torrents of words pour out upon his brothers instructing them what to say and do to his father, and as he ardently embraces them and lets them also release the tension of their consciences stretched to breaking point.

45:16-28 Pharaoh's pleasure in the arrival of Joseph's brothers is indicative of his pleasure in Joseph. We do not know what Pharaoh knew of Joseph's personal history. Hearing that the brothers had arrived, he may have feared family ties might persuade Joseph temporarily to return home, and rob him of the grandest vizier king ever had, especially in years of crisis. Whether or not there was self-interest in Pharaoh's suggestion, there was certainly generosity. There was nothing in Egypt too good, not only for Joseph, but for Joseph's clan. It appeared that they would have the choice of the land, and in a time of emergency and widespread famine that was almost unbelievable magnanimity. How different in a later day when a king arose who 'did not know about Joseph' (Ex. 1:8)! Such are the extremes God's people may encounter in their earthly pilgrimage.

The brothers returned replete with gifts from Egypt's king, and wagons in which to bring the family back. Joseph had sent his brothers away with a shrewd word of counsel not to quarrel by the way (24). Was Reuben still carping at their high-handed action in selling Joseph to the Ishmaelites? Or was Joseph's concern lest the question and nature of the confession they would make to their father lead to strife on the way home? There is no record of a confession to their father at all, and some scholars assume that it was made though not included in the narrative. However, it is difficult to believe that Jacob could have taken such news in his stride. Certainly the news that Joseph was still alive would overwhelm all other considerations including how Joseph had ended up in Egypt, but the question remains as to precisely what it was that stunned him into numbness (26).

We suppose that the seemingly futile longing of twenty years had so inured Jacob to his broken heart, that the shock of putting it together again almost killed him. We can hardly doubt his mind must have darted like quicksilver from the fact of Joseph's life to that torn and bloodied coat. What did that mean? The sacred record has drawn a veil over what transpired, and we must not try to probe. Not that to form an opinion would be necessarily to depart from Scripture, but to establish a precedent of going beyond the record could easily become a habit which in some cases could lead us seriously astray. Is not sufficient revealed?

It is good for us, especially for the questing spirit of youth, to accept limits to speculative and imaginative thought, if only to afford us humbling balance. The fact of Joseph's greatness, not lost on the old man, scarcely seems to register with him at all; but Joseph's invitation does. His mind is clear enough to know what he will do. Time may be short. Joseph is yet alive: if he can go and see him before he dies, that is all he desires. He will die happy then in the satisfaction that life has not cheated him of its legitimate fruits. We rejoice in the glorious truth that God is good, but we also note with sober reflection that the last (and surely most painful), deception visited on the arch-deceiver (cf. 29:25; 31:41) is now ended.

Chapter 46

Jacob Goes to Egypt

46:1-4 Jacob presumably departed form Hebron and came to Beer-sheba, the place of the last Jehovistic altar in the land. This was where Hagar met God when she fled with Ishmael (21:14), where Abraham (21:31-33), and Isaac (26:23), retired from the Philistine Abimelechs of their day. Isaac had ultimately stayed there after his westward excursion when God had said, 'Do not go not down to Egypt' (26:2). Now as the aged Israel anxiously seeks God at the outpost of the land given to his grandfather Abraham, his father Isaac and to him also, the Lord is saying to him, 'Do not be afraid to go down to Egypt' (4).

Jacob's fear was complex. It sprang positively, from God's promise of the land, with the implication that the chosen race were not to leave it. Negatively, it came from what had happened to Abraham in Egypt together with God's command to Isaac not to go there. Perhaps, most of all, his fear arose from the Lord's dark prophecy to Abraham of four hundred years of slavery and ill-treatment (15:13). But Joseph was there, and had prospered incredibly. Now God himself seemed to be reversing all his previous guidance by commanding him to go there, not only assuring him that he would be with him, but also that at last he would bring his people home again to the promised land.

Here is a sermon and lesson indeed. It can only be built, however, upon a full understanding of God's promise and prohibition, and it will show how God may seem to contradict his former guidance to accomplish the grace and glory of more inscrutable purposes. Joseph had not been appreciated in his own land, therefore God took him to pagan Egypt, not to lose his faith there, but that it should be developed in adversity so that he might make deep impressions upon the life of a great nation. This is the mighty triumph of grace over evil which can be wrought when God is honoured in righteous living. Now God is saying to Jacob, 'Go down to Egypt, for I will make you a great nation there, and will bring your people back again.'

Moreover – perhaps it is this which most delighted the human affections of the old man – Joseph his lost and favourite son would close his eyes in peaceful death. What more could human heart crave for? Thus the mighty purpose of God is advanced, and the pleasure of his aged servant fulfilled – all in Egypt! What spiritual treasure is here for those who have the godly wit to unearth it, and to lay it for confirmation alongside similar profound truths in other parts of the Word! The lesson extends even to the Apostles' Creed: 'He descended into Hell.'

46:5-34 We look at the list of Jacob's descendants who went down into Egypt, then resume the delightful story. The total number is seventy (cf. Ex. 1:5, and Deut. 10:22). First comes a list of Jacob's sons and grandsons by Leah, then lists of the same by Zilpah, Rachel, and Bilhah. These totals are: Leah's descendants (including Jacob himself), thirty-three (15); Zilpah's, sixteen (18); Rachel's (including Joseph and his sons), fourteen (22); Bilhah's, seven (25). The total of sixty-six given (26) excludes Jacob: 'All those who went to Egypt with Jacob', and Joseph and his two sons. It has been computed that Perez (12) was four years old when he came to Egypt; his sons, like Joseph's when he came to Egypt, were still 'in his loins' (AV), 'still in the body of his ancestor' (NIV). (Cf. the same expression in Hebrews 7:10.)

It is largely left to our imagination to picture the migration to Egypt.

They are bound for the land of Goshen (more about that later), and Judah rightly has the honour of going before to Joseph to prepare the way. Never were external, worldly differences so swept aside as when the lord of Egypt stepped from his chariot before which all Egyptians bowed the knee (41:43, marginal reading) to fall on the neck of his aged father. What a reunion! What could the brothers then have felt? We hope they felt how wonderful it was that the heinous sin which caused such bitter separation was altogether swept away, and the evil one's long-held purpose overthrown.

How typical is Israel's remark! His cup is full and, knowing that his days are numbered, he could now die happy. Perhaps he feels that this would be the most fitting, as it would certainly be the most dramatic, climax to the moving meeting. But Joseph has other ideas. It is so with our beloved aged. They keep referring to their imminent demise, perhaps with more than a little wistfulness and trepidation, lest they should survive to become a burden, whereas the last thing their loved ones want to think about is their departure. Not that sensible Christian people ignore the inevitable. Rather do they want, without presumption, to enjoy the happy survival of their venerable dear ones as long as God wills.

Joseph's next thrill will be to introduce his father to Pharaoh, or, rather, Pharaoh to his father! Different reasons are given for the Egyptians' abhorrence of shepherds (or cattle-dealers). The most convincing is the religious one, that they abhorred those who ate animals which they worshipped (e.g. the cow was sacred). It is not so likely therefore that they despised cowherds; but nomad shepherds from Palestine might be difficult to contain. However, Joseph knew his Pharaoh. Nor do we believe that he has only in mind the settlement of his family in the best pasture land of Egypt. Rather is he concerned that they should live in a separate, border province for the greater preservation of their racial purity. If the Egyptians had religious reasons for keeping separate from them, Jacob – indeed, Joseph too – was more anxious for the same reason that they should not be contaminated with heathen blood.

This reveals the long-sighted shrewdness of Joseph, not to say the vision and inspiration of his faith. 'By faith Joseph when his end was near spoke about the exodus of the Israelites from Egypt...' (Heb. 11:22). Consider then Joseph's masterly poise, anxious that his people should remain separate from the Egyptians, and yet himself living and ruling in the midst of them and making himself so acceptable to them that it was unthinkable to Pharaoh that he should lose him. In all this Joseph remains true to the Lord. Only men of the first rank of faith could live such a pin-poised life so successfully and fruitfully.

Chapter 47

47:1-6 Notice Joseph chose five of his brothers to meet Pharaoh (2). Recall how he gave Benjamin a portion of food five times greater than anyone else's (43:34) and gifts of new clothing five times more than to the rest of his brothers (45:22). It would seem the number five had particular significance in Egypt.

See the wisdom and skill with which Joseph makes arrangements for his family's settlement in Goshen. He has no doubt of Pharaoh's abundant generosity towards him and his family, but he wants the negotiations to be conducted properly, even while he has motives in view which he does not divulge. That Joseph knew his own superiority was from God is clear by his whole walk and witness, but he does not expect Pharaoh to understand this, nor does he attempt to explain it to him. It would appear that Pharaoh regarded Joseph's excellence as residing merely in himself, (notwithstanding 41:38f.) and, though he saw his good works, did not glorify his God (cf. Matt. 5:16). Joseph accepted this, and wisely proceeded to advance the long-term interests of God's chosen people without attempting to instruct Pharaoh in it or convert him to it.

This provides a major lesson in discernment for us. How sad to see Christians breathing out their evangelistic effusions indiscriminately in the pathetic hope that some good, willy-nilly, hit-or-miss, may be done! Such are prepared to go on for years with their self-satisfying 'service' and never see one particle of fruit for it. For all its (often frenetic) activity, it is a lazy way to evangelise, which could be done as well by some sort of mechanical 'distributor', without human understanding at all!

Doubtless Joseph selected his five brothers carefully, and fully instructed them how to behave and what to say. Pharaoh asked their occupation, to which they answered directly. Perhaps it is intended to convey that they have happened into Goshen and have found its pasture lands suitable for their occupation (4). They are sojourning in the land, presumably for the duration of the famine. However, all this meticulous, careful tact is swamped by Pharaoh's repetition of his generous promise to Joseph (45:17ff.). The land is at their disposal (6). Indeed, if any of the brothers are, in Joseph's estimation, worthy cattle-breeders, then let them be employed with the royal herds. This last offer does not seem to have been taken up, and it is perhaps not too much to assume that it was not acted upon. If not, we suspect why. Joseph may well have had no confidence that any of his brothers, with the possible exception of Judah, would preserve themselves from the corruptions of Egyptian heathen life. There are not many Josephs, who can successfully steer a hazardous course on a dangerous sea.

47:7-10 Perhaps we dealt too cursorily in the previous note on 47:1-6 with Joseph's hidden sense of superiority from which he acts in faith to preserve and prosper Israel in a pagan land. To miss this is to miss all that makes the record sacred history. Yet if we do not discern the superiority arising from the divine purpose behind the astuteness of Joseph, we cannot fail to see it in the humble grandeur of Jacob's bearing as he towers morally above Pharaoh. The king would have been prepared to be gracious to Joseph's father whatever sort he was, but he was obviously impressed by the old man, and asked his age. With the serene self-possession of ripe old age Jacob replies, humbled by the king's grace to recall how ill his life compares in length and virtue with his fathers.

Quite spontaneous as Jacob's words undoubtedly were, nothing was so calculated to discompose the man on the throne. Here was a decrepit old man, probably carried into his presence on some kind of litter, who made the king and his courtiers look like lackeys by sheer magnificence of bearing, and yet who when questioned took the lowliest place in his heredity. What is this? It is to the worldling whose glory, such as it is, resides in himself the complete contradiction. Yet to the discerning, whose 'highest place is lying low at the Redeemer's feet', it is the perfect integration of humility and confidence. Jacob's glory derived from his God, Pharaoh's from himself, and the one in comparison with the other is as honour in the presence of shame and regality in the presence of meniality.

There is no record of Pharaoh having replied after he invited the old man to speak. This may be significant. Can we doubt that the old man's humble words, carrying a breath of the Eternal and a conception of the long purposes of God, created an atmosphere redolent of conversations the king had had with Joseph, and yet of a new power and pointedness which Pharaoh had never known? When the old man assumed the initiative and blessed Pharaoh, the glory of Jehovah must have shone so transparently through his frail flesh as to humble the king to the dust, and stupefy him with a confusion that could only be borne in silence. This is the divine authority devolving upon all who are called to the presence of kings for God's sake (Matt. 10:18), of which many examples are found subsequently in the scriptures: e.g., Nathan before David (2 Sam. 12), Elijah before Ahab (1 Kg. 17:1; 18:18), and Paul before Felix (Acts 24:24ff.). Solemnising, and encouraging.

Joseph and the Famine

47:11-26 This interesting passage needs practically no comment or explanation. After stating that Joseph saw to his own family's settlement and needs in the land of Goshen, the district of Rameses (11), the record goes on to recount his statesmanlike measures to provide corn for Egypt and Canaan by bringing the whole people into serfdom. We should not understand 'that year' and 'the following year' (18) to mean these were the first and second years of the famine (cf. 45:11). It is likely that they were towards the end of the seven-year shortage, when the need was desperate and the people entirely dependent upon Joseph's granaries. The fact that they formerly possessed money, livestock and land of their own shows in what dignity and independence they lived under Pharaoh. That was to be changed because God had given Egypt and Pharaoh himself into the hands of his chosen Joseph who himself had come to Egypt as a Hebrew slave boy.

We must not lose sight of this, because the passage is teaching us how God in the course of time and in the rhythms of history causes the whole world to eat out of his hand in utter dependence upon him and his appointed servants. Note the exemption of the priests (22), which suggests Egypt's religion, such as it was, was held in high esteem by the throne. Note also the 20% tax upon food grown from the free distribution of seed (24). We see how prophetically true Joseph's dreams were, that not only his family and his father, but practically the whole civilised world were at his feet (37:5ff.). We can perhaps excuse youthful Joseph telling his dreams when we see how convincing this prophecy must have been to him. He must have believed in his coming exaltation as if it had then been accomplished. Did his father and brothers also remember his dreams and recognise the clear fulfilment of them? Read Psalm 105:18f. Faith, wonderful faith!

47:27-31 Seventeen years Jacob survived in Egypt, although on arrival there he was apparently carried into the presence of Pharaoh. But his time is running out, and he sends for Joseph to request of him that he should not be buried in Egypt, but in Canaan in the sepulchre at Machpelah with his fathers (25:9). This Joseph swore by a vital oath, as Eliezer to Abraham (24:2, 9). Then Jacob worshipped God. We have already dealt with the question of the 'bed-head' or 'staff' (Heb. 11:21) at 32:31f. It had been assumed that the word 'staff' was necessary to the view of Jacob's permanent crippleage at Peniel, but we suggest from the earlier passage that this is not necessarily so. The important point is not whether the original word means 'bed-head' or 'staff', but that he worshipped.

In this oath about his burial, Jacob is acknowledging the sweeping purpose of God which is only in its earliest stages of fulfilment (15:13ff.). Having reached the third, fourth, and fifth generations, it will continue for hundreds of years of bondage in a foreign land, until as a mighty nation Israel returns to the land of promise. The significance of Jacob's renewal of his faith in God is not measured by his feeble act of worship or the comparatively unimportant question as to where his bones shall lie. The crucial point is that, while he perforce must die in a strange land, he does not accept the exile as permanent, but verily believes God's promise that his seed shall yet possess the land of Canaan and mightily influence the future course of history. It was this the old man saw, and to which he was clinging tenaciously, perhaps even when his children and grandchildren were odiously comparing (often) barren Canaan to this fruitful land of Goshen. It is in faith of this he makes Joseph swear the most sacred oath (notice that both here and in 24:2 the oath concerns posterity), that he will not bury him in Egypt, but in Canaan.

The mind of any intelligent person can revel in the Genesis stories, but only faith sees the thin red line of God's almighty purpose. Does this come naturally – I mean *spiritually* natural – to you? 'Here we do not have an enduring city, but we are looking for the city that is to come ... the city with foundations, whose architect and builder is God' (Heb. 13:14; 11:10). In spite of every apparent indication to the contrary, the purposes of God are moving inexorably forward.

Chapter 48

Manasseh and Ephraim

48:1-22 Jacob's eyes are dim so he cannot recognise his grandsons. The text might seem to suggest that this is their first meeting (11), but it is not necessary to understand it so. The general tenor of the passage implies, however, that the meeting is near Jacob's demise towards the conclusion of his seventeen years in Egypt (47:28). The lads would have been about twenty years of age at the time. Notice that the writer puts Ephraim before Manasseh (5, 13) in anticipation of Jacob's reversal of their primogeniture. The reference to Luz (Bethel) is not Jacob's flight from Esau, but his return from Haran (35:10ff.). When he says, 'Ephraim and Manasseh will be mine' (5), Jacob means that Joseph's two sons by his Egyptian wife are to be of equal rank with the eldest of Jacob's own sons, Reuben and Simeon. Subsequent children will be counted as merely members of the tribes of Ephraim and Manasseh (6). Jacob makes moving reference to Rachel's death. Rachel 'died by me' (AV, 7) should read as in NIV, 'to my sorrow Rachel died'.

When Jacob understands who the lads are, they are brought between his knees, suggesting his ritual acceptance of them as his sons, after which Jacob blesses Joseph and then them. We must not lightly pass over the profound respect Joseph shows to his aged father (12), surely a far cry from the cavalier (and often heartless) way in which elderly parents are too often treated today. Thereafter the two young men are presented for Jacob's blessing.

Although it requires a little 'plaiting' of the mind to follow the complexity of this criss-crossing of the hands, the import is clear. Jacob by insight of faith is setting the younger Ephraim before the elder Manasseh (cf. Jacob and Esau, 25:23). This is no mere prediction, but the prophetic declaration that Ephraim shall be the leading tribe of Israel (see our comments above on 35:22-29 for the sequence by which the primacy of the tribes passes from Reuben to Ephraim and thence to

Judah). Observe that as with Isaac's blessing of Jacob, so here Jacob speeds his blessing of Ephraim before Joseph has opportunity to protest. When Joseph does protest (18), his father sweeps aside his objection for he knows what he is doing. Thus the Almighty gets his high elective way, transcending traditional primacies which at other times he chooses to honour.

The great thing to note is that we may never presume to know the divine will. God always sees more clearly than we do where he is going, therefore wisdom learns to defer to him always. It is not only a daring thing to 'correct' the Almighty when he speaks, whether directly or by his servants, it is foolish for he always knows best. The accuracy of v. 22 is questioned on the ground of what happened at Shechem (33:18-19; 34:25-31). However, there is no reason to suppose that the brief history may not bear this interpretation, Jacob claiming the land both by purchase and by destruction of the Shechemites. For subsequent references to the area and fulfilment of the prediction, see Joshua 24:32 and John 4:5.

Chapter 49

Jacob Blesses His Sons

49:1-12 Jacob assembles his sons to sum up their characters and predict their future, in relation to their past, and to the overarching sovereignties of God. We have seen the rejection of Reuben (3f.), and the reason for it (35:22). We have also considered the dreadful action of Simeon and Levi (34:25-31), but the punishment for their sin (5ff.) is now given (7b), namely that Simeon became absorbed in Judah (Josh. 19:1-9), and Levi had no portion of the land, only cities in the provinces of the other tribes (Josh. 21:1-8). Note that, on the analogy of our Lord's sin-bearing which it typifies, the calling of Levi to bear the sin of Israel (Num. 18:1f., 6 etc.) cannot be regarded as a punishment, but as a privilege.

We may reflect on the glorious prediction concerning Judah (8ff.), so soon after the primal blessing has been conferred on the younger Ephraim (48:19), especially comparing his blessing with Joseph's (22-26). Some scholars regard the passage as much later than Jacob. The attachment of his name to these predictions is seen as coming long after they are well on the way to fulfilment and is therefore assumed to be a poetic licence presumably to preserve the father-figure of the nation. Without adopting a rigid and unimaginative attitude to the text, we cannot accept the allegation of such fraudulence in its purport (cf. v.1f.). It does astonish us that the sin of Reuben is visited upon his tribe while the vile sin of Judah (ch. 33) is not. Does the dramatic difference between the two blessings lie in the very different characters of the two men, Reuben's sin being consistent with his character and Judah's not with his? Also, did Jacob learn of Judah's mercy towards the youthful Joseph (37:26f.)? He certainly knew of his noble initiative concerning the safe return of Benjamin to his father (44:33f.).

It might be argued that this eulogy of Judah derived from his noble deed, without reference to the primacy just bestowed upon Ephraim. But this is not in accordance with v. 10, and besides it excludes the supernatural prophetic element inherent in the record. The prediction of his supremacy among his brothers is plain enough (8). For the fulfilment of the lion metaphor see the reference in the New Testament to Christ as the 'Lion of Judah' (Rev. 5:5), but also note the references to Christ as the complementary Lamb (Jn. 1:29; Rev. 5:6, 8; 6:1, 3, 5, 7 etc.). The note of expectation of the coming of him to whom the sceptre belongs (10) is often repeated in the Old Testament scriptures (e.g., Ps. 110:1ff.; Ezek. 21:27). Shiloh (10, AV, see NIV marginal reading, *until Shiloh comes;* or, *until he comes to whom tribute belongs;* cf. RSV margin), can mean none other than Messiah. The words 'blood' (11) and 'red' (12, AV, RSV, translated 'dark' in NIV), must not make us rush to the conclusion that here is hidden reference to the death of the Saviour. The blessing at this point is describing the prosperity and joy that follow the fruitful wine harvest and most naturally applies to the prosperity of the reign of Judah. Recognising and acknowledging this, some may prefer not to exclude the possibility of a symbolic reference to the passion of our Lord. At the very least we would conclude that he would have a wooden head indeed who could read these verses and not fill into them some of the glorious history of royal and messianic Judah!

49:13-33 As the reference to Zebulon takes note of geographical location, 'Zebulon will live by the seashore...' (13) – follow this up with the aid of Bible maps – so, it would appear, does that to Issachar. Taken up with the pleasant and prosperous agricultural land which was her portion, she settled down like a beast of burden between two panniers or saddlebags (14) laid upon its flanks. But, presumably becoming the envy of the nearby Canaanites, Issachar suffered for her self-indulgence.

Dan has two portions of land marked in the Bible maps, because of her migration north in the generation after the conquest of Canaan (Judg. 18). The phrase, 'will provide justice ... as one of the tribes of Israel' (16) simply indicates that although he is small and descended from Bilhah the handmaiden, he will play his full part as a tribe judging his own people. The description of Dan as a viper biting the horse's heels so that the rider is thrown does not necessarily suggest furtiveness (though see Judg. 18:27f.), but rather the vigour and victoriousness of a small tribe facing formidable foes. Samson, the most illustrious Danite, is the supreme example and personal embodiment of this ideal (cf. Judg. ch. 13-16).

There is no knowing the precise reference of the unexpected, brief interlude in the blessings when Jacob appears to pause in his flow of words to invoke the Lord's deliverance (18). It may be that at this point he senses he is being empowered by the Spirit of God to utter spiritual mysteries and calls on the Lord to continue the inspiration. However, it also fits in with any situation in which God's people are being overwhelmed, see that their extremity is beyond them without divine aid, and therefore are driven to wait on God in the conviction he will certainly act to help them.

The name 'Gad' in the Hebrew suggests a band of raiders (19). Jacob foresees this tribe being attacked by such raiders, but driving them off in a counter-raid. RSV translates, 'Raiders shall attack Gad, but he shall raid at their heels.' This will be the consequence of this tribe's exposure to the pagan kingdoms on the East of Jordan, the Ammonites in particular, because Gad – with Reuben and the half tribe of Manasseh – like Lot, chose land on the principle of narrow self-interest to his cost (Deut. 33:21).

The land of Asher (20) was a fertile strip by the north west coast. The second half of the blessing, '...will provide delicacies fit for a king', may refer to provisions for the royal courts of Phoenicia, or Samaria, or Jerusalem, with the distinctive implications and interpretations which each of these three powers suggests – in the case of Phoenicia either oppression or disloyal friendliness with a foreign power. The reference to Naphtali as a 'hind' or 'doe' that bears beautiful fawns is puzzling. Both NIV and RSV give as a marginal reading 'he utters beautiful words'.

The blessing of Joseph (22-26) is the most expansive of them all. Ellicott suggests that Jacob is struggling to bestow more than is in his power. His comment is understandable in the light of the rich blessings heaped on Joseph. Yet there can be no doubt whatsoever as to his remarkable fruitfulness, not only in numbers but in influence. This is perhaps most simply proved by the use in later times of the name 'Ephraim' as a designation for Israel, the northern kingdom. From the future extension of the tribe of Ephraim 'over the wall' (22), Jacob turns back to the sorrows of Joseph's youth and God's championing of his cause, and even beyond to his own chequered youth, God's revelation of himself to him at Bethel and God's subsequent faithfulness to him (24b-25). The fulfilment of God's prophecy both to him and to Joseph in the teeth of bitter adversity expands the old man's faith and hope, and he sees how the same God in spite of every future opposition is able to pour out manifold and superlative blessings upon the offspring of his favourite son (26a). The assumption that he will be 'the prince among his brothers' is either the prophesied primacy of Ephraim or may be a reference to Joseph as a type of Christ, despised and rejected, yet glorified. (Note that the primacy of Ephraim was lost through disobedience and given to Judah. See Ps. 78:9ff., 67f.)

The vivid picture of a ravenous wolf devouring the prey (27) makes reference to the tribe of Benjamin's warlike tendencies. The left-handed Ehud was of this tribe (Judg. 3:15ff.), and Benjamin is praised for his part in the victory over Sisera (Judg. 5:14). Saul also, who began with such promise and evident military ability (1 Sam. 11), was of this tribe; his disastrous history must be attributed to his disobedience to God rather than the failure of any natural warlike traits of character. Another rather different view of the tribe is given in Deuteronomy 33:12, which may well refer to Jonathan's protection of David (1 Sam. 20:16f. and 23:16ff.).

The Death of Jacob

When Jacob had ended his blessing of his sons, he drew up his feet into his bed and departed this life. What a dignified and blessed passing from this scene of time! O, that we might live thus to end our days in fulfilment of the will of God, and with magnificent, humble dignity depart to be with Christ which is far better.

Chapter 50

50:1-26 The last chapter of this mighty book of beginnings commences with a moving scene, then goes on to describe briefly the peculiarly Egyptian practice of embalming (2f.), and finally concludes with the same embalming practice (26). The results of this may be seen in the British Museum thousands of years after, but Joseph's use of the practice had a somewhat different purpose from that of the heathen Egyptians. His concern was to preserve the body until it could be carried to the family tomb at Machpelah. As to the burial place, see Acts 7:16.

The period of mourning for Joseph's aged father for seventy days was unusually long, even in the east. Why Joseph's indirect approach to Pharaoh through his 'court' (4)? Had another Pharaoh succeeded? If so, was Joseph's hesitation a foretaste of Israel's misgivings concerning their sojourn in Egypt (46:3)? Whether or not this was so, God will let nothing stand in the way of Joseph's purpose because in it was the promise of all Israel's mighty future. Jacob shall be buried in the land of promise, as at last Joseph shall be also. It must have been a magnificent procession, and there is more than a touch of irony in the Canaanites' regard of it as an Egyptian's funeral. Why, they might have asked, take an Egyptian funeral to Canaan? It appears the procession took the route east of the Salt Sea and Jordan.

Joseph Reassures His Brothers

On their return, Joseph is doubtless surprised to be faced with his brothers in a new act of obsequiousness (15-18), though the reason is not far to seek. They had assumed that Joseph's forgiveness of them was in the sight of his father, and that after Jacob's death he would take vengeance. Unfortunately, how true to life is the fact of strife in families hidden until the demise of parents. Happy is that family who can lay their parents to rest and yet regard one another with that charity which was their parents' joy.

How wrong the brothers were about Joseph! This, as we have previously remarked, is unhappily typical of sinners' incredulity of grace. Nothing so proves our guilt as the sense of condemnation which refuses to admit the possibility of mercy, and nothing so proves our blindness to the love of God as our blank unbelief of his real, complete and final forgiveness. For his part, Joseph is not only able to dispel their fears but to offer them an interpretation of their misdeeds which gives free rein to the sovereign purposes of God, while excusing nothing. God knows what he is doing when he allows sin to have its way. He can endure and manipulate it all (this is the very essence of Christ's victory on the Cross), making the ugly thing serve the beauty of his holiness.

Nothing can daunt a faith which sees this. True, in its trials it can whimper as pathetically as the most cowardly soul. Yet it can never be absorbed in its grief, for its faith in the sovereignty of God pierces time's thickest gloom and knows, not only that God will triumph in the end, but also that faith will triumph with him. As God caused Joseph's adversity which began in Canaan to turn to prosperity in Egypt, so God would cause Israel's coming adversity in Egypt to turn to the prosperity of redemption into the promised land. This is the significance of the embalming of Joseph's body when he had died. When the children of Israel were at last delivered from the bondage of Egypt, as an emblem of the triumphant will of God, they carried the body of this man, who, following his father, perceived the tortuous but undeviating design of God, and therefore made provision for its advancement (Exod. 13:19; Josh. 24:32).

ROMANS

It would appear that Paul's Letter to the Romans was written from Corinth as his three month visit there, near the end of his third missionary journey, was drawing to a close. It was written possibly in the Spring of AD 58, before he had visited Rome.

CHAPTER ONE

1:1-4 The apostle Paul begins by calling himself a servant of Jesus Christ, a designation he doubtless learned from the Lord Jesus, whom the prophet Isaiah prophetically called 'the servant of the Lord' and who himself willingly owned the designation. The nature of Paul's service was that of being a sent-out one, an apostle of the gospel of God, to which he was called and set apart.

These barely stated facts only hint at the magnitude of his calling. But Paul immediately establishes the gospel's harmony and identity with what was promised beforehand by the Old Testament prophets in the Holy Scriptures. For the Son came as the seed of David as to his human nature, and was designated the Son of God with (in) power according to the spirit of holiness by resurrection from the dead. Here we have the ancestral nature of our Lord's humanity, along with his divinity, expressed not – as in the Prologue to John's Gospel – from all eternity but in terms of his victory over all evil. This is the Man who overturned a whole universe of evil; he is more than sufficient for our needs!

1:5-7 Through Jesus Christ our Lord, Paul received grace and apostleship to bring about the obedience of faith among all nations, as did those to whom he is writing, and all who belong to Christ. The grace comes before the apostleship, for it is in the context of guilty sinners made right with God that the call came to him to go to all nations in obedience to the faith which was God's gracious gift to him.

Paul identifies with those to whom he writes as also called to belong to Jesus Christ, and he greets them together with all in Rome who are loved by God and are therefore called to be saints. The greeting is one of grace and peace from God our Father and from the Lord Jesus Christ.

We ought not to miss the fact that it is in virtue of Paul's apostleship that he has the right to greet the Romans in this way. The greeting (while penned either by the apostle Paul or by his secretary) is from God the Father and from the Lord Jesus just as surely as if it had come in a divine visitation. This is the high privilege of those who are called

to go out with the gospel: they bring greetings to needy humanity direct
from the throne of God. It is as if approaching the letter box one morning
one found on the mat a letter from God addressed personally to oneself!

Paul's Longing to Visit Rome

1:8-10 The grace that Paul has already spoken of twice is seen in the
manner in which he addresses the Romans. Their faith, he says, has
been spoken of by many in various places. He could have omitted that
and gone right to the point of his burden. But, no; he almost always
begins by saying what is good about people, however rigorous his
subsequent words may be. This is sheer grace; its exercise is only
possible (apart from those who simply want cunningly to appease those
they have hurt) for those who have at least glimpsed the grace of God.

Nor is it a mere compliment that Paul pays them. His commendation
is part of his thanksgiving to God for the divine goodness, and is
therefore an encouragement to the Roman saints (who had to endure
Nero around this time after Claudius had expelled Jews from Rome –
and included Christians in that expulsion, Acts 18:2). The apostle's
commendation also reminds them, and us, that all Christian
relationships should be seen in the light of our thankfulness to God for
his mercies. In such thanksgiving to God for his goodness to us we
should often thank him for the wonderful gift of friendships in Christ,
which have a unique quality.

Paul now goes on to assure the Romans of his constant remembrance
of them in prayer. That is also the privilege of those of us who are
bound together in the bonds of Christ, to help each other with our
prayers. He testifies before God that this is an essential part of his
spiritual service in the gospel of the Son. On this particular occasion it
is geared to his request that, within the will of God, he might have a
happy journey to come and visit them. This leads him to tell them that
he longs to see them, and to explain why.

1:11-15 Whatever tender bonds of affection Paul expects to enjoy when
he meets the Romans, the reason he expresses here for his longing to
visit them is intensely practical: it is that he might impart some spiritual
gift to them to establish them.

Did the apostle have some knowledge of weak areas in their faith, which are apparent in the subsequent letter? It would appear so. But lest they think him presumptuous, he immediately goes on to say that he hopes they would be mutually encouraged in the faith by such a meeting. He wants them to know that he had planned many times to visit them in Rome (the centre of the world of his day), but so far had been prevented; and he then goes on to repeat what he had every right to say, on the authority of his apostleship. In addition to the harvests of souls God had given him among other Gentiles (and he was writing from one of the harvest fields, namely Corinth, see Acts 18:10), he desires a fruitful harvest among the Romans also.

This, of course, is part of the burden of debt Paul felt he owed both to Gentiles of the cultured Greek sort and to the uncultured barbarous (Paul's word!) peoples – to those who regard themselves as wise and those who are regarded by others as foolish.

That was bold talk in a letter to Rome, for if any Christian community in the world of Paul's day would have been of mixed races it would surely have been the Roman church. Thus to identify Greek culture so openly was brave of the apostle indeed.

Before Paul reaches these Roman believers, he wants them to know (although their local circumstances would surely have convinced them of it), that the appeal of the gospel is universal: 'whosoever will' may come; there is a welcome in Christ for everyone who responds to the gospel. That is why the apostle is so ready, willing and eager to preach the gospel to those who are in Rome also. Indeed his pride in the gospel – which permits no shame on its own account – will be immediately apparent.

1:16 You see how the apostle introduces the two verses which serve to sum up both his message and the gospel. In face of the whole world, not only Jews but Greeks and Barbarians, he is so proud of the gospel that there is no possibility of his being ashamed of it in any circumstances or in any association.

It is entirely like Paul immediately to give his reason for this brave statement. The gospel is the power of God for salvation to everyone who believes. Here is how the power of God works: he who made all things, and controls and governs all, directs the greatness of his power towards this end: to every soul who believes salvation is granted.

Paul's 'everyone' indicates that it is impossible to believe without receiving salvation, because God has inexorably annexed man's salvation to faith. He will fully explain what he means by salvation in due course.

The offer of salvation through faith is given first to the Jews, because they were God's chosen race to bring in his salvation; it was to them at first that he gave the oracles of the Word of God (see Rom. 3:2). But the same offer is made also and equally to the Gentiles who are not to be regarded as a lesser breed in the kingdom, but as fellow citizens with the saints (cf. Eph. 2:19-22).

1:17 In verse 17 the reason why the gospel is the power of God is further unfolded. By it the righteousness of God is revealed, a point which will require the bulk of the letter to expound. But already it is clear that it has to do with the divine character – which itself takes the bulk of the Old Testament to set forth.

The divine righteousness here is closely related to the desire of the Almighty to impart his righteousness to fallen creatures. Thus, as it is revealed, it has everything to do with faith as a gift of God, and with faith from first to last. That is to say, the righteousness which God wills to impute and to impart to fallen men whom he has chosen and whom he calls to himself has everything to do with faith – and nothing to do with anything other than faith! This point Paul immediately clinches by his citation of Habakkuk 2:4: 'the righteous shall live by faith.'

This quotation is used three times in the New Testament: here, and in Galatians 3:11 it refers to that righteousness which is imparted by faith; but in the third instance, Hebrews 10:38, the sense which is emphasised is, rather, 'the righteous shall survive (in an evil day) by faith!'.

The statement thus has both a justifying and a sanctifying aspect. That is to say, faith has to do with the whole of the Christian life from beginning to end. We are saved by faith, and we continue to be saved by faith until faith is lost in sight (cf. 1 Cor. 13:8-13).

God's Wrath Against Mankind

1:18 The wrath of God which is also revealed in the gospel is the antithesis of the righteousness of God so revealed, because the righteousness seen in verse 17 turns out to be sheer mercy, whereas the wrath is sheer, inexorable justice.

Is God, then, divided? No, not at all. He is so great that he contains both of these seemingly contradictory elements, and in such wise that both are fully exercised. But the seeming contradiction is resolved by the costliness of God's judicial action, of which much more later.

In the meantime, it is God's wrath which is revealed from heaven. It is there that God is angry with both the irreligious unrighteousness among men and their immoral wickedness in the totality of its offence before Almighty God.

Note the order of these words (godlessness, then wickedness) which indicates that it is turning away from God as our Maker and Saviour which leads to our turning away from man as our brother, and failing to treat him as we ought to. The same order is apparent in the Ten Commandments (Exod. 20; Deut. 5), which call for our devotion to God in the first four commands as the basis of our devotion to our fellow man in the next six (beginning with our duty to our parents).

Paul now goes on to characterise the nature of such unrighteousness and wickedness: it is quite deliberate. Men hold down the truth of God by their irrational suppression of it. Here man stands as the enemy of his Maker – a fact which is so appalling and heinous as to be almost unbelievable, if it were not true! It is – perhaps strangely – this truth which comes home to us at Christmas time, since it is the Christmas hymns and carols which speak most plainly about what God did in the birth of Christ to remedy this huge fault and the dire rebellion of man against God.

1:19-20 The fact of God's wrath having been revealed (v.18), the reason for it is now declared. It is because the godlessness and wickedness of men are in sheer violation of their knowledge of God. This is incontrovertible since God has plainly revealed his character to them.

Undoubtedly men in their sin will seek to argue against this, but in the light of the apostle's authoritative declaration from God, what excuse has man? Whatever excuse he may think he has will be swept away at the final judgment, where all will be judged according to eternal truth.

Paul now proceeds to explain the nature of God's revelation of himself, which thus leaves man without excuse for his deliberate suppressing of the truth about God by his godlessness and wickedness. Creation itself is the reason for the inexcusableness of rebellious man. For since God wrought all that is (cf. Gen. 1), the creation has been its own incontrovertible witness both to God's power and to his divine nature. Paul repeats that, because these elements in the divine being and nature are clearly seen and understood, men are left with absolutely no excuse for not acknowledging him as God.

It follows that when men proudly declare that they are atheists and deny that there is any evidence for belief in an almighty and eternal God, they are pitting their wits against clear evidence to the contrary. It is for this reason that we often say that there cannot be such a person as an honest atheist. He may not know it, and may need to be told, but in asserting his professed atheism he is pronouncing himself a liar in God's sight.

This is, of course, what lies behind the incarnation. It is the reason why Jesus came to earth, so that, for one thing, in the fulness of time, God would give to the apostle Paul these very sentiments. That God should have opened our eyes to these truths, so that we do not live our lives under false pretences, is sufficient to make Christmas a very happy time for us, since we understand more of why the Lord Jesus came.

1:21 This verse begins with the repeated assertion that men know God! Since most of them would vigorously deny this to be true, who are we to believe, God or men? The answer is obvious. The reality then turns out to be that men have their own reasons for seeking to deny both the existence and the attributes of God. The truth about the sinner is that he must spend his ungodly life trying to run away from God. And to every assertion that there is such a Being, he must answer back his vigorous, vociferous and repeated 'No!'

Even Bernard Shaw admitted that men early discover that there is a God whom they do not like, and so they spend the rest of their lives running away from him. This must be true, given the premises above, and this is what the apostle now says. It is, surely, a fearful thing (although men have little awareness of it) that having known God through nature, instead of glorifying him as he is revealed in the wonders of his creation and thanking him for them, they develop an attitude of mind which is going to lead them into lives of futility. Such darkness so engulfs their hearts that it renders them crippled and barren souls desperately seeking to find a role, but missing it entirely because they have denied the reason for their own existence, that of glorifying the God they now proceed to reject.

The truth then is that, apart from those who have been enlightened to acknowledge God in their lives, men are living manifestly false lives. Not much wonder, then, that the world is in a mess. Men have 'fallen' from the God who made them. Everything must then go wrong. It is a wonder that, by the mercy of the Eternal, the world is not in a much worse state, and that it is possible to live a comparatively normal life, even while denying God. But that is only because God is so full of mercy and patience.

1:22-23 Thus all the proud pretensions of unbelieving man – all the elaborate denials of the existence of Almighty God – are seen to be a perversion of man's undoubted intellectual gifts. It must make such men, if they died as they lived – atheists, fools of their day and generation. That is what God's Word says. And so such men in their 'wisdom' (which Paul tells the Corinthians is 'foolishness', 1 Cor. 1:18-31) turn their backs on God, and proceed to make gods of their own.

The truth is that man must have a god, for so the Almighty has constituted him. He must worship something even if it is his own self – a fact which both shows his intelligence and his admitted subservience to something higher. But when he turns away from the Highest, and proceeds to worship himself – man – an interesting development takes place. He then views man (now running away from God) as ever lower and lower, until, in the depravity of his carnal heart, he sees himself as simply one with the beasts. But then, this desire to worship something, when the true object of worship has been denied, leads man to extremes of animal worship until nothing less than the snake is his choice.

Little does man know that in all this process he has been silently and hiddenly led by the devil himself, whose aim is to have men worship him, until he has them in his grasp. But at the last he will wickedly laugh at them for being so foolish as to give themselves to him. If Satan in hell is able to be distracted from his own severe pains, he will spend his time laughing at how he has duped the citizens of that nether realm of fire and brimstone whom he has brought there to their utter dismay.

Yet there will be one source of the devil's amusement for which there will be absolutely no justification, and this is that none of his fellow denizens of hell were ever destined for any other place. God will prove to be deprived of not one of the saints chosen in Christ before the foundation of the world. No one will be as the devil spitefully wished it to be, but all as the Eternal One planned it to be from before the beginning.

1:24 The consequence of men deliberately turning their backs on God, who made them and all things, defiantly to worship fellow creatures instead of their Maker is so subversive as to occasion divine retribution. The term 'to give up' or 'give over' is terrible, for it implies that the Almighty deliberately consigns persistent sinners to wallow in the sin they have chosen. But this is really to confirm them in the choice they themselves have made.

In fact, this divine 'giving up' is to confirm them in two choices, for their immoral state which here has to do with sexual impurity is that which has arisen by reason of their irreligious turning their backs on God. The decision to do so, whether men realise it or not, leads to another inevitable choice: immorality. This bears out the order of words in verse 18 concerning God's wrath from heaven: it is vengeance first at irreligion and then at its inalienable consequence, immorality.

It cannot be too strongly emphasised that irreligion is bound to lead to immorality. We see that clearly in our own day. The abandonment of religion in our land, seen in the desertion of the church, has inevitably resulted in the abandonment of morals in our nation. Now almost anything goes, and rules, written and unwritten, become laxer and laxer until men become quite unshockable at the most atrocious evil deeds and words.

It is significant that the forms of immorality which the apostle fastens on here are those concerning sexual relationships, in which men and women lose all sense of restraint as to what they permit. They indulge in various forms of bodily sin, so that their degradation arises by degrading the bodies of one another. One example of this is that what in one age might become clandestine adultery becomes so outrageously open and affronting that men and women purposely engage in wife-swopping and regard it as such a joke that they freely confess it and rejoice in it. This would seem to suggest that they have passed beyond the realm of shame and restraint. This, in turn, implies that the divine action of giving up or over has taken place: they are now abandoned to their wickedness.

1:25-27 This verse returns to the thought of verse 23, that of wantonly exchanging the glory of the immortal God for mere images in a downward spiral of choices from possibly noble man to begin with, to ever more bestial man, until the beasts themselves are worshipped, possibly from the noble to the vile until Genesis chapter three's representation of the devil as a serpent is reached. And this is Satan's delight, as we see so obviously when he sought to make Jesus bow down and worship him (Matt. 4:9).

What has thus happened is now described in verses 26-27 in terms of ultimate truth. But, which 'truth of God' is involved here? Is it the truth which God himself is, or the truth which, belonging to him, he has made known? Surely the latter, since the truth which God has revealed about himself and all things is set over against the lie – a lie which excludes the Creator (who is verily blessed for ever), as if he no longer existed. In his place are set his creatures, of ever baser sorts.

It is a monstrous iniquity on the part of men in God's own universe to exclude him; the heinousness of such an act is such that God has no option, if he is just, but to consign them to their evil deeds and confirm them in the same – as if to say, 'You have chosen to turn your back upon me, the Creator of the universe, and prefer to worship my creatures? Then in a judicial action I deliberately turn you over to the vile passions which belong to such perversion.'

This is a fearful thing – that what godless and immoral men choose to do in their revulsion against their Maker becomes their lot, as if they were already in the vestibule of hell!

Here the action of females is mentioned before that of males, albeit less explicitly than the description of males in verse 27. Paul refers to the homosexual vice of prostituting the normal and natural use of the female sexual functions for the unnatural ones of women burning in sexual lust for women (v.27), then proceeds to describe the action of depraved men in burning in lust for their own sex rather than for the female sex.

Sexual desire is natural, since it is by the sexual functions of men and women that God in his wisdom has ordained to perpetuate the race of humankind. The command is given to Adam in Genesis 1:28 to 'be fruitful and multiply'. This is abandoned by both men and women who turn the natural use into the unnatural and vile; which then – since God ultimately confirms men and women in their unnatural deeds – becomes a judgment of God upon them.

1:28-32 The following verses are among the most awful in the Book! They simply say for the third time (vv.24, 26, 28) that because men have turned their backs upon their Maker and sought to do what is utterly repugnant and abhorrent to the One who made them, he has judicially turned his back upon them and has consigned them deliberately and definitely to do that of which he absolutely disapproves. What they formerly dabbled in tentatively is now made their meat and drink, for they are filled with every kind of wickedness.

Paul's list is hideous and long. Every kind of badness conceivable is here. This is a list which makes righteous people tremble and shudder, and determine to run as far and as fast as they can away from all such appalling evil.

The chapter now ends with a damning re-emphasis on the deliberateness of men's transgression. Earlier the apostle wrote that 'although they knew God, they neither glorified him as God nor gave thanks to him'. Now he writes, 'Although they know God's righteous decree that those who do such things deserve death, they not only continue to do these very things but also approve of those who practise them'. This is the last stage of abandonment, when all sense of the consequences is lost in the overwhelming wave of evil desire to do as much wrong as it is in their wicked power to do. Such a state must be very near the state which our Lord describes as having committed the unpardonable sin. We take that to mean a state in which one has gone so far in wickedness that one is completely possessed by the devil and is so absolutely committed to his disastrous will that no turning back is possible. The die has been cast, and the soul is lost ere it dies, like Esau and Judas!

CHAPTER TWO

God's Righteous Judgment

2:1-2 The first question which usually arises in interpreting Romans 2 is whether or not Paul is addressing Jews throughout the chapter, even if he does not address them by name until verse 17. It may not be vital to decide this issue, since there are many scholars on various sides of the argument. In any case, Paul's strictures are against those who judge others for doing precisely the same things as they do themselves. This the Jews with the divine oracles would be naturally prone to do, although the passage could certainly apply to high-minded Gentiles.

Obviously there can be no excuse for anything so hypocritical because, as verse 2 states, God's sentence on such is based on truth. But it is part of our sinnerhood that we seek relief – and almost some self-justification – in condemning our own sins when they are manifested in others.

This is a mark of the depth of the perversity and iniquity of the human heart; for it is clearly a wicked, lying and malignant thing to do. Yet we must all confess that there is a proneness in the guilty human heart to do just that, although it can occur only where there is deliberate blindness, not only to the truth of God but to the truth about our own sinfulness. There can surely be nothing that God is so hard on as Pharisaism! And yet, it is the sin to which the Christian church is most susceptible, since the truth of God is so uncompromising about sin that we seek relief from our own stricken consciences in the cunning of condemning others for sins of the same sort as our own. 'God be merciful to me a sinner' – the cry of the tax-gatherer – is surely the highest we dare seek. As the old hymn says: 'My highest place is lying low at my Redeemer's feet.'

2:3-4 There could be no possible exoneration of the sinner who condemns others for committing the same sin he is guilty of himself. And for this reason, as we have noted, God's judgment is according to truth.

We may be inclined to think that harsh. But if there were in the heart and mind of God variations of standards with regard to the truth we would not be able to trust him, and our whole life would hang on the variableness of a God who could not be depended upon to be the same at all times to all persons. That would be no foundation for any kind of stable life. And so we must be glad that the *Confession of Faith* speaks of God's 'glorious justice'; for it is not only safe and secure, however severe, but it is the basis of all our security. And that is far from all; for such divine integrity is the foundation of all the blessings which flow from it.

Think here of the solid rocks which are the foundation of so much of the earth. But deeper down in the bowels of the earth the rocks are molten. There is a parable here. The cold, hard crust simply overlays a wealth of liquid fire, which we may see spewing from volcanoes. And that speaks of a warm, loving, 'liquid' heart underneath all the seeming hardness of the law, a heart full of tolerance, patience and kindness which God loves to pour upon his erring children in the hope that they may see themselves in all their sinful ingratitude, and repent.

Do we fail to see the tenderness of God behind his strictures? If we do we have completely misunderstood him.

2:5-6 If the goodness of God conduces to repentance, why is it, the apostle is asking, that God's unique goodness to his chosen people Israel has far from led them to that? It is because they have despised his goodness and thought that it was mere indulgence. They have thought that they had no need of repentance (as those horrid Gentiles had!). They were the chosen, favoured people of God – indeed, but they were not chosen in order to be indulged as if a lower standard of righteousness was permitted them than others – the very reverse! They were set, like a city on a hill, to give light to the whole Gentile world (cf. Isa. 42:6; 49:6), and they had failed.

There are no favourites with God as far as the lowering of his standards is concerned. The greater the favour the greater the responsibility. To think otherwise is simply to store up heaps of condemnation against the day when all rights and wrongs will be revealed and when God will render to every man according to what he has done.

Paul states this very clearly, not only here in verse 6 but also to the Corinthians when he says that 'we must all appear before the judgment seat of Christ, that each one may receive the things done in (that is, *through*) the body, whether they be good or bad' (2 Cor. 5:10). John says it again in the Revelation. After having stated that death determines our eternal state, he goes on to say: 'And behold, I come quickly; and my reward is with me, to give every man according as his work shall be' (Rev. 22:1).

Again, in 1 Corinthians 3:15, Paul shows that the fact that all mankind will be divided on that day between those who are to be with God in heaven and those who are not does not preclude the fact of the judgement of the individual deeds of each man. The saints of course will be with Christ in glory, but there is still to be judgment of the deeds of their Christian lives – not to condemnation, but to reward or loss. Whatever we may regard as reward or loss (and it is too great a subject for now), there is no doubt that our Christian lives down here are to be measured and assessed and reward given or loss sustained.

2:7 That deeds springing from the quality and character of each person's life are to be judged is now made plain. There are, clearly, two categories: the just and the unjust. This distinction answers questions which might be raised as to whether works were now the essential criterion with regard to human destiny. Not at all! The just will be with Christ, the unjust banished from him, but works will be judged in either case. Those who patiently persist in doing good do so because the Lord is with them energising them in seeking the glory of God in all their work done to his honour and towards immortality and incorruption. They will reach the goal which is eternal life. This is the way of life for the true believer. However he may be from time to time distracted by Satan's wiles and the deceitfulness of his own heart, his bent and intent is towards those higher things which will then merit the Lord's 'Well done'.

It is otherwise with those who live for self and who pursue policies of self-advancement and who refuse and disobey the truth. Their perverse obedience is altogether towards unrighteousness. They are willing slaves to all that is wrong (see 1:32 again), and of course they will incur the wrath and anger of Almighty God, so that affliction and anguish will come upon them, every one who works evil, whether Jews (for they should know better), or Gentiles. But there will be glory, honour and peace for everyone who does good – again, first to the Jew, then to the Gentile.

I love the way Paul comes down, from the heights in the promise of blessings to those whose hearts being right do good, from glory and honour to the exceedingly practical and down-to-earth blessing of peace. That may refer to blessings and fruits and rewards down here as well as hereafter; for it is better to do right down here than to do wrong. The righteous have a better life, even down here in this vale of tears!

2:11-12 That the eternal God can be so impartially just that there are no favourites with him, and yet that he should be the source of divine election, is a marvel that is simply too deep for us. Certainly we can understand this only in terms of him dealing with mankind in a fallen state and therefore as objects of his wrath unless his mercy lights on us. But that his final judgments run right through both categories of saved and damned, so that not even in hell can he be accused of injustice, is an awesome thing, and should for ever humble us in our attempts to understand what it is that makes him Almighty God.

At verse 12 Paul now proceeds to show the impartiality of God's justice, and he does so in respect of the damned who possess or are ignorant of the law. The only difference is that the wicked who did not have the law of God in any formulated or conceptual form will be judged according to their uncurbed lawlessness. They are those Paul has already described in chapter one as turning their backs upon God. In face of the evidence of creation alone they have no excuse.

The other category – those who, like the Jews had the written formulation of the Mosaic law – will be judged on the basis of their having had floods of spiritual and moral light thrown upon their paths by that repository of eternal truth, the Ten Commandments. They express first the abiding character of the Almighty, before these same commands enjoin obedience from creatures who are furnished with his laws. Their case would therefore appear to be infinitely worse than the ignorant heathen, for they have less excuse for their lawless wickedness since they possess the very oracles of God.

2:13-16 Paul now goes on to show that the Jews' possession of the law does not give them an automatic advantage over other men. In fact it only increases their liability if they do not obey the law that has been given to them. The greater their advantages, the greater their responsibility to use them for betterment, and the greater the shame and disgrace if having them they ignore them or set them up as mere idols ignorantly to be worshipped, but not to be kept in daily life.

The fact that the writer says that it is not those who have the law but those who obey it who are declared to be righteous is not to say that any have been declared righteous by keeping the law. No one has ever done so completely except the Lord Jesus Christ. The verse is simply limiting its scope to the fact that having the law does not ensure that a man will keep it. Paul will go into this much more thoroughly in the next chapter. But even now in verse 14 he shows us a remarkable thing. It is possible for Gentiles who have never had the Mosaic law to do by instinctive response to a partly enlightened conscience the things prescribed by the law. This shows that the law is already written on their hearts. Searching and groping in the darkness for moral and spiritual light, they are able to approve or disapprove their actions according to their response to the standards which their degree of enlightenment has reached.

That all this is contained within the life of the unregenerate shows that the dividing of mankind into the saved and the lost does not constitute two 'hold-alls' of saints or sinners, undifferentiated within their own categories. As there will be a judgment of believers to receive rewards for faithful service, or loss for lack of faithfulness in service (1 Cor. 3:10-15), so justice will be meted out exactly to the damned according to the degrees of their wickedness, or will be withheld to the extent that moral standards have been attained.

This does not mean and cannot mean that any individual can attain to salvation through such moral achievement – think of the sinful pride of those who attain even comparative morality as Paul will unfold it soon – but simply means that a just God recognises such distinctions in men, saved and lost.

The Jews and the Law

2:17-24 The Jew is now identified as having the advantages of the Mosaic law, and these are listed. There is no doubt that the Jew relied on his possession of the law to establish his moral and spiritual superiority to all Gentiles and was not slow to despise them as 'dogs'.

However, the responsibility devolves on the Jew to keep the law in which he is instructed because he claims to know the divine will and is able to know and approve what is superior. If he therefore accepts and boasts of the advantages, if he is convinced that he is a guide to blind Gentiles by bringing light to those who sit in nature's darkness, if he is an instructor of the foolish and a teacher of infants because the law he possesses embodies the knowledge of the truth; then the question needs to be asked, 'Do you who teach others also teach yourself?'

Is it the case that those who know by the law that it is wrong to steal actually steal? Is it the case that those who know by the law that it is wrong to commit adultery actually do so? That those who know and are taught to abhor idols actually become so fascinated by these heathen objects as to rob pagan temples? All these contraventions show that the Jew is in fact guilty of dishonouring the law of God by breaking it, and that this was well known in the Gentile world. The result: God's name was blasphemed among the Gentiles on that account.

Here the clear inadequacy of an outward knowledge of the law to produce right living is manifest. Unless the law is written on the heart, all the placarding in the world will make no material difference. The heart is the element that makes the difference between mere knowledge and actual practice.

2:25-27 The apostle now drives the guilty Jew into his last stand of defence against accusations, namely the fact of his circumcision, which he claimed was a divine right, setting him apart from other men. What he forgot, however, was that circumcision was a covenant to be kept, a covenant of grace first given to Abraham to be kept by faith (cf. Gen. 17:9). Its value then could be none other than the value of observing its terms, not legalistically, but as provisions of grace.

Thus to break the law in any of the particulars already listed, such as stealing, adultery, or idolatry, was virtually to uncircumcise oneself, and therefore to render the outward rite of no value before God at all. Indeed, says Paul – referring back to those (described in verses 14 and 15) who seek to obey the law written on their hearts although they do not have the oracles of God – may not such regard themselves as circumcised without the rite, because they are seeking to fulfil what circumcision represents? And may they not rise to condemn Jews who, despite their circumcision, unlawfully and in an ungodly fashion, flout the law, when those without it seek to keep its precepts?

The same may be said of baptism although modern commentators do not make this point. Calvin does, however. The greatest harm is done to covenant baptism by the misuse of it by unregenerate church members who are of course incapable of instructing their children in its privileges. Where covenant baptism of the infants of true believers is taken seriously, however, the children are brought up in the Lord as little Christians, by the disciplines of prayer, precept and example. And as is clear from the context of Paul's statements here on circumcision, it is possible for the children of believers to be brought up as little Christians although water has not been used, although there is no greater reason for withholding water from them than for withholding circumcision from Jewish covenant children.

2:28-29 Paul now commits himself to this striking statement: A man is not a Jew if he is one outwardly, for circumcision is not merely outward and physical, but inward, of the heart and by the Spirit. As we underlined above, this is equally true of baptism, although that affords no ground for neglecting the ordinance as enjoined in Scripture (Matt. 28:19). The outward rite when trusted in materially can be – as with the bread and the wine – a real barrier and hindrance to faith. The physical rite then belongs to the realm of the law which is outward and has no inherent power to sanctify the soul, but only to enjoin what ought to be done. It takes the Holy Spirit to fructify what the law enjoins.

Paul returns to this in the wider context of the ninth chapter, when he discusses the rejection of Israel following her rejection of Christ. He says, 'It is not as though God's Word had failed. For not all who are descended from Israel are Israel. Nor because they are his descendants are they all Abraham's children' (Rom. 9:6-7).

The last remark of chapter two is about the spiritual man's praise being from God and not from man. This is very apposite, for while men may greatly rejoice and take pleasure in their submission to outward rites, those whose hearts are regenerated by the Holy Spirit and who enjoy circumcision of the heart and baptism of the Spirit (Gal. 2:11-12) recognise that this is a work of God and they give praise to him and not to those who merely require outward rites.

Writing to the Galatians, Paul brings out the same point (cf. Gal. 2:12-15), ending, 'Neither circumcision nor uncircumcision means anything, but what counts is a new creation.'

CHAPTER THREE

God's Faithfulness

3:1-8 The assault on the prevailing practices of Judaism has been so strong that we might be left wondering what advantage the Jew has over the Gentile when the Jew is so heedless of the Mosaic law.

Paul nevertheless asserts the advantages; they are real. The Jews were entrusted with the oracles of God. That privilege and priority is God-given. No one and nothing can take it from them. Of course they have not always been faithful and true, but does that negate and nullify God's faithful Word to them? Never! God cannot lie though the whole world prove false; he must prove true.

Paul supports this by a quotation from David's psalm of penitence written after his sin with Bathsheba. It was David himself who, following his confession, declared: 'So you are proved right when you speak and justified when you judge' (Ps. 51:4). In fact the righteousness of God stands out so far that the more unrighteous man is, the brighter the righteousness of God appears, just as the moon and stars shine the brighter the darker the night.

Is God then wrong to be wrathful at the sin of man when by contrast man's sin intensifies the glory of God's righteousness? No! God's righteous wrath cannot be 'bought off' because man's sin serves as a foil to divine righteousness. Otherwise, God would be prevented from judging his sinful world, and that could never be right.

Yet someone might still argue: If the sinner's falsehood enhances God's truthfulness and thus increases his glory, that should be regarded as imposing an obligation on God not to condemn but to commend him. After all immunity is, sometimes, offered to 'super-grasses'!

But see what that would mean: it would be tantamount to saying, 'Let sinners do evil in order that God may bring good out of it.' It is true that God sinlessly uses evil for his glory (as in the death of his Son), but that cannot mean that evil is any less evil. It must still be punished, or else God would be unjust. The bonus cannot belong to sinners, but to God who permits but still punishes evil, as is his right. All who say otherwise are to be utterly condemned.

No-one is Righteous

3:9-19 So the Almighty is justified; for his law is perfect. But what of the Jews? Are they any better for having the high privilege of the oracles of God? Not at all; Paul has already consigned all men to guilt (1:18-32), and now the implication is made clear that this includes the Jews.

Paul now proceeds to gather from the Old Testament, and particularly from the Psalms, a number of indictments of man's guilt before God.

The first (v.10) is from Psalm 14:3; the second (v.11) is from Psalm 14:2 and Psalm 53:1; the third (v.12) from Psalm 53:3; the fourth (v.13a) from Psalm 5:9 (although see Ps. 52:2), and the fifth (v.13b) from Psalm 140:3; the sixth (v.14) is from Psalm 10:7; the seventh (vv.15-17) is from Isaiah 59:7, 8; and he eighth (v.18) from Psalm 36:1. Together these form a total indictment from which no man could possibly escape. Each is like another nail in the coffin of man's claim to respectability. Is it not remarkable that such a radical impeachment should be culled from the Old Testament? How integral the Testaments are!

Paul then sums up his conclusion at verses 19-20. He is still thinking of the Jews, who seemed to regard themselves as above the law since it was given exclusively to them. No: what the law says it says to those who are under it. Since there is no doubt about the Gentiles' guilt, and the Jews are even more guilty because they have sinned in face of their advantage, every mouth is silenced before God and the whole world becomes altogether guilty in his sight and accountable to him.

3:20 But why will no one be declared righteous in God's sight by observing the law? Because no one can attain to it? Of course. But that would have been true of the Gentiles also if they had had the law.

The reason is not only that no man can attain to the law's perfection, but that the possession of the law explicates and makes plain how far from perfectly fulfilling the law even the most devout Jews are. As Paul puts it to the Corinthians (2 Cor. 3:6), the letter of the law kills, because it makes plain how far short the best of men fall from its perfections. And Jesus makes that failure even plainer when he seeks to show the Pharisees that the sum of the law is to love the Lord God with all the heart and soul and mind, and our neighbour as ourselves (Matt. 22: 34-40). This no man has ever done perfectly, nor can anyone but the One who said these words – the perfect Lord Jesus.

Nonetheless, the law of God shows us the way to God, even although it condemns us in doing so. This is what Abraham said to the rich man who suggested word be sent to his five brothers lest they also come to the place of torment: 'They have Moses and the Prophets; let them listen to them.' 'No,' said the rich man, 'but if one from the dead goes to them, they will repent'. But Abraham answered, 'If they do not listen to Moses and the Prophets, they will not be convinced even if someone rises from the dead' (Lk. 16:27-31).

The law as first given, of course, was to be a means of sanctifying those who had been saved by the blood of the Passover. But they could not keep that law, so it turned out to be the means of the conviction of sin. But it is still the law of love to those who have it written on their hearts (Jer. 31:33) and who are therefore made able more approximately to fulfil it. Nevertheless, as we are about to see, the blood of the Passover was but a type of the precious blood of Jesus by which alone the guilty sinner of any dispensation can be absolved. This is now made plain from verse 21 onwards.

Righteousness Through Faith

3:21-24 This is the heart of the gospel: the only way guilty man can possibly fulfil the law is by being shown a righteousness he may aspire to, apart altogether from any law framed as a requirement. This is the 'law' of righteousness which comes from God to man as sheer, pure gift. It is the gift of faith which is to be directed towards Jesus Christ our only Saviour.

Of course this is not new, in the sense that it had been already made known in the Law and Prophets of the Old Testament, by which the ancient Patriarchs and Prophets were accepted by God as having been declared righteous by faith (cf. Heb. 11). But it is entirely new, in that it comes through Jesus Christ. Indeed, it is only through Jesus (whom Abraham saw by faith and was glad, and whom Moses, David, Isaiah and all the prophets saw by faith) that any man can be saved. Although our blessed Lord came late in the day, he was made a sacrifice for the sins of the saints of all ages – those before him as well as those after him, including ourselves.

This righteousness, which comes to those who by the gift of faith receive Jesus Christ, makes no distinction between men, for, as Paul has already shown in this chapter, Jews and Gentiles alike have fallen short of that glory of righteousness for which they were created. In their helplessness they are justified (that is, declared to be right), by the totally free gift of faith, the gift of God's grace. And that gift of grace and faith is theirs through the redemption – that is the deliverance from the pollution, guilt, and penalty of sin – which comes solely and only through Christ Jesus.

This is a gospel of the sheerest grace and mercy, which leaves nothing for guilty man to do for himself but helplessly cling to Jesus Christ. All honour, glory and thanksgiving be to him!

3:25-26 In the fulness of time, God publicly presented his Son, Christ Jesus, to be a propitiation. That is the word in the original text with which we must stay despite all the attempts of modern translations to 'explain' it otherwise.

The word 'propitiation' clearly implies the wrath of God on account of man's sin, and the act of divine justice in providing a propitiatory sacrifice for that sin, which is effectual for him only through faith in Christ's blood. This act of providing a propitiatory sacrifice for man's sin in the fulness of time was in particular a demonstration of God's justice – a demonstration which was necessary to justify God's forbearance of the sins of all the former saints.

Up to the time of Christ's sacrifice, no sin of man had ever received its due punishment in accordance with the justice of God. That is a tremendous thought! Think what it means: Abraham's sins were not punished until Christ bore the penalty for them, and this was due to the great forbearance of a patient and yet faithful God who must deal with sin, but who would save the repentant sinner from the consequences of his sin.

God waited long – from Adam to Christ – to fulfil what was written in Genesis 3:15 about 'bruising the serpent's head'. The death of Jesus, then, was the public setting forth of God's justice in open demonstration, a justice, held in reserve over the centuries by the Almighty's mercy in temporarily overlooking the sins of the Old Testament saints.

Nothing could show as well as these words the retrospective efficacy of Christ's death to deal with the sins of the Old Testament saints. Thus he is both the just God who must punish sin, and, at the same time and in the same composite action, the justifier of those who have faith in Jesus' sacrifice on their behalf. Wonderful!

3:27-29 Mankind in its totality is at the mercy of God. That mercy waited long to endure and expunge the penalty for the sins of the saints that all might go free and be justified by the exercise of faith as the gift of God's grace. Absolutely no room is left for boasting – least of all from Jews. Indeed, they are the more incriminated because of their failure to avail themselves of the advantages of the law, in order to walk in it.

But boasting is excluded not only negatively, on account of man's failure to keep God's law, but positively because the remedy for such failure is the free gift of God's grace, namely the gift of faith. Boasting is therefore utterly excluded by reason of the fact that man is justified by faith. And that faith is the absolute antithesis of any observance of the law, since it is purely and only the act of helplessly clinging to God and pleading for mercy, on the grounds of Christ's propitiatory death.

John Murray calls such faith 'self-renouncing', but 'self-surrendering' also appeals as an appropriate description. Faith looks to God, observance of the law to self. It was seeing this that led Martin Luther to the end of all his efforts to please God by acts of penance. 'Nothing in my hand I bring, Simply to Thy Cross I cling' (Augustus Montague Toplady).

3:30-31 The oneness of Almighty God was dear to the Jews, which made it hard for them to accept the deity of the Son. But if there is one thing about which the Scriptures are adamant, it is the unity of the Trinity. The Almighty will therefore act consistently with himself. In bundling all mankind together as in need of his mercy and making no distinction between Jew and Gentile as far as justification is concerned, no material difference is to be sought or found between the prepositions '*by* faith' and '*through* ... faith'. All have sinned and come short of the glory of God, and therefore with the law, or without it, they are bereft of shelter, because none have observed it as perfectly as was necessary to be justified by it.

Paul then ends the chapter with a most astonishing and seemingly contradictory assertion. If the law is absolutely excluded from the justification of any, may we not legitimately ask what purpose it serves, since none can fulfil it acceptably to God? Ah, concludes Paul, that is where you must not run on to condemn the law. It is because of the perfections of God's holy law in its entirety that mankind has been arraigned as guilty of failure to observe it. Although he is not prepared here to discuss the justification of the law, as he does in chapters 6 and 8, he nevertheless declares its justification with astonishing boldness, and leaves it there in this blunt verse for the time being. This is undoubtedly one of the apostle's seed thoughts, from which he will yet harvest a rich crop. But for now, in chapter 4 he returns to the antithesis between faith and observance of the law as a means of justification. He draws his illustrations from the Old Testament itself, in a way that is calculated to convince Jewry.

CHAPTER FOUR

Abraham Justified by Faith

4:1-10 The first example given of justification by faith apart from the works of the law is that of Abraham. If, hundreds of years before the law of Moses was given, Abraham had been justified by works he would have had something to boast of. But had he? Not before God. Scripture (Gen. 15:6) says plainly that 'Abraham believed God [the circumstances are described throughout Genesis 15] and it was credited to him as righteousness.' Faith, then, is the justifying requirement, not works; and as we have already learned at 3:28, faith is apart from any observance of the law.

Paul now proceeds to discuss cases in which works call for wages, since wages are not a gift but an obligation, since they have been worked for. But in the case of the man who does not work, but trusts the God who justifies the wicked, as Abraham obviously did, that trust is reckoned as righteousness.

The apostle then moves from Abraham to David, and quotes Psalm 32:1-2 to stress the blessedness of the man to whom God credits righteousness apart from works: his transgressions are covered, his sins forgiven and against him the Lord will never count sin.

Here then, a thousand years apart, are two of God's chosen race, both of whom are justified by faith apart altogether from works. Surely that should convince the Jews!

Even so, they might be flattered and think that, since this was the case with Abraham and David, it was a peculiarly Jewish requirement for God's chosen, circumcised race. Not at all! In fact Abraham believed God and was declared to be righteous long before circumcision was given. The prior event took place in Genesis 15:6, whereas circumcision was not given by God to Abraham until Genesis chapter 17.

We see, then, the astonishing priority of faith in the annals of the Old Testament patriarchs. All refuge in works is therefore excluded in every way.

4:11-15 The sign and seal of circumcision was given to Abraham as the external token of the righteousness he had while he was still uncircumcised. He, then, is the father of all who believe, Jew or Gentile, circumcised or uncircumcised, so that righteousness might be credited to them as they walk by the faith exemplified in the steps of believing Abraham.

The stunning thing for Jews then to realise is that Abraham's justification by faith was prior to the law of Moses by hundreds of years. But that is not all. In calling Abraham from Ur of the Chaldees God made promises to him which were prior to any kind of explicit law (see Gen. 12:1-3; 13:14-17; 15:4, 5, 18-21; 17:2-21; 22:15-18).

It was thus as an uncircumcised man called from a heathen background that Abraham received God's promises that he would be the heir of the world. This is an astonishing thing, for it means that the heirs of God are not those who seek to please him by efforts of law-keeping, but those to whom God is pleased to make promises before any question of law or response to law is involved.

If it were otherwise, and the promises were given to those who had attained to some fulfilment of a system of law, then faith would be excluded as a completely fortuitous exercise. But in fact it is through faith alone, apart from any law, that righteousness is established. For law has to do with the threat of divine wrath, and where there is no law, there cannot be any transgression of law.

4:16-18 Faith comes by grace, whereas works come by law. The good effects of faith are guaranteed to all Abraham's offspring, that is, to those who believe. That includes those who are of the law and of circumcision – as long as their stand is not upon the law which has to do with works and wrath, but upon faith, following the example of Abraham who is the father of all who are saved by believing, not by fulfilling works.

The apostle therefore appeals to the Scriptures of Genesis 17:5 where God declares, 'I have made you a father of many nations.' This, then, is true 'in the sight of God' since he has so singularly declared it. What is in view must be as universal as the jurisdiction and supervision of the Almighty, so that none who believes is excluded from the 'sonship' of Abraham. Anyone who believes is his son inasmuch as he believes unto righteousness, as father Abraham did.

Furthermore, this faith is placed in a God who gives life to the dead. In view here is no mere resuscitation such as happened to Lazarus or the son of the widow of Nain, but resurrection, as in Christ's case (cf. Eph. 1:19, 20).

But God not only gives life to the dead, he calls things which are not as though they were. Which things, we might ask? If we go back to creation, this is true of everything that exists. Everything has been created by God out of nothing, in order that it might have existence. Is the reference to that? John Murray thinks that in this context it has prophetic reference to things which at the time of writing did not exist but which, having been called by God (and chosen in him from before the foundation of the world, Eph. 1:4), are regarded as already in existence. So that these things to come are not merely in the realm of the 'possible', but are potentially already accomplished.

Paul goes on to show this by his illustration from the life of Abraham, who believed that, even although he was a hundred years old, God would give him a son. His faith was practically equivalent to the existence of the child before he was born, it was so sure.

4:18-22 This is the nature of true faith, the gift of the Father, that it enshrines a hope which persists against all competing hopelessness. It cannot be daunted, because it has seen into the realm of the divine will sufficiently to know that what it believes shall indeed be, without dubiety. It was thus that Abraham became the father of many nations, as God had promised: 'So shall your offspring be' (Gen. 15:5).

Of course, all this sounds as rarified as if it had taken place in a heavenly sphere. But no: Abraham faced – indeed had to face – the fact that at the age of one hundred his body was as good as dead as far as procreation was concerned, and, at ninety, Sarah's womb as past bearing by many years. He faced these facts squarely, but did not allow them to weaken his faith. He stood on the promise of God, and therefore was strengthened in faith and gave the glory to God, because he was fully persuaded that Almighty God was able to do what he had promised.

The result of such invincible faith was not only that in the fulness of time Abraham received Isaac the son God promised, as Hannah and other biblical women did, but God also honoured his faith by crediting it to him as righteousness.

This is the nature of true faith, that it so enters the realms of its giver, God, that it is bound to partake of a measure of heavenly knowledge – especially relative to itself. It knows itself forgiven, and justified with the righteousness in which those who believe are accounted and declared by God to be righteous in his sight.

Faith, then, is the great 'introducer' of souls to the potent realm of God's saving power, of which the first great part is to provide incontrovertible assurance that one is accepted by God as righteous. Such faith, which is God's free gift, looks to God, and believes God's declaration (Gen. 15:6) just as surely as Abraham in his old age looked to God and believed God's promise.

4:23-25 Paul now proceeds to apply this great lesson drawn from Genesis 15:6, that Abraham was accepted by God as righteous through faith, to those who follow on, including those to whom the apostle is writing – including ourselves! We are reminded that Paul wrote to the Corinthians: 'Now these things happened to them by way of example, and they were written for our instruction, upon whom the ends of the ages have come' (1 Cor. 10:11). The faith God gave to Abraham concerning the miraculous birth of Isaac is the same gift he gives to all his chosen ones (Eph. 1:4) in any age.

The lesson of Abraham, therefore, in circumstances vastly different from our own makes no difference. It applies equally to us, so that as we appropriate the gift of faith and exercise it towards God in Jesus Christ, righteousness is imputed to us, just as it was to Abraham.

The content of that faith is now described in verses 24 and 25. Its essence is the resurrection of Jesus Christ from the dead, because that is the climax of the work of our redemption. Jesus Christ who was delivered up to punitive death for our offences, having borne that penalty, is raised by his Father from the dead. This resurrection simply seals the efficacy of his atoning work, and therefore effects our justification.

It would therefore be incomplete to say that we are justified by the death of Jesus, if we did not include in that observation the statement that his death inevitably issued in his resurrection. So important is the resurrection for our justification that John Murray calls it the basis of it. Nor is he excluding the death from that statement, because it would be impossible for there to be a resurrection if there had not been, beforehand, a death.

It is also important to see that in both these acts – Jesus Christ's death and his resurrection – it is the Father who is the Actor. This is not to deny the willingness and co-operation of the Son (cf. Jn. 10:18), but he was 'delivered over' and 'was raised' by the Father. It is on this basis alone that we come to the great statement of justification in Romans 5.

CHAPTER FIVE

Peace and Joy

5:1 Justification having been based on the death and resurrection of Jesus Christ, we now go on triumphantly to its fruits. The first and greatest fruit of being justified is that we have peace with God. This is not primarily our peace, but God's – although it must issue in our peace. He is at peace with us on account of his Son having suffered the punishment for all our sins; this mediation extinguishes the wrath of God.

As long as our faith in Jesus Christ remains – for it is not a single act on our part but a sustained attitude – God is at peace with us. This has very important practical considerations for us. The first of them is that we do not base our assurance on any feelings of peace that we might cherish towards God, seeking to live a life of faith on the basis of our subjective feelings. That would be a fickle basis for peace! John Campbell Shairp's hymn brings this out well:

Twixt gleams of joy and clouds of doubt
Our feelings come and go;
Our best estate is tossed about
In ceaseless ebb and flow.
No mood of feeling, form of thought,
Is constant for a day;
But Thou, O Lord, Thou changest not:
The same Thou art alway.

I grasp Thy strength, make it mine own,
My heart with peace is blest;
I lose my hold, and then comes down
Darkness, and cold unrest.
Let me no more my comfort draw
From my frail hold of Thee,
In this alone rejoice with awe –
Thy mighty grasp of me.

The poet does not go into the basis of that peace as Paul so wonderfully does, but he is quite clear that it lies in God and not in ourselves. Nothing could be more helpful for maintaining a steady life of assurance, which in even the greatest storms of personal doubt and uncertainty is built on the immovable rock of what God has done for us through Jesus Christ.

As long as our faith holds to that, and we rest in God and his Son, whatever our feelings may register at any point in time, we may know that God is still at peace with us. He has not only given us the ground and basis of such peace by the work of Jesus Christ; he also gives us the gift of faith by which we hold on to the divine fact, and therefore centre our assurance on what God has done for us once and for all. The result of that, which should increase constantly is that we may have the peace of God in our souls. This is so deep that it 'surpasses all understanding' (Phil. 4:13). This is the rightful heritage of the children of God by faith in Jesus Christ.

5:2 The grace to which we have access through faith in the Lord Jesus Christ is, of course, justification, which, as John Murray says, 'is an abiding and immovable status arising from a past action'. There is nothing in language which can fully express the wonder of any guilty sinner that God accepts him as for ever justified in his sight. It simply magnifies and exalts beyond all expression the work of the Lord Jesus Christ in being delivered over to death for our sakes.

It is not only the fact that, by faith in his finished work, we are declared by God to be inalienably righteous in his sight that is quite overwhelming. The Lord could rightly accord us that privilege almost *in absentia* by sending it as an accolade from afar, from his throne to our human condition. But by the blessed gift of righteousness declared, we have access to the throne of God in a permanent standing. It is this that is so overwhelming. We should therefore constantly marvel at the high privilege of drawing near to God (James 4:8 says he will also draw near to us). We should consider such access as an extraordinary blessing, not least because of the coordinate joy which comes with it, namely that of the hope of glory to come.

We have, then, this series of blessings as the fruit of our justification: the knowledge that God is at peace with us, that we have access to him by this inestimable grace, and that in this invulnerable position we may exult in the hope of seeing the glory of God in the future. The joy is in the hope and prospect of seeing God's glory, since John says 'we shall be like him because we shall see him as he is' (1 Jn. 3:2).

That phrase 'as he is' is quite out of this world, and promises us such a sight and experience as we can only faintly glimmer now. But the hope that we are to see the Almighty and Eternal God as he is should transport our souls into realms of the quietest and yet most exultant ecstasy. Yet it is all based on the primary blessing, that we know that God is at peace with us. When that knowledge envelops our souls it is undoubtedly something so deep that it passes understanding.

5:3-5 Paul now points us to a further fruit of justification which we all find much harder to reach. We marvel that the apostle is so ready to say not merely that he understands the reason for tribulations but that he glories or boasts in them.

This is possible only because he maintains a thoroughly unified vision of his Christian life, and links the hereafter so climactically with his life down here that he does not see the one except in the light of the other. This is such an integration of earth and heaven as is bound to stabilise the soul, and give it a balance and settlement which is bound to make faith immovably strong.

To rejoice in sufferings is completely healthy. To rejoice in sufferings for their own sake would be unhealthy and indeed sick. But to do so for Christ's sake, whose sufferings were so fruitful, is a very different thing. (The fact that these sufferings are for Christ's sake, and for the church as the body of Christ, is brought out most wonderfully in Col. 1:24, which should be consulted.)

Paul now proceeds to enumerate the sufferings, and demonstrates logically how in their sequence they issue in the building of Christian character. The first fruit of affliction for Christ's sake is patience, perseverance or steadfastness; and patience produces what can best be called proof or approvedness; and approvedness produces hope. You see, therefore, how patient endurance produces character, and does so by these two stages of assurance and hope. It is these which make the apostle so steadfastly sure of himself in Christ. There is absolutely nothing to be ashamed of in this hope, because it is produced by God himself in his love for us imparted to our hearts by his Holy Spirit.

The truth is, of course, that Paul cannot go on to unfold the fruits of justification without more than hinting at the subjective fruits of it in our experience of the Lord in our hearts. I have felt for long that this aspect of Paul's teaching in Romans 5 is not acknowledged sufficiently by scholars; some even go so far as to say that Paul continues to deal with justification right through to chapter 8. No: the fruit of justification is sanctification, since what Christ has done *for* us must lead naturally to what he does *in* us. That is why we see chapter 5 as transitional, pointing in two directions, back to what we have learned of justification in chapters 3 and 4, and forward to what we are to learn of sanctification in chapters 6 to 8.

5:5-8 We cannot leave the great fifth verse, with its tremendous summation of the fruit of justification, without taking careful note of the objective ground of our hope in Christ. It is not, of course, our love for God, but his for us, leading to all the painful means to our salvation, which are referred to here.

Note with what emotive language the apostle describes God's love: it is 'poured out' into our hearts. The very flowing nature of the description shows the livingness as well as the lovingness of its action in taking possession of us. The reason for the assured hope which this affords us is now given. It was just at the right time that Jesus died for the ungodly, while they were still powerless to help themselves. This indicates the quality of God's love for us: it is not only full of pity, but of help.

The proof of that unique quality of love is the fact that while in human experience as Calvin puts it, 'it is a very rare occurrence indeed among men that any should die for a righteous man, although this may occasionally happen; but even if we admit that this may happen, none will be found willing to die for the ungodly, as Christ did.'

It is surely following Calvin that John Murray plays down any distinction between the righteous and the good man, as other scholars also do. It is clear why: the great contrast is between what men at their best might do and what God does at man's worst! That is certainly the point being made, and the contrast is huge and endless in its implications. Nonetheless, it seems to me that there is no need to ignore the distinction between the right and the good man since it is there in the text. It is also a fact of life that there can be a substantial human distinction between what a coldly correct righteous man might do and what a man of ripe and gracious character would do. Why, we often see this in our Lord's dealing with pharisaical souls! Of course the proportions of the gap between the two men (righteous and good) and that between them and what Almighty God does can hardly be exaggerated. It is while men were sinners, weak and helpless, and ungodly too, that Christ died for them. He took the initiative, and bridged the gulf which none but he could do, and none but he would think of doing. This is tremendous news! That God cares for sinners who have insulted him and rebelled against his goodness, as in Adam we all did, and cares for them sufficiently to send his Son to die for them ... that is love unimaginable. Yet it is true!

5:9-11 Christ's death as the specific shedding of his blood has not been mentioned since 3:25, and John Murray wonders whether there is here a fine distinction between the blood as justifying by faith and the blood as the ground of justification. Possibly it is the ground of justification that is in view here, since the beginning of the statement suggests a foundation upon which something is to be laid.

It is not until verse 10 that the life of Christ is mentioned, but verse 9 does make the beginning of a distinction between his blood and himself. This as we have already noted seems to be transitional, moving from justification itself to the fruit of it. If, then, justification is by his blood, something tremendous flows from that, namely that we are saved from God's wrath through him. Here we proceed from the blood that justifies to the person saved by the extinguishing of God's wrath. Not only is blood shed, but that which kept two beings apart – man's sin which incurred the wrath of God – is removed. Thus, as verse 10 tells us, reconciliation is effected.

You see what the apostle is straining every nerve to say: the ground of justification by the shedding of blood being accomplished, the relationship between the sinner and his God is re-established, and from God's side. We therefore move from the ground and the truth to the personalities involved. While we were yet sinners and therefore enemies of God because of his hostility to our sin, Christ died for us to reconcile us to God by the extinction of his wrath. Thus the Christ who became the ground of our reconciliation is now the one through whose resurrection life that reconciliation is enjoyed.

The movement of salvation from the death of Christ to his life shows how integral the death and resurrection of Jesus Christ are to our full salvation. This naturally leads to the joy of verse 11, because the Jesus whose blood effects our reconciliation himself rises from the dead to become our active Mediator as our great High Priest at the Father's right hand. This, then, is a whole salvation, justification pointing to its fruit – not only deliverance from sin, but entrance into the personal enjoyment of reconciliation. We are the Father's children, through the Son, our Mediator.

Death Through Adam, Life Through Christ

5:12 We must not read 5:12-21, or even verse 12 as a digression or parenthesis, although the argument of verse 12 is broken off and never completed (see the dash in *The New International Version* at the end of verse 12). Up to this point in his letter the apostle has been dealing with our salvation from sin through justification by faith in the blood of Jesus. He now goes on to show the nature of the solidarity which exists between Adam and his sin and all who sin in him.

The astonishing thing here is that the verse makes absolutely no reference whatsoever to the individual sins of any man beyond Adam. It is Adam's one sin that is imputed to us; no other sin is allowed to come into consideration. The reason for being so dogmatic about this will appear later, although it can be stated here that it is the application of our solidarity with Adam to our subsequent solidarity with Christ which the apostle intends to bring out. Leon Morris has a clarifying statement on this whole passage: 'The one man and his sin and the one Saviour and his salvation are critical to the discussion.' It is wonderful indeed when we realise that we are saved solely because we are bound up in solidarity with Christ's manhood.

Before Christ came into our lives, we were solidly implicated with Adam and with his sin as the head of our race. We belonged to his world of sin, which is totally at variance with what God intended for man, although he foresaw it and has made all provision against it. The whole Adamic framework of human life from the Fall is therefore such a disaster that it must be dispensed with and set aside, so that another order of humanity may take its place. Since the Adamic order is headed up in the one man Adam, it is he and his whole order of manhood which must be disposed of, and another Man sought to establish a new order of humanity absolutely free from the bondage and contamination of sin.

This other new Man is Christ. We are therefore now concerned with the radical exchange of humanities, that of Christ's for and instead of Adam's.

Sin came into the world through one individual man, Adam. Our relationship with him in that sin is so solid that we inherit his sinful nature, being conceived in sin and brought forth in iniquity (Ps. 51:5). We all continue to sin because we are descended from him. But it is not with these individual sins that the apostle is concerned here, but rather with our solidarity with Adam in his one sin. What Paul is really saying in verse 12 is that there has only been one sin to ruin the human race, and we are as much involved in that one sin as Adam was: we sin not only after Adam, but in Adam.

Paul says 'in Adam all die' (1 Cor. 15:22). Obviously everyone does not believe that; we only inherit sin from Adam, it is contended. But that does not do justice to what the apostle proceeds to unfold in the following verses. It is from this platform in verse 12, namely that we all sinned solidly in Adam, that he goes on to his argument in verses 13 and 14 to show historically how God has dealt with our sin in Adam.

5:13-14 Sin was in the world from the Fall, and death reigned through sin from Adam to Moses because the whole of mankind was vitally implicated in Adam's one disastrous sin. Mankind's individual sins during that period could not be imputed to them because there was no explicit law against them until God gave Moses the law (cf. 4:15). Yet death reigned during that period by virtue of mankind's solidarity with Adam in his one all-pervading and all-incriminating sin. Thus, although men could not be accused of their own sins since there was no law against them then, they were condemned by virtue of the fact that death reigned because of their solidarity with Adam in his one sin.

This solidarity of Adam and mankind in his one original sin because of our federal union with him is not easy for some to grasp and others to accept; but James Philip in his excellent commentary on Romans uses two illustrations to make the point clear. The first is biblically based. When David challenged Goliath to a duel before the armies of the Philistines and Israel, it was understood that a victory for either man was a victory for the whole army and nation (cf. 1 Sam. 17). The nations were 'solid' with their warrior representative. The other illustration drawn from *The Confession of Faith* says of our first parents: 'They being the root of all mankind, the guilt of this sin was imputed, and the same death in sin and corrupted nature conveyed to all their posterity, descending from them by ordinary generation' (VI.3). The point is that the root, trunk and branches of a tree are a single entity; they belong together as one. The reign of sin from Adam to Moses was not on account of the actual sins of mankind subsequent to Adam (although they inherited the propensity for sin from him). It was grounded in Adam's one sin only, imputed to them in solidarity with him.

That is why Adam is a type or pattern of Christ for, if we may anticipate verse 19, just as by Adam's one act of disobedience the many were made sinners, so by the one act of Jesus Christ's obedience the many are made righteous.

5:15 Paul now proceeds to develop his comparison of Adam with Christ. Adam is the type or pattern, Christ is the anti-type. He begins with the negative: 'the gift is not like the trespass', and goes on to the 'how much more' of God's grace that came by one man, Jesus Christ.

The freely-given gift is, of course, justification. By it we are declared by God to be righteous. The comparison of the gift with the trespass demonstrates that the gift is absolutely superlative. Adam's one sin led to the death of many through the imputation of his guilt and the subsequent reign of death from him to Moses. By contrast the gift of God's grace which came by Jesus Christ abounded and overflowed in excess.

The tragic disaster of Adam's sin has appalling repercussions for mankind. But the gift of God by the grace of Jesus Christ overflows so superabundantly that, for all the parallels between Adam and Christ, the gift and the trespass are as unlike as any contrast could possibly be – black versus white, light versus darkness, death versus life, heaven versus hell.

That these two acts, typologically similar and standing in juxtaposition to one another – Adam over against Christ – should issue in such diametrically opposite results is, of course, not surprising. Since the one act was so heinous and dire in its universal consequences and the other so gracious, glorious and wonderful, it takes the uttermost extremes of thought and word to describe the contrast. But there is this balance between them: the one answers the other – and in the most glorious, unimaginable way!

5:16 The next comparison also commences with the negative. The gift of justification by grace is not like (the result of) the one man's sin.

The one sin, in all its far-reaching heinousness and by itself alone, brought judgment to condemnation. But the gift of justification is so expansive in its overwhelming mercy and grace that it takes into account what dare not be considered until now, namely the actual sins of men which, alas, followed the one sin imputed to mankind. Justification, then – God's declaration of our righteousness by faith alone, whose ground is undoubtedly our absolution from the guilt of participation in Adam's one sin – takes into consideration every sin a man has committed. We may therefore rejoice in complete freedom from the guilt, penalty and shame of them all.

Many wisps of gospel hymns run through one's mind here, all expressing the point of William Booth's great hymn, 'O boundless salvation' whose second verse is:

My sins they are many, their stains are so deep,
And bitter the tears of remorse that I weep;
But useless is weeping, thou great crimson sea,
Thy waters can cleanse me, come roll over me.

Another began,

The mistakes of my life have been many,
The sins of my heart have been more,
And I scarce can see for weeping,
But I'll enter the open door.

And again:

My sins rose as high as a mountain,
They all disappeared in the Fountain;
He wrote my name down for a palace and crown,
Bless His dear Name, I'm free!

Not the most exalted of versification! – but it indicates something of the wonder of having all one's sins forgiven!

5:17 In verse 17 we have a similar argument to that in verses 15 and 16. The chief difference is that this verse takes us further along the road towards the positive results of justification – from death reigning over all mankind because they are embroiled in Adam's one sin, to believers reigning in life.

Paul goes over the ground once more: the one act of Adam's sin led to the reign of death over the world and upon mankind; but God's abundant provision of grace in the one act of Jesus Christ bestows on us fantastically much more, even the gift of righteousness. Thus we are enabled to reign in life everlasting, through him. Reigning grace! What an expression! And what an experience!

But the two arms of the proposition are not equal. While it is death which reigns in the one, it is not life that reigns in the other. Rather, in the latter it is the persons who receive the abundant provision of grace and the gift of righteousness who reign in life. In the one, the person is the victim of death which is reigning; but in the other, it is not life that is reigning, but the person who is reigning – in life. This speaks of a transfer from victimhood to a regal revelling in the lavish fruits of justification.

The abundant (indeed, overflowing) oceans of grace are characterised specifically as co-incident with the gift of righteousness, and this must imply far more than mere exoneration. This is not merely a being cleared of penalty, guilt and shame. The gift of justification (as in verse 16) is one thing, but the gift of righteousness must be a donation of that quality of righteousness which God is, and which he is able to bestow on those destined for his favour. To be reigning in life with the gift of righteousness suggests such a command of all that is good as to fill the soul with sheer ecstasy and delight, opening up as it does the way to endless blessing, in which the notion of eternal beatitude is far from absent – bliss indeed!

5:18-19 We note that the form 'just as' which we first saw at verse 12 is resumed at verses 18 and 19, whether a link-up is seen between these verses or not. The 'So then', or 'Consequently', indicates that there is now a summing up of what has been said from verse 12. It is stated with remarkable clarity and succinctness. Just as one trespass led to condemnation for all men, so the result of one act of righteousness was justification, which brings life to all men.

The vital matter here is to see that the 'all men' in the second part of the verse cannot be identical to the 'all men' of the first part. All men are condemned, but not all men are saved. The second 'all' is governed by the justification which is in Christ. In verse 19 the one act of Adam which made all men sinners is now characterised as disobedience; whereas Christ's one act is characterised as obedience to the will of the Father in the shedding his precious blood. The result is that many are constituted as righteous, for we are not merely declared by God to be righteous, but he so regards us, otherwise justification would not be unto life.

All this is still in the realm of justification, not sanctification, so that being constituted righteous does not refer to any subjective righteousness that we may think we have, but solely to how God regards us. We are still in the realm of what Christ does *for* us, not yet in the sanctificationary realm of what he does *in* us.

5:20-21 Paul returns to Moses here and to the fact that sin and death reigned from Adam to Moses all because of Adam's one dreadful act. But with the coming of Moses the law was added. Mankind could now be convicted by law of their actual transgressions and sins as well as of their complicity in Adam's one fateful act. And the apostle adds, 'Does this lead to complications, since man is now additionally condemned?' Can the grace of God in the justification of the sinner who is implicated in Adam's one awful act extend to that increased condemnation?

Triumphantly the apostle concludes the chapter. Where sin abounds and overflows, grace all the more and with far greater superfluity exceeds, in order to reign through the accomplishment of the righteousness of the believer. This ensures for him nothing less than eternal life through Jesus Christ our Lord. What a glorious climax! Grace not only reigning, but superseding and transcending all that the law could muster to voice its condemnation of our many actual transgressions and sins.

These last verses give an impression of the grace of God as a great flight of reigning love soaring far above all that could ever straiten or tether the human spirit. It has received the gift of God's righteousness for eternal life, and nothing on earth or in heaven or hell can alter it. Grace reigns unto everlasting life. Hallelujah!

CHAPTER SIX

Dead to Sin, Alive in Christ

6:1 Verses 20 and 21 ended chapter 5 on a magnificent note, namely that where sin abounded by the introduction into the human situation of the Mosaic law, grace overflowed all the more through the righteousness secured by Jesus Christ. Thus reigning sin is utterly overwhelmed by reigning grace. This has been wrought by the substitution of Christ's manhood for that of sinful Adam, so that those who belonged to sinful Adam now belong by faith to Jesus Christ.

The thought, therefore, that grace is able to overwhelm sin so powerfully – even where sin has increased – now leads the fertile mind of the apostle Paul inspired by the Holy Spirit, to discern an argument which opposers might put forward. The more sin is manifested, the more grace is called for and available in the divine storehouse to deal with it. On the surface, this appears to be an argument for increasing sin so that greater grace might be required to deal with it. God forbid! Paul exclaims. Far be it from the Almighty to be in the business of increasing sin – whatever grace might be manifested in the situation.

There is, of course, no doubt that it is the emergence of sin in the world which the Almighty has used sinlessly to manifest grace to a degree which man could never have known but for the sin of Lucifer and Adam. But sin is always sin to God and must be seen to be a disastrous interposition. Our aim in Christ must be to have as little of it as possible – indeed, that it might be done away – lest we become the manufacturers of sin for the purpose of the production of superior grace.

The inherent contradiction in such a cunning argument must now be exposed. For the inspired apostle this is simple: even if more sin would lead to more grace, how could those transposed from the world of sinful Adam into the world of Jesus Christ go on sinning, even as a supposed policy of increasing grace? This would not merely employ sin and Satan to serve God's grace (which God is able to do sinlessly); it would involve his approval of sin in order that it might be used towards the end of greater grace. This is diabolical reasoning, Paul says.

The one thing that must be clear is that God's use of sin and evil is never by deliberate design, as if he were the Author of it – else he would be a devil himself! – but by permission, even while he loathes the sin that has intruded into his universe. God must always be against sin, however much he uses it for his own purposes, or else we have nothing less than a collusion between God and the devil, which is the most monstrous thought, surely, that could occur to man!

Thus Paul ruthlessly exposes the demonic nature of such an argument. But what is the ultimate proof of its invalidity? It is that Jesus died to deal with sin and Satan, and that finally, so that whatever use God still makes of sin is on the understanding that sin is to be done away with for ever. Furthermore, those whose sins are covered by the blood of Jesus Christ are also in the same act initiated into the death of Jesus Christ in order that they might be raised with him to a life of holiness.

6:2-5 We return to the argument hitherto hidden in Paul's ingenious unfolding of the two races of Adam and Christ. What God has done for us in the substitution of Christ as our justification in place of Adam as our condemnation is the seed plot from which the bud and blossom of a fuller harvest now appears. Christ, in place of Adam, not only works justification but also sanctification. For what Christ has done for us is now ours as a gift.

This gift is in fact Christ himself by the Spirit in the power of his death and resurrection. If we have received by the Holy Spirit as an indwelling gift the death and resurrection of Jesus Christ, in him we are therefore dead to sin and alive to God. Being dead to sin, how can we continue in sin? It is a complete contradiction of all that has been done and given to us.

But how did we die to sin? Paul answers in terms of our initiation into Christ. He had no need to die to sin on his own behalf, for he was sinless. He died for us. We in turn were baptised vitally into Christ as the one who died to sin on our behalf. Therefore those baptised into him are baptised into that same death to sin. To emphasise how important it is to grasp that the death of Christ to sin was an elemental reality, Paul adds that we were therefore buried with him through baptism. That baptism (whatever the mode with regard to water baptism) is a vital baptism by the Holy Spirit.

It follows, therefore, that if Christ who died to our sin (that we might follow him into that experience by his Spirit) was also raised from the dead, then we must follow him into his risen life also. It would be incredible that we should follow him by baptismal initiation into the one but not into the other. This we do by the glory of the Father's love, in order that we may live a new life in him. We are risen with him, having died with him to sin. We are therefore united with him in both his death (to our sin) and his resurrection (on behalf of our resurrection).

The important thing to realise here is that Jesus Christ did not need to go through any of this for himself. He, the sinless One, had no such need: it was all for us. It would, therefore, once again be incredible if we were not united or, as John Murray says, 'grown together' with him in both experiences.

This is too good not to be true!

6:6-7 Paul goes on to discuss further implications of our union with Christ which are so inherent in what has been said already that he affirms 'we know' them. But exactly what it is 'we know' has to be explained. It is that in union with Christ in his death and resurrection our old self, the totality of the old nature which became susceptible to Adam's sin and went astray from God in disobedience, has been crucified with him with a radical finality which leaves no room for thinking it remains. It is gone, just as surely as Christ actually died bodily on the cross.

The old nature is called 'the body of sin' because it is in the body that we sin. But the word 'body' does not exclude the spiritual element in sin, since it all takes place in the human body. It is destroyed that it may have no power over us to enslave us to sin.

Now, knowing ourselves, we are at once bound to question the radicalness of such a statement. We are not absolutely free from sin. Is Paul using a verbal fiction here, to try to impress us, since he surely knows that we still sin even though we are united to Christ? Not at all, as we shall see abundantly later.

It is necessary here to pre-introduce the fact of what *The Confession of Faith* calls the 'remnants of corruption', the dregs or residue of sin which remain in us after the body of sin has been destroyed (as may remain in a vessel which has been emptied of its contents). The radicalness and finality of our break with the old nature, as the body of sin, is proved by the fact that if we have died with Christ to our former sin-dominated nature, we must necessarily be freed from it. Its rule over us exists no more.

One of the further proofs that this is so will be seen shortly with the positive effects of our resurrection with Christ, which replaces the old desires and aims and ambitions with new desires and new purposes. This is a test of the reality of Christ having come into our lives. If he does not make an immediate difference, whatever struggles ensue, the implication must be that nothing as radical as the new birth has taken place. Anything as radical and final as a death is bound to make a whole world of difference, although it still leaves subsidiary problems to be solved. It is important that we honestly face these, as Paul makes us do with his rhetorical question at 6:1. As we grapple with them we will in due course come to a more satisfying understanding of what has been done, not only for us, but in us.

6:8-12 At verse 8 the apostle is still concentrating on our union with Christ in his death and resurrection; but now the thrust is more towards the resurrection.

The resurrection of Jesus Christ was no mere revivification of his former, mortal life (as in the cases of Lazarus and the son of the widow of Nain). Rather it is a translation and transformation into indestructible eternal life. This is the first miracle of the new creation and the beginning of Christ's own kingdom. He cannot die again, since death no longer has mastery over him; it is done with, in his case, for ever. His death is final and brings to an end the dominion of sin once and for all. As the new Man he has crushed it out of existence. The life he lives thereafter is the immortal and eternal resurrection life of his new Manhood, which he lives to God.

This being so, the same applies with complete and final application to those for whom he died and rose again. Incorporated into Christ by union with him in his death and resurrection we are to reckon ourselves also to be dead to sin and alive to God.

This is surely the most important crux of the Christian life – not only for what it says, but for what is not said until later. If in Christ we are dead to sin and alive to God why should sin remain in us any longer?

The beginnings of the answer actually come in the next verse (v.12). By the death of Christ the reign of sin is ended for those who are baptised into his Name (cf. v.3). But that is not to say that sin is dead in us! We know by bitter experience that it is not so. There are still some 'remnants of corruption' in our hearts as long as we are in these mortal bodies. Nevertheless, by the new birth the power is given to us not to let sin reign in our bodies so as to obey its evil desires (v.12).

6:13-14 The meaning of verse 12 is now amplified. Since it is in our mortal bodies that we sin, the members of these bodies must no longer be dominated by sin. The wording of verse 13 is striking: it says, 'Neither be presenting your members as weapons of unrighteousness to sin.' The word 'weapons' is often translated 'instruments' but this conceals the first hint of the conflict now upon us as we approach the truth which will be expounded in chapter seven. The mood of the verb is imperative ('be presenting'), commanding the believer not to allow the members of his body – eye, hand, or foot – to be employed as weapons of unrighteousness in the service of sin. That is to say, we must not play the enemy's game and fight battles against the new nature – as David did when he deserted Israel to fight on the Philistines' side (1 Sam. 27:1). Treason!

There can be no going back to the old ways: on that way lies sin, sorrow and, alas, an embarrassed entrance to heaven! (See 1 Cor. 3:15).

The reason why turning back to sin after having been united to Christ in his death and resurrection is unthinkable is that sin has been mastered once and for all. The believer is no longer under its servitude but under the freedom of grace. Indeed, it is this very freedom within the realm of grace which tempts the mind to think of libertarianism; and that is what the apostle proceeds to tackle in the second half of the chapter.

Slaves to Righteousness

6:15-19 Remember that Paul, having shown at the end of chapter five that grace is ready and willing to overwhelm sin however great its increase, commences chapter six with a question which would occur to many a thinking mind: If grace is able to overwhelm sin, does this not imply that more sin will lead to the manifestation of more grace – with all the libertarian implications of such an equation?

The apostle answers by stressing the finality of the change wrought in us by union with Christ in his death and resurrection: we cannot go on sinning for that would be to prove false to our renewed nature.

Paul has declared that we must not yield our members to sin since in Christ we have died to sin and its servitude and now live in the world of grace not of law. But the thoughtful person might say: Since we are under grace, not law, let us then do as we like and sin if we choose! 'Perish the thought!' is the apostle's reaction. To do so would prove that you were still enslaved to sin which leads to death (and the evil master of sin), and not to that obedience whose fruit is righteousness. For Jesus said, 'Every one who sins is a slave of sin' (Jn. 8:34); and 'No servant can serve two masters; either he will hate the one, and love the other; or he will be devoted to the one and despise the other. You cannot serve both God and Money' (Lk. 16:13).

Our thankfulness to God for you, says Paul to the Romans, is because although formerly you were slaves to sin, you have been set free from it, wholeheartedly to obey the form of teaching to which you were entrusted (v.17). But what is that form of teaching? It is the body of doctrine which is to be gathered from a close and thorough study of the Bible, which in view of our new nature, instructs us on biblical principles of conduct.

At this point (v.18) the apostle feels it necessary to say that in speaking of slavery and emancipation he is using understandable terms as a concession to human frailty so that they may be in no doubt as to his meaning. Paul sees our human body as under either malign or benign slavery; under sin with its dire consequences, or under that world of grace whose economy is that of willing obedience to the righteousness which is the essence of biblical truth.

6:20-23 The argument here takes a curious turn, the point of which is found in verse 21. To be a slave of sin is to be free from the constraints of righteousness to do whatever one likes. This the worldling would think is the ideal for life. But let us ask those who have pursued such a course: What does it produce? Was there any lasting benefit from a life of 'glorious' lawlessness giving vent to all one's passions and free rein to all one's faculties and propensities without restraint? Ask the ruined soul on the verge of suicide, all his powers wasted and he himself exhausted and reduced to a shell of his former self. Nothing but shame ensues from such a course, and in the end unless it is halted, ignominious death.

However, rescued in time and set free from the bondage of sin and having become a willing and free slave of God, the benefits are enormous and infinite, even holiness of life, which includes true wholeness, with the eventual end eternal life. Talk about freedom! Who is free? The person who, having broken loose from the wise bounds of reasonable restraint, finds himself in bondage to several kinds of ruin of body and soul? No; the hard-earned wages of that way of life is to find oneself on the brink of shameful and despicable death. But to be set free from the hard-won bondage of sin, with its ruin and endless despair, in order to receive the gift of God is to enter the Elysian Fields of life in Jesus Christ our Lord.

The contrast is thus complete. There can be no comparison. It is the difference between a living death, and a life of endless, infinite and luxurious satisfactions with an abundance of all kinds of healthy and useful fruit, all of which abides.

CHAPTER SEVEN

An Illustration From Marriage

7: 1-6 Before the apostle continues, he makes appeal to what, by now, his readers ought to have known. At 6:14 he declared that those who are in Christ by death and resurrection are no longer under law but are now under the canopy of grace. They are therefore set free within the realm of willing obedience to enjoy the fruits of righteousness.

They are in fact not only dead to sin, as 6:11 has declared, but are also dead to the law and therefore free from bondage to its constraints. For the law has authority over a man only as long as he is alive. When he is dead, the law ceases to have any jurisdiction over him whatsoever.

Paul then uses an illustration which has led to endless discussion. On the surface it seems simple, but it has to be handled with care. A married woman is bound to her husband only as long as he is alive. When he is dead, she is free from the binding constraint of that marriage. This being so, if she married another man while her husband was still alive she would be committing adultery. But after her husband is dead she is perfectly free to marry another.

Notice how the apostle applies this. It is not the law that is dead, but we that are dead to the law by our identification with Christ in his death; just as in 6:11 sin is not dead in us but we are dead to sin. Thus, being dead to both sin and the law, we are set free from both bondages to be married to another husband than the law, even Jesus Christ, who was raised from the dead in order that we might bring forth fruit to God.

Paul now goes over this again in the contrasting verses 5 and 6. He begins strikingly. When we were in the flesh (he means, when we were living under the influence of our fallen nature) the passions of our sins operating through the law in our members brought forth fruit for death. But now that we are discharged from the law, having died to that in which we were held fast, we serve in newness of life and not in the oldness of the letter of the law.

Struggling With Sin

7:7-13 The next question, after all that has been said about the law is: Is the law sin, since we needed to die to it as well as to sin? Ah, no! Dead to sin is one thing, but dead to the law quite another. We are dead to sin because sin is a thoroughly bad thing. But dead to the law is vastly different, for the law of God cannot be bad. It is the misuse of the law by sin which calls for our death to it.

We must be grateful to the law for making us aware of sin, for apart from the strictures of the law we would have known neither sin nor that we were sinners (see 5:13). Lustful though I was in the flesh, I did not know it until the law said, 'Thou shalt not covet', and then I realised that this was what I was doing in exercising my coveting, lustful nature.

But this was not the fault of the law convicting me of my sin, but of sin itself, which took occasion from the strictures of the law to work in me all kinds of rebellious evil desires. This means that apart from the law, sin (for all its hideous reality) is dead—as far as I am concerned. In that sense I was alive before the law came (see 5:13 and 14 again), but when the law in the form of the commandment came, sin revived, and I became aware of it. Because of it, I 'died', becoming aware that I was in fact 'dead in trespasses and sins' (Eph. 2:1). Thus the commandment, which God ordained to be a guide to life, I found to lead to death.

We need to pause here to consider the statement in verse 10, that the law was ordained to life. The first use of the law of God given to Moses at Sinai was to offer life to the people of Israel recently saved by the blood of the passover Lamb sprinkled on their door posts. The law was unto life for saved people; it was sin that turned it into an aggravation of sin, and, as verse 11 says, deceived by instigating rebellion to its strictures.

The law therefore slew Paul in the sense of making him aware of sinfulness. But that is not the fault of the law, which is only doing its God-appointed work, as holy, just, and good. We cannot blame the law for the fact that what is good became death to us. Sin is the guilty party. By the coming of the law, however, sin comes to be seen as exceedingly sinful, using what is good to work death. This, of course, is all in keeping with the cunning malignity and perversity of the devil, as we shall see!

7:14-16 There is no doubt that verses 7-13 look back to the pre-regenerate state, recalling how sin operated to enlist the law to our undoing. However, the remnants of sin within us (regenerate although we are) are still as ready as ever to use the law to incite us to sin. Therefore the whole question of sin and the law has to be sorted out in order to protect our regenerate life.

The first thing to be noted, which has already been hinted at, is that the law is spiritual. It was given not only as a way of life for the Lord's people but primarily as a transcript of the character of Almighty God. 'But', says the apostle, 'I am unspiritual, sold under sin'. Why does he say that now, and what does he mean? Some think that such strong expressions must refer to his unregenerate state; but no! It is simply a fact that he is a fallen creature (who had been sold to the devil, if you like!) and the remnants of corruption still lurk in his mortal being.

As the apostle proceeds with his argument about the tensions between the old life and the new it is clear that he is referring to the struggles of a regenerate man. Sometimes he is even bewildered as to who he is. The tension between who we are now and who we once were – and the remaining dregs of that old life – can be exceedingly perplexing.

The truth is that, for all the tension and struggles he endures, Paul betrays himself as on the side of the new life and not on that of the old, which he obviously deplores. The second half of verse 15 and verse 16 make this clear. Despite the increasing intensity of the language as the apostle proceeds towards the climax of his argument at the end of chapter seven, the truth that these are the struggles of a regenerate man becomes clearer, until there can be no doubt as to the reality of the situation: the attainment of true holiness is an uphill battle all the way.

7:17-20 Verse 17 with verse 20 are a crux in the apostle's argument. He recognises that he is prone to do what he knows is not right and which he does not want to do. He is, therefore, obliged to conclude that the tendency to sin no longer belongs, but by the blessed work of Christ within has become an alien and interloper in a life which has died to sin and is now alive to God.

This is a tremendous discovery. But the thought instantly occurs: If it is no longer I who am doing these things but sin which still indwells me, then am I not responsible? Oh yes I am! We have been commanded in 6:13 not to let sin reign in our mortal bodies to obey its evil desires. We must not yield the members of our bodies to sin, but yield ourselves once and for all to God and not allow ourselves to come under bondage to sin, 'for sin shall not be your master because you are not under law but under grace' (6.14).

Paul then goes on to discuss what this means for him now. In doing so, we must see that what he still calls his 'sinful nature' (NIV) or his 'flesh' has been demoted and reduced to 'remnants of corruption'. We must therefore not accord to it so high a profile that it assumes itself to be a life competing with our new life in Christ. The old is gone, since it is crucified with Christ; therefore what Paul here calls his 'flesh' or 'sinful nature' is nothing more than the remnants or dregs which admittedly still remain and lurk within him.

Nevertheless we must not think of ourselves as born again with two natures. The old, 'sinful nature' (NIV, Greek *sarx*, flesh) is gone and we are dead to sin, although sin is not dead within us. Therefore, as verses 17 and 20 say, what has been demoted from being our entire former nature and is reduced to a mere intrusive force or power (even if Paul calls it the 'flesh') must never be dignified with any name which suggests that it is anything other than an objectionable intrusion into a new life to be yielded to God.

At the same time, Paul finds this evil force so strong that despite the command not to let sin reign within him (6:13) it takes over and causes him to do what, as newborn in Christ, he does not want to do. The fact that he does not want to do those sinful things is proved by verse 19, and creates a great dilemma for him.

At this point, it may be helpful to advance the theory discussed elsewhere, that the struggle with inbred sin, now reduced to 'remnants of corruption', would seem to begin to take on the proportions and magnitude of a tussle with a greater than human force, even that of the enemy of souls himself. But that would take at least another reading to unfold.

7:21 The sum of these verses from verse 14 is simply that what was formerly our sinful nature, although still designated as the 'flesh', is no longer our true personality but an incubus attached to us. It has been set aside by divine action and by the coming of our new nature in Christ. It has become, as we have described it elsewhere 'an old, unwanted baggage ready to be put out and taken away in the morning when Christ comes in power and glory'.

But, as we have already hinted, there is a growing sinister element about this evil appendage, which, as the apostle's argument proceeds, takes on an increasingly menacing tone. While it no longer represents the true self born of God but an evil encumbrance, it does seem to take on something of a personality until in these later verses of chapter 7 it becomes a raging foe waging war against our life in Christ.

Although the devil as a personality is not mentioned in this passage, evil is mentioned in verse 21. We are therefore bound to see that there is at least a sinister shadow of the evil one cast upon our lives, and it would seem impossible not to detect the smell of brimstone about the working of this demoted 'flesh'. From this, one is obliged to conclude that Satan is lurking in the background, although not named and frontally dealt with, as he is in Paul's instruction on spiritual warfare in Ephesians 6:10-18. A new battle now engages the soul consecrated to Christ, since what is hiding in the folds of this sinful encumbrance is the power of Satan himself. His malign office is to stir up the remnants of our old sinful nature and so reinforce their power that they grow threateningly stronger than they have ever been before. We feel we are getting worse, not better, and thus the reality, freedom and power of our new nature in Christ is challenged.

Read verses 21-23, and see if this does not illuminate the tussle described by the apostle here. As *Towards Spiritual Maturity* puts it: '*sin is characterised in increasingly personal terms*'. In 6:14 it is dominion; from 6:16-23 it is a tyrannical master, a slave-driver; in 7:8 and 11 it is an unscrupulous and wily opportunist standing ready to use what is good (the Law) for its own evil purposes; in 7:13, 17, 20, and 23 it is a deadly enemy warring against the new man in Christ.'

We need to see that although Satan is not mentioned here by name, he has to be reckoned with as reinforcing that which has been demoted to an appendage. So, by his hidden power lurking in the folds of the remnants of sin, he constitutes himself the third dimension of evil which can be dealt with only by the power of Christ's cross. On the basis, therefore, of Christ's victory over Satan we must first detect his horrid presence and nefarious activity, and then command him to go. Get thee behind me, Satan!

7:22-25 'When I want to do good, evil is right there'; and so we have characterised that evil as Satan lurking hiddenly in the folds of our remnant sinfulness, reinforcing its power phenomenally, so that because of our struggles we feel that we are growing worse not better. Are we truly regenerate? The proof that we are, and that the battle we are engaged in is that of our new Christ-born nature against what has been demoted from a nature to a power, is found in the fact that Paul says he delights in the law of God in his inner self. No unregenerate sinner could say that, which is incontestable proof that we are born again of God.

But this does not diminish the warfare, as we see in verse 23. It leads to such a cry of despair as would rend the heart, and so Paul shouts to high heaven: 'Who will deliver me from this body of death to which I am tied?' But notice that what was formerly the real, sinful self is now reduced, desecrated, and cursed as a most evil thing. But how then can it be so powerful as to master the power of the Christ within?

As Paul's answer makes plain, the truth is that this 'body of death' to which he is tied will remain as a horrid incubus as long as he is mortal: only death will completely deliver him from it. Consequently the apostle concludes this stirring chapter almost paradoxically with an acknowledgement that his regenerate condition on earth is this: with his sanctified mind he serves the Lord as a willing love-slave of God's holy and perfect law, but as far as this sinful incubus is concerned, it can only serve as a slave to the law or principle of sin.

The hidden truth in all this, which is found explicitly only in such a passage as Ephesians 6:10-18, is that while the sinful incubus of the remnants of corruption within us, the 'flesh', or dregs of the sinful nature, must remain with us while we are in this mortal body, the fact that this can be so malignly reinforced by Satan's hidden power must constantly be reckoned with. When we come to terms with this fact and bravely recognise that Satan is our deadly foe in the matter of sanctification, and that he has to be dealt with by faith in Christ's victory, we can come through to a measure of victory over him and so prevent him poking in the remnants of our sin. Thus we achieve a degree of peace in our daily lives which is quite wonderful.

CHAPTER EIGHT

Life Through the Spirit

8:1-4 The key to the understanding of chapter 8 is surely the significance of these words 'now no condemnation'. That there is no condemnation to those who are justified in Christ Jesus was made plain as early as 5:1. What other condemnation could the justified believer then suffer? Ah, it is one thing to be delivered from the guilt, shame and penalty of sin, but as the struggle enunciated in chapter seven makes plain, there are still lurking in the depth of the regenerate heart seeds or dregs or remnants of sin. These can arise to discomfit and even discountenance the believing soul – if he has not learned how to deal with them.

But as chapter seven has made out, these also have a remedy in Christ. It is that fact which is now stated, and in terms which show that no power whatsoever should incur for us a sense of condemnation, because we are now indwelt by Jesus Christ through the Spirit of God. He who is within us is greater than he who is in the world (1 Jn. 4:4) and is therefore capable of conquering every foe who can assail us. How are we so sure of this? Because the law (or principle) of the Spirit of life in Christ Jesus has made us free from the law (or principle) of sin and death.

But how can the Spirit of life in Christ Jesus be so powerful when we have seen how strong the power of sin's remnants still are within us? They took occasion from this confrontation by the holy law to incite us to fresh sin! But what the law could not do because of remnant sin within, God did! And he did it by sending his Son in the likeness or similitude of sinful flesh to condemn not only sins committed by the flesh, but the very nature of sin in its residue still lurking in the flesh.

The blessed result of that dual condemnation – of sin's power as well as its guilt – is that we are enabled to fulfil the law – not by looking to the law, but by looking to the almighty Spirit of God within us in whose power we are to walk.

If this, or what has gone before, still appears to be exceedingly complicated, we have the blessing of two lines from the hymn *Rock of Ages* by Augustus Montague Toplady who clinches the matter in one of the most succinct epigrams outside of Scripture:

> Be of sin the double cure,
> Cleanse me from its *guilt and power*.

8:5-10 By sending his own Son in the likeness of sinful flesh, to be sin for us (2 Cor. 5:21), God condemned sin in the flesh in order that the righteousness of the law might be fulfilled in us. This cannot be realised by walking according to the flesh and carnally looking to the law. Despite its holy nature, it has no power to help because of the flesh. Rather it is accomplished by walking according to the Spirit who is the Spirit of Jesus Christ who has fulfilled the law perfectly for us.

Paul therefore proceeds from verse 5 to show how radical this difference is. There are two lives. There is life according to the mind of the flesh, the old nature; and there is life according to the mind of the Spirit, the new nature in Christ. They are so different that the former, the mind of the flesh, is in fact death, whereas the mind of the Spirit is life and peace. But how is it that these two lives are so radically different? Because the fleshly mind is at enmity with God – and that can only lead to death – double death! Since that old nature is not subject to the holy law of God, nor ever can be, those who are in the flesh cannot possibly please God. Yes, but how can we know which life we are in? By this infallible criterion: if the Spirit of God dwells in us, we are not living a flesh dominated life, but a life empowered by the Spirit.

This is the only test. Either we possess the Spirit of Christ, or we do not; and if we do not have the Spirit of Christ dwelling in us, we do not belong to Christ at all.

8:10 Paul has already said at verse 6 that the mind of the fleshly nature is death. He now returns to the theme to say that if Christ by his Spirit is within us our body is dead because of sin. That can only mean that sin has sown the seed of mortality in our natural bodies so that our inevitable destiny is death. This has already been stated in different language both at 5:12 and 6:23. But that is only half the story. The body is destined to death because of sin; but Christ is in us, and Christ in us cannot be destined to death; for his Spirit is life (not 'alive', NIV) within us!

Yes, but how does Christ's Spirit come to be dwelling in us? Because Jesus wrought righteousness on the cross for us. Many believe the word *pneuma* (spirit) in verse 10 refers to our human spirit which is 'alive' because of righteousness. Even *The New International Version* renders it with a lower case 's', as 'your spirit'. This is nonsense. How could our human spirit be righteousness if Christ had not wrought righteousness for us by his finished work? Christ's Holy Spirit is life within us because of his work of righteousness accomplishing our redemption. It is Christ who is our righteousness, and therefore his Spirit is life within us just because (and only because) Christ wrought righteousness for us by his redemption.

There is a sense in which Christ, even dwelling subjectively in our mortal breasts cannot surrender the objectivity of his unique work. He is still the regnant Christ although dwelling by his Holy Spirit in our breasts. He retains his sovereignty, even there.

8:11 Twice in this verse the Father is referred to as raising the dead. It is, first, the Spirit of the Father who raised Jesus from the dead who now dwells in you. And it is he, the Father, who raised Christ from the dead who, at the general resurrection, will also quicken your mortal bodies ('mortal' because, although still living, given over to death). The Father will do this by the agency of the Holy Spirit who is even now dwelling within your mortal bodies.

Here then is the assurance that, at the return of Christ, the three Persons of the blessed Trinity working as One will effect for all true believers what the Father and the Holy Spirit accomplished in the resurrection of Jesus himself. This is fully set forth in the great resurrection chapter, 1 Corinthians 15, and also in Ephesians 1:17-23. We shall have bodies like Christ's resurrection body. The guarantee of that is the fact that we have the Spirit of this same Jesus dwelling in our mortal bodies now (see Eph. 1:13-14).

8:12-13 Paul therefore returns to his practical argument in verse 12. If this is all true, then our debt and obligation is not to what is past, to the former, totally sinful condition of our fleshly nature. Rather, as verse 13 goes on to say, it is to the Holy Spirit already dwelling in our regenerate breasts.

The reason for this is stated, namely that the end of living according to the flesh is death in the fullest sense, not only mortal but eternal death. On the other hand, if, drawing upon the power of the indwelling Holy Spirit, you put to death the practices that belong to a body destined to death, you shall live – that is gain in the fullest sense of the word – eternally.

This is a matter of mortifying what Christ has already slain. That paradox may seem too contradictory to make sense, but such mortification is still necessary because of these remnants which remain after the old nature has been put to death. While we are in our mortal bodies there are still those dregs which have to be dealt with. Paul says in 1 Corinthians 15:31, 'I die daily.' At that point he is referring to 'deaths' which come upon him through others; but his words may also be applied, as we are sure the apostle would admit, to mortifications to self, sin, and Satan as he operates through the temptations of the remnants of his fleshly nature.

8:14-16 The test is this: if in our mortal life we are led by the Spirit of God and are enabled to put to death the dregs of our guilty past and mortify the deeds that belong to that former sinful body, then we prove ourselves to be sons of God. All such are sons of God; and the beneficial effects of that are now unfolded in verses 15-17.

The Spirit we receive which makes us sons of God is not a Spirit of bondage which inspires in us an attitude of dread towards God our Maker, as if we were shut up to the demands and threats of the law (cf. Heb. 12:18-24). It is none other than the Holy Spirit himself who is the Spirit of adoption, or of 'the placing as sons'.

Strictly speaking it is the Father who adopts, but his willing Agent in the adoption is undoubtedly the Holy Spirit, and it is he who, working within us, authenticates the 'natural' cry of the son to the Father: 'Abba' – practically the first cry of an infant!

Verse 16 goes on to explain how this works. It is the Holy Spirit himself who co-witnesses with our human spirit that we are 'children' of God. The Greek word 'children' (*teknon*) is different from 'son' (*huios*). Translated into Scots it is 'bairns'(= born ones). This union of the Holy Spirit and our regenerated spirit is also mentioned by Paul in 1 Corinthians 6:17 where he says 'he who is joined to the Lord is one spirit with him'. The Holy Spirit, therefore, together with our regenerated human spirit bears this common witness to the fact that we are indeed children (born ones) of God.

8:17 The practical conclusion of this amazing relationship takes us into realms so high that it might turn our heads; but by the end of the verse we are down again to earth, and yet instantly away to glory! The high privilege of our relationship with God, being the creatures we are, held in tension with what it is going to cost us to gain our inheritance in glory by following our Lord into our share of his cross (Col. 1:24), so taxes our thoughts that there cannot be a complacent inch in us anywhere. If we are born ones – see how he goes beyond the image of 'adoption' – then we are heirs, heirs of God, since he is our Father.

It seems so logical, and yet to think of ourselves as royal children of God who were so rebellious (until he seized us and took us over) is so astonishing that it sounds like a fairy tale. But it is not. It is absolute truth, the reality of which will be proved to us one day in experience so transcendent that human language can scarcely contain it. Indeed it takes the book of the Revelation to try, since even Paul confesses, 'Eye has not seen...' (1 Cor. 2:9)!

'Heirs of God' is now explained in terms of this other amazing thought that we become the younger brothers and sisters of Christ, and our heirdom is held jointly with him. That we should be spoken of in the same breath as our Redeemer is astonishing – even if we remind ourselves that we never partake of his deity. Yet, as Peter says, we partake of his divine nature (2 Pet. 1:4). This is heady truth, and doubtless that is why the apostle felt that it had to be matched with the corollary and other side of the coin, the test of our sonship, which is sharing his sufferings.

The truth is, that sharing Christ's sufferings is the only way to share his glory. That is a very profound thought, and although we must not seek morbidly to look for causes of suffering and self-consciously inflict pain on ourselves, we should know that taking up our cross – our share in his sufferings (see Col. 1:24 again, which needs to be pondered deeply!) – is something which is bound to come our way in the ordinary course of our Christian duty. Only it may be so painful and unattractive when we are faced with it that we may not see it, or want to see it, as our blessed Lord calling us along that road. God help us!

Future Glory

8:18 In his monumental commentary on Romans, John Murray suggests that, in the remaining verses of our chapter, there are three grounds of encouragement to support and console the children of God in their sufferings for Christ's sake.

The first (vv.18-25) is the great disproportion between sufferings in this life and the weight of glory hereafter. The second ground (vv.26-27) is the help of the Holy Spirit to sustain us in our infirmity. The third (vv.28-30) is the consolation and assurance to be derived from the fact that all things work together for the good of those who love God. He adds with regard to verses 31-39 that 'This triumphant conclusion to the consolation unfolded in the preceding verses is, in Philippi's words, "the highest rung in the ladder of comfort which from verse 18 onward, writer, like reader, has been mounting".'

So to verse 18: our 'present suffering' is not merely the suffering of anyone's lifespan, but the entire suffering of the whole Christian age and era until Christ comes. When weighed against the glory which is then to be revealed, our suffering is not to be compared with it.

Of course we do not know the glory yet to be revealed, as Paul says ('Eye has not seen...' 1 Cor. 2:9) but the Spirit reveals it to us. And faith believes that the cost of all the suffering – that of Christ and his church – is such that the reward must be beyond all understanding, let alone comparison, to make it worth the Father's while to send his Son to save us at such a price.

The attitude of John to what was revealed to him in the Revelation shows that it was hardly possible for mortal man to support the glory revealed to him then, as to Moses, Isaiah, Daniel and Paul, earlier. They fall down speechless before it all, for the weight is too great to bear. Hence the need for new bodies to support not only what we shall see, but what we shall become. For the glory which shall be revealed towards us will actually reach us – that is to say, we shall share it. This is the difference between the glories revealed heretofore to those men of the past and what shall be revealed to us all then: we shall not only see it; we will become part of it.

8:19-21 It is surely consideration of the incomparable majesty of the glory to be revealed (described above) which makes the apostle declare that the creation (non-rational, animate and inanimate) is anxiously watching and waiting for the manifestation (apocalypse or unveiling) of the sons of God.

The 'manifestation' of which he speaks is the glorification of the saints in their resurrection bodies at the coming of Christ. But why is the creation waiting and longing so anxiously for this? Because by the Fall the natural creation was dragged unwillingly into ruin by man who had dominion over it (Gen. 1:26-28).

The creation thus defined had no part in the evil of the Fall, and was therefore made subject by it unwittingly to vanity, emptiness and futility. Thus creation is subject to man, and in the transformations promised at the coming of Christ the change of creation's condition must attend and wait upon that which will be wrought upon man, the crown of creation. Note that while neither 1 Corinthians 15:51-52 nor 1 Thessalonians 4:16 mentions creation, the suddenness of the coming of the Lord and the instantaneousness of the transformation described in these passages suggest the priority of man in resurrection.

The creation is subjected 'in hope', because God did not wipe out his fallen creation after the Fall. In fact, in imposing his judgmental will on man (Gen. 3:17-19) yet not destroying him, he naturally afforded the same hope to the creation under him. Thus the creation itself will be delivered from the slavery of its corruption into the liberty of the glory of the born ones of God – but after them. First man, then creation.

8:22-23 The fact that there is hope for the whole of creation – God being so merciful – is proved by our knowledge of the groaning, sighing, throbbing birth-pangs of its fallen condition. This is the 'sad music' which has attended the fallen existence of the natural universe in all its parts right up till now. It will continue until man has been changed. We thus see the prior importance of man, and creation's experience as attendant upon what will happen to him. That of course is not fully apparent now, because man lost his dominion over creation by the iniquity of the Fall.

While that loss is potentially recovered in Christ, the ignorant world of fallen men certainly does not know the power invested in Christ on behalf of his saints. Indeed it is doubtful if the saints themselves know the potential that is theirs now in respect of the beneficial dominion of the natural creation available to them, especially by the prayer of faith through their great High Priest, the Lord Jesus Christ. Consider our Lord's command of the wind and waves on the sea of Galilee, all in the interests of the welfare of man.

However, the groaning is not confined to the natural creation, and Murray sees a suggestion of surprise that it should be found also in the saints, who have the firstfruits of the Spirit. But it is because they have only the firstfruits of the Spirit that the groaning of the saints continues, as it does in Paul's words at 7:24, 'Wretched man that I am! who will rescue me from this body of death?' But this is followed by the immediate cry, 'Thanks be to God [for deliverance] through Jesus Christ our Lord!'

But that deliverance will come only with the return of Christ, when our full adoption as sons will take place by the putting together of risen bodies with immortal souls (cf. Eph. 1:13-14). Until then we groan because, as we are to see shortly (vv.26-27), the Spirit himself is groaning within us for our full redemption.

8:24-25 This whole argument concerning present, expectant groaning, especially of the saints, is brought to a climax by reference to hope. For in hope we were saved. Despite all that has happened to God's beautiful universe to spoil it and drag man in particular away from his Maker, God has not given up hope. This is already hinted at in Genesis 3:17-19. The image of God in man has been defaced, but not destroyed; therefore the work of the firstfruits of the Spirit within regenerate man inspires this longing and eager waiting for full redemption.

It is part of the essential property of faith in Jesus Christ that one sees and glimpses and longs for a deliverance which is not possible down here while, as Paul says in Romans 7:24, we are tied to these 'wretched' bodies. But that is the nature of hope. It looks towards that which is not yet attained but is confidently expected, as the writer to

the Hebrews says (Heb. 11:1). And since the hope which the work of
the Spirit inspires within us is sure hope, the eager expectancy is all
the more intensified because the desire for that which is promised grows
with every realisation that it is ensured by the Word of God.

Yet, because it is sure, there is an element of quiescence about this
hope which mediates sweet peace and patience. Nor is the peace which
is generated an empty peace as is the case with the mere acceptance of
denial or refusal. Rather it has in it all the quickening of ultimate
expectancy, to foster ever greater hope (cf. Isa. 26:3-4).

8:26-27 Here we have what John Murray calls the second ground for
encouragement to the children of God to endure suffering. We have
learned that the world on its own level groans; the saints also, possessed
of the firstfruits of the Spirit and with their eager, hopeful spirit, are
certainly groaning; but now that is surely because the Holy Spirit within
them is groaning, for better things. He takes a share and helps us in our
weakness; for we do not know what to pray for as we ought (an example
of this being found in the apostle's own experience in 2 Corinthians
12:7-10); but the Spirit himself intercedes for us with inexpressible
groanings. This is a work of the Trinity, since the Son, our great High
Priest seated at the Father's right hand, is also constantly interceding
for us (as verse 34 will say; see also Heb. 7:25; 1 Jn. 2:1).

The inexpressibility in view in the description of these groans can
hardly apply to the Holy Spirit: he cannot be unaware of, or be unable
to express, our need since he knows all things. The inability is ours, so
that all the Holy Spirit within us can do is to groan unutterably as to
our present need. This is the most wonderful thing, for the Holy Spirit
engages us in a form of expression which involves us in groans beyond
articulate expression since we are quite unable to express what he sees
and knows of our need.

We said above that the Trinity is involved in this wonderful exercise;
and this we learn in verse 27. The Father who searches the heart of
man knows the mind of the Spirit, which means that although we may
pray inarticulately, the Father in heaven who receives the prayers of
the Spirit through the Son (who is also interceding! v.34) understands
what to us are inarticulate and inexpressible groanings.

This is even more wonderful; but it is made possible because the

Holy Spirit supplicates on behalf of the saints according to the Father's will. So although this is something altogether too high for us, yet we are personally and intimately involved in it, because the subject of all this intercession is the need of our souls as the indwelling Holy Spirit knows it.

It is good, then, that we do not forget that the indwelling Holy Spirit knows our need far better than we do (cf. Eph. 3:20); it is always wise in view of our own ignorance to defer to him. Surely this is why we say in our intercessions, 'Thy will be done.' Remember that in his earthly life even our blessed Lord said to the Father, 'not my will but thine be done', although we are sure there was no deviation in him from the Father's mind and will. It was an admission of human weakness, which endears us to him unspeakably.

More Than Conquerors

8:27-29 Here we come to the third ground for encouragement in the midst of suffering. Paul says, literally, 'we know that, to those loving God, all things he works together for good, to those called according to his purpose.'

This is very wonderful if we take the 'all things' absolutely as far as the believer is concerned. It means that there is nothing in heaven or earth or hell which can frustrate the good and perfect will which the Lord purposes for his children. All evil is under his power, control and direction. Although he hates evil with a perfect hatred, that does not prevent him manipulating it sinlessly to serve his high and holy purposes – as he did in the crucifixion of his dear Son. And all because those who love him know that they are called according to his purpose.

Paul now proceeds at verse 29 to show how this operates. He foreknew them (as the apostle also implies in Eph. 1:4), since they were chosen in Christ before the foundation of the world. Peter also says we were chosen according to the foreknowledge of God the Father (1 Pet. 1:2). He could not have chosen us if he had not known us, and this he did before the world began.

This is almost too wonderful to contemplate and certainly to understand. Surely it will engage our minds and hearts throughout all the days of our earthly life and still fascinate us up yonder and be a cause of enquiry and research for endless ages to come, whether there is any possibility of discovering the hidden truth, or not. Possibly we will never know when and why and how he knew us before the worlds were born. That will simply make it all the more mysterious and intriguing!

8:29 See how closely foreknowledge belongs to divine election and foreordination. Foreknown, chosen and foreordained (or predestined) are simply steps towards the end God has in view, which is to conform his chosen ones to the image or likeness (the Greek word is the root of our word 'icon') of his Son.

Likeness to Jesus is the end; and nothing in the world could be simpler to understand, and yet more taxing to achieve. This views the eternal Son of God as the 'firstborn' of many 'brothers', which is for saved sinners the most astonishingly daring designation. Paul tells us in Colossians 1:15 that Jesus Christ is the 'firstborn over all creation', and in verse 18 that he is the 'firstborn from the dead'. But here he is the 'firstborn of many brothers', and that links with the way in which Hebrews 2:10 speaks of God 'bringing many sons to glory', and goes on to say that he therefore makes the 'Pathfinder' or 'Pioneer' or 'Captain' of their salvation 'perfect through suffering ... for which cause he is not ashamed to call them brothers'.

We have sometimes been chary of the designation 'brothers' of Jesus Christ. Addressing our Lord, 'O Christ, our Elder Brother' may make us tremble; but there is no need to be over-scrupulous, if we hold such a wonderful relationship in equipoise with Christ's deity and his Saviourhood. We must let him come close: it will not damage or injure him, and it will – as Paul says – change us.

8:30-31 Here Paul goes back to the temporal beginning of the process leading to complete conformity to Christ, and continues it towards its glorious climax. Those who are foreknown, elect and predestined in eternity are, in time, called, justified and glorified. But these divine acts are here expressed in the past tense in order to indicate the certainty of that which was purposed before all worlds.

Note that no reference is made here to man's response in faith, because these are the sovereign acts of God. Of course man has to respond to the call, and of course he has to believe in order to be justified and then glorified. But these are not in doubt where God is acting sovereignly, and therefore do not need to be discussed here.

We have now reviewed the three major grounds of encouragement for suffering saints outlined from verse 18 onwards: (1) the disproportion of suffering to glory hereafter (vv.18-25); (2) the help of the Holy Spirit in our infirmities (vv.26-27); (3) the fact that all things work together for good to them that love God (vv.28-30). Paul will now reach his 'triumphant conclusion' (John Murray) in the remaining all-glorious verses of this wonderful chapter.

8:32-37 Paul begins his 'triumphant conclusion' with an all-confident 'What then shall we say to these things?' In view of the overpowering grounds for encouragement adduced, he answers by questions which evoke irrefutable answers.

The first question, 'If God be for us, who can be against us?' is answered with a resounding, 'No-one!' But Paul nonetheless goes on in verse 32 to show why this is so. If he who is indeed God's own Son was not spared but was delivered up for us all – how will the Father not with him also give us all things freely? Is there any doubt that a God who goes the length of sacrificing his only begotten, beloved Son to death for us can be trusted completely? The answer is again a resounding, 'No!'

Who, then, will bring any charge against those whom God has chosen in such unique circumstances (v.33)? It is God who justifies them, sovereignly, as we have seen. Is there therefore anyone who can condemn, when God justifies (v.34)? Why, the apostle goes on – turning now to consider the Son – Christ Jesus is the one who has died, and moreover, has been raised from the dead to sit at God's right hand to intercede for us.

Who, then, shall separate us from the love of such a Christ (v.35)? Will anything, such as affliction, distress, persecution, famine, nakedness or sword? Surely not, when Psalm 44:22 describes the lot of God's people as facing death all day long for the Lord's sake, and being considered as sheep for slaughter! No: in all these testing experiences we are, in fact, more than conquerors through him who loved us.

8:38-39 More than conquerors 'in all these things'? You cannot be more victorious than that. The 'all' indicates that there are no exceptions, because the victory is secure through his love for us, and that love is measured by the cross. This is borne out by verse 38, which specifies an exhaustive range of possible adversaries: death, life, angels, rulers, dynamic powers, present or future things, height or depth or any other creation. None of these, Paul says, will be able to separate us from the love of God in Christ Jesus our Lord.

The range of these possibilities is staggering. Death we can understand as a means of separating us from God and Christ, if the second death is in view (Rev. 20:14; 21:8). But life? What kind of life could separate us from the Lord of life? Perhaps we should not ask, since this seems to be the Holy Spirit's way of ranging from one extreme to the other.

Angels would seem to refer to fallen angels, since holy angels are surely no threat, but Murray, citing Meyer, says 'it is questionable if the term "angel" without any further qualification is ever used in the New Testament of evil spirits. Hence the evidence would favour the view that "angels" are the good spirits'. This is not easily taken and may not be conclusive.

Whatever we may say about the hostile potential of 'life' and 'angels' (and the mystery remains!), no such question arises concerning rulers, dynamic powers, present or future things, or height or depth or any other conceivable or inconceivable creation. Any of these could be potentially hostile to God's love for us in Christ Jesus, but absolutely without success.

8:39 This is the 'tremendous climax' to these eight chapters, showing the mercy of God in Jesus Christ. We are justified by Christ, as chapters three to five have displayed; and within that kernel of justification the bud, blossom and fruit of sanctification are gloriously and beautifully unveiled to us in chapters six to eight. Our blessed Lord is not only for us, but he is in us as our sure hope of salvation, which no creation can foil or even threaten.

It is marvellous to be so secure. But if you cast your mind back through the earlier chapters and recall how the Jews in particular were bundled together with the rest of mankind as 'guilty' before God (3:20), you may begin to understand that there are outstanding questions Jews may ask which demand explanation and answer. In the next three chapters (9-11), Paul addresses these questions. He begins at chapter 9 with a cry of deep distress, which shows how much he cares for the people of his own race, of whom he has had to say such scorching things. He therefore seeks now to explain why God's promises to Israel have such a convoluted answer.

It might be helpful before we address ourselves to chapter nine to read through these three chapters even cursorily and preferably at one sitting, or at least chapter nine, in order to gain some understanding of the complexity of the divine plot. It may be that, once absorbed in the argument, it will prove impossible to desist until one has read the whole section. If so, not only will it be seen where the Jews fit into Paul's total argument in respect of his theme – the righteousness of God imparted to man; but the reader will also be given an invaluable insight into future things, perhaps more conclusively than from any other passage of Scripture. Happy hunting!

CHAPTER NINE

God's Sovereign Choice

9:1-3 To understand Paul's heart-cry here, we must recall that while in 1:16 he said the gospel was the power of God to everyone who believes, to the Jew first and then to the Gentile, he had to recognise the harsh reality of the unbelief of the Jews – from which he himself had suffered! He was therefore obliged to try to resolve the seeming contradiction; a task which he now sought to do. Nor was this a mere assignment, but a labour of love, even if an anguished one in view of what his race had done to his Saviour and their Messiah, Jesus Christ.

In fact Paul's desire for his race to see the light which once so blindingly shone on him on the Damascus road is so strong that he chooses the severest asseveration and strongest protestation in which to express it. He speaks the truth in Christ, not a lie, and his conscience confirms it in the Holy Spirit, that he has great grief and incessant pain in his heart. Indeed, such is his desire for the salvation of the Jews that he takes up what Moses had said in his despair lest God wipe out ancient Israel for their sin. Moses would have had himself blotted out of the book of life if that could have persuaded the Lord to forgive Israel's sin (Exod. 32:32). In similar fashion, Paul says he could wish himself accursed if that would bring his brethren, his kinsmen according to the flesh, to Christ. He does not say he *would*, but that he *could*, so great is his distress. It is a breathtaking statement, as was Moses' similar declaration.

This is Paul's first answer to any patriotic Jew who would charge him with contempt for Jewry. It would surely be calculated to incline any fair-minded Jewish critic at least to listen to his argument. The challenge to us is this: Do we know such deep, heart-burning desire for the conversion of our race, our nation or community or family, as that?

9:4-5 Paul proceeds to enumerate Israel's advantages before God as the measure of his sorrow that they should have rejected their Messiah. 'Theirs is the adoption as sons' (cf. Exod. 4:22). This is not yet the full adoption in Christ (cf. Rom. 8:15) as is clear from Galatians 4:1-7, where Israel's adoption as children under the law is distinguished from that in Christ. But it points inevitably to it for true sons of Israel.

The 'glory' is the shekinah glory of God which appeared on Sinai (Exod. 24:16-17) and filled the tabernacle (Exod. 40:34-38) and eventually the temple (1 Kgs. 8:10-11; 2 Chron. 7:1-2). This was the visible manifestation of the presence of God which preceded Jeremiah's prediction of the law written upon the heart (Jer. 31:33) and was fulfilled by the coming of the Holy Spirit with inflaming power at Pentecost to indwell the saints.

'Covenants' – in the plural – raises the question of the relation of these to the one covenant of grace in both Testaments. The plural doubtless refers to different dispensations of the one covenant – twice to Abraham (Gen. 15:8-21; 17:1-21); to Moses (Exod. 2:24; 6:4-5; Deut. 8:18); and to David (2 Sam. 23:5), although to others also, such as Noah (Gen. 9:9) and Joshua (Josh. 8:30ff.).

'The giving of the law' obviously refers to the events described in Exodus chapters 19 and 20; 'the service' ('temple worship' NIV) refers to the worship of the sanctuary; and the 'promises' undoubtedly focus upon the Messiah; while the 'fathers' would refer at least to Abraham,

Isaac and Jacob, but might not exclude David in view of what follows: 'from whom comes the Christ according to the flesh, who is over all, God blessed for ever, Amen'.

Here is a recital of Israel's advantages, full enough to show both the apostle's appreciation of them and his sorrow that the Messiah, who is the culmination of them all, should have been rejected.

9:6-9 But how could there be such apostasy among the Israelites when they had received so many advantages and privileges? Does the fact of it not contradict the confident Word of God which has given so many covenant promises of blessing to his chosen people? No, not at all: the Word of God has not failed. But how has it not failed? In the sense that not all descended from Israel are Israel. Nor because they are descended from Abraham are they all children of Abraham.

For instance, says Paul, You remember how distressed Abraham was at Sarah's intolerance of Ishmael after Isaac was born. But God said to the patriarch: 'Do not be so distressed, but listen to Sarah because it is through Isaac that your seed will be reckoned' (cf. Rom. 4:1ff. again for a lengthy corroboration of this). Paul goes on to explain the principle in view here: it is not the children of the flesh who are the children of God, but the children of the promise. Isaac was promised – against all nature; whereas Ishmael (whom Paul does not mention by name) was born of mere flesh.

One wonders whether Paul's use of the word 'flesh' (*sarx*) here has more than a physical connotation. He often uses the word to denote the sinfulness of the flesh, and certainly it was an act of sinful unbelief that caused Sarah and Abraham to adopt the stratagem that led Abraham to have a son by Hagar the Egyptian maid – producing the Arabs!

The fact of the promise is now stated in terms of Genesis 18:10,14. God said (over against the seeming impossibility of Sarah having a child at the age of ninety), 'I will return at the appointed time, and Sarah shall have a son.'

So, the Word of God has not failed; it is we who fail to understand the selectivity of the Word of God. Indeed, as early as Abraham the father of those who have faith, we have a hint of God's eventual intention (in the light of Israel's sins) to work, not through the nation any more but, following the Babylonian captivity, through a remnant.

And this idea is carried over and continued in the concept of the Christian church as a remnant (the meaning of the word 'church' [Greek: *ekklēsia*] is a 'called out' company). This is why we say the church is growing and the kingdom is coming.

9:10-13 There is not only a radical distinction between the children of Abraham (Ishmael and Isaac), but also between the sons of Isaac (Jacob and Esau), 'that the purpose of election should stand'. Here we are faced once again with the mystery of the divine elective will, for as Ishmael was born before Isaac, Esau was born before Jacob; yet intimation was given to Rebecca before the birth of the twins that 'the older would serve the younger' (Gen. 25:23). This means that Jacob, and those of the true Israel, were not elect on a mere national basis, but with respect to salvation, since we know, alas, that Esau was a rank unbeliever (Heb. 12:16-17). Thus it is the purpose of election which determines the radical distinction between the two brothers, not anything they do in life: 'not of works, but of him who called'.

This is even more dogmatically stated in the quotation from Malachi 1:3: 'I have loved Jacob, but Esau have I hated.' Does that mean that what they did in life does not matter? Of course it cannot mean that; but it is the divine election which determines the lifestyle and destiny, not the lifestyle which determines the destiny.

To those who know more about morals than about religion, this seems the wrong way round, but that is because they tend to start from man, and not from God. It is he who made us, not we ourselves. We must start from God, even if what we learn appears to our arrogant minds overbearing and dogmatic. We must learn that God can do as he wills with his own and dispose of them as he pleases. 'Shall not the judge of all the earth do right?'

But we may say we do not understand, and that what is dogmatically stated sounds unjust and unfair. Well, it is not; and we had better get accustomed to it, since the things we are about to read in this amazing chapter are even more challenging than those we have read thus far.

9:14-21 Paul's supposed interlocutor asks the question: What, then? Is God unjust? Not at all! In answer he quotes the Lord speaking to Moses: 'I will have mercy on whom I will have mercy, and I will have compassion on whom I will have compassion' (Exod. 33:19).

Thus he intends to complete the argument. No one is likely to object to the declaration on the compassionate side when Paul says, 'So you see, it does not depend on man's desire or effort, but on God's mercy.' But when the apostle goes on to declare the other side of the argument and quotes God's judgment on Pharaoh (of whom the Lord says, 'I raised you up for this very purpose, that I might display my power in you and that my name might be proclaimed in all the earth'), it is another story. For we know how God displayed his power in Pharaoh's case – by destroying him for persistent defiance. The one is easy to accept; it is the other which causes concern.

But the apostle pursues his conclusion relentlessly. 'Therefore God has mercy on whom he wants to have mercy, and he hardens whom he wants to harden.' This is a statement so uncompromising that the apostle expects objection, which he proceeds at once to meet. 'Someone will say, "Then why does God still blame us? For who resists his will?"'

It is here that many may be disappointed that Paul does not pursue the argument further. And there may be those who think he ought to have done so, as *The Confession of Faith* seeks to do (III. 7-8). But even after a serious discussion of the matter it says no more than is stated here. Apparently the Holy Spirit had no more to say on the matter; for all that Paul says is, 'Who are you, O man, to talk back to God?' That is to say: Know your place, and keep to it, when abstruse things are discussed which go beyond your understanding, or your faith.

This is now stated in Scriptural terms from Isaiah 29:16; 45:9 and Jeremiah 18:1-6 in terms of the analogy of the potter and the clay. Even if, with *The Confession of Faith*, we speak of election to damnation as the divine passing by, this obviously remains a mystery which we may never understand, hidden in the heart of God. What if this is kept from us as an essential part of our creaturehood? Peter says, 'God resists the proud, but gives grace to the humble' (1 Pet. 5:5). Let us not dispute with the Almighty his eternal decrees – even if Paul goes on to develop the argument further, in one of the most abstruse passages in the Letter.

9:22-26 The 'What if' of verse 22 commences a long sentence (to verse 24) which remains unfinished, but is full of import. The essential meaning is that vessels of wrath and vessels of mercy are equally in the hands of the divine Potter. If we accept the divine will in respect of God's mercy, we must equally accept the divine will in respect of his wrath, since these both express elements in the integration of God's mind and heart with regard to his creatures. This is not to say these disparate elements of the divine will, his wrath and his mercy, are equal to the Almighty. Consigning to destruction the vessels of wrath fitted to or prepared for destruction is not to him equal to his making known the riches of his glory to the vessels of mercy. Indeed the one is a kind of clearance in order to the second. Judgment is in the interest of salvation, not salvation in the interest of judgment. But although they are not of equal importance to the Lord, they are equally determinative in the divine will, so that neither is to be disputed in favour of the other.

Nonetheless, it is the calling of his elect people, both Jew and Gentile, to become his people which thereafter occupies Paul's mind. He goes on to speak in particular of God's sovereign choice of the Gentiles employing the language of Hosea to do so. The prophet has in view Israel estranged and then reconciled, whereas Paul applies this to Gentiles as those 'not his people' sovereignly called to be 'the people of God', and those 'not his beloved' called to be 'his beloved'.

Note the reference to 'place' in verse 26, which obviously has in mind the possibilities of universal change on the part of Gentiles all over the world. God's grace will reach them where they are, and name them his people there. This surely is exemplified in our Lord's great commission to the apostles to 'go and make disciples of all nations, baptising them in[to] the name of the Father and of the Son and of the Holy Spirit' (Matt. 28:18-20).

Israel's Unbelief

9:27-33 In keeping with the above universal appeal to the Gentiles upon Israel's refusal of her Messiah King, Paul now quotes appropriately Isaiah 10:22-23 concerning God's judgment on unbelieving Israel in the days of the Assyrian invasion of their land. Only a remnant will be saved. Indeed (now quoting Isa. 1:9), if the Lord Almighty had not made his inviolable promise to Abraham, Isaac and Jacob, they would all have been wiped out like Sodom and Gomorrah.

This is a fearful statement and is surely made in particular and in the first instance to any sceptical Jews associated with the church in

Rome, appealing to them to reconsider their precarious position vis-a-vis Jesus Christ. It matters not how great and prestigious Israel may have been, and proud of her numbers – as computed either in the beginning or ending of the book of that name (Num. 2:26). Those destined to be called by the name 'sons of the living God' will be few. It therefore behoves every Jew to ask, in view of these passages in Isaiah, 'Am I of the remnant to be saved or not?'

'Ah,' Paul's imagined interlocutor asks, 'What are we to say, then? That the Gentiles who did not seek after righteousness grasped it, namely a righteousness from faith; but that Israel seeking a law of righteousness, did not arrive at it.' Why not? Because they pursued it not by faith, but from the standpoint of the self-effort of works. Thus if they had attained righteousness that way, it would have been, 'Glory to me', not to God. Such a spirit and attitude had to be excluded. In their case it was because they stumbled over the stumbling stone which calls for faith as a gift of God and not as a work of man's carnal self-effort. Isaiah had a word for that also. In Isaiah 28:16 we are told that the precious cornerstone has been laid. No one who trusts in it (Christ) will ever be dismayed.

In verse 33 Paul conflates two verses, starting with Isaiah 28:16 but going on to quote Isaiah 8:14, which says that the Lord Almighty, who is meant to be a sanctuary for his people, will nevertheless become for both houses of Israel a stone of stumbling, a 'rock of offence' (literally 'scandal'). Yet, the one who trusts in him (he goes back now to 28:16) will never be put to shame.

Thus Paul justifies God setting aside the Jews yet remaining true to his promise to Abraham in that (as he shows from their own Scriptures) a remnant will always be saved.

CHAPTER TEN

10:1-4 The theme here is the same as in the latter section of chapter 9, namely Israel's seeking righteousness in the wrong way, by works instead of faith. But into that argument Paul here interjects another deeply felt cry: 'Brothers, my heart's desire and prayer to God for the Israelites is that they may be saved.'

But the apostle has just shown from the prophet Isaiah that only a remnant will be saved. Does he not accept it? It is easy to say that we must accept the inevitable, but that does not stop us longing for the salvation of those we love. This is surely what God uses to constrain us to pray at least a remnant of them into the kingdom.

Thus in love the apostle seeks to see the best he can in them. They have a zeal for God, but it is not informed. The demands of the law have blinded them to the fact that the law was given by God, and he is therefore the Author of the righteousness they are called upon to attain. He has not laid down the law and departed to leave them to live it out by themselves. But instead of submitting themselves to the God who requires humble obedience to these laws, they have gone about carnally trying to obey them. To the extent that they have succeeded outwardly, they have filled their hearts with pride, which in God's sight is a greater violation of the law than the grossest sins. So Christ came that they might cease to seek righteousness by such pride-instilling efforts, and find it instead by believing the perfect righteousness to be procured by his death for sin.

Christ, then, must be to us the 'end' of sinful effort and the beginning of faith in him. The word 'end' can mean 'fulfilment' as well as 'cessation', but here it must have the latter meaning: the end of the law as a means of attaining righteousness. The way to righteousness is not by self-effort, but by receiving Christ, who by his work has constituted himself as, and is, our righteousness (cf. Jer. 23:6 where, in *The Authorised Version* the words are printed in capital letters!).

There is no other way to attain God-accepted righteousness than by Christ, the only righteous One in person and deed.

10:5-9 Paul now adduces Moses to support the distinction he has made between the righteousness of faith and that sought by legal law-keeping. He quotes Leviticus 18:5 which (like Deut. 4:1; 5:33; 8:1; 16:20), says that a man shall live by keeping the law.

It is important here to note that this oft-repeated statement shows that the Mosaic law was given unto life for Israel, saved as the people were from Egypt's bondage by the blood of the lamb being sprinkled on their door posts. It was undoubtedly the divine intention that they should obey the law by faith and not by mere external, carnal, legal righteousness – that is to say, by the strivings of the flesh. But, alas, they did not attain to that righteousness of faith which Moses describes so evangelically in Deuteronomy 30:11-14. This could only be accomplished when, by that same faith, they had attained the circumcision of their hearts as promised in Deuteronomy 30:6.

But nothing could express the fleshly arduousness of seeking righteousness by self-effort better than this passage from Deuteronomy 30:11-14. The former part (v.12) suggests (as John Murray brings out) that Christ did not come down from heaven so that devout souls would seek to scramble up to heaven themselves by their own efforts to try to attain righteousness. The latter part (v.13) on the other hand suggests that righteousness-seekers would have to descend into the pit to look for it since, as far as they are concerned, Christ never ascended from the grave! No: the trouble is it is too simple to understand. Men in the ingenuity of their fallenness seek to do the hard thing to establish their own ability, but they find themselves climbing the wrong mountain which, so far from being the hill of God and of his holiness, leads to dizzy heights of carnal self-seeking, from which they must surely crash to the ground.

By contrast, the 'word of faith' is a gift, just as surely as the law is a gift, proffered by grace, and all we have to do is to look for it on the tip of our tongue or at the door of our heart. And that leads to confession and saving faith – or, as in verse 10, saving faith and confession. More about the order of these two words later.

10:10-13 The order of the words 'mouth' and 'heart' is that of Deuteronomy 30:14. But because the heart is before the mouth in religion – what we know must come before what we speak – the apostle reverses the order in verse 10. In order to be justified, one has to believe with the heart that Jesus was raised from the dead by his Father. For this is the climax of the gospel, which includes, because it implies, all that has gone before: his birth, life and death. Jesus is not only alive. He is Lord!

There is an immediacy about such a realisation which calls for vocal confession. This was David's experience in Psalm 39:1-3. He could not hold his peace about the wonder that, notwithstanding the fact that his mortal life was fleeting (vv.4-6), his hope was in the Lord.

But what does it mean that salvation attends and follows confession?

Surely the apostle is referring to salvation in its subjective effects upon our lives. For example, a certain man earnestly believed in his heart, but there was no change in his life until he was pushed into an open-air ring and obliged to confess his faith: his spiritual life sprang from that moment.

Paul quotes Isaiah 28:16 which begins with the Lord saying he will lay a precious cornerstone in Zion, well tested and of a sure foundation, and the one who trusts in that living Stone (that Rock of eternity) will never be dismayed. But he changes the wording slightly from 'one' to 'every one', which he needs to do, because he is about to return to the subject of Jew and Gentile, and to declare (on the basis of 1:16; 3:9, 19, 22, 23, 29, 30; 4:11-12; 9:24) that there is no distinction in the call to Jew and Gentile – the same Lord is Lord of all and richly blesses all who call on him; 'For [and here he finds another Scripture in Joel 2:32, ready-made for his purpose] everyone who calls on the name of the Lord will be saved.'

10:14-18a It has been declared and attested that 'everyone who calls on the name of the Lord will be saved'. Then, that is the thing to do. But how to do it? You can hardly call on a name of which you know nothing. It has to be declared, and its significance presented, before there can be any legitimate commitment to it. Who then will declare it with intelligence and understanding? A messenger is needed, but unless he is commissioned his heralding the Lord's name will be without authority. An appointed messenger is therefore called for. And when one is found, how beautiful are the feet of such a carrier of good news to needy ones!

Ah, but throughout Israel's history many messengers were sent as we see in Hebrews chapter 11. 'Beautiful' indeed may have been the feet of messengers such as the patriarchs and prophets, but their beauty, like that of Messiah himself (Isa. 53:2), was not seen. They were hated: 'O Jerusalem, Jerusalem, you who kill the prophets and stone those sent to you. How often I have longed to gather your children together as a hen gathers her chicks under her wings, but you were not willing', was our Lord's lament (Matt. 23:27). So the apostle similarly laments the unbelief of Israel, taking up the first statement of Isaiah 53, 'Who has believed our message?' He concludes, 'Faith comes from hearing the message, and the message is heard through the word of Christ.'

The message must be proclaimed before it can be heard by the needy. And the message is none other than the word of Christ: he is the Saviour of the world. If men will not have him when they hear the truth concerning him, they cannot be saved.

But the main trouble with Israel was that, although there were times of drought and famine of the Word, they heard but would not heed.

10:18-21 They heard but would not heed; for 'their voice is gone out into all the earth, their words to the ends of the world'. This quotation from Psalm 19:4 refers not to preaching words, but to the wordless voice of God's creation silently but eloquently sounding forth his praise (cf. Rom. 1:19-20). Is this quotation not inappropriate, since Paul has been speaking about the message of the gospel? Not really: the apostle is going to extremes when he implies that not only have Jews in any part of the world heard something of God's Word – how otherwise would they know they were Jews? – but even the Gentiles are without excuse for turning their backs on their Maker since the creation itself declares the eternal power and deity of Almighty God. So the Jews are doubly indebted to God, for they have had the witness both of nature and of God's written Word.

This second point, against any suggestion that Israel did not understand the Word, Paul now proves by quoting Deuteronomy 32:21. There Moses had said that God was so angry and jealous that his chosen people had rejected him that he purposed to make them jealous by turning to people who had practically no nationality and were devoid of understanding, and making them respond. This is then clinched by a quotation from Isaiah 65:1, where the prophet finds God saying that he was found by those who had not the sense to go seeking him, because he deliberately revealed and manifested himself to them, although they were not asking for him. And that is divinely justified, the prophet implies in Isaiah 65:2, because the Lord grew tired of holding out his hands to a disobedient and contradicting people. The Jews therefore have no excuse.

CHAPTER ELEVEN
The Remnant of Israel

11:1-5 The unbelief of Israel, which has been manifest through this section of the letter if not all through it, raises this pertinent question: Has the Lord become so tired of the Jews (10:21) that he has cast them off, his own people? Never! 'I myself am an Israelite' says Paul, 'a descendant of Abraham'.

God has not put away his people whom he foreknew! How could he un-know a people whom he had before created in love (as Paul says we are 'chosen in Christ before the foundation of the world'). It may look like it, sometimes because of his righteous anger against them for their backsliding and waywardness, but it is never so. Indeed, Elijah in his day thought he was the last of the true sons of Israel as his enemies plotted his death. He told God: 'Lord, they have killed your prophets and dug up your altars; and I am left alone and they seek my life' (1 Kgs. 19:10, 14). But what was God's answer?: 'I have reserved to myself seven thousand men who have not bowed the knee to Baal' (1 Kgs. 19:14-18).

That was one of Israel's direst crises. The apostle does not mention here the Babylonian captivity after that, when many thought it was the end of Jewry – not to speak of Jewry's rejection of Christ and their subsequent dispersion which lasted until the recreation of the State of Israel in 1948. May we not be certain, therefore, that there will always be a remnant whom God reserves to himself? Even to this present time, the apostle says, there is a remnant according to the election of grace.

Ah, the remnant idea! It began to dawn on the Lord's people, especially after the Babylonian captivity (cf. Ezra 3:8; 9:8, 14; Neh. 1:3; Isa. 1:9, etc.). This must at first have been an exceedingly humiliating notion to proud Jewry, but it was to prove to be the lasting truth, that God was to preserve his people by remnants (having no care for the taunts of his enemies at various times that they were almost finished as a people) until all the remnants of the election of grace would be brought together in the new Kingdom.

Any Christian who does not see this as God's will now will lose heart for Christ's church. God is building his church through the centuries and he does not care what it looks like in the meantime to undiscerning and critical eyes who have no understanding of what he is about. He plods on, building brick by brick and storing the living stones in his unseen Repository – Upstairs. Only suddenly will he reveal his whole church and kingdom. Hallelujah! Until then we must be patient.

11:6 Grace is the very antithesis of works. This is Israel's great stumbling block – and ours, especially nominal church members who answer the question, 'Are you a Christian?' by saying, 'I am doing the best I can.' Because the law of God is couched in terms of doing and not doing, they assume it is self-effort that is called for, thus affording every encouragement to human pride, such as we see in the Pharisees: 'The Pharisee stood and prayed to himself, "God, I thank thee that I am not as other men, rapacious, unjust, adulterers, or even as this tax-collector. I fast twice in the week; I give tithes of all I possess"' (Lk. 18:11-12).

The question is: Who does the saving? It is either God, or man. If it is God, then that is a work of purest grace, and no man can take the credit, however responsive it is necessary for him to be to the grace of God. Response is possible only where there is something to respond to, and that is grace.

We should never be lulled by Satan into thinking that when we are launched into the Christian life by the sovereign inauguration of God's electing purpose, thereafter all we do in response to grace is self-effort. Why, the very ease (comparatively speaking) of our flight heavenward when grace is in control should tell us that it is his yoke which is easy and his burden which is light (Matt. 11:28-30). Consequently, our thankfulness, when we feel we have done a good job for God should be first to thank him and not ourselves for enabling us. For he is not churlish with respect to our effort and what it costs us to respond to his grace: in heaven he will reward us for all effort on our part. This he is able and willing in his generosity to do, because he knows that it was all inspired by his grace. Paul sums this up succinctly to the Ephesians when he says: 'For by grace you are saved through faith, and this [faith] is not from yourselves; it is the gift of God: not of works, lest any man boast' (Eph. 2:8-9).

11:7 The first six verses of chapter 11 deal with the question of whether God has cast off his people. The answer is that the vast majority of Israel failed to obtain what they sought so earnestly. Instead of boarding the 'band-waggon' of God's grace, they wilfully thought to please him by their unaided walk, assuming that since God had given the law to them it was theirs to fulfil it in their own strength.

The Jewish people thus failed to realise that this was an exercise calculated to increase pride in their own self-effort, almost as if in competition with God! They responded as little children do to their parents when given a hard assignment: 'Hands off! See what I can do on my own?' This is the essence of self, and is calculated to stifle all grace and enlist self-consuming pride, since the relevant exercise is not human achievement, but salvation.

Of course, as we noted earlier, God does not ignore the costliness of our efforts, but down here the proper drill is not to stand apart from him and try out our personal strength, but to lean hard on his grace in order to feel the delicious sense of being buoyed up and borne onwards by the strength that he supplies (cf. Peter's words in 2 Pet. 1:21, 'carried along by the Holy Spirit').

This in fact was the experience only of the elect, the select band who saw what God was seeking to do and gave themselves up to it with the complete co-operation of loving obedience, and with high admiration for the wealth of power the Lord delights to bestow on his own. They alone saw what he was seeking to do. But it has not been so with the majority. For all their professed faith in their God, and their attendance to his laws and rules, they have taken their stand over against him with grim, private thoughts, as if to say, 'He challenges me by his commandments, and he may think I am not able to do what he asks, but I will let him see!'

This is the essence of sinful independence. For example, it is easy to see that world-class sportsmen set themselves with exclusive determination to achieve their aim and fame and become completely absorbed in their self-effort so that all else is excluded; this makes them exceedingly hard. However, there are two elements to the particular hardening which Paul describes, and we must look at them further.

11:8-10 Both elements of the hardening of men's hearts conspire to the same end. The first and overarching element is the sovereign will of God. So far from the apostle apologising for this, we have seen already in 9:18 that he explicitly says that God hardens!

With regard to the non-elect *The Confession of Faith* says: 'The rest of mankind, God was pleased, according to the unsearchable counsel of his own will, whereby he extends or withholds mercy as he pleases, for the glory of his sovereign power over his creatures, to pass by, and to ordain them to dishonour and wrath for their sin, to the praise of his glorious justice' (III.7).

Aware that this statement will be received with awe, the Westminster divines go on: 'The doctrine of this high mystery of predestination is to be handled with special prudence and care, that men attending the will of God revealed in his word, and yielding obedience to it, may, from the certainty of their effectual vocation, be assured of their eternal election. So shall this doctrine afford matter of praise, reverence, and admiration of God, and of humility, diligence, and abundant consolation, to all that sincerely obey the Gospel' (III.8).

This is the point of Paul's quotations from Deuteronomy 29:4 and Isaiah 29:10 about the 'stupor', and that from Psalm 69:22-23 about the 'table' which becomes a 'trap' (which speaks of God's bounty being spurned by the ungodly).

The second element in the hardening is that of the sinful will of apostate man. If we look at 9:31-32; 10:3, 16, 21, we shall see that these all speak of man's sinful will. Nor should we forget that our God, in choosing by his grace to save even one soul, is acting with the greatest magnanimity. In view of the sin of Adam of which all partake (Rom. 5:12) it is by mercy alone that such a soul is saved.

In this connection, it is interesting to consider the references to hardening in God's dealings with Egypt in respect of the plagues. (See Exod. 4:21; 7:3, 13, 22; 8:15, 19, 32; 9:7, 12, 34, 35; 10:1, 20, 27; 11:10; 14:4, 8, 17.) In these many references you will find the divine hardening entwined with that of man's self hardening. The two belong together. The overarching will of God must always be kept in mind, and yet the fact is that since the Fall all men are culpable. 'It is of the Lord's mercies that we are not consumed, because his compassions fail not' (Lam. 3:22).

Ingrafted Branches

11:11 John Murray points out with his usual lucidity that there are two answers to the dread question, 'Has God cast off his ancient people Israel?' The first answer in 11:1-10 is that the rejection is not complete, there is always a remnant; the second answer which the apostle now tackles is that the rejection is not final; it has an end.

This rejection because of sin has a positive purpose – indeed, two positive purposes, which are both tremendously encouraging. *The New International Version* describes their 'fall' as 'not beyond recovery', which is helpful. They did stumble and fall, but God's first positive purpose by that transgression was that salvation should come to the Gentiles. That is a glorious purpose which confirms all that God had said from Genesis 12:1-3 right through the Old Testament to Isaiah 42:6 and 49:6 about choosing a special people to be a 'light to the Gentiles'. But although Israel failed to be such a light, God's purpose is not frustrated, for he is ready even to use their darkness to the very end that, paradoxically, it becomes a means whereby he turns to the Gentiles that they may be saved.

But God's positive purpose is not only that the Gentiles be saved; it is that this ingenious intention should provoke Israel to jealousy, so that in the end they also might be saved. It would therefore appear that during these gospel ages God is preparing to show Israel that the Christian faith is superior to their Jewish faith: thus one day they will see, and we are to pray its hastening, every day!

This is one of the most profound and complex revelations in the New Testament, but a failure to understand it has led to far greater obscurity than need be among Christians about the future purposes of God for both Jew and Gentile. The ultimate salvation of Israel, for all her sin, is ensured in that God uses this 'loop' in his will to get at them by this paradoxical way.

What this is saying – and the only thing it can be saying – is that God has a purpose for the Jewish race, beyond the conversion of the Gentiles throughout Christendom's history thus far. It is amazing how obtuse Bible students and scholars have been over this issue so comparatively clearly stated in verse 11, preparatory to the great statement of verse 12.

If verse 11 is accepted wholeheartedly, the more complex verse 12 and its companion verse 15 should tell their own message, and lead that all-perceptive 'shuttle' between Jew and Gentile one step on, namely to a further outpouring of God's grace on the Gentiles following the conversion of Israel to himself. So the pattern repeats itself thus: the Jews rejected, the Gentiles saved; the Jews thereby made jealous and saved. They thus fulfil their original 'remit' from Almighty God to be a light to the Gentiles so that multitudes of them should be saved. Not much wonder Paul ends this chapter with the glorious doxology of verses 33-36!

11:12 Here we must distinguish clearly between the two 'sides', Jew and Gentile, in a sentence which calls for logical understanding and rigorous clarification. The difficulty with the verse is that Paul repeats his statement before reaching his conclusion.

Try reading this verse without the repetition, thus: 'If their trespass means riches for the world ... how much greater riches will their fulness bring!' Then ask: Greater riches for whom? The answer can only be: for the world! And since the two parties are Israel and the Gentiles, the sentence can only mean, 'If the trespass of the Jews means riches for the Gentile world, how much greater riches will the fulness of the Jews bring to the Gentiles.'

The apostle is speaking of the rejection of the Jews becoming a blessing to the Gentiles; and so what he goes on to say is that when Israel is restored as a nation and the time of her fulness has come, much greater riches of blessing will then accrue to the Gentiles.

Now read the whole sentence, adding the repetition thus: 'If the trespass of the Jews means riches for the Gentile world, and the loss of the Jews means riches for the Gentile world, how much greater riches will it mean for the Gentile world when the fulness of the Jews is come.'

Paul goes on in verse 13 to say that he is talking to the Gentiles, so the statement can only promise that after Israel has returned to the Lord, her conversion to Christ will result in far greater blessing for the Gentiles than formerly: 'how much greater riches' can only mean phenomenal blessing to the Gentile world after the nation of Israel has turned to the Lord.

This is such a wonderful prospect that it should fill our hearts and minds with awesome wonder at the amazing permutations of God's purposes of grace for his church in the future. If we would live with that definite prospect in view, whether we ourselves ever see it down here or not, it would give such a fillip to our faith, despite all the discouragements in this present evil world, that our hearts would constantly sing for joy!

11:13-14 These two verses belong together, because they simply make a parenthetical statement between verses 12 and 15, in which Paul emphasises his appointment by God to be the apostle to the Gentiles.

Paul does not want anyone to be in doubt about his sense of responsibility to the Gentiles, for the drift of verses 11-15 is all towards the blessing of the Gentiles following Israel's conversion (fulness). Nonetheless, given his understanding that blessing to the Gentiles during Israel's rejection is divinely intended to make Israel jealous, the dear apostle is able to derive satisfaction from a course which enables him to look forward with joy to the day when that jealousy in Jewry will be aroused. Then Israel will rise up in a body as a nation and demand of the Gentiles that they do not keep the Christ their very own Messiah to themselves, but share him with those who ought to have been the first to inherit his blessing!

So Paul is able to hold in view a double ministry. He is apostle to the Gentiles, and yet he sees beyond them, at least to make individual Israelites jealous, that envy might drive them to Christ. And we may assume that this took place in Paul's experience.

In fact there is a sense in which Paul did not renounce his preoccupation with his own people (see the beginning of chapters 9 and 10 for the anguish of his desire for their salvation) until the Jews who came to him in Rome rejected the gospel (see Acts 28:17-27). Thereafter, in what he writes in his prison letters and subsequently, there is an absence of preoccupation with the conversion of the Jews. But the fascinating thing is this (if Paul were ever tempted to be envious of Peter appointed apostle to the Jews; see Gal. 2:7), that the best he could do to win the Jews was for him ardently to seek the Gentiles, and thus make the Jews jealous!

Who could have thought of such a 'telescopic' purpose but those inspired by the Spirit of God? So Paul returns to his theme of verse 12 at verse 15, to which we will come.

11:15-16 Paul now repeats this wonderful 'telescopic' idea, revealed to him by God. The rejection of Jewry from God's blessing because they rejected their Messiah (and their appalling dispersion throughout the world as a despised and persecuted people, cf. Hitler's destruction of the Jews) leads to the gospel coming to the Gentiles. It is Gentiles largely who have composed the Christian church during the almost two thousand years since Christ came. This Paul calls the 'reconciliation' of the Gentile world.

In an analogous way, the acceptance of the Jews by God, when they realise that Jesus of Nazareth whom they crucified and will then mourn is their Messiah (see Jn. 19:37) and turn to him, will mean life from the dead. The consequence will be a resurgence of blessing to the Gentile world.

Now there are those who cannot see verse 15 thus, especially because they give the phrase 'life from the dead' another meaning. But to do so is to throw overboard all that the apostle has been laboriously trying to say since verse 11. The whole complex statement must hang together. Nor is there any doubt that a balanced reading of it will make it do so.

However, verse 16 which follows uses an idea drawn from Numbers 15:17-21 and seems to veer from the theme of the Gentiles to that of the Jews. Yet it does so only to bring out the same theme as before – as the succeeding verses will show. But it now presents a new challenge to Gentile believers. For verse 16 seems to be speaking of the ancient patriarchs (Abraham, Isaac and Jacob), the 'root' of Israel, and going on to say that if the root was holy so will the branches be – converted to their Messiah at any subsequent time, especially at their national conversion.

Paul then proceeds to the next stage of his argument concerning the great 'shuttle' of Jew and Gentile; and that argument, taking in the following verses 17-21, requires that we take them together.

11:17-21 The 'you' of verse 17 refers to the Gentiles, addressed sternly in view of their privilege: although 'wild olives' (like figs and the vine, the olive tree is a symbol of Israel) they have been grafted into the true olive root when its own branches are broken off. They must never allow their enjoyment of that nourishment drawn from the genuine olive tree to cause them to crow over the rejection of the Jewish branches by which they were brought in. Such an attitude would be short-sighted; for, says the apostle, it is the root which supports you, as it supported the branches. You may say: But the branches were broken off so that I could be grafted in. Ah yes, but they were broken off because of their unbelief, and such a fate could happen to you too! Since you stand only by faith and these branches have been broken off because they departed from genuine faith in their true Messiah, it behoves you Gentiles to be humble lest you do the same. There is therefore no justification for any pride or arrogance on your part whatsoever. Indeed, in view of Israel's sad and sorry declension, you ought rather to fear lest as God was brave enough in the interests of his perfect standards not to spare the true branches, he might not spare you either!

This leads the apostle to a consideration of both the kindness and severity of God, a theme of perpetual and abiding interest, which must constantly exercise us as we see the workings of God among men, including ourselves!

11:22-24 The test of predestination to glory is faith. All the divine kindness in the world cannot brook unfaith – that would be to abandon the divine character. God's grace is incalculable in its generosity, but it cannot abandon itself to persistent unfaith: this is to ask the impossible and the utterly irrational.

If God is to maintain his character, then, as long as man opposes him, grace must appear in the guise of severity. For the aim of grace is to get man on God's side in order to bless him. When it does not, there is no question of God failing; it is simply that men then ask for second best, which of course turns out to be the worst. What would the Lord desire more than that we continue in his kindness so that he might bless us more and more? That is to his pleasure as well as to ours, and has – we are sure – a completely satisfying all-round outcome.

The Jews in their rejection of their Messiah failed to see this. But when long centuries of God's goodness to Gentile believers does its purposed work of making them jealous, and they see what they have missed and begin to seek it afresh, they will be re-grafted into their own olive tree. God, who can do anything, is able and more than willing to accomplish this. Indeed, to graft the natural branches back into their own olive tree is a more natural proceeding than grafting the wild olives of the Gentiles into the Jews' own olive tree.

Do you see what the apostle is doing here? Anyone who knows anything about anti-semitism (hostility to the Jews) knows how hateful to Gentiles the Jews have often been. Witness the holocaust by Hitler. Paul's appeal therefore encourages those who are in Christ develop an attitude of profound respect for God's chosen people, and to hope, pray and work with all our powers to bring the Jews back to their own Messiah so that they belong to the Lord Jesus Christ their rightful King and Saviour.

All Israel Will Be Saved

11:25-27 Paul is still talking to Gentile believers about their attitude towards Jewish believers: there is a mystery in the divine dealing with his own people which all Gentiles should seek to understand.

The apostle has just said that it will be more natural for the Lord to regraft Jews into their own olive tree than to graft Gentiles into it. This should evacuate all conceit from the minds of Gentile believers; for it cannot be that the Lord of glory has less regard for his chosen people than for Gentile foreigners. Rather, he has had a more tortuous purpose for them, in order to clear their minds of all pride.

This helps us to understand the reason for the partial hardening that has led them away from the only source of their true life, their Messiah King. But this is not to go on for ever, although to Gentiles living in the midst of the hardening (which has gone on for nearly two thousand years) it may seem interminable. It is to last only until the fulness of the Gentiles arrives.

'Fulness' should be read here, not 'the full number' (as *The New International Version* and practically all modern versions say). But the 'fulness', whatever number is included, does not exclude the blessing of Gentiles after the Jews have come in, as verses 12 and 15 undoubtedly predict. So 'all Israel' shall be saved. This does not necessarily mean every single Israelite, but the mass of God's chosen people.

The term 'all Israel' has been given various connotations and extensions, strangely enough including Gentiles, but this is to impress upon the words an unnatural meaning. But why does the apostle put it this way? Surely to assure both Gentile and Jewish believers that God never had any intention of rejecting his people, only of ridding them of unwarrantable conceit in their being the chosen people of God. But see what that conceit has cost them! Nevertheless, the tenor of Isaiah's prophecy at least shows, as Paul brings out, that God is able to surmount all their godlessness by the strength of his covenant (cf. Isa. 59:20-21; 27:9). This he will do when he rises to take away all their sins by the deliverer, even their own Messiah, when he comes to convert them to himself amidst mingled mourning and rejoicing.

11:28-32 Verse 28 could be wrongly construed and deeply misunderstood. The 'gospel' here must mean the good news of Jesus Christ as the Jews have rejected it. But in the blindness of their conceit they did not realise that something deeper even than their rejection of the gospel was mysteriously operating, namely election. Yes, the Jews had proved to be enemies of the gospel for the sake of the Gentiles, but that was temporary and could in no way overturn God's covenantal decree by which he chose his own people from the time of the patriarchs, and even before that.

Israel in its totality was always beloved, for God does not change his mind about those of whom Paul speaks so eloquently in 9:4-5. They are his for ever, although he has this tortuous way of going about their conversion. It is well therefore for Gentile believers to remember that as in the past they disobeyed God but have now obtained mercy, so now the Jews have disobeyed, leading to God's mercy to the Gentiles. And this is in order that eventually the Jews might obtain mercy also, as Hosea says (Hos. 1:4-11).

But one all-important point calls for attention before we are 'lost in wonder, love and praise' at the great doxology of verses 33-36. The 'alls' of verse 32 are not like those of Galatians 3:22, embracing all men without exception. They can only refer to the 'alls' of God's mercy, referring strictly and only to his own, his elect, those eternally chosen in Christ. Note this very carefully!

Doxology

11:33 We have remarked above on the mystery of God's ways with men. But it is not what we do not know of them, unsearchable though his ways are, which draws from Paul, and from ourselves, such ecstatic exclamation. Rather it is what we have been able to understand of the divine ingenuity, the sheer complexity of purposes wrought with such exquisite finesse. We have marvelled again and again at the elaborate fabric of his will for his wayward and contorted people, Israel, as well as his determined love for the Gentiles.

It takes our breath away to contemplate the divine grasp of the whole human situation. It is indeed the observed depth of wealth of God's wisdom and knowledge which prompts us, with Paul as our human guide, to consider the unsearchable celestial bourne whence all this sagacity emerges – the place of the divine judgments where in eternity the counsels of the Trinity took place.

It is not only the complexity and ingeniousness of the divine will as revealed which prompts such inspired response, but the fact that back of it all is the divine mercy, as verse 32 says. The saying 'Necessity is the mother of invention' could be applied here to the obvious fact that Almighty God has such compassion for his own in the midst of their fallen plight that he employs the illimitable resources of his power and love to devise means to rescue them. And this he does to the accomplishment of a pattern so rich that it puts all tapestries to shame. Not much wonder therefore that Joseph Addison broke out in his hymn,

> When all Thy mercies, O my God!
> My rising soul surveys:
> But O! eternity's too short
> To utter all thy praise.

11:34-35 It is what we know of what we are sure is infinite deity which leads us to contemplate what must still be for us to discover here and hereafter in the Eternal and in his purposes which as yet is unseen and unknown. Whatever happens in glory and however much we learn then of his ways, hidden from us now, we can well imagine that there will still be untraceable tracts of his pathways and purposes which even then will remain undiscoverable, since we shall never be God, however long eternity lasts.

Paul is driven to the Old Testament to ask his unanswerable question in terms of the words of Isaiah 40:13. Who indeed has known the full mind of the Lord to enable him to be his counsellor? The thought is incongruous and utterly unacceptable! No one could reach the depth of his mind, let alone counsel him about his ways.

The apostle then takes up words from the Book of Job. Few men have known the depth of the unknowable as Job did because the Almighty led him by a way which was beyond understanding, not only for its pain but for its fruitfulness. Yet the Lord is saying to that man humbled to the dust, 'Who has ever made a claim on me that I must pay?' (Job 41:11).

11:36 Thus we come to the three immense prepositions, 'from', 'through' and 'to'. These have sometimes been related respectively to the three Persons of the divine Trinity: the Father ('from'), the Son ('through') and the Holy Spirit ('to'). But the very reference to 'all things' at the climax of the utterance surely shows that the three Persons are to be taken together inclusively as the one Eternal God.

We know that the Scriptures are infinitely careful to distinguish the Persons of the divine Trinity and never confuse them; but since there are times when it is the 'aggregate' deity which is in view, it is good at such a time of mingled understanding and incomprehensibility to give glory to the Triunity of the Godhead. He is one God, blessed for ever. Amen.

CHAPTER TWELVE

Living Sacrifices

12:1-2 The 'therefore' with which this chapter begins connects not only with the riches of grace expressed in the doxology of 11:33-36, but with the teaching on sanctification of chapters 6 to 8. The challenge to practical holiness is based on our union with Christ in his death and resurrection, and follows the apostle's usual practice of presenting Christian truth in teachable form before exhorting to obedience to it. These are the mercies or compassions of God unfolded in the whole of the foregoing eleven chapters, which are the ground of Paul's earnest challenge to present our bodies to God a living sacrifice, holy, acceptable and our reasonable service.

It is our bodies which are to be presented because the human body is the casket in which the soul presently resides, and the whole life of the human person is lived within it. It is, therefore, in the human mind and body that the transformations of grace are to be wrought out.

The language of presentation is that of ritual sacrifice. But this is the sacrifice of the living, not the dead, because the principle of Christ's death and resurrection operates to enable us to present our regenerate body, not the body of sin and death, to God. We are constantly to present our bodies to him so that the renewed life of Christ within us might operate in the fulness of his grace and power.

This is in complete contrast to our former life, in which we were conformed to the spirit of this present fallen age. Being renewed in Christ and by him in his death and resurrection, we are commanded to submit to his transforming power. We are intelligent beings whose bodily life is to be controlled and guided by the working of minds renewed by the Holy Spirt of God. The application of these means of grace will furnish us with the full proof of what is the good, perfect and acceptable will of God. We will therefore know by the outpouring of his blessing upon us that this is not only our necessary obligation as renewed creatures in Christ Jesus, but our highest joy.

12:3 What has been said above applies to all believers, but from verse 3 the apostle begins to differentiate, and starts with himself. He is a recipient of grace, and it is out of the abundance of the gratitude of his heart that he speaks to everyone who will listen to him or read him, earnestly exhorting them to guard against the great all-consuming sin of pride.

Pride here would be claiming to be what one was not, and therefore assuming a place or position to which one was not entitled. That is the essence of falsehood, and utterly misleading to oneself, to others, and especially deeply displeasing to God. The responsibility is upon every child of God to think with that sobriety which seeks to know the facts about oneself before God and man, and make claim only on those as in the sight of God. More particularly, this would be to consider the measure of faith which God accords to each saint, and to abide by that.

It surely stands to reason that in the intimacy of our private encounter with God through Christ and its effects upon our human relationships, the good Lord is bound to indicate to us the measure and bounds of the gift of faith he has accorded us as appropriate to the life he desires us to lead. Of all things, we ought to know how far he calls us to follow him in that life and service which is his will for us to exercise by his power. Therefore, to exceed the Lord's will for us would be to part company with him and his pleasure and power, and become rebels against the purposes of his proffered grace.

12:4-6a As believers, we who are in Christ's church are members of one another, as the body of Christ. Therefore the gift of faith and the measure accorded to each individual saint is bound to stand in relation to our life in that fellowship, as well as in relation to the world.

The measure of faith accorded to each is, of course, part of the sum total of faith given to the church from the inexhaustible store of the Lord Jesus Christ, whose faith is without measure (cf. Jn. 3:34). This has all to do with our individual uniqueness in Christ, which is indispensable if the body is not to be incomplete. And as we are each personally indispensable to the body, so is our contribution to the life and work of the body. None can take another's place; for even to try will lead to displacement, if not disposal.

This is supremely important not only in that we perform the divine function or office purposed, but also that we serve each other. Our gifts, therefore, if we are to be incorporated in the whole, are bound to differ. This has infinite advantages: it not only accords unique dignity to each saint, but also a distinctive place and function, so that the interplay of the whole by grace leads to harmonious activity. Paul writes at length of this elsewhere (cf. 1 Cor. 12:11-26).

12:6b The apostle now goes on to enumerate some of the gifts which Christ has given to his people (cf. 1 Cor. 12:8-10, 28-29; Eph. 4:11). There are seven gifts specified here; nine in each of the passages in 1 Corinthians; four or five in the Ephesians passage according to whether we view 'pastors and teachers' as one office or two. Not only the number of gifts but their order is suggested by these lists. Apostles where included are always first and prophets second, an order which is preserved in Ephesians 2:20; 3:5 and 4:11. No apostle is mentioned here, presumably because there was none in Rome at the time of writing.

The first gift mentioned here is prophecy, which may be either foretelling or forthtelling. What it means may be inferred from the phrase 'the proportion of faith'. The word for 'proportion' in the original is 'analogy', which has to do with the comparison of things which are similar or parallel. A prophet does not speak into the air whatever comes into his head, but in accordance and agreement with what has already been revealed. This may suggest the general English translation 'proportion'; for the prophet would prophesy according to the measure of his faith, which would require him to tell all that had been revealed, but no more.

We see this supremely in the Great Prophet himself, the Lord Jesus Christ, who made known what he might and might not reveal, and even what had not been revealed to him, for example the day and hour of his second coming (cf. Matt. 24:36).

Since in the New Testament the word 'apostle' is generally used in the unique sense of one who has seen the Lord (Paul was qualified by his Damascus road experience), the question arises whether 'prophets' also belong exclusively to the early church, or whether the gift of prophecy continued beyond the closing of the canon of Scripture. If one believes that prophets have arisen in the church beyond apostolic times, as some Christians do, the 'proportion' or 'analogy' of faith accorded to them would undoubtedly be related to the closing of the canon of Scripture (cf. Rev. 22:18-19), lest anyone thereafter should claim to have a revelation which proves not to be in accordance with the biblical truth already given and received.

Without settling this much discussed question here, however, suffice it to say that so much has been revealed (which we may not yet understand, as well as what we do understand) that it is surely better to concentrate on what is divinely revealed, in all its mystery, than seek to be agents of what purports to be new truth, which would be hazardous for any saints subsequent to the great apostles!

12:7 The next gift enumerated is that of 'ministry' or 'serving'. Does this refer to the ministry of the Word or works of mercy? The Greek word is *diakonia* which is actually used more frequently in connection with the Word than with deeds of mercy. However, the offices in this list are not set in order of rank, as in other places (1 Cor. 12:8-10; Eph. 4:11-12), so that the ministry of the Word may not be intended here. Besides, there is perhaps a 'gut' reaction which tells us that it refers to works of mercy.

Since these are concerned mainly with physical things a double danger arises in connection with them: either a tendency to exclude that which is spiritual – although the proper exercise of this gift calls for true spirituality as in the choice of 'deacons' in Acts 6:1-7 – or becoming arrogant because works of mercy are so evident.

In a day when new truth was still being revealed prophetically by apostles, teaching might be regarded as a lesser gift. But following the completion of the canon of holy Scripture it is one which becomes highly important, because its chief office by the Spirit is to afford understanding of the holy text so that its blessings might be imparted to the flock.

Those who have been engaged in the spiritual task of teaching the Word of God can best testify to its manifold effects upon those who receive it, purifying and establishing their lives in Christ and building that character with which they soon begin to be equipped for different kinds of service. To see the Lord apportioning responsive listeners to the Word of God to their several vocations is a marvellous thing. And even in the smallest fellowship of saints the tasks appointed may be various!

12:8 The next gift, that of 'encouraging', involves exercising functions specifically belonging to the Holy Spirit. Indeed, the Greek word Paul uses means, 'to call another in to speak for one, to support and comfort', and is applied to the Spirit himself as the Paraclete in John 14:16, 26; 15:26;16:7 and to Jesus in 1 John 2:2. While this suggests a wide function, including exhortation, it may be regarded as generally providing comfort and encouragement – like a lawyer standing by someone at the judgment bar, or an interpreter using his or her skills when important matters have to be communicated in another language.

We can think of few more blessed tasks in a fellowship than that of encourager, not least because people today seem to be so preoccupied with their own concerns that little thought may be given to encouraging others. In the midst of a busy fellowship those who go out of their way to provide encouragement to others, especially those who may be uncertain of their vocation or who may be in need of cheer and kindly counsel, are a godsend!

The gift of 'giving' or 'sharing' seems to refer to individual

contributions towards the help of others, rather than those made from
the church treasury, which may be included in what is in view in verse
7 under the diaconate. Such giving or sharing has to be exercised 'with
simplicity'. Modern translations have departed almost *en bloc* from
The Authorised Version in translating the word *haplotēs* by
'generously' against all lexical reference. But what is really meant is
that whether the giving is generous or not, it is to be given simply, that
is, without fuss or publicity, not seeking acclaim for one's generosity.
The simplicity here surely refers to a personal response to an undoubted
need, which is made at once and without any consequential
accompaniments. We constantly see in the media those who have
undertaken some arduous task to gather money for a good cause; they
are pictured handing over a cheque with such evident glee and public
satisfaction that the 'shine' is taken out of the deed (see Matt. 6:3-4).

12:8 The rule and government of the church is the task of the
officebearers, of whom Paul has much to say in 1 Timothy 3. Two
orders are designated: those we call deacons, who according to Acts
6:1-7 care for the material welfare of the church and its people; and
elders who care for the spiritual welfare of the church and its members.
In 1 Timothy 3 Paul gives careful thought to the selection of these
officebearers, so that their diligence will be assured. Only responsible
men should be chosen who will serve the church as serving the Lord
himself.

The exhortation to show mercy with cheerfulness is so general that
it could apply to any believer, with perhaps special reference to those
either in positions of responsibility in the church, or to those who have
the means and the leisure to care for the unfortunate. It is a challenge
to us all that in Christ we ought to become aware of the needs of others,
and to be ready, not as a matter of mere duty but as a privilege, to help
to succour them.

The manner in which we dispense largesse or meet the needs of the
unfortunate is exceedingly revealing. There is a way of patronising the
needy which almost makes the gift or service an insult. How
independent-minded people detest charity! On the other hand there is
a way of helping which makes the recipient feel they are conferring an
honour on the giver by being there to be served. The true Christlike
attitude would be very near that of the simplicity advocated already in

this verse. Its aim would be to honour the recipient and to play down the merit of the giver as simply fulfilling the command to love one another and so fulfil the law of Christ.

Of these seven gifts, the first four deal with the range of their activities, whereas with the last three it is the attitude of heart and mind which is stressed. This latter is of supreme importance, for it is the spirit in which we perform our duty which marks the Christian quality of our service. It is this which conveys the grace of God and the love of Christ to others – not the deed only, but the spirit in which it is done.

Love

12:9 The apostle proceeds from those specialised duties given to particular individuals (vv. 3-8) to those enjoined on all believers. The original reads 'let love be unhypocritical'. That is a mouthful! What could be more reprehensible than hypocrisy which feigns love, the highest of the virtues! Let love at least be genuine. Yet love is such a powerful motivation that there is the greatest temptation to use it for unworthy and selfish ends. But this is treachery at its very worst, and speaks of a degree of deceit which is exceedingly wicked. From such wickedness we ought to shrink, says Paul. Rather we are to cleave to what is good, as a young man leaving his father and mother cleaves to his wife (the same Greek word, cf. Matt. 19:5).

It is the combination of these two, shrinking and the cleaving, which reveals the character. There are many temptations and we can easily be bewitched and deceived. But if we are alive and awake to the difference between the two worlds of good and evil (which our first parents became completely confused about by listening to an alien voice) we will show it in our daily lives by shrinking instinctively from the evil and choosing and cleaving to the good. This is the test of whether we have passed from death to life in Jesus Christ.

Have we, by this standard?

12:10 It is love chiefly which keeps families together. We have seen to our sorrow that law will not do so. Laws can be broken, but love can not. Is it not also true in the church that love is the only force which will keep the Christian family together? We have seen where lack of love and differences of opinion – sometimes on important matters, but more often on secondary matters – have led to division. But love can keep people with differing views together, because it recognises that the family is more important than differences within it.

The sweetest emanation of what we call love is affection, which is a tender regard for the feelings as well as the thoughts and opinions of our brothers and sisters. Thus, even when we disagree (and we may do so conscientiously and earnestly), there is still an element of tenderness in our dealings with one another which is not violated.

Indeed, so important is the preservation of tender affection for our brothers and sisters that we are obliged to see them as more important in the family 'hierarchy' than ourselves. And lest we violate the law of love, which both Jesus and Paul say sums up all the virtues (Matt. 22:34-40; Rom. 13:8-10), our aim should be to prefer our brother and sister and seek to advance them. Otherwise by pushing ourselves forward we deny them their rightful place, since in God's eyes and man's they may be more worthy than we are.

If this spirit prevailed generally, it could then be safely left to others to advance us, as we deserve and need. What a beautiful circle of preference that would be, in which the spirit of the music hall duo 'After you Claude'; 'No, after you, Cecil' would not be a joke but a sweet and loving reality.

12:11 Take the last of Paul's three exhortations first: serving the Lord. It is in that service – and in making sure that it is the Lord we are serving and not some other furtive, personal cause which moves us – that we are to be on guard in two ways. Negatively we are to see to it that our zeal for serving the Lord does not flag, and positively that our spirit should remain fervent (which means that it should remain 'on fire', burning). No mere self-inspired motive will accomplish this if our zeal has become slothful for some carnal reason. Although it is our human spirit which is meant here in 'spiritual fervour' (NIV), it will only remain fervent where it is constantly inflamed by the Holy Spirit; and that, in turn, will be possible only where there is no hindrance in our lives capable of distracting us or dissipating our spiritual energies.

Of one thing we may be sure: there is always a spiritual reason for our zeal beginning to flag and our spirits ceasing to burn. It must be because there has been a withdrawal, whether conscious and deliberate or not. Satan could have a hand in this and needs to be watched constantly. But the Spirit himself will never depart: 'I will never leave you nor forsake you' he has promised. But our mind and heart may have been deflected from that specific dependence upon him which comes when clouds of sin or Satan, however 'filmy' and tenuous they begin to appear, subtly and gradually shift our attention from his glory, and from the fact that it is the Lord and him alone we are to serve.

Whatever changes may come in our inward or outward life, there is no reason why our spirits should not always be fervent, since his fire never goes out. There is always a specific cause if this happens; and when we cease to glow we must investigate it as a matter of urgency. If we insist on this always, then, despite every trial or testing, our lives will continue to tell!

12:12 From verse 9 the apostle is considering virtues which apply to all believers: loving and honouring each other sincerely, serving the Lord zealously without sloth but with fervency of heart, rejoicing in hope. This hope looks forward to the glory of God and is the prospect of seeing and sharing in that glory (in a manner that befits creatures, not the deity). This affords us great joy.

Without this hope, especially in times of sorrow and trial, we could lose heart – if we did not know that beyond all trials and earthly loss there is the divine prospect of seeing and sharing in the glory of God, with all its attendant blessings. Thus Paul exhorted the Thessalonians in connection with those who had fallen asleep in mortal death that they were 'not to sorrow, even as others, who have no hope' (1 Thess. 4:13) because the risen Jesus would bring them with him when he returns.

With such a prospect from the living hope burning in our hearts, it will be all the more tolerable to endure afflictions, which the apostle often refers to, not least his own trials and persecutions (cf. 2 Cor. 1:4, 8; 2:4; 6:4; 7:4; Eph. 3:13; 1 Thess. 3:7). 'All who will live godly in Christ Jesus shall suffer persecution' (2 Tim. 3:12; cf. 2 Cor. 4:17; 8:2; 1 Thess. 1:6; 3:3; 2 Thess. 1:4; 2 Tim. 3:11). It was thus that Paul confirmed souls during his first missionary journey, 'exhorting them to continue in the faith, and that we must through many afflictions enter into the kingdom of God' (Acts 14:22).

It surely goes almost without saying to those who know anything about the cost of the Christian way that such experiences as instanced in the above references are bound to drive us to prayer. The pity is that too often it takes trials to do so, whereas the exhortation here is to continue steadfastly in prayer. Doubtless that has particular reference to trials, but must we not see prayer as something more than a last resort in times of need? W. W. Walford's hymn 'Sweet hour of prayer' puts it thus:

> The joys I feel, the bliss I share
> Of those whose anxious spirits burn
> With strong desires for thy return!
> With such I hasten to the place
> Where God, my Saviour, shows his face,
> And gladly take my station there,
> And wait for Thee, sweet hour of prayer.

But the true life of prayer is not intermittent and occasional – nor, for that matter, merely frequent. It is a matter of living the whole of one's life in the Lord's presence.

12:13 The verse begins, literally: 'To the needs of the saints having common cause'. The root verb is *koinoneō*, 'to have things in common', often translated 'having fellowship with' others. It is a matter of sharing; but what? Surely whatever brothers and sisters need, and that could go beyond material things, although these may most often be the need (cf. 15:27; 1 Tim. 5:22; Heb. 2:14; 1 Pet. 4:13; 2 Jn. 2; Phil. 4:14). One who makes common cause with the needy is called a sharer (examples of this are found in Matt. 23:30; 1 Cor. 10:18, 20; 2 Cor. 1:17; Phlm. 17; Heb. 10:33; 1 Pet. 5:1; 2 Pet. 1:4. See also Lk. 5:10; 2 Cor. 8:23; Phil. 4:14; Rev. 18:4).

Akin to this is 'pursuing hospitality', which suggests a calling, for the word literally means 'love to strangers' or 'entertainment of strangers'. All do not seem to have this gift, but what they miss becomes clear in Hebrews 13:2, because those who practise it may entertain angels unawares (cf. also 2 Tim. 1:16-18).

The practice of hospitality, it must be admitted, is open to many abuses, on both sides. We must not allow others to invade our homes, for the home is the sacred shrine of a family of God's people. But in well-regulated homes it is possible to 'pursue' this gift, even where facilities and means are limited. It is amazing what some people are able to do in this regard, and all so quietly, almost with stealth, because it is seen as a calling of God. However, there is no hint in the exhortation that it is a specialised gift, but one for all Christian home-occupiers.

12:14 We are coming now to demands of a more exacting nature. Paul has outlined how we should behave, mainly among the saints, but extending that to include strangers. He now abruptly turns to consider how we are to regard our persecutors. We are to bless them.

On the face of it, this seems hard, but if we trace the Christian faith back to its origins, what is God's grace but mercy to the sinful and guilty? This is how he has won us! Should we not practise it also, in the hope that we may win our detractors and those who would use us despitefully? And if we say: But what about dealing with those who misuse us? Are they to get off scot-free? The answer is obvious: 'Vengeance is mine, saith the Lord, I will repay' (cf. v.19). We may complain that the Lord takes his time to do so; but, then, that is his affair. He is doubtless waiting for repentance on the part of the sinner, and surely also for a spirit of forgiveness on the part of the insulted.

But what is called for here goes far beyond restraining resentment! We are to bless those who persecute us, and that means nothing less than speaking well of them. But how can we speak well of those who do us ill? Well, the same language is used for God's blessing of us and our blessing of him in Ephesians 1:3. Ought we then to bless those who mistreat us? We can only do so if we wish them well, and the best way to do that is to invoke God's blessing on them, which would hopefully lead to their repentance. That is undoubtedly something like what is intended here. It is the very antithesis of cursing, for instead of seeking to consign them to perdition, we recommend them to God's mercy and grace – a much better proceeding.

12:15 If it is costly to bless those who persecute us, it requires almost an equal detachment from self-interest to rejoice with those who rejoice, for two reasons. We may not be in a rejoicing mood or frame of mind, and we may be tempted to be jealous of our brother's or sister's cause of rejoicing. In either case we need to be so crucified to personal interests that by entering fully into the situation of the joyful one we share their joy and feel something of the pleasure they are experiencing.

Of course, it is perfectly possible to put on an act, and by histrionics give a perfect imitation of pleasure even while privately we are fuming, or sneering. This is not it: it calls for 'a heart at leisure from itself, to soothe and sympathise'. Some might think it harder to mourn with those who mourn than to rejoice with those who rejoice, but perhaps it is easier. Certainly it is easier to patronise the sufferer than to rejoice with the joyful; but again, that is not it.

The degree to which we enter into the mourning and suffering of other souls will be determined by the extent of our understanding of their condition. Those who have entered into the fellowship of Christ's sufferings to the deepest extent will certainly be sufficiently detached from selfish self to do so. With their experience of sharing in the suffering of the greatest Sufferer of all, our blessed Lord (Rom. 8:17), they will be more able to enter into the mourner's situation. They will be able to share with an honesty and restraint devoid of patronage or self-commendation.

12:16 Both John Murray and *The New International Version* use the delightful word 'harmony' to express what this verse says. It is a beautiful idea, because since we are all different, it is impossible for there to be a complete identity of thought on many things. But as in music the combination of various sounds contributes to pleasing concord where otherwise there would be discord, so the interplay of thought among Christians can produce intriguing fellowship where there is give-and-take. This may not seem to be what is meant by 'Be of the same mind toward one another' (AV). But the apostle could never have meant that we are all to think the same thing, but rather that we need to be in total agreement on fundamental matters such as our common faith.

However, there could be total agreement on all important matters and yet tension and strife on lesser issues remain. This is where we learn by grace to agree to differ on secondary matters, which is perhaps the supremest of the social virtues. *The Good News Bible* reads, 'Have the same concern for everyone', which is rather different, but would allow for trivial differences and yet sweet harmony.

This leads on to attitudes towards those who may be of unequal social status or station, where the grace of the Lord Jesus Christ is seen in what Paul calls considering others better than oneself and looking not to one's own interests but to those of others (Phil. 2:3, 4). We cannot think ourselves superior to others and at the same time inferior to them: we must make up our minds! Perhaps looking for the good in them is the best way to begin to achieve harmony: we will not necessarily look for identical but for different virtues in others, and find pleasure in their complementarity. As in music the combination of various sounds played together produces harmony not discord, so we shall have the pleasure of appreciating what is best in others. This will prevent us from thinking all wisdom resides in us, and none in others; which very thought should inspire a healthy sense of humour – itself a saving grace!

12:17-18 It is important (as John Murray points out), to distinguish the next group of verses from what follows at the commencement of chapter 13. Here the apostle is dealing with private relationships, which are very different from the duties and obligations of magistrates functioning in public and judicial capacities.

In personal relationships, we are not to repay anyone evil for evil. This, if we may say so, belongs to the realm of grace, which seeks to prevail over evil and its deserts. As James says, 'mercy triumphs over judgment' (Jas. 2:13). This indeed is how lost and sinful souls are won for Christ! In the judicial realm, by contrast, God appoints men to act as governors to preserve order in society. The law must take its course. But we may not do as private individuals what would be our duty to do if we were magistrates.

The next exhortation is of a general nature, for to behave honourably before all men would call for one thing as a private citizen and another as a public official. Our behaviour must be appropriate to the person or persons we are involved with, thus commending ourselves to everyone (cf. 2 Cor. 8:21; 1 Tim. 3:7). This does not necessarily mean that everyone will approve of our behaviour, but that we seek to have a good conscience before God that we have acted in respect of everyone according to the divine will.

It follows therefore that, as far as it is within our power, we will seek to preserve peace with our fellows, whoever they are. This, of course, will lie only within the orbit of the divine will. What others may do to disturb the peace is not under our control, but when things go wrong and there are fractured relationships it is good to know in our conscience that peace was in our heart (cf. Matt. 10:34-36; Jas. 3:17; Heb. 12:14).

12:19-21 Here, intriguingly enough, the gracious approach in personal relationships is linked with the judicial function of the Lord himself. For the chief reason why we are not to repay evil for evil, or take revenge on our adversary, is simply that God will attend to these issues in the area of personal relationships. When they become public offences it is delegated to the judge appointed by God to deal with them (see 14:1-7). Thus the words quoted from Deuteronomy 32:35, 'Vengeance is mine, saith the Lord, I will repay' (which originally applied to Israel's enemies), in this context would refer particularly to offenders in the area of private and personal relationships, since the judge could hardly say that vengeance is not given to him, under God!

The sinner, therefore, who offends in the matter of personal relationships ought to fear the gracious believer who leaves retribution to the wrath of God far more than fearing the person who hits back, inasmuch as divine wrath is more to be feared than the wrath of any man!

But that is only the negative side as far as the injured believer is concerned. His love of his enemy, as Jesus enjoins, should be such as to enable him to show compassion and practical care to the extent of feeding him and giving him drink when thirsty (cf. Prov. 25:21, 22).

I have always thought the burning coals descending on the head of the sinner as a 'retribution' was nothing else than the love of God shed abroad in the regenerate heart which knows no end and is able to love its enemy just as Jesus sought to appeal to Judas to the very end. The hope would be that the 'heat' of such extreme kindness in face of provocation would bring the sinner to abundant repentance, as nothing else would do. In Judas' case it was fruitless, as Jesus knew it would be, but that did not stop our Lord from appealing to him by means of the sop from the common dish – surely a token of fellowship! – as well as addressing Judas in the garden as 'Friend' or 'Comrade'.

The last verse commands us not to be overcome by the evil of retaliation, but by acting graciously overcoming the evil with good. This would include the victim's personal victory over a spirit of vindictiveness, thus foiling the intent of the evil one to lead him or her into sin.

CHAPTER THIRTEEN

Submission to the Authorities

13:1 This section stands in its own right as part of the obligation of believers to find out and perform the good and perfect will of God (12:1-2). But it also contrasts with the 'pacifism' exemplified in our Lord's own life (as a lamb led to the slaughter he did not open his mouth, Isa. 53:7). The personal application of this to us has been explained already in 12:14-21.

Paul's teaching found specific application in Rome. The Jews were a proud, independent race despite – perhaps because of – long servitude. They longed to throw off the Roman yoke, as we see in the Gospels and in Acts 5:36-37. There was also the fact that Christians were given such royal freedom in Christ that subservience would not come naturally (cf. Acts 18:2). But everyone must submit to the governing authorities for this reason: since all men are under the governance of Almighty God because they are present in his world, they are in fact under his power. All authority in heaven and in earth is bound to be under the supreme authority of the Maker and Governor of the universe. All lesser authorities are under his authority, and exist by his permission. This gives him absolute authority over them and requires everyone's compliance with them as established and ordained by him. It is better to accept this fact and work with him than to rebel and clash with his sovereignty!

The extent of this magisterial authority is brought out by *The Confession of Faith* when it says that even 'Infidelity, or difference in religion, doth not make void the magistrate's just and legal authority, nor free the people from their due obedience to him: from which ecclesiastical persons are not exempted; much less hath the Pope any power and jurisdiction over them in their dominions, or over any of their people; and least of all to deprive them of their dominions or lives, if he shall judge them to be heretics, or upon any other pretence whatsoever' (XXIII.4).

13:2 Of course, there is another side to all this with which Paul does not deal here: the right of any man to obey his conscience in the sight of Almighty God. This we see clearly in two places in Acts (4:19-20 and 5:29) in both of which we have a godly man daring to defy the powers that be. This is recognised in many civilised nations and communities as the right of conscientious objection.

However, allowing for this proviso and under that conscientious limitation of power, the magistrate has the right of judgment and punishment of those who rebel against the authority of the state, because it is under the established authority of God. The full weight of the law of the Almighty is therefore behind the magistrate if he has been duly appointed, whatever his personal moral condition. He must be obeyed and his judgments carried out, on the understanding that he who rebels against the strictures of the law is rebelling against the ordinance of God and must receive due punishment for his contumacy. This, of course, is provided (as we must say, although it is not discussed here) that there is not a higher law of God which takes precedence to the law of the land.

13:3-4 Rulers are appointed under the overarching sovereignty of God, not to be a terror to those who do right but to those who do wrong.

There is no need to feel fear or terror at lawfully appointed authority if one seeks to do right, for the magistrate has no quarrel with the well-doer. But he has every right to punish evil, since 'he is God's servant'. God is on his side when he deals faithfully and according to properly constituted law with the lawbreaker.

This is something which can be almost forgotten in these rudderless days when even the judiciary may subscribe to the freedom of the individual to 'do his own thing' even if it interferes with the liberty or well-being of others in the community. The ruler who is so lenient on wrongdoers that they are permitted to go scot-free brings himself under the condemnation of Almighty God, for he is failing in his God-appointed duty. Wrongdoers therefore should be afraid of lawfully appointed authority, and the only way to avoid such fear is to seek to do right. Otherwise it is right to expect punishment.

On reflection it was a good thing for us when we were small to stand in awe of the policeman who used to parade the streets, and who made us ask ourselves whether we had done anything wrong. It instilled in us an awe of the law, even when we were not contravening it. We would stop in our play as the policeman approached and wonder. We would look at him with slight trepidation, as if we expected him to confront us and say, 'Are you being good children and not breaking the law?' He never did, but it was good that as children we were confronted with the law in the person of the local policeman in this way. Nowadays the policeman glides by in his limousine and, unless he draws up and stops, we take scant notice of him!

Remember the disciples at the last supper: 'Lord, is it I?' (Matt. 26:22) which is surely a healthy response by innocent souls. Nor does it need to occasion guilty fear, unless there is conviction of wrongdoing and therefore feelings of guilt. As to commendation (or 'praise' in the original) for doing right, this is perhaps implicit rather than explicit, but it may be that in lawbreaking days such as ours there is probably more call to commend law-abiding citizens than in more orderly and law-abiding days.

13:5-8a So much has been said about the law that it would be possible here to see the law as the sole authority. No; the chief authority, who lends his authority to the law and to the dispenser of the law is God. The chief regulator of our lives, then, ought to be our conscience in the sight of God. To submit to the law legally is right and proper as far as it goes, but to submit to the Lord because he is our Lord is far more noble and lifts our way of life to a far higher plane, that of a personal relationship with our Maker and our God.

The apostle immediately applies this to the mundane matter of taxes. Why ought we to pay taxes? Because the law says so? Yes. But much more because God says so. The law concerning taxes, like every other legitimate law for the welfare of society, came in the first instance from God. This is the deepest and highest reason for being law-abiding citizens, with respect for every legitimate sanction of the law and for those called upon to administer it.

This sets the Christian way of life far above mere legalities, and recommends a quality of life and behaviour which not only sees rectitude as its aim, but asserts the dignity of mankind in the sight of God as its standard. This will mean that we leave nothing undone that the law requires, because to do so would be to fall below that standard which lives its life in the light of God's all-seeing eye. The result of that will be that mere slavish legalism scarcely comes into consideration, since we are living on a level of grace which, as James 2:13 hints, transcends bondage to the law.

Love, for the Day Is Near

13:8b-10 But however high our standard in the sight of God, there are debts we cannot repay. The first, not mentioned here but obviously implied as the ground of all others, is our debt to God for our salvation. Before that supreme debt we must say with the hymnwriter, Isaac Watts:

> But drops of grief can ne'er repay
> The debt of love I owe;
> Here, Lord, I give myself away;
> 'Tis all that I can do.

It is within that great debt that our debt to our fellow man stands, not so much as unpaid (although it could be read thus), but as a continuing obligation. It may be said to be 'unpaid' in the sense that as long as we are on the earth and in contact with him, we have an obligation to love him. And the great thing about seeking to do so is that we not only attain the highest in terms of human relationships, but in the by-going we fulfil the law, as Jesus tells us to do (Matt. 22:34-40).

It is this which the apostle now illustrates by enumerating certain of these laws. The first four laws of the Decalogue comprise our duty to God, and the remaining six our duty to our fellow man. It is with these remaining six that Paul is concerned here. And the negative proof Paul offers that love to our fellow man leads to the *plerōma*, the fulness or fulfilment of the law which is that love does no harm to its neighbour.

This may seem to be rather a negative result of love, but as Leon Morris points out, the law is mostly concerned with the things we ought not to do. Eighty per cent of the Decalogue comprises negative commands. But Jesus turned them round by seeing them summarised in the two positive commands, to love God, and our neighbour as ourselves. We are doing much more than abstaining from doing harm to our neighbour by loving him: we may very well be winning him for Christ, and nothing could be more positive than that!

13:11-12 The suggestion that in loving our neighbour we may be winning him for Christ is exceedingly apposite to what follows, for here the apostle is concerned with the darkness of this present evil world, which is just as prevalent today as ever. We are living in the dark night of sin and Satan's power, despite the fact that the witness to Christ has been in the world for well-nigh two thousand years. There will be no more light until the Light of the world himself returns in blinding and transforming power.

Paul neatly suggests that night is the time when people normally sleep, and he fears that mankind is asleep during this dark period of the world's continuing ignorance of Jesus Christ. But the night is far spent (and if it was 'far spent' when Paul dictated these words, what of now?). Morning is near, and it is time to awake, because our ultimate salvation of body and soul is nearer than when we first believed. We must rouse ourselves and equip ourselves for the battle against the darkness by girding ourselves with the whole armour of light (cf. Eph. 6:10-18).

13:13-14 Paul's exhortation to 'put on the armour of Christ' (v.12) is to do nothing else than don Jesus Christ in the full armour of his victory over all evil. That is a very different way to live from that of professed Christians so deeply asleep in the indulgences of the world and the flesh that drunkenness, sexual immorality, debauchery and bitter strife and jealousy take over. For want of strong accoutrement in the armour of Jesus Christ horrid evils are in command. The only cure, as Paul tells the Ephesians (Eph. 5:14) is to awake and rise up from among the dead ones of this present evil world so that Christ may afford light to see how far astray one has gone.

It was the stirring words towards the end of our chapter which roused Augustine from his stupor of fleshly indulgence and made him the saint he became. The positive putting on of the armour of Jesus Christ as both defensive and offensive (as in Eph. 6:10-18) must leave absolutely no room for return to the gratification of fleshly indulgences.

As Paul says to the Colossians, 'you are dead, and your life is hid with Christ in God' (Col. 3:3). You are therefore 'to set your affection on things above and not on things of the earth'. Paul goes on: 'Put to death therefore whatever belongs to your earthly members, sexual immorality, impurity, lust, evil desire and greed, which is idolatry. Because of these the wrath of God is coming' (Col. 3:5-6).

In simple terms, the positive must leave no room for the negative. But what in down-to-earth terms is the positive life? It is putting on Jesus Christ, and clothing ourselves in his life. It was a simple life he lived: all his life of activity was geared to frequent resorts to his heavenly Father – for strength. His personal relationship with his Father was everything to him. Only what his Father ordained for him was to be considered. It must be so with us, through our relationship with the Son.

CHAPTER FOURTEEN

The Weak and the Strong

14:1-3 There are implications in the foregoing which must seem shocking to some within the Christian church. But what is the Christian church? It is a gathering of sinners being saved by Jesus Christ, and since salvation is in three tenses (we have been saved, are being saved and shall be saved), we must not assume that because a person has acquiesced in acknowledging Jesus Christ as their Saviour that all is immediately well. One has only to read Paul's epistles, especially those to the Corinthians, to see how far from ideal was the life that prevailed among that group of growing Christians!

It is perhaps too easy to class all Christians as belonging either to the weak or the strong, but it is a handy classification nonetheless, and serves Paul's purpose. If verse 1 were accepted *simpliciter* in many Christian fellowships, there would have to be a radical readjustment of basic attitudes to strangers and backsliders – to those who one day are in the place, and the next have gone back to the world. Many Christian groups would not tolerate such inconsistent behaviour. They regard their church as consisting of Christians who have 'arrived' – more like a showroom than a factory! But surely that is heaven, not earth!

Paul therefore proceeds to deal with the general problem of the weak and the strong by relating it to what must have been a burning issue among early Christians (and still may be), namely what is lawful for Christians to eat. There are three particular contexts in the New Testament where such subjects are dealt with; that of the asceticism of Colossians 2.16-23; that of eating food first offered to idols in 1 Corinthians 8; and the more general matters dealt with here.

The first matter was that of vegetarianism, an issue which apparently divided fellowships, although that may seem incredible to us. The remarkable thing which the apostle brings out here is that the weak person is the one with the greater scruple, whereas he would regard his asceticism, we are sure, as his strength. But the penetrating mind of the apostle, guided by the Holy Spirit, pronounces that this kind of stricture is a sign of the weakness which separates itself from the generality of the fellowship, and on grossly insufficient grounds. It is not strength which inspires the faddist to separate himself and stand superior to his fellows who indulge more freely in a variety of foods; rather, it is weakness.

14:4 The matter of judging is now related to the domestic scene of a household of master and servants: it is not done to interfere with another man's servant. That is his master's business. If he does well or ill his master will attend to the situation. And so it is in the household of faith also, for the Lord will enable his servants to stand, for he is there to help them. Has he not declared himself to be the Servant of his servants (Lk. 22:27)? Here is a clear word, expressed in the gentlest terms, to warn us not to judge each other. The self-righteous critic may condemn the personal liberties of another without in the least understanding him and his situation, whereas his Lord and Master knows all and understands as none other can whether his heart is right, however unsophisticated his action may appear to be.

Even for one in a position of Christian leadership to seek to assess where another stands morally and spiritually requires us to know whether the person is on the way into Christ, or on the way out! The benefit of the doubt ought to be given until one sees whether the soul is advancing from the far country, or is already straying towards it.

14:5 Paul applies the general consideration of judging to the specific matter of the observance or non-observance of days, presumably holy days. He states that it is more a matter of conscientious knowledge, acted upon wisely and well, than the rigid observance of particular days. The important matter as to observances is to have a good conscience towards God.

This is true even in the matter of observing the Lord's Day, which we believe we are, on the basis of God's abiding injunction, to keep. It is possible to violate the law of love by condemning another who breaks the Christian sabbath and thus sinfully arrogate to oneself the place of God as judge. Jesus said to the adulteress, 'Neither do I condemn thee; go and sin no more' (Jn. 8:11).

The test of all such observance or non-observance is the relationship to the Lord. It is what is done to please the Lord that is all-important, not merely the external observances, which can easily become idolatrous. It is a matter of conscience before the Lord and since some consciences are more enlightened than others we must allow the Lord to assess whether his children are acting conscientiously or not. The one thing that must never be done, as Paul shows in 1 Corinthians 8, is to force a weak conscience. That is a great sin.

14:6 It is astonishing to those trained in strict observance, whether observing days or abstaining from certain foods or whatever, to be told that it is the strict observer who is the weak person! Why should that be? Simply because he is the more likely to come under bondage to forms of legalism and fail to enjoy the liberty that is in Christ. But he is not to be despised. Indeed, as 1 Corinthians 8 shows, he is to be shown patience. Nor must his conscience be violated. It is to be hoped he will be enlightened. But if he is abstaining to the glory of God, that is just as much to his credit as partaking is to the person who does so to the glory of the Lord.

The important thing is this: for whom is our strict or liberated behaviour observed? All must be done to the glory of God. Thus there may be in the same Christian fellowship those who indulge and those who abstain nevertheless living in amity and concord with one another because they are equally serving the Lord. At the same time, that is not to say that observance and non-observance are equal, for the one thing the legalist still needs to find in his experience of the Lord is liberty, as Galatians 5:1 says. But even that verse warns that liberty must not become a carnal yoke of bondage or, we might say, a cloak for carnal indulgence.

The apostle goes on in verses 7 and 8 to extend this principle to the whole of life – and to death! As we are to live to the Lord in everything, so we are to die to him also. Doubtless it is actual physical death the apostle is referring to here. But what he says could be applied to being self-denying with respect to whatever is inconvenient or inexpedient for our faith. That may be considered an intrusive thought here, but the terms of verse 7 and following imply such dying to self. This is what Paul expounds so revealingly in his love-letter to the Philippians, especially in 1:20-21.

14:7-8 It may perhaps seem a rash intrusion to apply Paul's words about dying to the Lord to ethical dying-to-self, when the climax of the passage refers to the last judgment. The apostle is actually saying that it is in expiring in mortal death as well as in living that the believer belongs to God, and that he must never forget that it is to the Lord he owes everything. But this means that we are never our own, or on our own, so that our every thought, word and deed must reflect that we belong to Another.

This paradoxically is the kind of 'bondage' which delivers from selfish considerations. It is true liberation, because now we do not bear final responsibility for ourselves, since we are indeed the 'property' of Another. This fact surely provides that air of detachment from care which makes life carefree in the best sense, because we have freely handed over all responsibility for ourselves to the Lord, and in everything right to the end of life and beyond, we look to him. It means that we have no independent judgment apart from him and consequently we are never on our own: we are under the care of Another. While that completely restricts every self-willed attitude and activity, it also delivers us from the care and anxiety that go with self-possession. This means that the whole question of how long we live and what content that life may have while it lasts is entirely within the Lord's jurisdiction.

It is this which Paul discusses so eloquently, as we have already noted, in Philippians 1:19-26. If we can live like that, as the apostle certainly sought to do, a whole world of care and burden will be jettisoned from our lives so that we are then able to get on with the responsibility of daily living literally without a care in the world in order to fulfil the immediate task – for him! This is the absolute difference between the servant, whose only care is to be obedient, and the master of the house upon whom devolves the care of the whole establishment and its people. Paul sums it up so decisively at the end of verse 8. The conclusion of every matter absolutely is: We belong to the Lord! That settles everything!

14:9-10 Paul here takes us back to the origin and inspiration of such absolute attitudes. They all stem from the actual death and resurrection of Jesus Christ; and this our Lord went through for the specific reason that he might be Lord of both the dead and the living. This he had to undergo. Otherwise, even although the eternal Son of God, he would have had no jurisdiction over us as far as redemption was concerned, but only as co-Creator with the Father. He had to gain and win Lordship of our redeemed condition by undergoing death and resurrection himself before he could be Lord of it.

The conclusion of the matter of our judging what another may do, the weak or the strong, the partaker or non-partaker, the day-observer or non-day-observer, is now clear. He, like ourselves, has a Lord and Master who governs and controls all that happens, both to the dead and the living (meaning the resurrection living, since Paul cites death first). We have therefore enough to do to see to it that we ourselves are living under the authority of the Lord of our death and resurrection, and therefore ought to leave what another may do to his Lord and Master also.

Verse 10 could be viewed as visualising us all in a queue awaiting our individual appearance before God's judgment seat. Like James and John, over against 'pushy' Peter, seeking to secure their place in the queue of the disciples, we may argue with ourselves and with one another where we will come with regard to the favoured places. But this is trivial in the extreme, because as we wait our turn we know that jurisdiction is not with us but with him. It is therefore futile for us to weigh ourselves against one another. In any case, our judgment is warped in our own favour since we are inevitably inclined to exonerate ourselves from our own faults and award high marks for our achievements in a way that makes nonsense of true judgment. We must await the pronouncement of the true Judge, and therefore all prejudgment is foolish and even sinful.

We must 'mind our own business' – which is the business of our own relationship with our Lord. That is more than enough for any or all of us to be getting on with!

14:11-12 It has to be pointed out that the 'all' of verse 10 specifically applies to believers, since the final judgment for all without distinction was dealt with at 2:5-16. Believers must not think they will escape judgment, as 2 Corinthians 5:10 and Philippians 2.10-11 also declare. But that judgment is as to their conduct, their persons having been accepted in and by Christ, as already explained in the context of 3:21-31. 2 Corinthians 5:10 specifically states that we shall all undergo judgment as to the things we have done (cf. Eccl. 12:14; 1 Cor. 3:10-15; Rev. 22:12).

The question could arise whether the 'knee' and the 'tongue' are co-extensive. We are sure that 'every knee' must be all-inclusive, including God's enemies – any other thought being outrageous! But whether the 'tongue' includes the sullen, grudging acknowledgment of the damned that they have been wrong, demanded before they go to their own place, may be beside the point, since the apostle is writing to believers. It is brothers, whether weak or strong, to whom the text quoted applies. Each brother will have to give an account of himself to God. It therefore behoves us all to be more taken up with how we ourselves will fare than by pre-judging our brother now, weak or strong.

14:13-14 Judging, in the sense of censoriously condemning another man for what he does in respect of his religion, should cease. Our critical faculties should be exercised in another direction altogether, to see to it that in our attitudes and actions towards our brother there is nothing which could become to him a stumbling block or obstacle.

To return to the subject of eating, the stumbling block or obstacle here could refer to the weak brother abstaining, and seeking to prohibit the strong (who is unaffected by what he eats) from partaking. That might be a legitimate understanding of the words of verse 13; but it will not do for verses 14 and 15, because the apostle goes on to warn the strong not to violate the tender, unenlightened conscience of the weak.

Of course the weak must not 'call the tune' for all, and so restrict the action of the strong that the latter loses the freedom he legitimately ought to enjoy in the Lord Jesus (for no food is of itself 'unclean'). But neither must the strong impose their freedom on the weak. If in all conscience the weak brother regards certain foods as unclean, but is made to eat against his tender conscience, this will hurt his soul and do him harm – possibly irreparable harm. (See 1 Cor. 8:4-13 which establishes the case for giving full consideration to the weaker brother until his conscience is more enlightened.)

We may extend and apply the matter of eating to other areas. The rule established by William Booth in The Salvation Army and observed when the writer was in it as a boy was that attendance at sport or entertainment occasions which charged for admission was forbidden, since this supported worldly organisations. But in my view, a stronger reason for abstaining is the example one sets to weaker souls, who may become enamoured of these things. This is still one's personal rule for not attending theatres, concert halls or sports arenas, lest the example set for others could become a temptation and snare. The same applies to believers who take liberties with alcoholic beverages, however moderately: think of the weaker brother watching you!

14:15-17 Our behaviour in respect of our Christian brother (to go no further) must be governed by Christian love. His 'distress' because he sees us indulging in that which he regards as sinful and harmful can be very great. In his unenlightened state he may become thoroughly confused and lose his way at a stage when it is important for him to abide by safe, clear and sure guidelines. Indeed, the terms the apostle uses go far beyond the weak brother's 'distress'. He speaks of a 'stumbling-block' and an 'obstacle'. The eating of the strong is said to 'destroy' a 'brother for whom Christ died'.

We need to see both the extent and the limit of what is implied here. Apostasy is surely ruled out, if he truly is a 'brother for whom Christ died'. In any case, the word 'destroy' can apply to the ruination of the life of a believer. We see how far he can sink into sin yet not be fully and finally driven beyond the pale of saving grace – a 'beyond' which is unthinkable.

The apostle goes on in verse 16 to appeal to the strong not to let his 'good' be evil spoken of. What is this 'good'? It is surely the freedom he enjoys as a liberated Christian. It is wonderful to be associated with and belong to a company of liberated Christians who within strong and free guidelines are not bound by narrow nit-picking scruples. But where is there such a fellowship which does not include, even if on its fringes, Christians of another sort or standard?

It could be that in certain confined circles it would be possible for such liberated Christians to use great freedom, but even so, there is always the fear that others hearing of their liberated exploits could be enticed into what would be *for them* harmful experiences.

But lest the theme become too pedestrian, the apostle at the right moment – at verse 17 – lifts the whole subject into its true realm and in doing so makes a great statement of universal application. The kingdom of God is not a matter of eating and drinking. These should – and will – find their own level when the platform on which we stand is that of righteousness, peace and joy in the Holy Spirit.

It may help us to apply the word 'righteousness' to practical situations if we shorten it to 'right'. The kingdom of God is a world of what is 'right' as God sees rightness. And this rightness is so full of blessing to the children of God that it should issue in peace and joy – not to say the other blessing already mentioned, namely love!

If in the realm of God's reign and rule we seek to please him, and our fellow-believers also, we would never dream of acting in a way that would grieve our Lord or harm our walk with him or our relationship of helpful love with our weaker brother.

14:18-21 Why does the apostle say that anyone who serves Christ in righteousness, peace and joy will please both God and men? We thought that to please God was to set us at odds with worldly men! Yes; it is true that friendship with God puts us at odds with worldly men, but there is nonetheless a walk of balanced judgment which cannot but command their respect as they see Christians show consideration for others. This is to bear the image of the Lord Jesus himself who went about doing good.

This did not prevent our Lord from being cruelly crucified, which men of judgment allowed; but it must have condemned them all the more that they saw such moral poise and exquisite kindness in him, yet did not lift a finger to save him!

This is the wisdom set before men which they undoubtedly see and at least privately acknowledge, but oppose only because it condemns them. This is an entirely different attitude towards men who are without from that which would witness for Christ by odd and extravagant behaviour – the flag-waving, noisy, over-exuberant conduct which embarrasses sober souls and makes them curl inwardly at the antics of grown believers behaving like silly children at their worst.

Our whole attitude therefore must be that of preserving the peace of the fellowship by helping to build each other up in the faith and not to tear down by selfish displays of extreme liberation. If by our eating and drinking, or whatever indulgence our fellow Christians see, we destroy the work of God in their souls there will be a price to be paid. When we come to our senses we will see what havoc has been wrought in the lives of others because we were selfishly uncareful and full of pride at our liberation.

As has now been stated frequently, for the sake of others we must generally live narrower lives than we personally need to, lest we cause others to stumble.

14:22-23 Ah yes, there is a private life we may all live before the Lord, which is no one's business but his and ours. Have that faith which is yours before the Lord and keep it to yourself before him, says the apostle. And if the Lord liberates your soul even to extreme freedom with regard to what you allow yourself, then rejoice in that, and be happy in it. But see that it does not exceed or go beyond the bounds of what your conscience says is right.

At verse 23 the apostle turns to the weak. If he sees the liberated soul unwisely parading his liberty and is tempted to go beyond his conscience, eating against his own scruples, he will suffer self-condemnation. That is injurious to his soul simply because his eating is not of faith, but of doubt.

Paul now pronounces this exalted definition of sin: whatever is not of faith, is sin. This sets the standard for mankind as God's highest creature at the zenith, and is in keeping with the statement in Hebrews 11:6 that 'without faith it is impossible to please God'. Faith here is nothing less than utter dependence on God, leaning hard upon him at every moment of life. That may seem an extreme and exacting demand (and impossible for the unbeliever); but yet it is surely perfectly in keeping with his status as God's creature. Who should he depend upon but his God for guidance as to each detail of his life? If conscience is the inbuilt monitor of mankind's relationship with God, a man ought to keep consulting his conscience at every point of decision, certainly every moral decision.

This is not only the best way to live; in the end it is easiest, with no unpleasant repercussions. Indeed, the whole of Hebrews 11 sets out the way of faith as the 'more excellent way' of which Paul also speaks in his introduction to his great 'love chapter' (1 Cor. 12:31). The way of faith is 'what the ancients were commended for' (Heb. 11:2; cf. 'these were all commended for their faith', Heb. 11:39).

Augustine apparently held that this statement was of general validity, whereas Chrysostom felt that it ought to be confined to the subject in hand, and therefore to believers only. Doubtless; but it is a great statement, and sets forth the truth with admirable brevity and impressive clarity.

Some have held that a shorter version of Romans concluded at this point, since in some ancient manuscripts the doxology in 16:25-27 appears at this juncture.

CHAPTER FIFTEEN

15:1-3 The same subject concerning the weak and strong continues, focused primarily on the question of eating or not eating food which had been forbidden under the Old Testament law. There is a clear state-ment of the obligation of the strong in the fellowship to bear (i.e., carry and help) the weak in every way, in their failings or infirmities.

This does not mean that the weak are to be pandered to so that they can 'call the tune'. But they are to be supported by an understanding of their weaknesses. All reasonable allowance should be made for them, even while they are encouraged towards a keener conscientious understanding of the irrelevance of food with regard to the spiritual life. Until the weak are so enlightened, they must be borne, almost like helpless children. That calls for sacrificial service on the part of others. We are not able to please ourselves while tending, caring for and 'carrying' others. The aim, however, is not that we should permanently have to carry the weak and yield to what may be their whims, but while carrying them to encourage them to learn to stand on their own feet and bear responsibility for themselves by a gradual enlightening of the conscience, which is never to be forced.

Paul sets before us the supreme example of Christ himself. He did not please himself but his Father. Not that he ever had another will than his Father's, but the way of suffering, sorrow and death is hardly enjoyable for any man, even the Son of Man. His attitude is summed up in the seemingly paradoxical cry, 'My Father, if it be possible, let this cup pass from me; nevertheless, not as I will, but as you will' (cf. Matt. 26:39). His will, therefore, was to do his Father's will, whatever it cost (cf. Phil. 2:3-8).

This, however, is to be interpreted in the light of the quotation which follows. It is taken from Psalm 69:9 where the psalmist David complains of the scorn even of his brothers, apparently because of his zeal for God's house. He says, 'the insults of those who insult you [God] fall on me'. The meaning as applied to our Lord must be that it is the reproach of his Father which Jesus bore, which he did gladly, however painfully. This ought to be the attitude of those who have come through to such enlightenment of conscience as prevents them becoming bogged down by irrelevant scruples. While thanking the Lord for their liberty they remember their weaker brethren and instead of sporting their freedom, hide it (see 14:22), and thus 'carry' them. This is exceedingly Christlike!

15:4-6 Having quoted the Messianic Psalm 69 (much cited in the New Testament) Paul now proceeds to emphasise the value of the ancient canonical writings for our learning and edification. This is also specifically taught in 1 Corinthians 10:1-11 (especially verses 6 and 11), and also in 2 Timothy 3:16-17. It is sometimes deplored that even evangelical ministries concentrate on the New Testament to the detriment of the Old. This is a major lack in the lives of many Christians. Does not the New Testament constantly throw us back upon the Old for remembrance and edification by the kind of allusions we find here? The New Testament is full of quotations from the Old.

Here Paul says the Old Testament teaches endurance and offers us encouragement. How true this is! We only need to read Hebrews 11 to see the phenomenal endurance and fortitude of the patriarchs, prophets and saints. As to the encouragement to hope, its prophetic elements amaze us as we see how sure these old warriors were about the future, now so wonderfully fulfilled in the coming of Jesus Christ.

The apostle goes on in verses 5 and 6 to express the desire that, by the endurance and encouragement taught in the Old Testament Scriptures, his readers (probably thinking particularly of the strong and weak) will develop a spirit of unity among themselves in following the Lord. The anticipated result is that the local fellowship may sound a concordant, harmonious and unified note of testimony to the world around, to the glory of the God and Father of the Lord Jesus Christ.

It is wonderful when the note that prevails in a fellowship is one of loving unity, mutual care and support, with an outgoing concern for the stranger and for those who may chance to come in, or are invited to join its gatherings.

15:7-13 Following the exhortation to unity, a new section commences at verse 7, dealing with the unity of Jew and Gentile. It begins generally enough. The basis of mutual acceptance is Christ's acceptance of us, to the glory and praise of God – it is his achievement, by grace!

You would hardly think at the beginning of verse 8 that the apostle was about to uphold the Gentiles along with the Jews, but that is his intent. His reason for declaring Christ to be the minister of the circumcision (*The New International Version* obscures the nuance of Paul's language by substituting 'the Jews' for 'the circumcision') is to drive the point right back to Abraham as the father of the circumcision (cf. 4:9ff.). Indeed, as we trace the references to the patriarch back to God's first promises to him in Genesis 12:1-3;15:6 and 17:1ff., we see that the divine purpose was to bless 'all nations' through him. And that, of course, includes the Gentiles. They were to be the recipients of God's mercy equally with the Jews although the oracles came to the Jews first (Eph. 2:11-22).

That Christ became a servant or minister to the Jews to confirm his mercy to the Gentiles simply emphasises that God chose Israel to be his evangelists to the Gentiles, a task which alas they never properly fulfilled until Christ came. That it is the joy of spiritual Jews to sing God's praise among believing Gentiles is witnessed to from a reference culled from David's song of praise in 2 Samuel 22:50 (= Ps. 18:49). This is but the first of several quotations testifying to the joy of spiritual Jews joining in the praise of God with believing Gentiles (cf. Deut. 32:43 [v. 10]; Ps. 117:1 [v.11], and Isa. 11:10 [v.12]).

After these thrilling instances of Jews and Gentiles singing praise to God together, the apostle ends the section by expressing the desire that the God of hope might fill them with all joy and peace as they put their trust in the Lord, so that they might overflow in hope by the power of the Holy Spirit. It is a fact that the richer the mixture of saints in concert worshipping and singing praise to God, the sweeter and holier and more blessed the experience. God loves a rich mixture of saints, which – alas – is not always how hidebound inturned fellowships see things!

Paul the Minister to the Gentiles

15:14-17 It is hard to credit the apostle with such generosity towards the Romans here after the many severe things he has had to say to them in this letter. But if we refer to his introduction again, we will see that he began by gracious references and by expressing his longing to visit them (1:8, 11-13). Here, having imparted the riches of the truth, which must have sifted their hearts and minds to the depth, he gives his final estimate of them. He is persuaded (he has not visited them yet) that as brothers in Christ they are 'full of all goodness, having been filled with all knowledge, so as to be able to instruct [warn and discipline] each other'.

These are astonishingly complimentary words for the discerning apostle to say to the Romans, but he doubtless means them. While his discernment appears in having recognised their attainment of superlative degrees of goodness and knowledge, he is yet able to see where they may still advance, and that is why he has written as he has done. Jesus says, 'To those who have, shall be given more, so that they may have abundance' (Matt. 13:12). So he writes even more boldly to put them in mind of further things they ought to know, drawn from the store with which the grace of God has furnished him.

Paul recognises his calling and the special knowledge that goes with it, and yet he freely acknowledges that this does not come from himself but from the grace of God. We are all, whether teachers or taught, recipients of God's good grace, and thus puts us on a common footing. We are not all the same, but we are of the same stock, each of us a suppliant of his mercy and grace.

This is Paul's gracious introduction to the subject of his calling to be God's minister to the Gentiles, for he desires that they might, with the Jews, have opportunity to offer praise to God for his goodness in Christ by the coming of the Holy Spirit to them in sanctification. This being so, he says he has something to boast about in Jesus Christ of things relating to God. We know, of course, that this boasting would not be of himself, but of the Lord. Doubtless he was astonished that the Lord had wrought so mightily through him, and he would therefore be all the readier to give the glory to the One to whom it belonged.

Should not this always be the attitude of those whom the Lord has been pleased to use?

15:18-22 The apostle is glad to boast in Christ Jesus of the service God has given him, since it is all to God's glory. But he is exceedingly careful not to encroach on the province of another servant of the Lord – even although he is the apostle to (all) the Gentiles. Yet the facts speak for themselves as they are documented in the extent of his travels described in the Acts and Epistles. Study of an appropriate Bible map will show how distant from the more familiar regions of his labours was Illyricum (present day Yugoslavia and Albania). His travels from Jerusalem through Asia Minor (Turkey) and Greece – to say nothing of his later sea voyage to Rome and lands he may have visited after his release from prison there (including Spain?) – show that he was given grace as a pioneer to lead many Gentiles to obedience to God.

Paul freely acknowledges that his mission was wrought by the power of the Holy Spirit in signs and wonders as he fully preached the gospel of Christ in these many places. Nor did he need to trespass on another man's territory, for practically the whole Gentile world was before him. However, his scruples are expressed in a way which could be misunderstood. He is after all primarily a church-planter, and if he returns to build up the converts he has won, that is not to say he would interfere with another man's work. His chief burden was for the lost.

This is why he quotes Isaiah 52:15 which stands at the penultimate point of entry into the famous fifty-third chapter. The suffering servant is there predicted to endure unspeakable agonies in order to make known the good news to those who had never seen or heard the wonders of God's grace. Indeed the apostle declares that this is why he has been hindered from visiting them in Rome: there has always been a prior consideration, that of reaching the unreached and untouched (cf. 1:13).

However, as we shall see, his intention to come to Rome is not primarily to do the very thing he has just disdained – to poach in other men's territory – but that he might visit them en route for far away Spain!

Paul's Plan to Visit Rome

15:23-28 The statement that there is no more place for Paul in his present territory must not be misunderstood. His desire is not to evangelise every soul in an area – he was far too wise a strategist to have that as his aim – but to see living churches planted where more and more souls could be reached. His work then was done in his present sphere. It is a mark of the divine sagacity of the man that he knew so definitely when his work was done in any quarter and was therefore ready to move on, whatever human considerations would have constrained lesser men to remain.

We can feel the suppressed excitement of Paul at the thought that at last, after years of longing to meet and greet the saints in Rome, the opportunity was now before him, even if only in as he was passing through. His delight at the prospect of the mutual encouragement it would be for him and them to meet and for him to be 'filled' with their company is apparent. But what a gracious way to put it! It would be a wonderful 'stopping-off' place, to visit the 'eternal city' and meet the saints of whom he had heard so much, and have them convey him on his way westwards.

At the moment, however, there is something else on Paul's mind. The saints of Greece, north and south (among whom he was ministering as he wrote this precious letter) have taken pleasure in gathering a contribution to the poor, struggling church in Jerusalem. He intended to carry this gift to them as a seal of the fruit of the Christian life of the Greek saints. Only then would he come via Rome on his way to Spain.

In the by-going Paul expresses (v.27) the reciprocity which ought to obtain between saints of different places, especially Gentiles who have received their living faith through Jewish evangelists. It is right, he says, that having received the spiritual good news by Jews the Gentiles should have a care for these saints in their struggles, and so minister to them in their material needs as they are able.

15:29-33 This dear man who attends upon the Lord in every particular, although he knows what he wants to do, is content to await the Lord's propitious moment. Nonetheless, he is sure that wherever he happens to be, he knows he will arrive in the fulness of the blessing of the gospel of Christ. This one thing he knows, that his life is committed to

Jesus Christ to be what he desires him to be at every time and every place. But it is not in his carnal self that he has this assurance, for he urges the saints in Rome also by their common love of the Lord and in the unity of the Holy Spirit to join him in his wrestling prayers that God may be all in all to him and that he might be in constant attendance on the Lord's will only. This may mean that Paul will land in places and situations in which he would seem to be at the mercy of unbelieving men, not least in Judea to which he now goes with the offerings of the Greek churches.

The principal prayer he invites is that the saints in Judea would be receptive to him personally as well as be willing to receive the offerings he brings. His desire is that God would bring him to these saints in Judea and that he would find them in a welcoming frame of mind. He wants to be preserved from those in Judea who hate Jesus Christ and persecute the saints there, and thus escape their wicked intent (he was almost lynched in Jerusalem on a subsequent visit, Acts 21:27-32). Then he will be able – at last – to make his way to Rome en route for Spain and enjoy that mutual fellowship he has so long desired to have with the saints in the great metropolis. Indeed, he expects to be refreshed by them in his travels before, as he hopes, embarking on that wonderful further adventure of reaching Spain with the gospel. In the meantime he ends this section of his letter with a prayer that the God of peace may be with them all.

CHAPTER SIXTEEN

Personal Greetings

16:1-2 Here we are brought back to the origins of the letter, written from Corinth, one of whose two seaports was Cenchrea. Phoebe was obviously travelling from there to Rome, and it is reasonable to assume that it was she who carried this all-important letter to the saints at Rome. We hope she had a more comfortable and safer voyage than did the apostolic letter-writer when he eventually made the journey as a prisoner to Rome (Acts 27:1-2:16)!

What a treasure to carry such a letter in one's baggage, especially if it was the only extant copy! Think how impoverished the church would be without it! How much less certain we would be of its illuminating arguments!

The question often raised here is: What position did Phoebe hold in the church of Jesus Christ? The word which is used of her (*diakonos*) is translated in Philippians 1:1 and 1 Timothy 3:8 as 'deacon', but it is often rendered 'servant' and can convey a wide range of service. Phoebe, like other women mentioned in the New Testament, could have rendered a considerable variety of service of an administrative as well as ministrative and compassionate order, without being accorded an ecclesiastical office. No woman was more influential in the early church than the lady next to be mentioned, Priscilla; but beyond being called a fellow-worker there is no hint of elevating her to an official position.

Whatever one may eventually think of feminine office in the church of Jesus Christ, it would be a complete anachronism to think of a lady officebearer then. Indeed, it would seem incongruous to accord to a woman such a place in that day, however commanding, authoritative and influential a figure she was. In view of this it is remarkable, when the wide range of activity of good women recorded in the New Testament is taken into account, that there was no call to appoint them to positions of ecclesiastical authority. Nonetheless, those of a concessive mind may conclude that these two women would have been the likeliest candidates, if such a thing had been considered. Certainly the apostle's recommendation that Phoebe should be well received and given every facility for the work she obviously loved to do, indicates how large a share women had in the work of the gospel even in the earliest days of the church.

Verse 2 also shows Paul's sensitivity to a church he had never visited.

16:3-5a So much for the lady, Phoebe by name, presumably bearing the precious letter. Now to the greetings to those who are in Rome.

It takes a wide search of the New Testament documents fully to 'write-up' the movements and activities of this pair, Priscilla and Aquila. We first hear of them after their expulsion from Rome by Claudius round about 49 A.D. (Acts 18:2), when they met Paul in Corinth on one of his earlier visits. They thereafter crossed the Aegean Sea to Ephesus, where they met Apollos from Alexandria and put him right on the richer substance of the faith (Acts 18:26). Paul writes of them being in Ephesus in 1 Corinthians 16:19; and then, after the relaxation of the Roman rule about Jews upon Claudius' death (A.D. 54), they must have returned to Rome where, perhaps, they had retained a townhouse.

Paul does not forget that they risked their lives ('laid down their necks', v.4) for him, very likely when he stayed with them in Corinth (Acts 18.3). These two had such a record of Christian service across the three land masses of the northern seaboard of the Mediterranean that 'all the Gentile churches were grateful to them'. There was a church in their house, and there is perhaps even a suggestion that Paul may have sent them back to Rome for service there.

With regard to the relative status of husband and wife, it is a fact that the lady is mentioned before her husband four times out of six, from which it has been deduced that she belonged to a higher social class than he. It has also been thought she was more able than her husband Aquila who was a tentmaker, like the apostle Paul. With regard to feminine service in the church as in other spheres, the dominance of women of quality and vigour is something which has to be accepted, and there is no doubt that men of a less forceful spirit are attracted to such. Does the Lord Jesus not take into consideration basic temperament in calling women as well as men into fellowship and service with him?

16:5b-11 The next in line to be greeted is Epenetus the first fruit (convert) from Paul's ministry in the province of Asia, for whom the apostle naturally had a particular affection. Next is a lady, Mary, who had worked hard for the church in Rome. But how did the apostle know all that he says here without having visited the city? As we traverse this long list of warm-hearted greetings, the apostle's memory and his knowledge of the situation in a church he had never visited are more than remarkable.

What the word 'kinsmen' or 'relatives' means as far as Andronicus and Junias are concerned is uncertain, but Paul also describes Herodion (v.11) and Lucius, Jason and Sosipater (v.21) in the same way. It may mean more than that they were Jewish, since Priscilla and Aquila were also Jews and he does not use this term (which can mean 'relatives') of them. They may have been of the same tribe as the apostle, Benjamin, or some degree of cousins, perhaps not of his immediate family at all. F. F. Bruce thinks Herodion may have had connections with the imperial household. Paul certainly mentions the 'saints in Caesar's household' in Philippians 4:22.

Andronicus and Junias also had the double distinction of having been in Christ before Paul and having been in prison with him. They were 'outstanding among the apostles'. Whether the word 'apostle' is here used in the general sense as a messenger (a 'sent-out one'), or as an official of the church we do not know. Paul usually thinks of 'apostles' as those who had seen the Christ (cf. 1 Cor. 9:1), a qualification he received, as we have seen, in his Damascus road experience. Whether one can say that this is the sole definition of an apostle in the New Testament is doubtful, but the title should certainly be reserved for those who have a distinct divine appointment.

Other names mentioned in verse 10, Ampliatus, Urbanus, Stachys and Apelles are either beloved friends or remarkable for their integrity or service in Christ. The clear distinctions Paul makes amongst his friends show how supremely discerning he was in the matter of character and service, and how accurately and worthily he is able to describe them without exaggeration.

Paul refers to households as if he had lodged with them, which of course he had not unless they had visited him in Greece or Asia. He mentions Aristobulus whom Lightfoot thought may have been a brother of Herod Agrippa I, who lived in Rome. Calvin thought Narcissus was a wealthy freeman of Claudius, and just as lascivious, but the grace of God nonetheless entered that household. Wonderful!

16:12-16 Verse 12 refers to a group of three women all of whom, like Mary in verse 6, 'worked hard for the Lord': Tryphena, Tryphosa, and Persis. Where does he ever write of men working hard for the Lord? Is this a concession to faithful women whose divine service was necessarily ecclesiastically limited in those days? He certainly would not dream of sounding patronising, for on so many occasions he is exceedingly ready to own the good qualities of women who had attended to him. He seems to have a great respect for the ministrations as well as the Christian character of such women, which is beautiful.

Rufus, the red-haired, is generally thought to be the person mentioned in Mark 15:21, whose father, Simon of Cyrene, was compelled to carry the cross of the Saviour. If so, could he be the same Simeon referred to in Acts 13:1? Acts 11:20 mentions that some who were scattered on the martyrdom of Stephen were from Cyrene. Could this Simeon's wife, Rufus' mother, be the one who mothered Paul in Antioch after Barnabas had been sent into Cilicia to Tarsus to find Paul who had been unheard of for nearly ten years (cf. Acts 11:25)?

Those listed in verse 14 are simply names, all men, possibly belonging to the same group or church. In verse 15 Julia may have been a woman (it is a common feminine name), and possibly the wife of Philologus. These five also may have been a distinct group within the church in Rome.

The 'holy' kiss (v.16) is a sign of proper intimacy with those beloved in the Lord. It is far removed from sensuality, and indicates the close personal bonds which ought to prevail among lovers of the Lord. Paul also refers to the holy kiss in 1 Corinthians 16:20; 2 Corinthians 13:12; 1 Thessalonians 5:26, as Peter also refers to the 'kiss of love' in 1 Peter 5:14. Even our Lord in Luke 7:45 misses the kiss as a sign of respect and affection in the house of Simon the Pharisee; and we see its perversion in Judas' action in the garden: 'Betrayest thou the Son of man with a kiss?' (Lk. 22:48).

The apostle's final greeting at this point shows both his knowledge of and concern for the infant church in every place. Paul would not have made so bold if he did not know that Christians in all the places he had been to, or had been in touch with, would greet the saints in Rome equally warmly upon his writing to them.

16:17-20 The mention of so many in Rome for whom Paul had affectionate regard is further emphasised by the next passage. It clearly indicates that, as in other places, there was the danger of agents of Satan entering in among the saints to disrupt and cause division. Whether this had already taken place is not stated, although it is suggested that if they had not entered the church, they would have been dealt with more definitely (cf. Gal. 5:19-21; Phil. 3:17-21; Col. 2:20–3:4; 1 Tim. 6:3-10). Certainly there is no place where the potential for such disruption would be more present than in cosmopolitan Rome. But Satan loves to plant his agents in the church wherever there are possibilities of growth and development. So much is this the case that Paul foresaw it in the Spirit and warned the church in Rome that Satan would attempt to do this among them. His malign efforts had to be forestalled.

What sort of tactics would such satanic emissaries espouse? Either a spirit of Jewish legalism, or the opposite, a spirit-abusing liberty in Christ by advocating anti-law libertinism.

It is interesting that Paul does not advocate confrontation with such so much as avoidance of fellowship with them (v.17b); for perhaps nothing would so discourage them as the 'cold shoulder' to dampen a spirit of naive ignorance of the moral law (the weak over against the strong again); or more likely (cf. v.18), deliberate attempts to seduce the fellowship into ungodly ways.

Something very beautiful is said in verse 19. There is a simplicity in Christ (2 Cor. 1:12; 11:3) which, for all its ability to plumb the depth, as it is set free in Christ to do, delights in obedience to God's holy law. Such gracious consistency affords the apostle perhaps the greatest joy of his life. He sees that it is born of profound insight into that good and evil which are completely separated by Christ's cross, so that wisdom is the wisdom of the Crucified, and folly is the hallmark of the enemy of souls. What our first parents did by eating from the tree of the knowledge of good and evil was to confuse the two, so that the one was subtly designated as the other ('good for food, pleasing to the eye and also desirable for gaining wisdom', Gen. 3:6).

Keeping as far away as possible from evil and from evil persons not only preserves our peace in God, which at its best surpasses understanding. This element of peace in the character of the Almighty also engenders the strongest resistance to Satan, and ultimately brings about his defeat (cf. Phil. 4:7).

A benediction in grace suitably ends the passage.

16:21-27 Paul now graciously includes greetings from the friends who were, presumably, present with him as he dictated his letter. Timothy obviously comes first, along with his three kinsmen, Lucius, Jason and Sosipater (whatever their exact relationship with the apostle, cf. above on verses 7 and 11).

Tertius is obviously Paul's secretary on this occasion, and saw to it that his name appeared before the list was ended! The apostle's practice of using a secretary may also be seen elsewhere (1 Cor. 16:21; Gal. 6:11; Col. 4:18; 2 Thess. 3:17).

The apostle's host, Gaius (a not uncommon name), had been baptised by Paul at Corinth (1 Cor. 1:14), and is very likely the person called Titius Justus in Acts 18:7. He was host not only to Paul and his relatives and friends but to the whole church. His home must have been a considerable establishment.

Erastus was a public official, which warrants the apostle saying to the Corinthians (1 Cor. 2:26) that 'not many' saints there were influential, rather than 'not any'! F. F. Bruce has suggested that Quartus (meaning fourth) may have been younger brother to Tertius (v.22, meaning third), but this is uncertain. It is touching that Paul calls this last named person 'our brother', which may simply mean that he is equally included in the fellowship with the others.

Finally we come to the doxology, which, so far from being a perfunctory ascription of glory, ranges deep and wide in the realms of Christian theology. To the only wise God is ascribed the ability to establish the Roman saints both in the gospel Paul preached and in its proclamation, which now reveals a mystery hidden for long ages but now made known through the prophetic writings of the Old Testament. This mystery was first hidden and then made known by the command of the eternal God. We see, therefore, the eternal sweep of God's purpose in a comprehensive movement stretching from eternity to eternity.

Now that the mystery is revealed, the task of evangelising the Gentile nations, which Israel by her manifold sins had failed to do, is to be accomplished so that the nations might believe and obey the saving truth.

It is a wonderful concept, that what Israel from the first was commanded to do (Gen. 12:3) but had failed to achieve, is now to be accomplished, mainly by converted Jews, with a view to the church in succeeding ages being largely composed of Gentiles – until at last the Jews as a nation are brought in (cf. 11:12, 15, 25, 26). Surely such a vast concept is worthy of all the glory that can be ascribed to such a wise and wonderful God!

Christian Focus Publications publishes biblically-accurate books for adults and children. The books in the adult range are published in three imprints.

Christian Heritage contains classic writings from the past.

Christian Focus contains popular works including biographies, commentaries, doctrine, and Christian living.

Mentor focuses on books written at a level suitable for Bible College and seminary students, pastors, and others; the imprint includes commentaries, doctrinal studies, examination of current issues, and church history.

For a free catalogue of all our titles, please write to
Christian Focus Publications,
Geanies House, Fearn,
Ross-shire, IV20 1TW, Great Britain

For details of our titles visit us on our web site
http://www.christianfocus.com

Books
by
R. C. Sproul
published
by
Christian Focus

A Walk With Jesus

376 pages   ISBN 1 85792 260 3   large hardback

A study of the life of Christ, based on the
Gospel of Luke, divided into 104 sections.

Mighty Christ

144 pages   ISBN 1 85792 148 8   paperback

A study of the person and work of Jesus.

The Mystery of the Holy Spirit

192 pages   ISBN 1 871676 63 0   paperback

Examines the role of the Spirit in creation,
salvation and in strengthening the believer.

Ephesians

160 pages   ISBN 1 85792 078 3   paperback

Focus on the Bible Commentary, useful for
devotional study of this important New Testament book.

The Gospel of God

256 pages   ISBN 1 85792 077 5   large hardback

An exposition of the Book of Romans

Books by Donald Bridge

JESUS - THE MAN AND HIS MESSAGE

What impact did Jesus make on the circumstances and culture of his time? What is it about him that identifies him both as a unique Saviour and the greatest example of gospel communication?

Donald Bridge challenges the way we view Jesus, and our portrayal of him to the world around us. He argues that walking with Jesus today means reading his words, welcoming the impact of his personality, embracing the provision he makes for us, and sharing his good news with others.

Donald Bridge combines a lifetime of study of the Gospels with an intimate knowledge of the land where Jesus lived and taught. He has been both an evangelist and a pastor, as well as working for several years in the Garden Tomb, Jerusalem.

176 PAGES   B FORMAT
ISBN 1 85792 117 8

SPIRITUAL GIFTS AND THE CHURCH
Donald Bridge and David Phypers

First published in the 1970s, when the Charismatic Movement became prominent in British church life, this classic study of gifts, the individual and the church has been revised and expanded in light of developments since then. The authors, Donald Bridge and David Phypers, give a balanced view of a difficult and controversial issue.

The baptism of the Spirit, with its associated gifts, is a subject which has perplexed and fascinated Christians. It is unfortunately one which also divides Christians who disagree over the extent to which gifts should appear in the Church.

Donald Bridge is an evangelist and church consultant and David Phypers is a Church of England pastor.

192 PAGES   B FORMAT
ISBN 1 85792 141 0

Reformed Theological Writings
R. A. Finlayson

This volume contains a selection of doctrinal studies, divided into three sections:

General theology
The God of Israel; God In Three Persons; God the Father; The Person of Christ; The Love of the Spirit in Man's Redemption; The Holy Spirit in the Life of Christ; The Messianic Psalms; The Terminology of the Atonement; The Ascension; The Holy Spirit in the Life of the Christian; The Assurance of Faith; The Holy Spirit in the Life of the Church; The Church – The Body of Christ; The Authority of the Church; The Church in Augustine; Disruption Principles; The Reformed Doctrine of the Sacraments; The Theology of the Lord's Day, The Christian Sabbath; The Last Things.

Issues Facing Evangelicals
Christianity and Humanism; How Liberal Theology Infected Scotland; Neo-Orthodoxy; Neo-Liberalism and Neo-Fundamentalism; The Ecumenical Movement; Modern Theology and the Christian Message.

The Westminster Confession of Faith
The Significance of the Westminster Confession; The Doctrine of Scripture in the Westminster Confession of Faith; The Doctrine of God in the Westminster Confession of Faith; Particular Redemption in the Westminster Confession of Faith; Efficacious Grace in the Westminster Confession of Faith; Predestination in the Westminster Confession of Faith; The Doctrine of Man in the Westminster Confession of Faith.

R. A. Finlayson was for many years the leading theologian of the Free Church of Scotland and one of the most effective preachers and speakers of his time; those who were students in the 1950s deeply appreciated his visits to Christian Unions and IVF conferences. This volume contains posthumously edited theological lectures which illustrate his brilliant gift for simple, logical and yet warm-hearted presentation of Christian doctrine (I Howard Marshall).

272 pages   ISBN 1 85792 259 X   large format

MENTOR TITLES

Creation and Change – Douglas Kelly
A scholarly defence of the literal seven-day account of the creation of all things as detailed in Genesis 1. The author is Professor of Systematic Theology in Reformed Theological Seminary in Charlotte, North Carolina, USA.
large format   ISBN 1 857 92283 2   *272 pages*

The Healing Promise – Richard Mayhue
A clear biblical examination of the claims of Health and Wealth preachers. The author is Dean of The Master's Seminary, Los Angeles, California.
large format   ISBN 1 857 923 002   *288 pages*

Creeds, Councils and Christ – Gerald Bray
The author, who teaches at Samford University, Birmingham, Alabama, explains the historical circumstances and doctrinal differences that caused the early church to frame its creeds. He argues that a proper appreciation of the creeds will help the confused church of today.
large format   ISBN 1 857 92 280 8   *224 pages*

Calvin and the Atonement – Robert Peterson
In this revised and enlarged edition of his book, Robert Peterson examines several aspects of Calvin's thought on the atonement of Christ seen through the images of Christ as Prophet, Priest, King, Second Adam, Victor, Legal Substitute, Sacrifice Merit, and Example. The author is on the faculty of Covenant Seminary in St. Louis.
large format   ISBN 1 857 923 77 4   *176 pages*

Calvin and the Sabbath – Richard Gaffin
Richard Gaffin of Westminster Theological Seminary in Philadelphia first explores Calvin's comments on the Sabbath in his commentaries and other writings. He then considers whether or not Calvin's viewpoints are consistent with what the biblical writers teach about the Sabbath.
large format   ISBN 1 857 923 76 6   *176 pages*

Focus on the Bible Commentaries

Exodus – John L. Mackay*
Deuteronomy – Alan Harman
Judges and Ruth – Stephen Dray
1 and 2 Samuel – David Searle*
1 and 2 Kings – Robert Fyall*
Proverbs – Eric Lane (late 1998)
Daniel – Robert Fyall (1998)
Hosea – Michael Eaton
Amos – O Palmer Robertson*
Jonah-Zephaniah – John L. Mackay
Haggai-Malachi – John L. Mackay
Matthew – Charles Price (1998)
Mark – Geoffrey Grogan
John – Steve Motyer (1999)
Romans – R. C. Sproul
2 Corinthians – Geoffrey Grogan
Galatians – Joseph Pipa*
Ephesians – R. C. Sproul
Philippians – Hywel Jones
1 and 2 Thessalonians – Richard Mayhue (1999)
The Pastoral Epistles – Douglas Milne
Hebrews – Walter Riggans (1998)
James – Derek Prime
1 Peter – Derek Cleave
2 Peter – Paul Gardner (1998)
Jude – Paul Gardner

Journey Through the Old Testament – Bill Cotton
How To Interpret the Bible – Richard Mayhue

Those marked with an * are currently being written.

THE CHRIST OF THE BIBLE AND THE CHURCH's FAITH

Geoffrey Grogan

This book is a theological study

In the main, the odd-numbered chapters are theological. The first five of these set out the biblical evidence for our understanding of Jesus, while chapters 11 and 13 reflect on this theologically at a somewhat deeper level.

It is an apologetic study

This is the function of the even-numbered chapters. They deal with the main difficulties that have been and still are raised by those who are interested in Jesus but are not yet committed to him. It is to be hoped that they will also be of help to the committed. Each of these chapters follows the theological chapter most closely related to it.

The book will be useful to ministers and theological students. It has however been written in such a way that many Christians without theological training may be able to benefit from it, plus other readers who have not yet come to personal faith in Christ but are interested enough to read a serious book about him.

304 pages   ISBN 1 857 92 266 2   demy

In this wide-ranging and well-written study, Geoffrey Grogan provides a clear, scholarly and reliable account of the identity of Jesus of Nazareth. The fruit of prolonged thought about the New Testament's teaching, *The Christ of the Bible and of the Church's Faith* is marked on every page by clarity of exposition and reliability of judgment. Here we have a careful and thoughtful sifting of evidence and a steady pursuit of conclusions which are in harmony with it.

While familiar with trends in New Testament studies during the past two centuries, and grateful for the work of fellow scholars, Geoffrey Grogan has listened first and foremost to the witness of the apostles. He concludes that there is only one answer to the ancient question which Jesus himself asked them, 'Who do you say that I am?'

The result is this sturdy volume. Theological students, Christian ministers and leaders will find it invaluable, but any serious reader to whom Jesus of Nazareth remains an elusive figure will also come to the conclusion that this is a book well worth reading.

Sinclair B. Ferguson
Westminster Theological Seminary
Philadelphia, Pennsylvania, USA

This is an apologetic and theological study aimed at preachers, theological students, thinking Christians and interested agnostics. It succeeds in its aims admirably.

Donald Macleod
Free Church College
Edinburgh, Scotland

This beautifully-written book is a feast of scriptural analysis and argument about our Lord Jesus Christ. With profound learning but with lightness of touch, Geoffrey Grogan discusses all the main lines of the presentation of Jesus in the Bible, and then skilfully relates these to the questions that trouble people today about him. So the book is an attractive combination of Christology and apology – explaining Jesus in a way that answers modern doubts and puzzles, cleverly arranged in alternating chapters. Hearts will be warmed and heads cleared by this book – and doubt and unbelief will be turned into confidence and faith.

Steve Motyer
London Bible College

Christian Focus titles
by
Donald Macleod

A Faith to Live By

In this book the author examines the doctrines detailed in the Westminster Confession of Faith and applies them to the contemporary situation facing the church.

ISBN 1 85792 428 2   *Hardback*   *320 pages*

Behold Your God

A major work on the doctrine of God, covering his power, anger, righteousness, name and being. This book will educate and stimulate deeper thinking and worship.

ISBN 1 876 676 509   *paperback*   256 pages

Rome and Canterbury

This book assesses the attempts for unity between the Anglican and Roman Catholic churches, examining the argument of history, the place of Scripture, and the obstacle of the ordination of women.

ISBN 0 906 731 887   *paperback*   *64 pages*

The Spirit of Promise

This book gives advice on discovering our spiritual role in the local church, the Spirit's work in guidance, and discusses various interpretations of the baptism of the Spirit.

ISBN 0 906 731 448   *paperback*   *112 pages*

Shared Life

The author examines what the Bible teaches concerning the Trinity, then explores various historical and theological interpretations regarding the Trinity, before indicating where some of the modern cults err in their views of the Trinity.

ISBN 1-85792-128-3   *paperback*   *128 pages*

Published by Christian Focus

60 Great Founders
Geoffrey Hanks

ISBN 1 85792 1402   *large format 496 pages*

This book details the Christian origins of 60 organizations, most of which are still committed to the God-given, world-changing vision with which they began. Among them are several mission organizations.

70 Great Christians
Geoffrey Hanks

ISBN 1 871 676 800   *large format 352 pages*

The author surveys the growth of Christianity throughout the world through the lives of prominent individuals who were dedicated to spreading the faith. Two sections of his book are concerned with mission; one section looks at the nineteenth century missionary movement, and the other details mission growth throughout the twentieth century.

Mission of Discovery

ISBN 1 85792 2581   *large format 448 pages*

The fascinating journal of Robert Murray McCheyne's and Andrew Bonar's journeys throughout Palestine and Europe in the 1840s to investigate if the Church of Scotland should set up a mission to evangelise the Jewish people. From their investigation, much modern Jewish evangelism has developed.

Territorial Spirits and World Evangelization
Chuck Lowe

ISBN 1 85792 399 5   *192 pages*   *large format*

Over the last decade, a new theory of spiritual warfare, associated primarily with the teaching of Peter Wagner, has become popular around the world. This teaching concerns the role of 'territorial spirits', who are said to rule over specific geographical areas. Along with this theory has come a new practice of spiritual warfare: ruling spirits are named, their territories identified, and they are then bound or cursed. evangelism and mission are then said to proceed rapidly with dramatic results. Chuck Lowe, who teaches at Singapore Bible College, examines the full range of biblical, intertestamental and historical evidence cited in support of this new teaching. He affirms the need to be involved in spiritual warfare, but proposes a more biblical model.

'This is a methodologically-clear, admirably lucid, and mission-hearted challenge; a challenge not merely to our theories about Strategic-Level Spiritual Warfare, but to our evangelical technocratic quest for successful 'method'. Lowe argues that the floodtide of confidence in this 'method' has swept away exegetical, historical and empirical caution, and that it has unwittingly produced a synthesis uncomfortably closer to *The Testament of Solomon* and to animism than to any *biblical* understanding of demonology and spiritual warfare. In place of this questionable construction, with its quick-and-easy answers, Lowe points to the grittier, more robust example provided by James O Fraser, a CIM missionary to the Lisu in China. A great read!'

Max Turner
Vice Principal and Senior Lecturer in New Testament,
London Bible College

'So easily do many accept the new and the novel! To all who care deeply about world mission, Chuck Lowe's evaluation of strategic-level spiritual warfare is a needed clarion call; a call to reject what is built on a foundation of anecdote, speculation and animism, and to walk in the established paths of biblical truth and practice.

'Lowe has set himself up as a target for those who follow the SLSW theology. It will be interesting to see how they respond to this book.'

George Martin
Southern Baptist Theological Seminary
Louisville, Kentucky

'I am pleased to commend this careful examination of a controversial subject. The new interest in demons and the demonic, lately fanned by Peretti's novels, obliges Christians to reflect carefully on the biblical basis of all contemporary thought and practice. Not every reader will agree with the conclusions, which are sharply critical of Peter Wagner and others. But you do not have to go along with their theology to take seriously the devil and his minions.'

Nigel M. de S. Cameron
Distinguished Professor of Theology and Culture,
Trinity Evangelical Divinity School, Deerfield, Illinois

'The evangelical community at large owes Chuck Lowe a huge debt of gratitude. With his incisive, biblical analysis of strategic-level spiritual warfare, he shows clarity and sanity. He thoughtfully analyses the biblical, historical and theological tenets of our times with regard to spiritual warfare, showing them to be the re-emergence of the inter-testamental period and the medieval age. He makes a complex subject readable and concise, while remaining charitably irenic toward other Christians with whom he takes issue.

'The greatest strength of this book is the author's dogged insistence that, whatever one's approach to SLSW, one must not build doctrine on vague texts, assumptions, analogies or inferences, but on clear, solid, biblical evidence alone. I fully endorse the contents of this exceptional work.'

Richard Mayhue
Senior Vice President and Dean,
The Master's Seminary, Sun Valley, California

'The Bible makes it very clear that the forces of evil are strong, and that the followers of Jesus are engaged in an unrelenting battle against them. But little attention is given to this struggle in a good deal of modern writing, so Dr. Lowe's study of spiritual warfare is important. He is concerned with modern approaches that do not do justice to what the Bible teaches about the forces of evil. Specifically he deals with those who advocate strategic-level spiritual warfare. His book clarifies many issues, and encourages readers in their task of opposing evil.'

Leon Morris
Ridley College,
Australia

You Can Learn to Lead
Stewart Dinnen
ISBN 1 85792 2824   *B format 176 pages*

A practical manual for missionaries, church leaders, or anyone in a position of leadership. The author was International Secretary of WEC and therefore had plenty of hands-on experience.

Patrick Johnstone says of this book: 'It was my privilege to serve under Stewart's incisive and courageous leadership. I commend this book as a means for equipping others with like vision.'

And Brother Andrew comments: 'Stewart, your book is a gem! Diamonds! I wish I had written it.'

Rescue Shop Within a Yard of Hell
Stewart Dinnen
ISBN 1 85792 1224   *pocket paperback 272 pages*

The remarkable story of evangelism by Betel among the drug addicts and AIDs sufferers in Spain. In addition to the strategies of the workers being explained, there are testimonies from converted addicts, some of whom became leaders in the church.

Faith on Fire
Norman Grubb and the building of WEC
Stewart Dinnen
ISBN 185792 3219   *large format 240 pages*

Norman Grubb 'inherited' the leadership of WEC from his father-in-law, C. T. Studd. Leslie Brierley said of Grubb, 'To experience his dynamic leadership ... was my unforgettable experience.'